ONE YEAR DEVOTIONAL

Walking in His Ways

CWR

SELWYN HUGHES

Revised and updated by Mick Brooks
Further Study: Ian Sewter

Copyright © CWR 2004

First published 2004 by CWR, Waverley Abbey House, Waverley Lane, Farnham, Surrey GU9 8EP, UK. Registered Charity No. 294387. Registered Limited Company No. 1990308. Reprinted 2012, 2016. This edition updated for 2018.

Issues of *Every Day with Jesus* written by Selwyn Hughes were previously published as follows: *Changing Times - Unchanging Truth*, Jan/Feb 2000; *God's Last Word*, Jul/Aug 1994; *The Surprises of God*, Nov/Dec 1994; *Bringing the Bible to Life*, May/Jun 1997; *The Peak of the Epistles*, Mar/Apr 1997; *The Final Word*, May/Jun 1999.

Further Study sections compiled by Trevor J. Partridge except *Changing Times - Unchanging Truths* and *The Final Word* compiled by Philip and Mary Greenslade.

For list of National Distributors visit www.cwr.org.uk/distributors

Unless otherwise indicated, all Scripture references are from the Holy Bible: New International Version (NIV), copyright © 1973, 1978, 1984 by Biblica, (formerly the International Bible Society).

Other Scripture quotations used: Amplified: The Amplified Bible © 1987 Zondervan and the Lockman Foundation; AV: The Authorised Version; Moffatt: The Moffatt Translation of the Bible , © 1987, Hodder & Stoughton; NKJ: New King James Version, © 1982, Thomas Nelson Inc.; RSV: Revised Standard Version, © 1965, Division of Christian Education of the National Council of the Churches of Christ in the United States of America; *The Message*: Scripture taken from The Message. Copyright © 1993, 1994, 1995, 1996, 2000, 2001, 2002. Used by permission of NavPress Publishing Group.

Concept development, editing, design and production by CWR

Printed in the UK by Linney

ISBN 978-1-85345-314-4

Contents

Introduction

Selwyn Hughes believed with all his heart that the most open time of receptivity in the soul is the devotional time. By 'devotional time' we mean allowing the mind to dwell on a biblically based thought then turning it to prayer. What point is there in reading Scripture unless we allow it to nourish and fire our souls with a deeper passion for God?

Selwyn wrote a devotional series of meditations called *Every Day with Jesus* for over 40 years. During that time the readership rose year by year and now numbers nearly one million.

Selwyn was often asked what was the secret of its success. His usual answer was that firstly, he believed it was something God had called him to do. He had felt this call as definitely as he did the call to Christian ministry. Secondly, whilst the meditations are divided into a page a day a definite theme is followed throughout. The page a day is not an isolated dab of unconnected ideas and suggestions but forms a consistent whole until the chosen theme is ended. This gives a sense of completeness and realisation, of having moved toward a goal.

Thirdly, a theme stretched out over two months seems to be a formula that fits well with most people. Three months would be too long and one month too short. Two months, it seems, is just right.

We hope and pray that this well tried and tested formula will once again enrich your personal devotional time as you journey with many others through the six great biblical themes that have been selected.

How to read the Bible

A question I am often asked, especially by young Christians, is this: why do I need to read the Bible?

We need to read the Bible in order to know not only God's mind for the future but how to develop a daily walk with Him. God uses His Word to change people's lives and bring those lives into a deeper relationship with Himself and a greater conformity to His will. For over four decades now I have spent hours every week reading and studying the Scriptures. God has used this book to transform my life and to give me a sense of security in a shifting and insecure world.

How do we read the Bible? Do we just start at Genesis and make our way through to the book of Revelation? There are many ways to go about reading the Scriptures; let me mention three.

One is to follow a reading plan such as CWR's *Every Day with Jesus One Year Bible* or *Cover to Cover Complete*. The great advantage of following a reading plan is that your reading is arranged for you; in a sense you are being supervised. You are not left to the vagaries of uncertainty: what shall I read today, where shall I begin, at what point shall I end?

A second approach is to thread your way through the Scriptures by following a specific theme such as *The Big Story* (also published by CWR). It is quite staggering how many themes can be found in Scripture and what great spiritual rewards can be had by acquainting yourself with them. When I started writing *Every Day with Jesus* in 1965, I decided to follow the thematic approach and I wondered how long I would be able to keep it up. Now, many years later, I am still writing and expounding on different themes of the Bible, and the truth is that I have more biblical themes and subjects than it is possible to deal with in one lifetime!

A third approach is by reading through a book of the Bible. This enables you to get into the mind of the writer and understand his message. Every book of the Bible has something unique and special to convey and, as with any book, this can only be understood when you read it from start to finish.

It is important to remember that all reading of the Bible ought to be preceded by prayer. This puts you in a spiritually receptive frame of mind to receive what God has to say to you through His Word. The Bible can be read by anyone but it can only be understood by those whose hearts are in tune with God – those who have come into a personal relationship with Him and who maintain that relationship through daily or regular prayer. This is how the Bible puts it: 'The man without the Spirit does not accept the things that come from the Spirit of God, for they are foolishness to him, and he cannot understand them, because they are spiritually discerned' (1 Cor. 2:14).

Praying before you open your Bible should not be a mere formality. It is not the *act* that will make the Bible come alive but the *attitude*. Prayer enables us to approach the Scriptures with a humble mind. The scientist who does not sit down before the facts of the universe with an open mind, is not prepared to give up every preconceived idea and is not willing to follow wherever nature will lead him, will discover little or nothing. It is the same with the reading of the Scriptures; we must come to it with a humble and receptive mind or we too will get nowhere. Prayer enables us to have the attitude that says, 'Speak, for your servant is listening' (1 Sam. 3:10).

If we are to grow in the Christian life then we must do more than just *read* the Bible – we must *study* it. This means that we must give time to poring over it, considering it, thinking about what it is saying to us and assimilating into our hearts and minds its doctrines and its ideas.

I have already pointed out that one of the ways of reading the Bible is by taking a theme and tracing it through the various books of the Bible. The pleasure this brings can be greatly enhanced by using this as a regular means of Bible study. When we study the Bible with the aid of concordances, lexicons and so on, we feed our minds, but when we study the Bible devotionally, we apply the Word of God to our hearts. Both exercises are necessary if we are to be completely rounded people but we must see that it is at the place of the devotional that we open up our hearts and expose ourselves to God's resources.

Let me encourage you also to take advantage of a reading plan as a further basis of study. Following this will enable you to cover the whole of the Bible in a set period. Those who have used this method tell of the most amazing spiritual benefits. One person who had read through the whole of the Bible in a year said to me, 'It demanded more discipline than I thought I was capable of, but the rewards have been enormous.' When I asked her what these rewards were, she said, 'I used to have a partial view of God's purposes because I dipped into my Bible just here and there as it suited me. Now, however, I feel as if I have been looking over God's shoulder as He laid out the universe, and I feel so secure in the knowledge that He found a place for me in that marvellous plan.' There can be no doubt that reading through the entire Bible in a set period enables one to gain a perspective that has tremendous positive spiritual consequences.

The third form of study – reading through a book of the Bible at a time – has the advantage of helping you understand the unity and diversity of the Bible. It is quite incredible how so many writers sharing their thoughts at different times of history combine to say similar things and give a consistent emphasis. Reading and pondering on this gives you such an appreciation of the wisdom of God in putting together this marvellous volume that it fires your soul and quickly brings praise and adoration to your lips.

I have found the best way to study a book of the Bible is to read it through once for a sense of the whole, and then to read it again, making a note of anything that strikes me, such as a principle to be applied, an insight to be stored away in my heart, or a thought to be shared with someone who is struggling.

One thing is sure, time spent with the Bible is not wasted. The more one loves God the more one will love the Bible. And the more one loves the Bible the more one will love God. Always remember that this unique volume – God's one and only published work – yields its treasures only to those who read it, study it and obey it.

Selwyn Hughes

Rev Dr Selwyn Hughes (1928–2006) was the founder of CWR and writer of *Every Day with Jesus* for over forty years.

Changing Times – Unchanging Truths

'Come let us sing'

DAY
1

For reading & meditation – Psalm 137:1–9

'How can we sing the songs of the LORD while in a foreign land?' (v.4)

These 'bashing crashing times', as one writer has described them, bring challenges to every one of us – Christians and non-Christians alike. Nevertheless, for Christians there are particular challenges, perhaps the greatest being that our society has become fiercely secular. You and I woke up today to a world that cares little for God. Secularism has spread everywhere. It fills our schools with books that have no room for divine truth, dominates our political systems, saturates the entertainment industry, and infiltrates morality with false definitions of power, sex, pride, and so on. If you speak out your convictions about God or the Bible you are ridiculed or labelled a fundamentalist. 'To believe the Bible,' concludes Calvin Miller, 'has become a kind of grand slur – an antiquated stumbling stone on the path to the brave new liberated world.'

FURTHER STUDY

Psa. 138:1-8;
Jer. 29:1-28;
Rom. 12:1-2;
Phil. 2:14-16

1. How can I best bless the unbelieving society I live and work in?

2. How can I not be conformed to the world today?

Jean-Pierre de Caussade said: 'It requires heroic courage and self-surrender to hold firmly to a simple faith and keep singing all the time.' The people in the psalm we have read today found that difficult. Surrounded by a pagan culture, they cried out: 'How can we sing the songs of the LORD while in a foreign land?' With us, it must be different. We must have the boldness to keep singing the Lord's song and refuse to be silenced by society. All may change, but God's truth – never.

Lord God my Father, give me the courage 'to hold firmly to a simple faith and keep singing all the time'. Baptise me afresh with Your Holy Spirit so that I may be all that You want me to be in the days that lie ahead. In Jesus' name I pray. Amen.

What is your name?

For reading & meditation – Hebrews 12:1–12

'... let us throw off everything that hinders and the sin ...
and let us run with perseverance ...' (v.1)

Despite increasing secularisation we must go on singing. And the song we should sing is that of the unchanging nature of spiritual truth. God's Word never changes. Paul's instruction to his son in the faith, Timothy, was: 'Continue in what you have learned and have become convinced of' (2 Tim. 3:14). What have we learned and what can we learn from Scripture that will help us develop a biblical framework for our thinking?

First, *we must put the past firmly behind us.* The writer to the

FURTHER STUDY

Num. 11:1-20;
Heb. 10:35-39;
11:13-16

1. Why was
nostalgia
dangerous
for Israel?

2. How does
Hebrews
challenge me
to be a disciple
of Jesus?

Hebrews encourages us to 'throw off everything that hinders and the sin that so easily entangles'. When much of my time was spent in counselling I discovered that three things often hinder people from moving on in their Christian life. These may well be preventing you from making a fresh start spiritually. We must deal effectively with the past before we can deal effectively with the future, or even the present.

At the ford of the Jabbok, Jacob had to confess his old name before he was given a new one (Gen. 32). He had to own up to his flaws ('Jacob' means 'supplanter', or 'opportunist') before he was given the name of Israel, 'God strives'. The past and the future are often separated by a river called Jabbok; it is a place of honesty, repentance and authentication. Jacob had to spend a while there before he was able to move on. I invite you to join me at the Jabbok. You may have wrestled with principalities and powers. Now it is time to wrestle with God.

My Father and my God, help me I pray to put the past firmly behind me so that I can move into the future with no weights or encumbrances. I would be free – free to accept Your plans for me. In Christ's name I ask it. Amen.

'Forget it'

For reading & meditation – Philippians 3:12–21

'Forgetting what is behind and straining towards what is ahead, I press on towards the goal ...' (vv.13-14)

The first obstacle to moving on is an inability to forget failures, blunders, tactlessness or, colloquially, bricks dropped.

I have been astonished at the number of people I have met who have overcome the great sorrows of life but have been unable to rise above the mistakes they have made along life's way. One woman admitted that two or three times a week she would go hot all over as she recalled a silly thing she did when she was a teenager. She had lived with this memory for over thirty years! Others have told me how some failure or tactless comment dogs their footsteps, and they cannot recall these incidents without feeling acute embarrassment.

Are you someone whose memory is filled with the stupid things you have done – so much so that you are unable to break free from them? You constantly say to yourself: 'Why did I ever do or say that?' Here's my advice to you: forget it. Assuming there was no evil intention (if there was then the matter comes in a category we will look at later) then put it behind you right now. All of us have slipped on occasion. I am aware that I have made some silly mistakes and said some foolish things, but I have learned from them and grown through them. I could make a long list of them, but there is no point. Brooding on your mistakes will only filch your faith, paralyse your potential and destroy your dreams. The race ahead demands the utmost spiritual fitness. Get rid of the weights that hinder your progress – now.

FURTHER STUDY

Isa. 43:14-21;
Jer. 31:31-34;
1 Tim. 1:12-17;
Heb. 12:1-3

1. How, for Israel, did God's new work outweigh the old?

2. How does Paul help us face up to our painful past?

Father, I place in Your hands whatever may hinder my progress in the race that is set before me. Help me deal with those things in my past that have to be resolved and then move on to new heights and new discoveries with You. In Christ's name. Amen.

'Made to forget'

For reading & meditation – Genesis 41:41-57

'Joseph named his firstborn Manasseh and said, 'It is because God has made me forget all my trouble ... '' (v.51)

Some may consider that my advice yesterday concerning past mistakes sounds good as theory but would be difficult to put into practice. How can one forget?

After Joseph became a man of substance in Egypt and was married, he named his firstborn son Manasseh, meaning 'God has made me forget.' What a moving moment it must have been for Joseph as, looking back, he realised that the pain caused by past events had gone away. You remember, no doubt, some of the terrible things that had happened to him: he was flung into a pit, sold by his own brothers, slandered by a lascivious woman, thrown into prison. But now the past was behind him and the bitterness had been siphoned off his spirit.

FURTHER STUDY

Gen. 50:15-21;
Ruth 1:20-21;
4:13-15;
Heb. 9:11-15;
2 Tim. 4:9-18

1. How did Joseph evaluate the past?

2. How did Naomi's misfortune turn to blessing?

Some believe Joseph was able to say 'God has made me forget' because time had healed him. But I believe something supernatural had taken place. The sharp edge does come off our memory with the passing of time as a result of natural forgetfulness, but also, I believe, when we invite Him, God will enable us to forget those things that impede our progress in the faith. Am I signifying that God will erase them from our memory banks? Of course not. What He does is to work in our minds so that we cease to be obsessive about them, and they no longer intrude into our memories to the extent that they interfere with our daily Christian life. God does not deliver us from the memory of the facts. It is the bitterness associated with those facts that He expunges from our minds.

Gracious and loving heavenly Father, how can I ever sufficiently thank You for the grace that takes the edge off painful memories? I bring every painful memory to You for Your healing and deliverance. Please heal me, my Father. In Jesus' name. Amen.

'No Fishing'

For reading & meditation – Hebrews 8:1–13

'... I will forgive their wickedness and will remember their
sins no more.' (v.12)

The second thing we must forget is our sins. We have all
sinned and we all need to repent. But once we have repented
and received forgiveness we must move on. What does God say
to repentant people? 'I will … remember their sins no more.' The
prophet Micah reminds us that God promised to 'hurl all our
iniquities into the depths of the sea' (7:19). 'Then,' as Billy Graham
has remarked, 'He puts up a sign that says 'No Fishing'.'

Many, however, still lash themselves for their sins (even though
confessed and forgiven by the Lord), and by so doing
they jeopardise their daily walk with Him. Since they
still hold on to their sins and refuse to relinquish
their guilt, they suffer so much pain that they are
prevented from living fully in the present moment.

A co-dependent is someone who prefers misery to
freedom. The wife of an alcoholic might, deep down,
prefer to carry on suffering rather than be released
from the problem. Co-dependency poses as other-
centred, but really it is self-centredness dressed up
as concern. Sometimes people who hang on to their
sins after they have been forgiven do so because
of a psychological need to browbeat themselves. They have not
accepted forgiveness – thus they still have a sense of guilt and
feel a need to punish themselves. Self-atonement is substituted
by them for Christ's atonement. Once we have repented of our
sins God forgives and forgets them. And you must forget them too.

FURTHER STUDY

Isa. 43:22–25;
Luke 5:17–26;
John 8:1–11;
1 Pet. 1:18–21

1. What sins can I
let go of today?

2. What
inherited habits
does the blood
of Jesus free
me from?

**Lord God, forgive me if I am trying to atone for my own sins instead
of accepting the benefits of Your Son's atonement for me on Calvary.
You forgive and forget. Now, with Your help, I will forget them too.
This I ask in Jesus' name. Amen.**

'Poison to yourself'

For reading & meditation – Luke 11:1-13

'Forgive us our sins, for we also forgive everyone who sins against us.' (v.4)

As well as forgetting our failures and the sins that have already been forgiven, we must put from our minds the sins that others have committed against us. In the Lord's Prayer we find: 'Forgive us our sins, for we also forgive everyone who sins against us.' God forgives us; now we must offer that same forgiveness to others.

Have you been sinned against? Search your heart now. Are you harbouring revenge? Forget it. I say this reverently for God's sake and your own sake, banish the thought of retaliation right now.

FURTHER STUDY

Mark 11:24-25;
Luke 7:40-50;
Acts 7:51-60;
Eph. 4:17-32

1. What is the source of great love?

2. Compose a prayer inspired by Stephen's example.

Whenever you hold resentment against another that resentment is poison to *yourself*. I realise that for some this is hard and that you are unable to do it alone. You need God's help. But His help is available. Claim that help now. Say something like this: 'Lord, I am struggling to forgive the person who has wronged me. Just as You have forgiven me, help me to forgive them. Deliver me from every trace of the memory of the hurt, which is damaging to recall. In Your mercy, help me to forget.'

You are facing a new future and need to muster all the courage you can for the days ahead. Press forward with the light step of a forgiven person. The apostle Paul had a past: the blood of the first Christian martyr, Stephen, was on his hands. But he went to God for forgiveness and faced the future with the words we have looked at: 'Forgetting what is behind and straining towards what is ahead, I press on towards the goal ...' (Phil. 3:13-14). So must you.

Lord God, if resentment has soured my spirit, help me now to forgive. In my own strength I simply cannot do so. But I am willing to be made willing. Take my willingness and add Your power. In Jesus' name I ask it. Amen.

No other name

For reading & meditation – Acts 4:1–12

'Salvation is found in no-one else, for there is no other name under heaven … by which we must be saved.' (v.12)

Now that we have put the past with its mistakes, sins and resentment behind us we concentrate on another important biblical instruction: *hold fast to the faith*. We live in times when pluralism has taken a firm hold. Pluralism claims that Jesus is in the same category as Buddha, Confucius or Thor. In today's world you can go into the supermarket of deities and select a god of your choice. The attitude of our age is that one god is as good as another.

Of course, there is much that is commendable in the different faiths. Many Muslims, for instance, are kind and devout, and some of Islam's teaching is admirable. Christians acknowledge what is good. We do not claim that world religions are of no value. That would be bigoted and foolish. What we claim as Christians is what God claims: that the only way a person can have a personal relationship with Him is through His Son, Jesus Christ. Other religions teach about God, and some of their teaching is true: He is all-powerful, all-knowing and all-wise. However, they stop short of the ultimate truth that only through the redeeming Christ can we be guaranteed an entrance into heaven. No other world faith can claim that its greatest teacher was God incarnate. Yet that is what we claim for Jesus Christ.

> **FURTHER STUDY**
> Deut. 6:4–25;
> Luke 9:18–27;
> John 14:1–9;
> Jude vv.3–4
>
> 1. What other gods am I tempted to serve?
>
> 2. How sure am I that Jesus is the way?

Let the pluralists accuse us of intolerance when we refuse to place Jesus in a pantheon (a temple dedicated to all gods). How can we, believing as we do that there are no gods or prophets equal to Him?

Father, thank You for reminding me once again of the truth that only through Jesus can we have a relationship with You. Help me guard this truth and hold on to it no matter how unacceptable it may be for this pluralistic generation. In Christ's name. Amen.

'Find us faithful'

For reading & meditation – Hebrews 10:19–38

'Let us hold unswervingly to the hope we profess, for he who promised is faithful.' (v.23)

Nothing can be of more concern to Christians than that our Saviour is being placed in a pantheon alongside other gods. In this materialistic age we have much in common with other theists, and are glad when they affirm in the face of militant atheism that there is a God. However, in contrast to them, as Christians we claim that Jesus Christ is unique, unparalleled and unsurpassed. Christianity is not one religion among others; it is in a category all by itself. Let us be clear about what we believe, for if we are not then the next generation may have nothing to sing about. John Mohr, in *Find Us Faithful*, wrote a verse which speaks directly to this point:

FURTHER STUDY

Josh. 24:14-27;
1 Chron. 16:7-36;
Hosea 11:1-11;
Acts 4:8-12;
Phil. 2:5-11

1. Why is God's name so crucial?

2. How significant for you is the name of Jesus?

Oh may all who come behind us find us faithful,
May the fires of our devotion light the way,
May the footprints that we leave
Lead them to believe,
And the lives we lead inspire them to obey.*

It has been said that we are always just one generation away from apostasy. We must make certain that we hold fast to the truth that Jesus Christ is God, and dismiss any thought that other prophets were anything other than good men. Like Martin Luther we must say: 'Here I stand, I cannot do otherwise.'

Father, grant me grace to be true to the faith 'that was once for all entrusted to the saints'. Despite the forces that are at work trying to steal its content, may I never weaken in my conviction that Jesus is the only way to God. For His dear name's sake. Amen.

A growing predicament

For reading & meditation – Matthew 28:16–20

'... go ... make disciples of all nations, baptising ... in the name of the Father ... the Son ... the Holy Spirit ...' (v.19)

We must not weaken in our conviction that Jesus Christ is God and humanity's only Saviour. We must be prepared to sing to the tune of divine truth. Consider with me how our age is deriding another essential of the Christian faith – evangelism.

This secular generation is not too critical when it sees us closeted in our churches, but when we attempt to put into operation our Lord's command to 'make disciples of all nations' we are faced with howls of protest. During a TV religious debate, one man said: 'Let's hope that the twenty-first century sees the Christian Church change its ways in relation to making converts. No one has any right to go up to another person and try to persuade them to become a Christian.' If that opinion were his alone I would not be mentioning it here, but sadly it isn't. Many people believe the same. And they pride themselves on believing it. Evangelism, by way of implication, is the work of bigots.

I have always liked the definition of evangelism as 'one beggar telling another where to find bread'. The souls of men and women are desperately hungry for the bread of life that comes from Jesus Christ alone. To make no attempt to offer that bread is to go against the instructions He has given us. In some countries, evangelism is forbidden or restricted by law. That is not the case here in the West. But who knows how long the door will remain open? We must go through that open door before it closes.

FURTHER STUDY

Exod. 20:22–24;
Isa. 45:20–25;
Psa. 47:1–9;
Rom. 1:1–6;
10:1–13

1. How confident am I in the message of the gospel?

2. Who can I pray for who is hungry for this message?

Heavenly Father, You sent Your Son to be our Saviour because there was no other way by which we could be saved. You have commanded us to spread the message. Help us do that. And give us the wisdom and the power to outmanoeuvre all obstacles in its telling. Amen.

Evangelise or fossilise

For reading & meditation – Acts 5:25–42

'Peter and the other apostles replied: 'We must obey God rather than men!'' (v.29)

Christ alone has the bread that satisfies. The following from Gerald May, a psychiatrist and a Christian, brought home to me the need to help people understand that what their souls are searching for can be met only through a personal relationship with Jesus Christ. Secular psychiatrists would benefit greatly from noting this.

'We all have secrets in our hearts … All my life I have longed to say 'yes', to give myself completely to some Ultimate Someone … I kept this secret for many years because it did not fit the image I wanted to present – that of an independent self-sufficient man. This desire to surrender myself had been at least partially acceptable when I was a child, but as a man I tried to put away childish things. When I became a physician and later a psychiatrist it was still more difficult for me to admit – even to myself – that something in me was searching for an ultimate surrender. Society … had taught me to say 'no' rather than 'yes', to try to determine my own destiny rather than give myself, to seek mastery rather than surrender.'

These feelings, so eloquently described, exist in every human heart. They are our ally when we seek to win others for Jesus Christ. Our Lord locked into this same desire when He talked to the Samaritan woman at the well (John 4). There is in every one of us a longing for something that only God through Christ can provide. Believing this, it becomes clear – evangelism is not an option but a necessity.

FURTHER STUDY

Psa. 131:1-3;
Isa. 55:1-5;
Matt. 18:1-4;
John 3:1-8;
6:25-35

1. How does my independence hinder me in doing God's will?

2. How can I become more dependent on God?

Father, we realise that if we fail to share the message of salvation through Your Son then the message will never be known. You have no voice but ours. Help us, despite the difficulties of an increasingly secular society, not to fail You in this. In Jesus' name. Amen.

Whatever happened to hell?

DAY
11

For reading & meditation – Isaiah 7:1–9

'If you do not stand firm in your faith, you will not stand at all.' (v.9)

Critical doctrines, such as the authority of Scripture, are being eroded, not only by those outside the Church but by those inside the Church too. Take the subject of hell, for example. John Blanchard, in his book *Whatever Happened to Hell?*, records this incident: 'When Martin Marty, a professor at the University of Chicago Divinity School, was preparing a Harvard lecture on the subject of hell, he consulted the indexes of several scholarly journals dating back over a period of a hundred years and failed to find a single entry.' His conclusion was that hell had disappeared and no one had noticed.

Though he was heavily criticised for doing so, C.S. Lewis took a biblical stand on the matter of hell. He wrote: 'I willingly believe that the damned are, in one sense, successful, rebels to the end; that *the doors of hell are locked on the inside*'* (emphasis mine). Mention of hell may be omitted from many pulpits today, but it is not omitted from the Bible.

And what about heaven? The concept of heaven is not so much disappearing as being broadened – broadened to include everyone who dies, whether or not they have had a personal relationship with Christ. In the light of what I have said over the past few days – and I have simply skimmed the surface – it is incumbent on us to hold fast to our faith, to be prepared to stand up and be counted. If we do not stand up for Christ how can we expect Him to stand up for us?

FURTHER STUDY

Psa. 1:1-6;
Mark 8:34-38;
John 3:19-21;
2 Pet. 3:8-18

1. Am I ever ashamed of Jesus?

2. What difference does the prospect of future salvation make to me?

Father, I am living in a world that, in general, is opposed to You and Your commandments. Help me to be willing to stand up for You and be counted, no matter what the consequences. I know I can count on You; may You be able to count on me. Amen.

**The Problem of Pain* by C.S Lewis copyright © C.S Lewis Pte. Ltd. 1940.

Alone - with Him

For reading & meditation – Mark 9:14–32

'The boy looked so much like a corpse that many said,
'He's dead.'' (v.26)

I f we are to face the challenge of these changing times we must be willing to be in the minority. The Bible makes it plain that the heroes of the faith were content to be in a minority. In Mark 9 we find Jesus casting an evil spirit out of a young boy. Before it left, the evil spirit convulsed the boy. As a result, 'The child turned like a corpse, so that most people said, 'he is dead'' (v.26, Moffatt). Notice the phrase *most people*. Had a vote been taken, the verdict would have been that the boy was dead and should be buried.

FURTHER STUDY

Judg. 6:11-16;
1 Kings 22:1-28;
Rom. 5:12-21

1. How did
God overcome
Gideon's
timidity?

2. What do
we owe to the
lonely bravery
of Jesus?

Nevertheless, the truth was in the minority of one. Jesus transformed the boy from a state of collapse to health, and restored him to his joyful father.

Following her conversion, Gladys Aylward, a London parlourmaid, believed God wanted her to go to China. Turned down by a missionary society, she remained certain of God's call, and in 1932 travelled to China independently. There she preached the good news and, when the Japanese invaded, led scores of refugee children to safety. She wrote: 'If God has called you to China or any other place and you are sure in your heart, let nothing deter you.'

You will not gain spiritual victory unless, when necessary, you are willing to reject the majority opinion. In Gethsemane Jesus was alone. At a short distance were His disciples, and further away a large crowd sent by the chief priests and the elders (Matt. 26:47). If you desire to be one of the multitude you will find yourself in the crowd farthest from Jesus. Alone, you are with Him.

Lord God, probe deep within my heart and see if there are hidden pockets of cowardice or fear. Dispel them lest they infect my whole system. Deliver me from concern about being in the minority. In Jesus' name I ask it. Amen.

The herd instinct

For reading & meditation – Acts 2:29–41

'... he pleaded with them, 'Save yourselves from this corrupt generation.'' (v.40)

Many people, some Christians included, are dominated by what some psychologists call 'the herd instinct'. We all like to feel we belong, but when society goes in the opposite direction to Christ then we must break away and follow Him. This is the point Peter is making in today's text.

At a meeting of Catholics and Protestants in Dublin, I mentioned the need to be emancipated from the fear of the herd. After I had finished my address, the presiding priest commented: 'The first step towards salvation is breaking with a society that is going downhill fast. At that moment you become a person. You are no longer saying 'Ditto', but 'I choose'. Wise words.

It was said that Zacchaeus could not see Jesus 'because of the crowd' (Luke 19:3). The herd instinct prevents many people from seeing Jesus. One of the common excuses of the day, especially among young people seeking to justify immoral behaviour, is: 'Everybody's doing it.' They are afraid of getting out of step, of being different. 'Society,' it has been said, 'demands conformity. If you fall beneath its standards it will punish you. If you rise above its standards it will persecute you. It demands a grey, average morality.' For this reason most people look around before they act. But in reality they don't act – they react. They are echoes, not persons with voices. You have three choices: you can be self-centred, herd-centred, or Christ-centred. Choose to be Christ-centred, no matter what the cost.

FURTHER STUDY

Deut. 30:11-20;
1 Sam. 15:12-23;
Col. 3:1-4,17-25

1. What excuse did Saul give for his sins?

2. How does Paul say we can stand out from the crowd?

Father, help me I pray to throw off the dominance of the herd and take instead Your yoke upon me. Though I am part of the herd and am willing to play my part, I do not want to be a slave to it. I would be Yours, and Yours alone. In Jesus' name. Amen.

The need to belong

For reading & meditation – Exodus 23:1-9

'Do not follow the crowd in doing wrong.' (v.2)

As my plane descended towards Zimbabwe, I could see herds of wildebeest feeding. I noticed four wildebeest facing away from the others as if watching for an enemy – one at each edge of the herd. The passenger next to me – a Zimbabwean – explained that this was not uncommon. The animals that stood on watch, he said, were called sentinels.

Human beings, too, sense they belong to a herd. The herd protects us, gives us a sense of commonality. We belong.

FURTHER STUDY

Deut. 1:32-36;
Dan. 1:1-21;
1 Pet. 2:13-20

1. Why did
Caleb gain
entrance to the
promised land?

2. How does
Peter say we
can dare to be
different?

Without that sense of belonging we are ill at ease. As social beings we cannot live without being part of society. Dr Overstreet, a psychiatrist, says that the human personality has several needs: the need to belong, the need for independence, the need for reasonable security and the need for personal significance. Of these, he claims, the strongest need is the need to belong: 'We must belong to something that gives us independence, reasonable security and personal significance.'

Christians, however, must realise that they belong first and foremost to God, and only then to the herd. And we belong to the herd as long as this does not conflict with God's purposes. We can be members of the herd but must not let ourselves be dominated by it, and we can be loyal to the herd if that loyalty does not compromise our loyalty to God, which is our supreme loyalty. Jesus identified with the herd, but was not controlled by it. Though He was the friend of sinners, His first loyalty was to God. Ours must be the same.

Father, give me the moral courage to be inwardly and outwardly different, to resist the herd when necessary, to elevate it when I can. Help me to be myself – in You. This I ask in Christ's precious name. Amen.

Beware of contagion

For reading & meditation – Matthew 14:1–12

'Prompted by her mother, she said, 'Give me here on a
platter the head of John the Baptist.'' (v.8)

King Herod made a foolish oath to give the daughter of Herodias
anything she wanted. When she asked for the head of John the
Baptist, Herod, we read, 'was distressed, but because of his oaths
and his dinner guests, he ordered that her request be granted' (v.9).
His overriding concern was not to appear foolish, and so became
a murderer of the man for whom I think he secretly had a great
respect. He killed his conscience when he killed John the Baptist
because John really was his conscience. The herd instinct snuffed
out the last little bit of light within Herod.

One Christian organisation has on its letter
head: 'Beware of the contagion of the world's slow
stain.' We need reminding that the stain of the
world can obscure our Christian faith. The religious
leaders of Jesus' day could have been the leaders
of the new order that He ushered in, but they were
more concerned about what others thought of
them. Everything they did was for people to see
(John 12:42–43). They looked around rather than up,
and when the kingdom was offered to them they
missed its meaning.

FURTHER STUDY
Isa. 52:7-12;
Acts 4:13-22;
1 Pet. 4:1-6
1. What urgent
actions follow
from hearing
that 'God
reigns'?
2. Why should
we live
differently
and who is
our example
for this?

You and I must not be like them. We must have
the moral courage to stand alone if necessary and
be willing to be in the minority. Sometimes the herd appeal is so
strong we can follow it blindly – to our destruction. The herd may
contribute to our life, but it must not determine our life. Vote with
your conscience even if you have to vote alone.

**Father, it is inevitable that my life be lived in the midst of society,
but the source of my life must be elsewhere. Grant that I may
always be motivated by You. In Jesus' name I pray. Amen.**

Free – to be different

For reading & meditation – 1 John 2:7–17
'The world and its desires pass away, but the man who
does the will of God lives for ever.' (v.17)

How powerful is the herd instinct in determining your conduct? Some people are like the dog that walks ahead of a procession – the dog looks back to see which way the crowd are going and then leads in the same direction.

One of the dynamics that put Christ on a cross was the herd instinct. 'But with loud shouts they insistently demanded that [Jesus] be crucified, and their shouts prevailed' (Luke 23:23). 'Wanting to satisfy the crowd, Pilate … had Jesus flogged, and handed him over to be crucified' (Mark 15:15). Peter was thrown into prison because of the herd instinct: 'When [Herod] saw that this pleased the Jews, he proceeded to seize Peter also' (Acts 12:3).

Since the herd is such a powerful driving force, what are we to do about it? There are four possible attitudes: (1) withdraw from it, (2) defy it, (3) succumb to it, (4) overcome it. If we withdraw from it we become antisocial. If we constantly defy it we breed defensiveness and antagonism. If we succumb to it then we are no longer a voice but an echo. The only way for a Christian to overcome its pull is by being totally committed to God. Surrendered to Him, you surrender to nothing else. If you are herd-centred you are insecure; if you are God-centred you are secure. We are destined to be surrounded by the herd, but we are not destined to be dominated by it. Don't be afraid of pulling away from the crowd when necessary. And always remember – one person with God is in the majority.

FURTHER STUDY

Psa. 57:1-11;
Dan. 3:16-18,28;
John 15:18-27;
Rom. 8:5-8

1. How does the psalmist find courage to stand alone?

2. How can we develop a spiritual mindset?

Father, I see that the herd can commend, but it cannot command. I'm the decider. Help me never to forget this. May I be emancipated from the power of the herd so that I can help it to be emancipated – from itself to serve You. In Jesus' name. Amen.

Creek-minded Christians

For reading & meditation – Judges 5:1–18

'Asher remained on the coast and stayed in his coves.'
(v.17)

We now look at another important aspect of daily living that I believe is in accordance with God's truth: *refuse to cling to accustomed ways in the face of the big and adventurous.* Some will find the year ahead to be one of the most exciting of their lives, and will be determined to respond to all the challenges God gives them. Others of us, I am afraid, will be like Asher who 'sat still by the seaboard, clinging to his creeks' (v.17, Moffatt).

Today's text is from 'The Song of Deborah'. Deborah was a judge who put into poetry her reactions when she heard the responses of the various tribes to the call to conquer Canaan. Some showed courage and determination whereas others were either filled with fear or were just disinterested. For instance, the tribe of Reuben stayed 'among the campfires to hear the whistling for the flocks' (v.16). When the call of adventure came they were caught by the shepherd tunes and the ease of the pastoral life. Dan lingered by the ships (v.17), unwilling to sacrifice business interests for the adventure of taking Canaan. Then there was Asher who sat by the seaboard clinging to the creeks. In the face of the big he settled for the little. He was creek-minded rather than ocean-minded.

FURTHER STUDY

Gen. 13:1–18;
Deut. 19:8–10;
1 Kings 19:19–21;
Eph. 3:14–21

1. How was Abraham's vision larger than Lot's?

2. How does grace expand our vision of what God can do?

What kind of Christian are you? Creek-minded or ocean-minded? Decide right now that you are going to accept all the plans God has for you. You are going to be an ocean-minded Christian who loses the little in order to reach out for the big.

Lord God, You who have set eternity in my heart and made me for enlargement, give me the courage in the year that lies ahead to leave the creeks and head for the ocean. I know You have some big plans for me. Help me to fulfil them. In Jesus' name. Amen.

Eternity in our hearts

For reading & meditation – Ecclesiastes 3:1–14
'He has ... set eternity in the hearts of men ...' (v.11)

Yesterday we reflected on the attitude of Asher who 'sat still by the seaboard, clinging to his creeks'. Some people find it more comfortable to stay safe rather than respond to the call of God's ocean.

Recently I read that Valparaiso, Chile, has a beautiful harbour. However, it is strewn with the wreckage of many battered vessels. When a storm blows in from the Pacific, the harbour is not safe. Many ships head out into the ocean where they ride out the storm, but those that remain in the so-called safety of the harbour are battered and broken by the huge waves. Safety for them lies in the open sea – in adventure upon the deep.

I want to urge you to reach out and grasp all that God has for you in the coming year. To cling to your creeks for safety and security is to miss the call of the big. Though I am not a prophet, I feel a strange pull to write words that first I hesitated to express. I am always concerned that what I write comes from the Lord, so if there is any doubt I hold back. For some of you reading these lines I think the Lord's word today is this: drop your littleness and watch it sink into the bigness of God's purposes. God has something bigger for you than you can imagine. Be open to that. Once again I draw your attention to today's text. He has set eternity in your heart. Something big and beautiful is going to happen to you in the days that are ahead. You'll see.

FURTHER STUDY

Psa. 117:1-2;
Isa. 33:17-24;
Luke 5:1-11;
Acts 1:7-11;
Heb. 11:23-24

1. How did Isaiah lift the sights of God's people?

2. How were Peter's horizons enlarged by grace?

Father, I feel You calling me to bigger and better things. And I must respond. Help me leave my littleness behind and open my heart to the big. I want to fall in with Your purposes for me. Reveal them to me and I will comply. In Jesus' name. Amen.

Seaboard poise or creek poise?

For reading & meditation – Matthew 15:1–20

'Why do your disciples break the tradition of the elders?
They don't wash their hands before they eat!' (v.2)

The Pharisees travelled from Jerusalem to Galilee to see what Jesus was doing. The sick were being healed, people were being changed. But they didn't pay attention to that; they simply observed that His disciples ate food with unwashed hands.

A similar mindset can be found among Christians when they miss what God is doing. A movement of Christian unity is sweeping across the world as denominations become less important and the truth of the one body of Christ becomes more significant. Sadly, though, many are letting unity pass them by, clinging to a particular point of view that is marginal rather than essential. We should never compromise the truth, but many are so intolerant that they foster ill will. They miss the big by focusing on the small.

FURTHER STUDY

Psa. 98:1–9;
Isa. 40:12–26;
Neh. 1:1–11;
Matt. 4:18–22;
Acts 16:6–10

1. How might the psalmist inspire me to praise God?

2. How were Paul and Silas helped to see the big picture?

Think again of Asher; he remained 'clinging to his creeks'. The creeks were *his*, and he wasn't going to let go of the accustomed in order to venture into the unaccustomed. A Christian told me he had not attended church while he was on holiday because: 'The churches in the town where I stayed had a different form of worship than I am accustomed to.' How sad. His 'creek' was the only thing for him. Had he been open to other forms of worship, a part of his soul which hitherto had remained untouched might have been opened up. To cling to our creeks simply because we are comfortable means that we may miss something God wants to do in us and through us. You can either have a seaboard poise or a creek poise.

God, forgive me if I am more concerned about staying safe and comfortable than I am about exploring all You have for me along the Christian way. I acknowledge my responsibility and ask You to help me to be an ocean-minded Christian. Amen.

Drowned in a duck-pond

For reading & meditation – Luke 9:57–62

'Jesus replied, 'No-one who puts his hand to the plough and looks back is fit for ... the kingdom of God.'' (v.62)

Sir Francis Drake was once caught in a storm on the River Thames. As he realised his boat was in danger of being sunk, he is said to have remarked: 'I, who have sailed the oceans, am I to be drowned in a duck-pond?' Many are drowned in duck-ponds when they should be out sailing on the ocean, which is big with possibilities.

Has God been speaking to you about something you are afraid to embark on? Go for it. Is there a new ministry for the Lord that you have wondered about but have lacked the courage to move into? Perhaps the Lord is using my words to challenge you today. Of course, it is necessary to follow the usual cautions, such as bringing the matter before the Lord in prayer, and talking it over with a spiritually minded friend or counsellor. Once guidance is clear, though, commit yourself to the venture. New ministries are waiting to be begun: there are Bible study groups to be started, youth projects to be undertaken, maybe another person such as Billy Graham to be converted and raised up as an international evangelist. Yet here you are clinging to your creeks.

FURTHER STUDY

Psa. 45:1–17;
Matt. 10:1–10,
40–42;
Luke 10:1, 17–24;
Rom. 15:17–29

1. What growth did the disciples see?

2. In what ways have I grown lately?

The people who cling to their creeks are invariably wrecked at the point of spiritual poise and satisfaction. They settle for comfort and the status quo, but deep down they realise they have not reached their potential in God – and that is a very unsatisfying feeling indeed. For we have been made for growth and creation. If we do not grow we groan – inwardly.

Lord God, infuse into me Your own spirit of adventure and creativity. May I launch out boldly for You and respond to the call of the big. I want to soar, not stagnate. Help me do so. In Jesus' name. Amen.

Launch out

For reading & meditation – John 2:1–11

'His mother said to the servants, 'Do whatever he tells
you.'' (v.5)

How do we break the habit of being creek-minded and become ocean-minded? First, we must break with all negativism. Go over your life prayerfully to see if there are any areas where you are still negative. They will not be easy to find for we all have blind spots. We build defences constructed of rationalisations around those blind spots. Push past those defences and root out the negativism.

Second, stop blaming others for your difficulties. Others may be partly to blame for what has happened to you, but you may have contributed to your difficulties by your wrong reactions – such as anger, resentment and self-pity.

Third, replace all negativism with positivism. The way to overcome evil, says Paul in Romans 12:21, is to overcome it with good. It is the same with negativism; the only way to overcome it is to replace it with a positive. Pause before responding negatively to a proposal to see if there is something there to which you can respond positively. One chief executive I know always tries to end a meeting

FURTHER STUDY

Neh. 4:1-23;
Rom. 4:16-25;
Heb. 11:17-19

1. How did Abraham overcome his doubts?

2. How did Nehemiah handle opposition?

on a positive note. By doing so he is following Jesus' example. The Pharisees criticised Him, complaining that He ate with tax collectors and sinners (Luke 15:1-2). That was very negative. Did Jesus meet a negative with a negative? No, He told three parables – the lost sheep, the lost coin and the lost son – a positive presentation of the truth that God is eager to save. He came out on the positive side of a negative situation. So can you.

**Lord God, there is a vast ocean of opportunity ahead of me; forgive
me if I have been clinging to my creeks. Now I want to launch out.
Show me what You want me to do, and I will do it. In Jesus' name.
Amen.**

'God has died'

For reading & meditation – Matthew 6:25–34

'... do not worry about your life, what you will eat or drink; or about your body, what you will wear.' (v.25)

Jesus emphasised in the passage before us: stop worrying. Much spiritual potential is destroyed because of worry. In my opinion it is legitimate to be concerned over issues or even upset by them, but it is not legitimate to let the mind dwell on them to such a degree that our daily functioning is brought to a halt. 'Worry,' argues one writer, 'is a form of atheism ... It says, 'I am not sure that God can take care of this so I am going to take control of it by worrying.'' The words 'Why trust when you can worry?' were placarded on a sign outside a church.

FURTHER STUDY

Psa. 56:1-13;
94:18-19;
Phil. 4:4-9

1. How, like the psalmist, can I maintain my trust in God?

2. What does Paul say we should fix our minds on?

One day, when Martin Luther, the German Reformer, was particularly worried, his wife appeared in the room dressed from head to foot in black. Luther asked: 'Has someone died?' 'Yes,' she responded, 'God has died ... God is dead.' 'Don't be ridiculous,' Luther retorted, 'God is not dead. How can such a thing be so?' 'Well,' explained his wife, 'the way you are behaving that is exactly how it seems.' Luther saw the point, put aside his worries, and began to praise God for all the good things that were happening in his life.

My father wrote this in one of my very first Bibles:

Worry is an old man with bended head,
Carrying a load of feathers he thinks is lead.

Believe me, when you *think* things are lead, they will *feel* as heavy as lead.

Lord God, forgive me if, even though I am a Christian, I practise a form of atheism. When I try to be my own god by fussing and worrying then I do not allow You to be God. I turn over to You right now all my worries. I am released. In Jesus' name. Amen.

The physical effects of worry

For reading & meditation – Luke 12:22–34

'Who of you by worrying can add a single hour to his life?'
(v.25)

Worry,' commented a medical doctor, 'is sand in the machinery of life. As we are conquering the physical side of disease we are losing the battle on the mental and spiritual side. We know almost everything about life except how to live it.' Another doctor admits: 'When I find a purely physical cause of disease I begin to feel like a doctor again.' The British Medical Association claims that 60 to 80 per cent of physical problems are rooted in our thinking. According to a heart specialist: 'It is not so much our arteries that are the problem as our attitudes.' The effect of worry on the body is well known to all who are involved in treating physical problems. One optician has discovered that worry can even distort vision, which makes the person concerned all the more worried.

FURTHER STUDY

Psa. 37:1-40;
Isa. 8:11-14;
John 14:1-14

1. How does Isaiah say God's people can be distinctive?

2. How do Jesus' words strengthen my trust?

John Evans, a pastor in Canada, tells the story of a business executive who suffered distressing symptoms for about six months. The problem was rooted in this incident. He copied out four long words from his medical records during the doctor's absence from the room. He did not know their meaning but believed they indicated he had an incurable condition. When another doctor explained the meaning of these terms he went away relieved and had no further symptoms.

Clearly, worry takes its toll on our physical system. No organ is immune from worry. So you had better stop worrying before your health and effectiveness as a Christian is weakened.

Lord God, come into my life and take away all useless worry. Reign in my life, for where You are, worry cannot be. Where You are not, worry and physical ailments increase. Through Your Holy Spirit come in. I consent. In Jesus' name. Amen.

'Shallow breathers'

For reading & meditation – Luke 8:1–15

'... as they go on their way they are choked by life's worries, riches and pleasures, and they do not mature.' (v.14)

In the parable before us now Jesus talks about the seed being choked by life's worries, riches and pleasures. We would have said that pleasures and riches are the main cause of difficulties. Jesus put worry first.

I once asked a number of people which they thought had the most negative effect on the personality: worries, riches or pleasures. All said that unrestrained indulgence in pleasures were the chief sources of arrested spiritual development. Yet

FURTHER STUDY

Psa. 20:1-9;
Prov. 3:1-8;
Rom. 15:7-13

1. According to Proverbs, what are the effects of trust?

2. What grounds does Paul give us for trusting in God?

ask any counsellor and I think they would agree with me that life does not bear this out. I would say more people are mentally, physically and spiritually debilitated by fear and worry than any other single thing. Worry not only chokes the Word of God but chokes the worrier. 'A worrier is always a shallow breather,' one doctor told me.

I used to be a chronic worrier. Many years ago a gypsy knocked at my door, and as soon as I opened it she commented: 'You are a worrier. I can see it in your face.' When I mentioned this to my wife her response was: 'I could have told you that, and I'm not psychic. I noticed it when we first met, and living with you has confirmed it.' There and then I made up my mind to stop worrying and largely, I think, I have succeeded. Oh, I have concerns, upsets, problems and so on, but few or no worries. How did I learn to stop worrying? That is what I will share with you over the next couple of days.

Lord Jesus Christ, no worries lurked within Your heart to cripple and hinder. You walked through this world unhurried, unflurried and unworried. Give me that same attitude to life for I want no enemies within. For Your own dear name's sake. Amen.

Overcoming worry

For reading & meditation – Romans 8:28–39

'And we know that in all things God works for the good of those who love him ...' (v.28)

Some say that to claim you can live without worry is merely academic. It sounds good but is impossible to put into practice. I disagree. Here is a digest of the principles I have followed for many years now that, by God's grace, have turned me from a chronic worrier to a man of faith and confidence. I am not talking about genuine concerns but nagging worries.

The first principle is: *face and feel whatever is troubling you and do not try to evade it.* Many Christians, when a problem arises, pretend that it does not exist and look for a way of not feeling it. Such denial is harmful to the personality. You must be willing to face an issue and feel its pain before you can do anything about it.

Second, *wherever you are and whatever circumstances you find yourself in, remind yourself that God is there also.* Each time something arises that might give cause for useless worry, God is there with you and has promised that all things will work together for good. It is possible to quote today's text in a condescending way and use it as a balm to console ourselves. We can quote the exact words yet possibly be saying in our hearts: 'All things *may* be working together for good to those who love God, but we will need to be a lot further down the road before we see how any good can come out of this.' You will gain no consolation from this. Believe that God can work in everything – your difficulties as well as your delights.

FURTHER STUDY

Psa. 46:1-11;
Isa. 46:1-13;
Hab. 3:17-18;
Acts 18:7-11

1. Are you conscious of being 'carried' by God?

2. What challenges face you, as they did Paul?

Father, help me to so live that though I still carry concerns, I do not dissipate my energies in useless worries. May I dwell deeply on the fact that You are with me in all things so that I throw off worry as a healthy body throws off germs. In Jesus' name. Amen.

'Lick the honey'

For reading & meditation – Hebrews 13:1–8

'... God has said, 'Never will I leave you; never will I forsake you.'' (v.5)

The third principle to help us overcome worry: *pray about everything*. Just repeating the Lord's Prayer delivers one woman from all her worries. When I was faced with the dilemma of either finding new power or giving up the ministry, many people encouraged me, but I found prayer to be the most powerful encouragement of all. Worries are not so much resolved as dissolved through prayer.

Fourth, *learn to meet today, today*. Jesus showed His penetrating insight when He said: 'Do not worry about tomorrow, for tomorrow will worry about itself. Each day has enough trouble of its own' (Matt 6:34). Troubles will come to us, but we must not bring forward tomorrow's troubles into today. If you do so then you will spoil today.

FURTHER STUDY

Psa. 34:1-22;
Hag. 2:1-5;
Luke 18:1-8;
John 10:22-30

1. How does Haggai answer the doubts of God's people?

2. What assurance does Jesus give me?

Fifth, *remind yourself that God will never let go of you*. 'The Lord your God is a merciful God; he will not abandon or destroy you' (Deut. 4:31). That verse has been a great anchor in my life. I may let go of God, but will He let go of me? Never.

A man fell down a well, but his fall was broken by his clothes becoming caught on a root sticking out from the side. Hanging there, he realised he might soon plummet to the bottom. Yet in that grim situation he noticed a leaf growing from the wall of the well, on which was a drop of honey. Reaching out, he licked the honey from the leaf and blessed God. Today's text reminds us that He will never leave us. So when life spins out of control, don't panic; lick the honey and bless His name.

Father, worry has played such a part in my life, but it shall reign no longer. I turn my life over to You afresh to be delivered from every useless worry. All my worries shall be dissolved in Your great quiet. I am eternally thankful. Amen.

'Much ado about nothing'

For reading & meditation – John 1:1-14
'Through him all things were made; without him nothing
was made that has been made.' (v.3)

In this fiercely secular age we should also *be convinced that we are made inherently for the Christian way.* The Christian way is the only way to live – period. Some unbelievers would have us believe that the Christian way is beautiful but unrealistic. This is how one critic expressed it: 'The Christian way of idealism breaks its delicate wings upon the hard facts of reality. It may work in some other world, but in this world we must not waste our time with the impossible ... that excites us with much ado about nothing.'

This scepticism is shared by most unbelievers, and you and I will not be able to advance one inch towards the heart of this secular age if we ourselves are not clear that we are made for the Christian way.

For most of my life I have been gripped by the fact that the Christian way is found not only in the texts of Scripture but in the very fabric of life itself. The text at the top of this page brings home to us the truth that the universe was made by Christ, so it follows that, having been made by Him, His character is stamped into every part of it. In Acts 9 we read about people belonging to 'the Way'. 'Way' is spelt with a capital W indicating that it is not just *a* way but *the* way. And not just the way of salvation either, but the way for everything. When we follow *the* way we go with the grain of the universe.

If we harbour any doubt about the fact that the Christian way is the only way that the universe backs then it is a fatal doubt; it will put to death all our highest hopes and possibilities.

FURTHER STUDY

Psa. 19:1-14;
Acts 17:16-34;
Heb. 1:1-14

1. In what two ways does the psalmist say God reveals Himself?

2. How does Paul present Jesus as satisfying a universal longing?

Gracious God, I see that the stamp of Christ is on everything; His is the way life has been made to work. Deepen my conviction on this matter, for if I doubt here I will have doubts all down the line. Please help me, Father. In Jesus' name. Amen.

No moral holidays

For reading & meditation – Acts 19:1–22

'... some of them became obstinate; they refused to believe and publicly maligned the Way. So Paul left them.' (v.9)

We cannot live effectively for Jesus Christ in this world unless we are working with the grain of the universe and not against it. The first time I discovered this truth – the truth that in following the Christian way we are following the way of reality – I remember saying to myself: 'Selwyn Hughes, by being a Christian you are not going against the thrust of the universe but with it!'

I long for this truth to lodge in your spirit also. If it does, then the conviction that your life is related to the sum total of reality,

FURTHER STUDY

Psa. 145:1–21;
Isa. 55:6–11;
Heb. 10:19–25

1. Am I convinced that to be a Christian is to go with the grain of the universe?

2. How has Jesus opened up the way of life?

and that that reality is working with you and not against you, will act as an anchor to your soul. You will not be thrown off balance when you see sinful men and women prospering in their sinfulness for you will realise that no one can live against the nature of reality *and get away with it*. Sinful men and women may appear to escape the consequences, but inwardly they are perturbed. In every possible situation the Christian way is the way to behave. There are no exceptions. You cannot take a moral holiday and say: 'I will live a Christian life for fifty weeks of the year and take a two-week holiday away from Christian principles.' An idea such as that will

not work. If we try to act in some way other than the Christian way then the sums will not add up. Life will become tangled and twisted. Life works only when we follow the way God ordained – *the* way.

My Father and my God, how can I ever cease to thank You that while others stumble I happened on this – the way? My doubts are now laid to rest. Deepen my conviction that there is no different way. This is the way for which I was made. Amen.

The great illusion

For reading & meditation – Psalm 73:1–28

'When I tried to understand all this, it was oppressive to
me till I entered the sanctuary of God ...' (vv.16-17)

Inherently we are made for the Christian way. When we see clearly that we are working with the nature of reality, we will be able to remain steady when faced with the difficult questions of life, such as: Why is it that such a large number of sinful people seem to prosper when those living honest lives have so little?

This question troubled the writer of Psalm 73. 'The arrogant,' he says, 'have no struggles; their bodies are healthy ... always carefree, they increase in wealth' (vv.3–4,12). Then he pleads his own virtue before the Lord: 'Surely in vain have I kept my heart pure; in vain have I washed my hands in innocence' (v.13). The psalmist felt peeved as he saw the prosperity of the wicked until he entered the sanctuary of God and came to realise that their pleasure was only temporary. The universe would have the last word, which was death.

Some US schoolboys were allowed to take a fruit machine apart to study its mechanism. They discovered the machine was designed to yield up one dollar in every ten. The machine's designer made sure it would work in the interests of those with evil intentions – those eager to profit from people's gullibility. However, when our Creator made this universe He designed it in accordance with His own character. Thus truth and righteousness will endure and evil ultimately fail. Wrong may seem to bring prosperity for a while but it is doomed. 'Evil,' it has been said, 'is the great illusion.' It is.

FURTHER STUDY

Phil. 3:17-4:1;
2 Thess. 1:5-12;
1 John 2:28-3:3

1. What are your deepest ambitions?

2. How does knowing the end help me live now?

**Father, I see You have designed the universe so that in the end good
is rewarded and evil punished. Your judgments are sure. No one
can escape them. How glad I am that I will not suffer Your wrath
because of Christ's gift of salvation. Amen.**

Allergic to evil

For reading & meditation – Colossians 1:15–23

'For by him all things were created ... all things were created by him and for him.' (v.16)

If we had eyes to see, we would read in all creation the words: 'Made By Him and For Him'. Sin, of course, has damaged this beautiful universe, but it is clear that the divine intention was for the world to work in Christ's way.

Sin, I believe, is unnatural. It is literally 'missing the mark' (Greek, *hamartia*), the mark for which we are made. That 'mark' is etched into every part of us. It is the will of God. 'The laws of our being,' argues one medical doctor, 'are none other than the laws of God – they are the laws of God wrought into the constitution of our being. To be true to them is to be true to God, and to be true to God is to be true to them.' Another doctor admits: 'I have come to the conclusion that we have Christian glands, Christian tissues, Christian organs ... my body functions better when Christ is in it.' 'Created by him and for him.'

FURTHER STUDY

Psa. 24:1-10;
John 1:1-5;
Rev. 21:22-27

1. How large, as John sees it, is the scope of salvation?

2. How does the vision of Jesus inspire my worship?

Sin throws into disorder every situation, both physically and spiritually, for evil is against the nature of reality. One preacher says of evil: 'It is the will to live put into reverse.' Human nature is allergic to evil. When we take it into our systems our inner selves revolt against it. This may not be obvious at first. A recent newspaper report tells of a woman who gave her husband a minute dose of arsenic every morning in his cereal. Eventually it killed him. It is the same with evil. Sooner or later it kills.

Father, You have made me for Yourself and I know that no part of my life will function properly unless it is infused with Your purity and love. Help me to work with the grain of the universe and not against it, and deliver me from evil. Amen.

The great crash

For reading & meditation – Matthew 7:24–29

'... everyone who ... does not put [my words] into practice is like a foolish man who built his house on sand.' (v.26)

J. Middleton Murray, a commentator on Christian issues, said in *Heroes of Thought*: 'If men and women do not care about the kingdom of God then they will find the same lesson taught by life itself. Life cannot be abused. To the judgment seat of God mankind will take with them only a life that was lived, and the judgment of God and the judgment of life are the same.' He predicted that one day science will state: 'This is the way to live, and not this.' And when that happens, people will respond: 'But the way you tell us to live is the Christian way, and the way you tell us not to live is the un-Christian way.' No doubt scientists will reply: 'Of that we cannot speak; we can only affirm that life has to be lived in this way if we are to experience its fullest potential.'

Jesus was surprised not so much at people's wickedness as their stupidity. 'Don't you see you are living against life and that when you do you will get hurt?' In the text for today notice the word 'everyone'. 'If you build on My words,' said Jesus, 'your house will remain standing; if you don't, it will go down with a crash.' There are no exceptions – this will happen to everyone.

Incorporate this truth into your life and, as you go your way, remind yourself constantly that the Christian way is not imposed on life but exposed by it. Let this be a conviction, not just an opinion. An opinion is something you hold. A conviction is something that holds you.

FURTHER STUDY

Psa. 107:1-43;
Isa. 50:4-11;
John 11:25-27;
12:37-50

1. How dangerous is it, according to Isaiah, to try to live by one's own light?

2. How crucial to us are the words of Jesus?

Father, I am so thankful I have found the way; not just the way to heaven, but the way to everything – period. What a difference this has made in my life. Help me hold this truth as a conviction, not merely an opinion. In Jesus' name. Amen.

A snare to avoid

For reading & meditation – John 17:1-19

'I have brought you glory on earth by completing the work you gave me to do.' (v.4)

Another important lesson is: *avoid the snare of over-involvement*. We must be adventurous for God but we must also make sure that our involvement in spiritual activities does not turn into over-involvement.

Today's text today goes to the heart of this issue for here we find Jesus telling His Father that He had brought Him glory on earth by doing the work He had given Him to do. 'I have completed the task *you* gave me to do' (v.4, Phillips). *You.* Our Lord did not allow Himself to be drawn into areas of spiritual activity that might have been commendable but were not right for Him. He finished His years of ministry on earth having done only those tasks that the Father had assigned to Him.

FURTHER STUDY

1 Kings 8:55-61;
Psa. 27:1-6;
Luke 10:38-42;
1 Tim. 4:11-16

1. What are the key elements of Solomon's blessing?

2. What priority did Mary choose?

I am making this point because many Christians I meet feel they are not pleasing God unless they are working to change everything they see that is wrong. But we are not called to set right every wrong. We are to do what we are able and leave the rest to God and others. Calvin Miller puts it like this: 'I often see a great deal of neurosis among evangelicals who have to wrestle the devil and pin him three times before they can feel like they are really the friends of God.' Frustration comes when we try to save the world. That is God's job. Watch that you don't stumble under enormous spiritual concerns that exceed the number God would have you carry.

Loving heavenly Father, I see that You have not put me in charge of correcting all that is wrong. Show me just what I should be doing, and how many concerns I should carry. Then help me leave the rest to You and to others. In Jesus' name. Amen.

Concerns versus control

For reading & meditation – John 5:16–30

'I tell you the truth, the Son can do nothing by himself;
he can do only what he sees his Father doing ...' (v.19)

The quickest way to experience frustration in your Christian life is to believe that God has called you to set right all the wrongs you come across. 'When we try to take the enforcement of New Testament morality into our own hands,' says one writer, 'we discover our utter frailty.' I am not suggesting we should turn a blind eye to glaring wrongs and be concerned only about those things that lie within our immediate circle of activities; I am simply saying that we must watch we don't take on more burdens than God wants us to carry.

A few years ago a zealous Christian in the United States shot and killed a doctor who had performed hundreds of abortions. The killer, according to one report, was otherwise a gentle and well-respected Christian who was troubled about the problem of abortion on demand. The hearts of many people in his local church reached out to him as they tried to understand such lunacy. But they had to recognise that he had allowed a concern to become an over-concern, which led him in due course to commit the act of murder. One commentator said of this action: 'Playing God is a game we are ill equipped to play.'

It is possible for Christians to 'care' themselves into neurosis. We must be careful that our concerns do not lead us to the point where we want to control others, because when that happens we ourselves will be defeated and frustrated.

FURTHER STUDY

1 Sam. 26:6-12;
Prov. 20:22;
John 14:23-31;
2 Cor. 10:12-18

1. What helps Jesus' disciples to focus on the right things?

2. How did Paul guard against 'over-concern'?

Father, in a world where hostile philosophies predominate it is too easy to be drawn into attempting to correct everything that is wrong. Save me from this, dear Lord. May my cares and concerns be always under Your control. In Jesus' name. Amen.

Intense peace

For reading & meditation – Philippians 4:1–9

'... the peace of God, which transcends all understanding, will guard your hearts and ... minds in Christ ...' (v.7)

Although God has called us to be people of moral integrity and to take a stand against immorality, He does not expect us to correct everything that is wrong. 'Many Christians,' I heard one preacher say, 'appear to be godly, but inwardly they are at sixes and sevens. The peace they pretend to have goes to pieces when they try to be something they are not – the saviours of the world.'

Well-known secular writer Alan Watts has made a case for combining Hinduism and Christianity. He applauds Christian truths such as submission to the will of God, but is of the opinion that Hindus have more inner peace. Is he right? Well, there is no way that Christianity and Hinduism can be synthesised. But Alan Watts has a point when he observes that Christians talk about peace a great deal but are so intense about it. I know some Christians, and I am sure you do too, who are like ducks on a pond; on the surface they appear peaceful and serene, seemingly floating along effortlessly, but beneath the surface their feet are going like crazy.

FURTHER STUDY

Psa. 94:1-23;
Isa. 26:1-11;
Acts 13:38;
Phil. 3:7-14;
1 Tim. 2:1-7

1. How does the psalmist view God?

2. On what does Paul focus?

A minister tells how he was delivered from regarding himself as a watchdog charged with preventing his congregation from sinning. One member of his church said to him: 'Pastor, you are so worried about the sins we may commit that no day is a happy one.' He accepted the rebuke and admitted: 'Just relinquishing responsibility for the sins of others and committing the whole matter to God took an immense load off me.' It always does.

Father, help me see that trying to save the world by myself is not only too much for me but thwarts and devalues the work of the Holy Spirit. May I be content to do only what You want me to do. In Jesus' name. Amen.

The rescuer syndrome

For reading & meditation – Galatians 6:1–10

'Carry each other's burdens, and in this way you will fulfil
the law of Christ.' (v.2)

A first step when training counsellors is to help them understand
the dynamics that may have drawn them into the counselling
ministry. A number are attracted to counselling because of the
good feelings they get as a result of rescuing people from their
problems. This is termed the 'rescuer syndrome'. Unless this is
identified and dealt with before trainees go any further, it can
cause major spiritual problems. We are to help others not because
of the good feelings this brings us but because it is right.

I said that some Christians 'care' themselves into
neurosis. Once in Japan I gave a talk to a group of
missionaries on the subject of emotional problems
that beset Christian workers. After my talk a woman
told me: 'Your words went like an arrow into my
heart. All my life I have thought God was not pleased
with me unless I was working myself to death,
carrying some sickness in my body, or agonising
over all the wrongs in the world. I have been like
Job who scraped himself with broken pottery and
sat among the ashes, but I have been doing so because I wanted
God and everyone around to see that I am sincere about the fallen
state of the world. Now I can understand why I have been doing
this: I have been persuading myself I care for others but really
what I have been doing is caring for myself.'

When we care too much, we are not really caring; we are
probably trying to meet some need of ours that God has not been
allowed to satisfy.

FURTHER STUDY

Psa. 103:1–22;
Num. 11:10–17;
Rom. 8:31–34;
1 Pet. 5:1–7

1. For what does
the psalmist
praise God?

2. How did God
answer Moses?

**Father, grant that I may never 'care' myself into neurosis. Help me
to be clear in my motives so that I minister to people not because of
the returns I get but because I am so filled with You that I can do no
other. In Jesus' name. Amen.**

Minding your own business

For reading & meditation – John 21:15–23

'... Peter ... asked, 'Lord, what about him?' Jesus answered,
'... what is that to you? You must follow me." (vv.21-22)

We can fall into the trap of over-involvement by being unduly concerned about what others should be doing instead of focusing on what God wants us to be doing. In today's reading Simon Peter is rebuked by Jesus because of his concern about his fellow disciple – John. Simon Peter had already been through a time of personal challenge – Christ had to ask him three times if he loved Him. So sensing a lack in himself he focuses his attention on John: 'Lord, what about him?' This is compensation – becoming curious about someone else to cover up a lack in oneself. Jesus says to him: 'What is that to you? You must follow me.' Or: 'Don't become involved in things you shouldn't be involved in – just keep your eyes on Me.'

FURTHER STUDY

Deut. 17:18-20;
John 1:35-51;
1 Cor. 3:1-9;
2 Cor. 5:14-21

1. How does Paul view his own ministry?

2. To what did Jesus call His disciples?

A counsellor tells how a politician he was counselling started to criticise the people who worked for him. So the counsellor opened his Bible to John 21 and read: 'What is that to you? You must follow me.' The politician slapped his knee and admitted: 'You've got me.' He realised his eyes were on others instead of on Jesus.

When you are busy being involved in what others are doing you are over-involved. You are concentrating on others instead of on Christ. So avoid all types of over-involvement. Make sure you are involved only in those things that God wants you to be involved in. Over-involvement leads to maximum weariness with minimum effectiveness. Appropriate involvement leads to maximum effectiveness with minimum weariness.

Father, if I am over-concerned about others then help me to take to heart Your rebuke: 'What is that to you? You must follow me.' Help me to keep my eyes only on You and the things to which You direct my attention. In Christ's name. Amen.

Free from stain

For reading & meditation – 1 Timothy 6:11–21

'... Christ Jesus, who while testifying before Pontius Pilate made the good confession ...' (v.13)

Another spiritual challenge is: *keep your commission free from stain.* 'In the presence of God who is the Life of all, and of Christ Jesus who testified to the good confession before Pontius Pilate, I charge you to keep your commission free from stain ...' (vv. 13–14, Moffatt).

Timothy is being told, first, to keep his commission in the presence of God, the One who contains in Himself all the resources we need. Second, he is to keep it in the presence of Jesus Christ, who before Pilate witnessed to the truth. It is not enough that we draw our life from God; we must witness to that fact, and live in the face of all antagonism. Pilate stands for anything that thwarts our Christian testimony. We are to meet that opposition unflinchingly, even though it may mean, as it did for Jesus, that life crimsons into a cross.

FURTHER STUDY

Matt. 10:17-20;
Mark 13:9-11;
John 18:33-38;
Acts 22:1-21;
Rom. 13:1-7

1. How did Paul defend himself?

2. When do I find it hardest to confess Jesus as my Lord?

The commission given to Timothy was the sum of the commands listed in verses 11 and 12: 'pursue righteousness, godliness, faith, love, endurance and gentleness. Fight the good fight of the faith. Take hold of the eternal life ...' As Christians, all of those commands apply as much to you and me. We are commanded to keep them free from stain and to live out the life God has put into us, even though sometimes it may be thwarted by opposition. Jesus was able to overcome Pilate because He was not like him. Pilate stood on one side of the truth, Jesus on the other. That was the route to His overcoming; it is the route to our overcoming also.

Gracious Father, I too have a commission from You – a commission to pursue righteousness, godliness, faith, love, endurance, gentleness, and to take hold of eternal life. May I be conscious of that commission every day of my life. Amen.

What a reflection!

For reading & meditation – Philippians 2:1-11

'Your attitude should be the same as that of
Christ Jesus ...' (v.5)

Like Timothy, we are commissioned to pursue righteousness, godliness and so on. We must keep that commission free from stain – of what?

First, we must keep it free from the stain of wrong attitudes. It is possible to do the right actions with the wrong attitude. Some Christians 'fight the good fight of the faith' with boxing gloves on. They take too literally the word 'fight' in Paul's command in 1 Timothy 6:12, and use a harsh approach in their attempt to make people good. Can we, by acting like the devil, cast out the devil?

In the Moffatt translation today's text reads: 'Treat one another with the same spirit as you experience in Christ Jesus.' How does He treat us? Gently, lovingly and with consideration. 'I appeal ... by the gentleness and consideration of Christ ...' (2 Cor. 10:1, Moffatt). Could there be anything more lovely than that phrase: 'the consideration of Christ'? There was nothing abrasive about Jesus. To all who arte burdened He issues this invitation: 'Take my yoke upon you and learn from me, for I am gentle and humble ...' (Matt. 11:29). His heart went out to the crowds because they were helpless (Matt. 9:36), and to the widow who had lost her only son (Luke 7:11–15). After He had preached at Nazareth we read: 'All spoke well of him and were amazed at the gracious words that came from his lips' (Luke 4:22). A sweet aroma of graciousness characterised everything our Lord did. His words and deeds reflected His character – and what a reflection!

FURTHER STUDY

Gen. 45:1-15;
Luke 9:46-56;
Eph. 4:20-24;
4:32-5:2

1. How gently have people treated you in the Church?

2. How can we deal with harsh attitudes in ourselves and others?

My Father and my God, deliver me from harsh attitudes that may stain the commission You have given me. Help me treat others with the same consideration that You show to me. In Jesus' name I pray. Amen.

'Wrapped in goodwill'

For reading & meditation – John 7:25–44

'... come to me and drink. Whoever believes in me ... living
water will flow from within ...' (vv.37-38)

I heard of a group of young adults – all Christians – who
took time out during the Christmas period to feed homeless
people on London's embankment. One of those they catered for
commented: 'Others give us better food and much more to eat, but
you Christians seem to wrap everything in goodwill.' It would be
wrong to suggest that non-Christian agencies doing similar work
are not motivated by goodwill, but the people whom the Christians
fed sensed there was a spirit in their giving that was different
from that of the others. It was the spirit of Christ.
The flavour lingered on long after the food had been
digested. So whatever you do for others, be sure to
do it in a Christian way – in the spirit of Jesus Christ.

Another thing from which we must keep our
commission free is the stain of emptiness. In the
passage we read from 1 Timothy 6 we noticed that
Paul charged Timothy to keep his commission free
from stain 'in the presence of God who is the Life
of all' (1 Tim. 6:13, Moffatt). The implication here is
that as God has endless resources, it is foolish not
to avail ourselves of those resources. A visitor to Texas remarked
to a local person: 'It looks like rain.' The Texan looked up at the
clouds scudding overhead and said: 'Naw, those are just empties
drifting by.' In God's name I implore all of you to make sure that
the same cannot be said of you morally and spiritually – that you
are just empties drifting by.

FURTHER STUDY

Exod. 31:1–11;
Psa. 16:1-11;
2 Cor. 8:1-9;
1 Pet. 2:13-25

1. What does
Paul encourage
the Corinthians
to give?

2. What was
Peter's counsel?

**Lord God, forgive me if, while unbelievers around me need the
refreshing rain of the Spirit, I am just an empty drifting by. You
have given me the promise of endless resources; help me avail
myself of them. In Christ's name. Amen.**

More stain

DAY
40

For reading & meditation – Leviticus 19:1–19

'Do not seek revenge or bear a grudge against one of your people, but love your neighbour as yourself.' (v.18)

After a speaker had finished giving the addresses at a conference, a minister confided in him: 'When you used the word "adequacy" it made me shudder. I feel I am not adequate for the task God has given me.' How sad.

'Life,' it has been said, 'is not only about attainment, but obtainment.' Many Christians are trying to attain the commission God has given them without first linking themselves to His resources. Two sisters were about to move into a lovely newly constructed house. In the kitchen the oven was ready for them to cook meals, but at the last minute they discovered it was useless, because it had not been connected to the main power cable in the street. Similarly, your life and mine will be useless unless we are attached to the life and power that is found in God.

Yet another thing from which we must keep our commission free is the stain of bitterness. There is nothing worse than to see a believer trying to live out the Christian life but eaten up by resentment. How can we get rid of hate? Frances Ridley Havergal, who wrote so many beautiful hymns, was at one time early in her life so bad tempered that during a tantrum she would lie on the floor and beat her head against the floorboards. So how did she rid herself of this temper and fulfil her commission? By doing what everyone with anger and resentment has to do: by bringing every resentment to God, asking forgiveness for them, and inviting Him to bury them miles deep at the cross.

FURTHER STUDY

Gen. 4:2–8;
Psa. 101:1–8;
Col. 3:1–14;
Heb. 12:14–17;
James 1:19–27

1. What are the Colossians urged to put on?

2. What does James define as 'pure religion'?

Father, I realise that the Christian faith is not sound if it is stained by resentment. Help me dissolve any resentment I have in Your love, for I want no corrosion in my soul. In Jesus' name. Amen.

Are your ears red?

For reading & meditation – Philippians 1:1-11

'... so that you may be able to discern what is best and may be pure and blameless until the day of Christ ...' (v.10)

Since every believer is still 'a Christian in the making', insincerity and unconscious hypocrisy can be found in the best of us. They are really the tributes we pay to truth and goodness. Even when we lapse from goodness and truth we simulate them, thus acknowledging that we ought to be true and good.

A painting of the Lord's Supper I once saw made a lasting impression on me. Jesus is depicted as telling His disciples that one of them will betray Him. Each disciple looks towards the Master questioning: 'Lord, is it I?' The painter has used a reddish hue for the ears of the disciples, and made those of Judas a little redder. When we come across the word 'betrayal' most of us think of Judas Iscariot. We feel indignant because of the way he treated our Lord. But does our indignation cover up our own betrayals? Maybe they are not as damaging as Judas' betrayal, but they hurt the heart of the Saviour just as much. If we have heard someone criticising Christ have we moved away and refused to identify with our Lord? Have we stood by when we have seen serious wrongs being done and not said a word? We who preach the gospel, do we do so for show or for the Saviour?

If you recognise some dualism in yourself then kneel down before God, confess it to Him, and ask Him to help you overcome it. From now on make it a daily commitment to keep your commission free from all stain.

FURTHER STUDY

Psa. 26:1-12;
Luke 13:10-17;
2 Cor. 6:3-10;
Col. 3:22-25;
2 Pet. 1:1-8

1. How did Paul commend himself to the Corinthians?

2. What does Peter say about goodness?

Lord God, help me to stand before You with open face and open mind and an open being. I want to be changed. Help me not to rationalise my insincerity but to face it and, with Your Spirit's help, to deal with it. In Jesus' name. Amen.

Harnessed to God's ends

DAY **42**

For reading & meditation – Galatians 5:1–15

'You, my brothers, were called to be free. But do not use your freedom to indulge the sinful nature ...' (v.13)

A further challenge: *discipline yourself for greater effectiveness.* The Christian way is the way of dependence – we draw our life from Another. Nevertheless, in order to do that, we must be disciplined.

'Discipline' sounds harsh to some, especially those who have suffered from overdiscipline in their childhood or those with a spontaneous type of personality. Once when I wrote on the subject of discipline, a woman who had read my writings for many years informed me: 'The word 'discipline' has so many bad connotations I just couldn't read that issue. I turned to another devotional and came back to *Every Day with Jesus* two months later.' But even if you have negative feelings about the concept of discipline stay with me because I think what I say may be helpful.

Throughout church history there have been those who have argued: 'Grace is free, disciplined living is no longer necessary.' Some have preached the message of grace in such a way that it has weakened character. Paul warns us in today's text 'not [to] make your freedom an opening for the flesh' (Moffatt). In the Galatian churches, liberty had become licence. Discipline was needed.

We must have done with the erroneous idea that to be disciplined means that you become a repressed person. That is a caricature. To be disciplined means that the forces that flow through your personality are all harnessed in the right direction. Unharnessed forces flow everywhere and get us nowhere – except into trouble. When they are harnessed to God's ends they are disciplined.

FURTHER STUDY

Deut. 8:1–20;
2 Tim. 2:1–7;
Heb. 12:4–13;
James 3:1–18

1. How does James deal with indiscipline?

2. How should I respond to the discipline of God?

Father, help me to be disciplined – disciplined by Your love and power, not by my strained trying. For I see that my soul, when disciplined, can dance along life's way. In Christ's name I ask it. Amen.

The future of the world

For reading & meditation – 1 Corinthians 9:19–27

'Run in such a way as to get the prize. Everyone who competes in the games goes into strict training.' (vv.24-25)

The future of the world,' said Ramsay MacDonald, a British prime minister, 'is in the hands of disciplined people.' I would amend this statement to: The future of the world is in the hands of disciplined people, *those who are linked to the highest goals*. Discipline, to be effective, must be linked to the divinely ordained framework of life.

Science, for example, is geared to extracting facts from the universe, but fails to take into consideration the sum total of reality. Scientists, in general, study such matters as the laws that guide the planets, but pay little or no attention to the fact that Someone laid down those laws in the first place. Scientists, of course, will claim it is not their task to go beyond the facts, but I would say that life was never meant to be compartmentalised. You cannot focus on the creation and leave out the Creator.

Similarly, psychoanalysts use the knowledge they gain from observing human behaviour to pick people to pieces, but fail to put them back on a higher level. Psychoanalysis without psychosynthesis (integration of disjoint elements of personality) cannot exert a total discipline. A Christian missionary with a background in psychology explains: 'Just as the spokes of a wheel hang loose without a hub, so the powers of life are at loose ends unless they come together into the central hub – the kingdom of God.' Yes, the future of the world is in the hands of disciplined people, but the discipline must be linked to the kingdom of God.

FURTHER STUDY

Psa. 86:1-17;
Matt. 6:25-34;
Rom. 14:1-23;
Titus 1:6-9

1. For what qualities is Titus urged to look?

2. How well do my relationships reflect Paul's vision?

Gracious Master, I see that life lacks complete meaning if I am not geared to the laws of Your kingdom. Teach me how to bring every thought and idea into line with the sum total of reality.
In Jesus' name. Amen.

Decrees become songs

For reading & meditation – Psalm 119:1–16

'Blessed are they who keep his statutes and seek him with
all their heart.' (v.2)

True discipline is not imposed on us; it is the inward discovery of
God's laws. Look again at our text for today: 'Blessed [or happy]
are they who keep his statutes and seek him with all their heart.'
The opposite could be expressed in this way: 'Unhappy are those
who follow their own inclinations, giving themselves a divided
inner self.' Later the writer of this psalm says this: 'Your decrees
are the theme of my song' (v.54). Decrees become songs. This idea
that a disciplined person is a disagreeable person is quite wrong.

FURTHER STUDY

Psa. 66:1-20;
Prov. 1:1-7;
John 8:31-42;
Acts 16:22-40

1. For what does
the psalmist's
example lead us
to sing about?

2. In what
difficult
circumstances
have I learned
to praise God?

The person who is disciplined to the laws of the
kingdom of God is a person who is full of rhythm
and song, for they are attuned to life.

It is true that Jesus, when talking about the
discipline of suffering in Mark 9:49, said, 'Everyone
will be salted with fire', but the fire of discipline
burns away only the encumbrances. When Daniel's
three companions were thrown into the burning
fiery furnace the fire did nothing to them except
burn away their bonds (Dan. 3). They were free in
the fire. We read that when King Nebuchadnezzar
looked into the furnace he saw the three Hebrew
youths accompanied by a fourth man. Who was that

fourth man? Some think it was an angel; others think it was Christ
in a human guise. All the fire did was to release them so that they
could walk in freedom with the divine visitor. Those who regard
discipline as fire must realise its end – freedom to be dedicated to
and in touch with the Worthwhile.

*Father, help me have done with this idea that to be disciplined is to
be disagreeable. I see now that discipline results in development,
and development in harmony. Your will is my freedom, my will
is bondage. Amen.*

A seed decision

For reading & meditation – Romans 12:1-21

'Do not conform any longer to the pattern of this world, but be transformed by the renewing of your mind.' (v.2)

'**B**eauty,' it has been said, 'is the purgation of superfluities.' Discipline confines us to that which is essential, and thus makes life beautiful. As Christians we must discipline our lives so that nothing remains except that which counts and contributes.

The reason why I have been able to keep writing *Every Day with Jesus* for many years is because I have learned to discipline myself to say 'No' to some things in order to say 'Yes' to the main one. Requests to sit on committees, to speak at meetings, sometimes even invitations to have dinner with friends have been turned down because they would have interfered with my highest priority – the writing of *Every Day with Jesus*. The whole secret of self-discipline is deciding on your priorities and sticking to them.

FURTHER STUDY

1 Kings 18:16-24;
Rom. 6:5-23;
Heb. 10:5-10;
James 1:2-12

1. On what basis should I, as a Christian, make decisions?

2. What am I double-minded about?

Decide, then, what is to have your primary attention. If you are a Christian obviously that must be fulfilling God's plans for your life. If that is your intention then be resolute. Don't be a 'Yes-butter' – 'Yes, Lord, I will do it … but not now.' St Augustine prayed: 'Lord, make me pure, but not just yet.' Concentrate your attention on doing the will of God and strip away everything that would hinder you. Discipline is as simple as that. Of course, this is easier said than done. The self will wriggle, look for some compromise, or beg to be let off. The resolve to do the will of God, whatever that entails, must be paramount. That decision determines all decisions – it is a seed decision.

Father, I would have an eye that is single so that my whole body might be full of light. Help me to say 'No' to the good in order that I may say 'Yes' to the best. In Jesus' name I pray. Amen.

Three powerful words

For reading & meditation – Deuteronomy 28:1–14
'If you pay attention to the commands of the LORD ...
carefully follow them, you will always be at the top ...' (v.13)

The secret of being disciplined is to decide what is to have your *primary* attention. A Christian woman who was bedridden for forty-four years made her bed a pulpit, for many came to her room, heard her tell how Christ ministered to her in her illness, and went away converted. She told one visitor that the three words she lived by were these: attention, meekness, power. What gets your attention gets you. If you give Christ and His will for your life the primary attention then everything will be arranged around Him.

Her second word, meekness, is important also because meekness is really surrender – the surrender of the self into the hands of God. And the inevitable result of this is power. This third quality is gained only as we understand and apply the other two. Power comes by discipline and by discipline alone.

The whole matter of discipline has to do with the self. The self must be disciplined to die as first in our scheme of things so that it might live as second. That is why, at the centre of God's kingdom, is a cross. Every one of us must go through spiritually what Jesus went through physically – we must die and be buried in order to experience a resurrection into a fuller and free-er life. A friend of mine has this motto: 'Severe with self, gentle with others, honest with all.' The disciplined you is not free to do what others may do, but is free to do what others cannot do – to be a contributive person full of light and power.

FURTHER STUDY

Num. 12:1-16;
Lam. 3:19-33;
Matt. 11:25-30;
1 Tim. 1:3-11;
5:1-2;
2 Tim. 1:7

1. How does the text describe the character of Moses?

2. What sort of person did Paul encourage Timothy to be?

My Lord and my God, I do not hesitate to put my head into Your yoke for I know that when I am in bondage to You then I am free to be the person You want me to be. Your yoke is my yearning, Your weight my wings. I am so thankful. Amen.

Excelling in love

For reading & meditation – 1 Thessalonians 3:1–13

'May the Lord make your love ... overflow for each other and for everyone else, just as ours does for you.' (v.12)

Make it your objective throughout life to *excel in loving*. Moffatt translates today's text: 'And may the Lord make you increase and excel in love to one another ... so as to strengthen your hearts and make them blameless in holiness before our God and Father.' The desire to excel in everything you do is commendable, and will yield earthly rewards; to excel in love, however, brings spiritual rewards – it 'strengthens your heart and makes it blameless in holiness'.

There is an old saying that he who loves not, lives not, and he who loves most, lives most. Professor E. Hocking, a medical specialist, said: 'The most radically creative attitude yet known to men is the determination to do what the Everlasting Mercy does.' The Everlasting Mercy, of course, is the creative, outgoing and generous love of God.

Love never fails, Paul tells us in 1 Corinthians 13:8. Many argue that love does fail, citing a loving mother whose son becomes a criminal, or a loving husband or wife who fails to stop their partner being unfaithful. But in such cases the failure is in the person who chooses to spurn that love. When the Bible tells us love never fails it means that to love is always the right thing to do. If the love is not received then you are still all the better for loving. Years ago some leading men in America were asked which was the saddest word in the English language. Many singled out the word: 'unloved'. I agree, but would add this also: 'unloving'.

FURTHER STUDY

Deut. 10:12–22;
Prov. 10:11–13;
John 13:31–38;
Gal. 5:6–15

1. Is my church growing in love?

2. How easily do I receive God's love through others?

Father, since I am loved by a love that is unlimited, help me this day and every day to love with love unlimited. For in doing so I will only be responding to Your love unlimited. Grant it in Jesus' name. Amen.

A greater sadness

For reading & meditation – Romans 5:1–11

'But God demonstrates his own love for us in this: While we were still sinners, Christ died for us.' (v.8)

Many people I have met who were cruelly deprived of love as children have managed to overcome the problems that lack of love produces and have gone on to be outgoing, creative and loving individuals. Though it is a great sadness not to have been given love, it is an even greater sadness to be unloving.

A question I have often been asked in the counselling room by people deprived of love in their developmental years is this: 'How can one love unless one has been loved?' One person made this

FURTHER STUDY

Hosea 2:14-23;
John 3:14-18;
Eph. 1:3-10

1. How does
Hosea picture
God's love
for us?

2. What saving
blessings flow
from God's
love, according
to Paul?

remark: 'I know I am supposed to be loving, and I feel inside me the need to love, but it is as if there is a wall of concrete around my heart and, hard as I try, the love will not come out.' Though there is truth in the claim made by psychologists that it is difficult to love if you have not been loved, I have known many such people turn into the most loving men and women once they have responded to the love of God.

So how do those whose hearts feel as if they are surrounded by a wall of concrete accept the fact they are loved by God, who is invisible, intangible and inaudible? I know of only one way. It is to focus on the cross, to linger there and remind oneself of the truth presented in today's text that He sent His Son as an atoning sacrifice for our sin. The Holy Spirit breaks down the 'wall of concrete' by bringing home to us what Christ has done for us on the cross.

Father, I accept that love is kindled by love, so I shall focus on the cross and allow the Holy Spirit to help me feel how much love lies in the heart of God even for me. In Jesus' name. Amen.

Awakened by God's love

For reading & meditation – 1 John 4:7–21

'We love because he first loved us.' (v.19)

A secular psychologist attending one of my seminars heard me say: 'One hour before the cross can do more for a person than endless hours on a psychiatrist's couch.' Turning to a colleague he whispered: 'This sounds too good to be true.' His colleague, also a psychologist but a vibrant Christian, replied: 'It's too good not to be true.'

Later, when the seminar was over, the Christian psychologist introduced his colleague to me and reported their brief exchange of words during my talk. I asked him to explain what he meant when he said: 'It's too good not to be true.' This, as I remember it, was his reply: 'I was brought up in a home where I was deprived of love. In fact it was more than deprivation of love, it was positive physical abuse. I was treated by a psychiatrist in my teens, and though I received some help for which I am grateful, my personality remained stunted as regards being able to love. But one day I found Christ – or rather He found me – and as I knelt at the cross, seeing how much I was loved, the scales fell from my eyes and my own love flamed in response. I found love for God and a love for others rising inside me in a way that I had never known or felt before.'

God's *agape* – His love – created and inspired *agape* within him. So I say again: an unloved person can become a loving person when awakened by the love of God.

FURTHER STUDY

Hosea 3:1-5;
Song 2:1-17;
1 Thess. 2:6-12;
Rev. 1:4-8

1. How did Hosea 'demonstrate' God's love for Israel?

2. How did Paul demonstrate God's love for the Thessalonians?

Father, open my eyes still more to the fact that I am loved by the world's most wonderful Lover. Your love conquers all my heart's antipathy and overwhelms all my suspicion and distrust. Let Your *agape* now create *agape* in me. Amen.

The highest ambition

DAY
50

For reading & meditation – 1 Thessalonians 4:1-12

'... live in order to please God ... we ask you and urge you in the Lord Jesus to do this more and more.' (v.1)

We return now to the challenge issued by Paul – to excel in love. Some believe that because the Christian faith teaches us to submit to God and involve Him in the running of our lives there is no place for ambition, for the desire to excel. Well, there is a place for ambition – the highest ambition of all being to excel in love: 'The Lord make you increase and excel in love' (1 Thess. 3:12, Moffatt).

In today's chapter, Paul instructs the Thessalonians to live a life pleasing to God and to do so more and more. Moffatt translates these words like this: 'You are to excel in it still further.' The word 'excel' appears again in Moffatt's translation of verse 10, in which Paul exhorts the Thessalonians to engage in brotherly love: 'We beseech you, brothers, to excel in this more and more.'

FURTHER STUDY

Prov. 15:9; 21:21;
Hosea 14:1-9;
Eph. 4:1-16;
2 Thess. 1:2-4

1. What response does Hosea say God is looking for from His people?

2. To what is God calling us, according to Paul?

So how do we *excel* in love? By being more interested in others than we are in ourselves. Self-interest must be replaced by interest in others. It is self-interest that snarls up our relationships. If we could take self-interest out of human nature, few problems would remain. A godly man once said: 'When you find yourself oppressed by melancholy the best remedy is to go out and find something kind to do for someone else. When you dig someone out of trouble, the hole left behind is the grave where you can bury your own sorrow.' Make it your ambition to do something every day that no one but a Christian would do. Then you will excel in love.

Lord God, You are always reaching after me to love me, awaken me, and bring out my potential. Help me this day to act in a similar way and quicken someone else's life by the touch of friendliness and love, for I cannot be too loving. Amen.

Would you love life?

For reading & meditation – John 15:1–17

'As the Father has loved me, so have I loved you.
Now remain in my love.' (v.9)

Leslie B. Salter, a Christian writer, says: 'Every normal man and woman longs more keenly for love, for warm friendship, admiration and human responsiveness from fellow human beings than for anything else in life.' Would you love life, he asks? Then start giving those about you the feelings they long for. Start passing out brotherly love and good cheer and see what happens. And seek to excel in this matter. The following lines by John Oxenham express the outgoing nature of love:

> Love ever gives, forgives, outlives,
> And ever stands with open hands,
> And while it lives, it gives,
> For this is love's prerogative:
> To give and give and give.

FURTHER STUDY

Psa. 139:1-24;
Acts 20:17-38;
Rom. 12:3-13;
1 Cor.16:13-14,
23-24

1. How well do we emulate Paul's love for the Ephesians?

2. Is God's intimate knowledge of me a threat or a comfort?

When you are more interested in giving than receiving, when you care more about another person than you do about yourself, you will receive in return a personal happiness you never thought possible. Throw your will on the side of excelling in love, and the universe will throw its weight of happiness on your side. You are made to live that way, and all the medicine you take, all the praying you do, will be ineffectual unless you throw your will on the side of outgoing love. So seek to excel in love, not for what you get, but for what you can give. It is the best of all ambitions.

God my Father, my Creator, You have fashioned me for love and You have made me a creator too. I share the power to make and re-make. Help me to be creative in love – to excel in it. In Christ's name. Amen.

Going down deeper

For reading & meditation – John 16:5–16

'It is for your good that I am going away. Unless I go away,
the Counsellor will not come to you ...' (v.7)

The penultimate truth of 'Changing Times – Unchanging
Truths' that engages our attention is: *resources are available
to you through the Holy Spirit.* Of all the resources available to
the Christian – prayer, the Scriptures, the fellowship of others,
personal counselling, and so on – the chief resource is the Holy
Spirit.

When a young US minister had a nervous breakdown a doctor
gave him this diagnosis: *'You are trying to build a million-dollar
house with just a thousand dollars of resources. You
are worried over inadequate resources. The cost of
this consultation is $100.'* That diagnosis would be
just as appropriate for Christians all over the world.
Is it true of you? Are you trying to do things beyond
your spiritual resources? Then you must learn how to
tap the resources available through the Holy Spirit.

When oil was first discovered in Texas, the
engineers drew oil from near the surface. Then an
oil worker dared to bore down 5,000 feet, where
they struck new levels of oil, producing new gushers.
Now almost all the oil is tapped at that level. It is
a parable. We Christians must discover the depths of the Holy
Spirit's power and tap the resources stored up for us in the heart
of God from all eternity. Then we shall be artesian and overflowing
– ready for anything. Believers can't make it through the Christian
life relying on their own experience or understanding rather than
on the Holy Spirit. No Holy Spirit – no progress. Period.

FURTHER STUDY

Psa. 143:1-12;
Joel 2:28-32;
Acts 2:1-4,14-21;
1 Cor. 2:1-10

1. How was
Joel's prophecy
fulfilled?

2. For what
does Paul say
we must rely on
the Holy Spirit?

Lord God, forgive me if I am living too near the surface, dependent
more on my own resources than on Yours. Help me to tap all the
resources available to me through the Holy Spirit's power.
In Jesus' name. Amen.

Imitation vs. impartation

For reading & meditation – Acts 1:1–11

'But you will receive power when the Holy Spirit comes
on you ...' (v.8)

How well do you know the Holy Spirit? In a modern translation of the Gospels, 'Holy Spirit' is printed without capitals – 'holy spirit'. This is symptomatic of what is happening in some parts of the Church. Some regard the Holy Spirit as a vague impersonal influence – to their impoverishment.

In the seventeenth century the Puritan John Owen said: 'The cardinal sin of the Old Testament was the rejection of Jehovah God; the cardinal sin of the New Testament was the rejection of God the Son; the cardinal sin of this age [speaking of his own day] is the rejection of God, the Holy Spirit.' Today, in what is being called the Charismatic Age, the Holy Spirit has been given great prominence. Fewer Christians claim that the gifts of the Spirit were for the Early Church only. But while the Spirit is evidently at work in many churches (perhaps most), multitudes of believers continue to think of the Spirit as a doctrine rather than the One who provides the dynamic by which the Christian life must be lived. They need to discover the actual resources of the Holy Spirit – not just His Name, but His nature.

I still meet people who talk about following Jesus' example. He is our example, of course, but merely following Jesus' example produces a weak type of Christianity. The Holy Spirit gives us the power not simply to imitate Christ; He imparts to us the energy by which Christ Himself lived. It's impartation, not imitation, that makes for effective Christian living.

FURTHER STUDY

Isa. 61:1-3;
Luke 4:14-30;
24:45-49;
Acts 4:23-31;
Heb. 2:1-4

1. How did the Early Church experience the anointing of Jesus?

2. In what ways do I need to draw on the power of the Holy Spirit?

Father, I am so thankful that You do not call me to strive to follow Jesus in my own strength, but impart to me through the Holy Spirit the power I need to be all that You want me to be. Fill me with more of that power. In Jesus' name. Amen.

Pleasing Him

For reading & meditation – 1 John 3:11–24

[we] receive from him [God] anything we ask, because we obey his commands and do what pleases him.' (v.22)

Is the Holy Spirit a doctrine or a dynamic in your life? Do you say, 'Look what the world has come to,' or 'Look what has come to the world'? It is easy to be pessimistic as we contemplate the state of the world. The disciples, prior to Pentecost, were pessimistic – they closeted themselves behind closed doors for fear of the Jews. But after Pentecost they became joyously optimistic. The presence of the Holy Spirit made all the difference.

A woman once wrote and told me: 'I have just stumbled across the meaning of the Holy Spirit. For years I have been trying to find what part He plays in the Christian life. Now I know.' How did she know? Her letter continued: 'Jesus made the statement that 'whoever believes in me, as the Scripture has said, streams of living water will flow from within him'. Streams of living water are flowing out from me – streams of purity and power.' I particularly liked the phrase 'purity and power' because some see the evidence of the indwelling Spirit only in terms of power; others only in terms of purity.

FURTHER STUDY

2 Sam. 23:1-4;
Ezek. 37:1-14;
Acts 5:1-11,27-32;
1 Cor. 6:9-11,
18-20

1. What inspired David's praise?

2. How well do I appreciate that my body is the Holy Spirit's temple?

Nine streams flow from those in whom the Spirit dwells: love, joy, peace, patience, kindness, goodness, faithfulness, gentleness, and self-control (Gal. 5:22).The account adds: 'Against such things there is no law.' You are not constrained by law; but when the Spirit fills your life, all you will want to do is to please the Lord. A truly Spirit-filled believer will not be pleased with anything that does not please Him.

Spirit of God, break down all the dams in my life and let the rivers flow – the river of power and the river of purity. When I am filled to the depths with the Spirit then I will not concern myself with superficial things. In Jesus' name I ask this. Amen.

Oil wells need oiling

For reading & meditation – John 4:1–42

'Jesus [said] ... 'If you knew the gift of God ... you would
have asked ... he would have given ... living water.'' (v.10)

An engineer was showing some visitors around some small oil
wells. As he passed by one of them he paused in order to oil
it because the machinery was squeaking badly. The visitors were
amused at the idea that an oil well should be oiled. Something that
is not so amusing, however, is a Christian who needs oiling when
they are trying to pump oil for others.

A minister said to me after a seminar in Australia: 'I need to
recharge my batteries. Can you help?' He continued: 'I'm not
bad, just empty. I am trying to pump oil for others
and I am dry myself.' We went into a room to pray
together, and I counselled him along two lines. First,
I talked about the need to repent. Why repent? A
lost spiritual blessing cannot be recovered without
repentance. If we have moved away from the
Lord and ceased to be dependent on Him then the
only way back is through the door of repentance.
We need to say sorry for losing the connection
between ourselves and the Lord. Next, we must
surrender. This involves letting go. Just as the
canvas surrenders to the painter, the violin to the
musician, the wire to the electricity, so we must put
ourselves at the disposal of the Deity. We substitute
His will for ours. When we do this, He has us and we have Him.

The Australian minister made a thrilling new connection with
Christ and the Holy Spirit. That advice, when followed, never fails.
Can the Holy Spirit put oil in the Christian worker's own life? My
experience says He can.

FURTHER STUDY

Isa. 63:7–14;
Rom. 8:22–27;
1 Cor. 12:1–11;
2 Thess. 2:13–17;
Jude v.20

1. What hinders
me drawing on
the resources of
the Holy Spirit?

2. Why did
Paul thank
God for the
Thessalonian
believers?

**Lord God, if I have been depending more on my own resources than
I have on the Holy Spirit then forgive me, I pray. I repent. Now, as I
surrender afresh to You, let the reconnection take place.
In Christ's name I ask it. Amen.**

Continuous surrender

For reading & meditation – Ephesians 5:1–21
'Do not get drunk on wine, which leads to debauchery.
Instead, be filled with the Spirit.' (v.18)

We have talked about needing repentance and surrender when we find ourselves lacking in spiritual power. Surrender is not once-and-for-all; surrender must be continuous. The literal meaning of today's text is 'be being filled with the Spirit'. Paul could say, 'I have been crucified with Christ' (Gal. 2:20), and yet he died daily (1 Cor. 15:31). Surrender is done, and yet it is never done – it is a continual yielding. Just as a man and woman in a happy marriage learn how to give themselves to each other and surrender their own thoughts and desires, so it is in our relationship with Christ. We surrender and keep on surrendering.

FURTHER STUDY

Isa. 44:1-5;
2 Cor. 1:12-22;
Eph. 4:20-30;
1 Thess. 5:16-24

1. What signs of
the Holy Spirit's
work are evident
in my life?

2. How may
we quench
the Spirit?

In her book Melva Libermore admits that for many years she lived a shallow Christian life. She knew everything about the Holy Spirit except how to yield to Him. Then she was told: 'Don't wrestle, just nestle.' So she got down on her knees and abandoned herself to the Holy Spirit. As a result He came and filled her in a way she never imagined was possible. She was transformed. After that experience she announced: 'Now I am no longer a thermometer, I am a thermostat.' A thermometer merely registers the temperature, a thermostat changes it.

The early disciples didn't go around registering the temperature; they went around changing it. The acts of the apostles were really the acts of the Holy Spirit working through the apostles. 'To be continued' could be written at the end of the book of Acts. To be continued – through you and me.

My Father and my God, I know the canon of Scripture has been closed, but grant that we Your people of this present day may continue what Your early disciples began. Forgive us that we have lapsed so much. Forgive us and restore us. In Jesus' name. Amen.

Unshakeable!

For reading & meditation – Hebrews 12:14–29

'Therefore, since we are receiving a kingdom that cannot
be shaken, let us be thankful ...' (v.28)

The last of the unchanging truths: *remember, no matter what
the future may bring, you are part of an unshakeable kingdom.*
Eugene Peterson paraphrases today's text thus: 'Do you see what
we've got? An unshakeable kingdom! And do you see how thankful
we must be? Not only thankful, but brimming with worship, deeply
reverent before God. For God is not an indifferent bystander. He's
actively cleaning house, torching all that needs to burn, and he
won't quit until it's all cleansed. God himself is Fire!'

The kingdoms of this world are shakeable and
will eventually fall. Paul speaks in 1 Corinthians
2:6 about 'the rulers of this age, who are coming to
nothing'. Moffatt refers to them as 'the dethroned
Powers who rule this world'. Secular powers are
dethroned in that the sentence of doom has been
passed upon them. They do not acknowledge God's
kingdom and so they will suddenly collapse or are in
a process of silent decay. Followers of communism
believed the system would last for ever, but now it
has largely been discredited.

FURTHER STUDY

Psa. 118:1-29;
Dan. 6:25-28;
Luke 1:26-33;
Rom. 9:30-33;
1 Pet. 2:4-10

1. What did the
angel promise
Mary Jesus
would become?

2. According
to Daniel, how
lasting is God's
kingdom?

In Luke 20:18 Jesus said: 'Everyone who falls on
that stone [Christ Himself] will be broken to pieces,
but he on whom it falls will be crushed.' For those who have
eyes to see, that crushing is taking place all around us. Nations
that refuse to build on Christ's righteousness stumble over it to
their destruction. Where now are the great empires of Rome, of
the Mongols, the Aztecs or Incas? Gone. They have received the
inexorable verdict of the final Word.

**Lord Jesus Christ, You are both tender and terrible, meek yet
masterful. The builders of civilisation have rejected You, but You
have become the cornerstone. My faith is in You. All glory and
honour be to Your peerless and precious name. Amen.**

The sword of the Lord

For reading & meditation – Isaiah 31:1–9

'Assyria will fall by a sword that is not of man; a sword, not of mortals, will devour them.' (v.8)

Kingdoms built on principles antithetical to God's laws are sowing the seeds of their own destruction. Today we have read: 'Assyria will fall by a sword that is not of man.' Whose sword is Isaiah speaking of here? It is, of course, the sword of the Lord. He saw that Assyria would fall not by the sword of mortals but by *the* sword – the Word of the Lord. In the same way that Assyria fell, other nations have fallen also – cut down by the sword. Evil, as we have already seen, is not only bad, but those who practise it are stupid; they attempt to live against the great design of the universe. 'Sin,' said one preacher, 'is plainly vandalism against life, a rebel flag of pride lifted up against the creation. So all sin and sinners, individual and collective, perish.'

FURTHER STUDY

Exod. 15:1–13,18;
Judg. 7:13–21;
Matt. 12:15–28;
1 Cor. 15:20–28;
Jude vv.24–25

1. How does being in God's kingdom inspire praise?

2. How does the future of God's kingdom give me hope?

When communism was apparently flourishing in Russia, a Christian commentator said: 'I am not afraid of their badness; I am more afraid of their goodness. There are some good things in it. And those good things will keep it going longer than it should.' The more oppressive a regime, the quicker it will fall. It is goodness that is enduring. Those who use the sword to destroy those who denounce their ideologies will themselves perish by the sword.

All nations that refuse to bring their laws in line with the morality by which the universe survives are on notice. Like the pillar of the Philistine temple pulled down by Samson, the pillars of their societies will be pulled down too. Maybe not immediately. But one day. One day.

Father, I am sincerely thankful I belong to a kingdom that is not merely unshaken, but unshakeable. My peace comes from You and is firmly based on Your promises, which can never fail. Amen.

No dead ends

For reading & meditation – Isaiah 9:1–7

'Of the increase of his government and peace there will be no end.' (v.7)

We must be genuinely grateful we belong to a kingdom that cannot be shaken. Look back at history; has anything remained unshaken? Only the kingdom of God. It cannot be shaken for its architect and builder is God Himself.

One morning, when I reached for my Bible, I read: 'Jesus Christ is the same yesterday and today and for ever' (Heb. 13:8). A line from a well-known hymn sprung into my mind: 'O Thou who changest not, abide with me.' Change can be found everywhere, but not in Him. He is the unchanging Christ in changing times.

Today's text tells us that 'of the increase of his government … there will be no end.' God's government is the only one that will not end. A Chinese saying is: 'He has gone up into the horns of a cow' – in other words, up something that has a dead end. You and I belong to a kingdom that does not have a dead end. It's sad that so many cling to the peripheral things (like Asher clinging to his creeks) and miss the central thing – the unchanging nature of the kingdom.

The ages have tested the foundations on which people have built, and only one has proved solid and dependable – the kingdom of God. From the depths of my heart I give thanks that I belong to the one kingdom that cannot be shaken. And so, I hope, do you.

FURTHER STUDY

Psa. 18:1-3,46-50; 127:1-5;
Isa. 40:8;
1 Cor. 3:11,21-23;
1 Tim. 3:14-16

1. How does the image of God as a rock stimulate faith?

2. According to Paul, how big is our inheritance as Christians?

Oh yes, Father, I am overflowing with gratitude because I am clinging to a Rock that can never break. I cannot thank You enough for giving me a place in Your eternal and unshakeable kingdom. All glory be to Your wonderful name. Amen.

Your kingdom come

For reading & meditation – Daniel 2:24–49

'... rock was cut ... not by human hands. It struck the statue on its feet of iron and clay and smashed them.' (v.34)

What better way than to end our exploration of the changeless truths that are ours in these changing times than to remind ourselves that the kingdom of God, as embodied in the Person of Christ, has the final say in human affairs?

Daniel tells Nebuchadnezzar that in his dream he has seen a huge statue with a head of pure gold, chest and arms of silver, legs of iron, and feet of iron and clay. Then he saw a rock that had not been cut by human hands strike the image on its feet, smashing them to pieces. After this the wind swept the fragments of the statue away without a trace.

FURTHER STUDY

Psa. 61:1-8;
Dan. 7:13-18;
1 Cor. 10:1-5,
14-17;
Rev. 11:15-18

1. When have I climbed to the 'rock that is higher'?

2. What is there about God's kingdom that makes us look forward to the future?

Daniel then gave the interpretation: the mixture of iron and clay represents a kingdom of strength and weakness, which will be broken by the stone not hewn by human hands. What is this stone – one not set up by humankind and therefore incapable of being overthrown by humankind? It is, of course, Christ, the builder of the kingdom that will one day break in pieces all powerful kingdoms with heads of gold but feet of clay. Proud civilisations point to their legs of iron, but seem unaware that their feet are a mixture of iron and clay. Every nation on earth is destined to fall. Christ and His kingdom will prevail.

When Christ taught His disciples to pray He instructed them to say: 'Your kingdom come' (Matt. 6:10). Would He have given them and us a prayer that has no fulfilment? Other kingdoms come and go. His kingdom is here now, and is here to stay.

My Father and my God, I have prayed the prayer You taught us to pray many times, but never with such enthusiasm and conviction as I do now. Your kingdom come. I await its coming with hope, expectancy, and great joy. In Jesus' name. Amen.

God's Last Word

'Speech without a stutter'

For reading & meditation – Hebrews 1:1

'In the past God spoke ... through the prophets at many
times and in various ways ...' (v.1)

We begin today a *devotional* study of the letter to the Hebrews. We cannot be sure who wrote the letter, but its theme is clear – the superiority of Christ over every other person and religious system. No other biblical book focuses upon Christ as does Hebrews. It is the clearest and most systematic presentation of Christ's adequacy and uniqueness to be found anywhere in the Word of God.

The letter is addressed to a group of Hebrew Christians who apparently were beginning to drift back towards Jewish ritualism. They were afraid that in turning to Christ they were losing too much – particularly the pageantry and ceremony of their Hebrew past. But the writer reminds them that in Christ they have far more than they have lost, and that Christianity is the perfect and final religion.

FURTHER STUDY

John 1:1-18;
1 John 1:1-3;
Rev. 19:13

1. What did the apostle John declare?

2. What did John testify to?

The letter begins by stating that God has spoken to all humankind through Jesus Christ in a manner far greater than when He spoke through the prophets. When you read the Old Testament and listen to the voices of the prophets you are hearing the incomplete message of God. It never brings you to ultimates and absolutes. In the New Testament, however – especially the Gospels – you find a new voice that gathers up the phrases in which God spoke in the Old Testament and merges them into one complete, final discourse. God's Word and message to humanity has been *fully* uttered in and through His Son. 'In Him,' as one great theologian put it, 'God speaks without a stutter.'

Father, when my eyes fall on Christ, Your own beloved Son, I know that all else is relative. He and He alone is absolute. May His supremacy become more real to me day by day. In Christ's name I ask it. Amen.

Nothing but the truth

For reading & meditation – Hebrews 1:1–2

'... in these last days he has spoken to us by his Son, whom he appointed heir of all things ...' (v.2)

Old Testament prophets brought God's Word to the people, but Christ was the *Word*. All others could point only to principles and ideas, but Jesus pointed to Himself and said: 'I am the way and the truth and the life' (John 14:6). He was the Truth, the whole Truth and nothing but the Truth.

The writer tells us also that Christ was appointed as 'heir of all things'. This shows us that everything will conclude at Christ's feet. Our Lord is the terminal point of the universe. Does this idea of everything terminating at Christ's feet mean the process is an arbitrary one – it happens because God wills it? No, not entirely, for everything that refuses to relate to Him will go to pieces by its own inherent inner conflicts. Those who can't or won't go Christ's way consign themselves to ultimate destruction.

A rather belligerent doctor once said to a missionary: 'I don't believe in Christ or God.' The missionary said gently: 'Go to hell then.' The doctor did not speak another word – he knew by instinct that that is where rejection of God and Christ finally leads.

Christ is the heir of all things because all things were made for Him and by Him. This means that the touch of Christ is on all creation; everything is made in its inner structure to work in His way. When it works in His way it works well, but when it works some other way it works to its own destruction. Live according to Christ and you *live*; live against Him and you perish – eternally.

FURTHER STUDY

Col. 1:16-20;
1 Cor. 8:6;
Eph. 1:19-23

1. What is Christ appointed to be?

2. List five things Paul declares about the supremacy of Christ.

Lord Jesus, You are heir of all things. All things that aren't placed at Your feet simply have no place. But everything surrendered to You is safe – including myself. I am eternally grateful. Amen.

The stamp of God's image

For reading & meditation – Hebrews 1:1–3

'The Son is … the exact representation of his being,
sustaining all things by his powerful word.' (v.3)

An old translation puts today's text: 'The Son who is the
effulgence of God's splendour and the stamp of God's very
being'. This is about as far as words can go in describing the Word.

The words 'the stamp of God's very being' dot the 'i's and cross
the 't's of our Lord's statement: 'Anyone who has seen me has
seen the Father' (John 14:9). People look to nature in the attempt
to see the image of God. They view sunrises and sunsets, rivers and
oceans, and wonder if God is like that. But storms rage, thunder
rolls, lightning strikes, earthquakes demolish whole
townships, and their concept of God is shaken. To
know God as He really is we must look into the
face of Jesus – the stamp of God's very image. The
question that then arises is not so much is Jesus like
God, but is God like Jesus? And because He is, then
despite any appearances to the contrary, we must
affirm Him as good.

This Christ, we are told, sustains 'all things by his
powerful word'. If there was any doubt about this
among the Hebrew Christians, all they had to do was to reflect
on the fact that when Christ was here on earth, He sustained
everything around Him by His powerful Word. He healed people
– with a word. He stilled the tempest – with a word. He raised the
dead – with a word. He did it in the microcosm, why not in the
macrocosm? I cannot imagine our Lord showing any greatness
unless He could have shown it in the little as well as the big.

FURTHER STUDY

Eph. 1:1–10;
2 Cor. 4:4;
Col. 1:15

1. Which God did
Paul serve?

2. What does
the 'image of
God' mean?

**Jesus, my Saviour and my Lord, You have shown us in the little
world around You the power of Your Word. We have seen it in the
minute and we see it in the magnificent. Thus we cannot doubt it.
Blessed be Your holy name for ever. Amen.**

'Staggering to a throne'

For reading & meditation – Hebrews 1:1–3

'After he had provided purification for sins, he sat down at the right hand of the Majesty in heaven.' (v.3)

Five things have been said about the Son in the opening words of Hebrews: first, God speaks by the Son; second, He is the heir of all things; third, He made the universe; fourth, He is the radiance of God's glory, the exact representation of His being; fifth, He sustains everything by His powerful Word. The sixth and seventh statements here are that He provided purification for sin, and sat down at the right hand of the Majesty in heaven.

The central purpose of Christ's coming to this earth was to be Saviour and Redeemer. 'You are to give him the name Jesus, because he will save his people from their sins,' was the divine prediction (Matt. 1:21). Not 'in their sins', which implies He saves us, but doesn't help us to stop sinning. 'From their sins' implies He frees us from the power that sin has over us. Christ's sacrificial death is an accomplished fact and now awaits my acceptance. The more definite my commitment, the more His power can affect my life.

The writer comes to the climax of climaxes: 'He sat down at the right hand of the Majesty in heaven.' Christ has been raised to the place of final authority. He has the last word – the Omega. No wonder that the early Christians, when looking for a declaration to sum up the Christian faith, settled on the words 'Jesus is Lord'! They saw that He is Lord not only by appointment but also by accomplishment. Some earthly potentates ride to a throne. Our Lord staggered to His. What a Saviour!

FURTHER STUDY

Acts 7:54-60;
Mark 16:19;
Luke 22:69;
Eph. 1:20

1. What did Stephen declare?

2. What is the significance of God's right hand?

Father, how grateful I am that Your Son came not as a Divine Executioner to destroy me but as a Divine Redeemer to deliver me. Help me to live so that in the face of everything my affirmation will be 'Jesus is Lord.' Amen.

Higher than angels!

For reading & meditation – Hebrews 1:4–9

'So he became as much superior to the angels as the name he has inherited is superior to theirs.' (v.4)

The thrust of the letter to the Hebrews is the pre-eminence of Christ over all people and all things. In today's passage we are introduced to the thought that Christ is superior to angels.

The sect known as Jehovah's Witnesses teaches that Jesus Christ was nothing more than the highest of the created angels. But don't these words demolish that theory: 'You are my Son'? 'To which of the angels did God ever say, "You are my *Son* …"?' (v.5). The passage goes on to say that when God brought His Son into the world, He commanded that all the angels worship Him. The worship of angels at Bethlehem is yet another clear testimony to the deity of our Lord. He is seen to be greater than angels by the demonstration of their worship.

What are angels? They are the servants and ministers of God – depicted in this passage as wind and fire (v.7). Wind and fire are powerful elements and not easy to master and control. They tend to leap over all barriers and restrictions, yet human ingenuity has learned to make them the servants of mankind. This is what God does with angels; though superior in some ways to human beings, their awesome power is channelled by the Creator into ministry to people. They are not as prominent today as they were in Bible days because the Holy Spirit is now resident in the world to lead and guide. But make no mistake about it – they are still around and at work. One of them might even be on a mission to help you this very day.

FURTHER STUDY

Psa. 91:1–11;
Dan. 6:22;
Acts 12:7; 27:23

1. What is promised to those who honour the Lord?

2. What did Daniel testify to?

Father, I am grateful first and foremost for the abiding presence of the Holy Spirit in my life, but also for the ministry of angels. Make me aware that whatever peril or predicament I find myself in – divine help is always at hand. Amen.

On and on, for ever

For reading & meditation – Hebrews 1:8–12

'But you remain the same, and your years will never end.'
(v.12)

The angels serve gloriously, but all they can do is serve. The Son exercises the rule of God by virtue of the fact that He sits upon heaven's eternal throne.

We have seen many monarchies turned into republics. The Communists, at the height of their power, said: 'We have toppled some of the kings of earth from their thrones; next will be the king of the skies.' Well, now they themselves have been toppled, and God's Word still rings out as clearly as it has throughout all the ages: 'Your throne, O God, will last *for ever and ever*' (v.8). Never forget that.

The inspired writer of Hebrews then describes the *nature* of Christ's rule. There is more than just authority represented by the throne of God – righteousness reigns there also. We need never be afraid of authority when it is guided by that which is right. Wrongdoing bears the stamp of death, for *right* (or righteousness) is on the throne. Be encouraged by that; God's day is coming.

Verse 10 reminds us that Christ sits upon the throne as both the Originator and Sustainer of the universe, and shares the eternity of God. Created things will perish, but that which is eternal will remain. Scientists often talk about 'the second law of thermodynamics' – the degenerative faculty in the universe. This is what the writer of Hebrews is talking about in verse 11. All created things will grow old like a garment, but the One who made them will not. He goes on for ever, and ever, and ever …

FURTHER STUDY

Psa. 45:1-6;
103:19;
Isa. 66:1;
Matt. 5:34

1. What was the psalmist's conviction?

2. What did the Lord declare to the children of Israel?

Father, it is impossible for me to comprehend eternity, but that does not stop me thrilling to the prospect. To share eternity with You – what more could I want? Thank You my Father. Amen.

Tongues that are stilled

For reading & meditation – Hebrews 1:13–14

'Are not all angels ministering spirits sent to serve those
who will inherit salvation?' (v.14)

Before we leave Hebrews 1, we pause to repeat that the writer
has held up two truths: first, the supremacy of Christ over
the Old Testament prophets; second, the supremacy of Christ over
angels. In relation to the latter, you may have noticed that the
writer reinforces his point by a remarkable selection of quotations
from the Old Testament – the literature recording what God had
said in times past. There are seven: five taken from Psalms, one
from 2 Samuel, and one from Deuteronomy.

The final reference to the superiority of Christ over
angels (the one before us today) puts the matter once
again in the form of an interrogation: 'To which of
the angels did God ever say, 'Sit at my right hand …'?'
(v.13). Here the Son is seen as eternally enthroned
and waiting for the ultimate subjugation of all who
oppose His rule. In the closing words of Hebrews 1
we are therefore brought back to the thought with
which we began – everything will conclude at
His feet. The feet of Jesus is the terminal point of
the universe. 'At the name of Jesus,' says Paul in
Philippians 2:10–11, 'every knee should bow … and
every tongue confess that Jesus Christ is Lord.' 'The rest,' said a
quaint Welsh commentator, 'have stilled their own tongues in
self-destruction.'

Thus the last thought of the chapter provides an impressive
keystone capping all that has gone before. 'What are angels?' the
writer is asking. Servants. But the Son? The Son – ah – He is God.

FURTHER STUDY

Phil. 2:1-11;
Eph. 2:1-10

1. What does
Paul declare
about the
position of the
unbeliever?

2. What does
Paul declare
about the
position of the
believer?

**Lord Jesus Christ, I exalt You and worship You as God of very God.
When I think God I think Jesus, and when I think Jesus I think God.
What a blessed Son You are to show me such a blessed Father. I am
so very thankful. Amen.**

Pay attention!

For reading & meditation – Hebrews 2:1–4

'... how shall we escape if we ignore such a great salvation?' (v.3)

The fact that the Son is God's final Word to humankind gives force to the exhortation and warning that begin Hebrews 2. Although angels are employed as God's ministering spirits, we do not need to rely on them to bring us the knowledge of God – that has been perfectly revealed in Christ, through whom God's final speech has come to the world. If angels uttered words that proved to be true, how much more should we value the Word that comes by the Son. And if people have been punished for disobeying the word of angels, what causes us to believe that we can get away by ignoring the Word that comes from the lips of Christ Himself?

FURTHER STUDY

Matt. 17:1-8;
Rev. 1:7;
2:11,17,29;
3:6,13,22

1. What did the voice from heaven admonish the disciples?

2. What was the tendency of the Early Church?

What our Lord had to say when He stood among us is the most authoritative Word the world has ever heard. It was confirmed by eyewitnesses, signs, wonders, miracles and gifts of the Holy Spirit. Because of all this, the writer is saying – pay attention! Christ is the One you should be listening to.

How sad that so many Christians seem willing to give their attention to anything but the Word of God. What can be more heartbreaking to a pastor than to preach the truths of God's Word to people week after week, and to see them miss God's best by their failure to pay attention? This is why Jesus had to say again and again: 'He who has ears, let him hear.' If we don't pay attention to what Christ says then we will have to pay attention to the difficulties that life presents. We either heed the helm or we heed the rocks.

Lord God, forgive me that I allow the focus of my attention to be taken up by things other than You. I know I am Yours – help me open my ears and heart to all that is Yours. In Jesus' name I pray. Amen.

Dignity vs. depravity

For reading & meditation – Hebrews 2:5–9

'But we see Jesus, who was made a little lower than the angels, now crowned with glory and honour...' (v.9)

Christ, who is infinitely higher than the angels, was made lower than them. Four reasons are given in the rest Hebrews 2 as to why our Lord became human. The first is: *He became human to recapture our lost inheritance.*

No angel could ever have taken Christ's place in becoming human, for God never gave angels the right to rule the universe; that prerogative was given to Adam and Eve and their descendants. As the psalmist said: 'What is man ...? You made him a little lower than the angels ... and put everything under his feet' (vv.6–8). Adam and Eve were placed on a disciplinary probation that, if kept, would have enabled them to attain much higher responsibilities and privileges.

'A little lower than the angels' means 'made for *a little while* lower than the angels'. When Adam and Eve sinned they forfeited that privilege, and as a result the whole human race now finds itself in futility. 'Yet at present we do not see everything subject to him' focuses attention on the state of the human race from Adam's day to this – we struggle to have dominion over the earth but the depravity in our hearts prevents us from fully exercising it.

The writer turns our eyes, however, to One who has come among us: He was 'made for a little while lower than the angels', lived in perfect obedience, overcame death, and has won the right to lift us to even greater heights than Adam and Eve would have reached had they not sinned. And who is that One? Jesus!

FURTHER STUDY

1 Cor. 15:42-49;
John 13:15;
1 Pet. 2:22;
Psa. 8:1-9

1. How is Jesus described?

2. What question did the psalmist ask?

Father, I see now why humankind has such an urge to climb mountains and conquer space – it is part of our racial memory. You built us for great things, but we have been ruined by sin. I am filled with gratitude, however, that in Christ all will be restored. Amen.

All one family

For reading & meditation – Hebrews 2:10–13

'So Jesus is not ashamed to call them brothers.' (v.11b)

Today's passage shows that our Lord's coming to this earth has resulted in us *recovering our lost unity.*

In being made lower than the angels *for a little while*, Christ (among other things) experienced to a deep degree the suffering that came into the world because of sin. In this connection the writer mentions our Lord was made 'perfect through suffering'. When He came into the world, the Saviour was perfect in that He was without sin, but not perfect in the sense that He had experienced firsthand the whole gamut of human suffering. Suppose Jesus Christ had simply spent one week among us. Imagine He went into the wilderness to be tempted on Monday, preached the Sermon on the Mount on Tuesday, worked the miracle of the feeding of the five thousand on Wednesday, gave the Olivet Discourse on Thursday, died on the cross on Friday – would He have been able in that time to enter into *all* our sufferings? Of course not.

FURTHER STUDY

Isa. 53:1-12;
Rom. 8:1-3;
1 Tim. 3:16

1. How did God send His Son?

2. How did Paul describe it to Timothy?

Because He fully entered into our fears and pressures, says the writer, He is now fully one with us. He is truly part of the human family and we, by His redemption, are truly part of His. The writer quotes from the Old Testament – 'I will put my trust in him' – to illustrate the point that the attitude and the relationship Christ had to God is the same as that we are to have towards Him and towards each other. When we have this attitude of trust then unity will no longer be a word; it will be a fact.

Lord Jesus Christ, You can speak to us in our condition because You have been in our condition – not for a week but for a lifetime. May the unity for which You came and died be more than an ideal one. May it be a real one. For Your own dear name's sake. Amen.

Satan's lost whip

For reading & meditation – Hebrews 2:14–15

'... that by his death he might destroy him who holds the
power of death ...' (v.14)

A third reason why our Lord became man is *to release us
from our present bondage*. The writer tells us that one of the
purposes of Christ sharing our humanity was to destroy the devil.
But has the devil really been destroyed?

Billy Graham tells the story of a boxer who was being hit all
over the ring by an opponent. During one of the intervals between
rounds he said to his trainer: 'He's killing me.' The trainer retorted:
'Don't be ridiculous; he hasn't laid a glove on you.' 'Well, keep your
eye on the referee,' said the boxer, 'for somebody is
knocking the living daylights out of me.' If the devil
has been destroyed then who is responsible for the
awful happenings in our world? Pick up a newspaper
and you will see abundant evidence that the devil
seems to be doing pretty well. How do we explain this?

Throughout the ages, the biggest single whip that
Satan has used to strike terror into hearts is the
fear of death. Our Lord tasted death for us, and by
so doing has taken the whip out of the devil's hands.
The word 'destroy' here does not mean 'eliminate', but 'render
powerless and inoperative'. The devil is still active in many ways,
but through Christ's victory on Calvary he has lost the power to
whip into subjection those who are His. The fear of death stops
many entering into the joys of life. But not a true Christian. When
Jesus went down into death, it was death that died, not He. In Him
we live – and how!

FURTHER STUDY

1 Cor. 15:50-58;
2 Tim. 1:10;
John 14:1-4

1. Why does
Paul say we can
stand firm?
2. What did
he declare to
Timothy?

**Father, I am so grateful that at Calvary You wrested from Satan's
hand the whip of the fear of death. Now he has no lash with which
to sting me. Death is not the end but the beginning – the beginning
of all things new. Amen.**

The sympathising Saviour

For reading & meditation – Hebrews 2:16–18

'Because he himself suffered when he was tempted, he is
able to help those who are being tempted.' (v.18)

The last reason why our Lord became human is that *we
might be restored in times of need.* Angels have no need of
a compassionate ministry (so I believe) because they never feel
in need of grace. *We,* however, do need ministering to in times of
need. When we think of the complex spiritual ills of our race, we
wonder how can Christ meet them all. But because He has felt the
whole gamut of human suffering, He can.

I have referred before to the painting by Charles E. Butler
entitled *The King of Kings,* which depicts Jesus Christ
standing at the foot of the cross and receiving the
homage of the crowned heads of the world. It is a
wonderful picture, but when I survey the wondrous
cross I do not see our Lord only as the King of kings
but also as the physician of souls. I prefer to think of
Him not encompassed by monarchs but surrounded
by struggling men and women such as you and me.

FURTHER STUDY

1 Tim. 2:1-6;
1 John 2:1;
Heb. 6:20

1. What is a
'mediator'?

2. What has
Christ become
for ever?

I see His eye falling upon the suffering and the
tempted, and penetrating to the core of their difficulties. And I
see His gaze beget a bold faith in their despairing hearts as they
realise they are looking at One who has worn their flesh, measured
its frailty, and knows exactly how they feel.

When beset by temptation, sit in the presence of Jesus and let
His power and your faith meet. Then, just as when the woman
touched the hem of His garment, the ancient miracle will be
worked once more. You will touch Him and be whole again.

**Jesus, my Saviour, you know my condition because You have been
in my condition. Just to sit in Your presence is to have my soul
restored. I am so very thankful. Amen.**

Greater than Moses

For reading & meditation – Hebrews 3:1–6
'Jesus has been found worthy of greater honour
than Moses ...' (v.3)

Hebrews 3 begins with the word 'therefore', to link us with the superiority of the Son over prophets and angels. We are to glance at prophets and angels, but our gaze is to be focused fully on Jesus – our Great Apostle and High Priest.

From here the writer goes on to deal with the superiority of the Son over Moses. As you know, God had spoken powerfully to His ancient people through Moses, and it was the conviction that he was the mouthpiece of God which had helped to hold the nation together down the running centuries. The main aim of the writer in this passage is to concentrate our attention on the concept of God's house, in which both Moses and Jesus served faithfully, but in a very different capacity. Seven times the word 'house' appears in this passage. So what is this 'house', which is mentioned so frequently? The word refers not to a building but to a community of people – the people of God. And all of God's people, both in Old Testament times and New Testament times, are considered part of His 'house'.

FURTHER STUDY

1 Cor. 12:12-31;
Rom. 12:4-5;
Eph. 1:22-23;
4:12-15; 5:23

1. How is the Church depicted?
2. What is Christ's relationship to it?

Now in this house of God, which is *people*, Moses ministered as a servant. Christ, however, is the Son. Because of this, the Son is much more to be obeyed, much more to be listened to, much more to be honoured and heeded than Moses. Jesus also is the *Builder* of this house – its Architect and Designer. All personalities, however great they are, have to take second place to Jesus. You do not select Him from rivals; He stands alone.

**Lord Jesus Christ, what a mighty and wonderful Saviour You are.
I not only worship You but give myself gladly to You – all I am and
all I have. Amen.**

A solemn warning

For reading & meditation – Hebrews 3:7-13
'See to it, brothers, that none of you has a sinful,
unbelieving heart ...' (v.12)

One of the characteristics of the letter to the Hebrews is that time and again the writer breaks off to issue a stern warning, as here. 'Today if you hear his voice, do not harden your hearts' (vv.7-8) is taken from Psalm 95, which refers to the rebellion of the Hebrew people in the wilderness under Moses' leadership. Consequently, the warning is closely connected with the point previously made, that Jesus is greater than Moses. Remember that this letter was being written to Hebrew Christians whose ancient leader was Moses, but they were now under the leadership of the Son – God's final Leader.

FURTHER STUDY

Hosea 10:1-12;
Jer. 4:3;
Prov. 28:14

1. What was the word of the Lord to the Israelites?

2. What sort of man is blessed?

The warning here is indeed serious. The writer sounds the alert against the possibility of them hardening their hearts. The terrible danger that the writer is pointing out is this: when truth is not acted upon, it has, after a while, the awful effect of hardening the heart, so that it becomes almost impossible to move in the direction of the Lord. This is what Jesus was referring to when He said: 'If they do not listen to Moses and the Prophets, they will not be convinced even if someone rises from the dead' (Luke 16:31).

Ought we not to pause now and apply this warning to our own lives? Are we failing to act on what we know is the truth? To continue like this is to live dangerously. There may come a time when the heart is not able to believe what it has consistently refused to act upon. *That* is the reason why we must encourage one another daily.

Lord God, drive this thought deeply into my spirit today – that if I
don't act on what I know to be true I may find it difficult to believe.
Help me always to put my beliefs into action, dear Lord.
In Jesus' name. Amen.

Calloused hearts

For reading & meditation – Hebrews 3:12–19

'... if we hold firmly till the end the confidence we had at first.' (v.14)

The failure of the children of Israel to enter into the promised land the first time they arrived at its borders is one of the great tragedies of the Old Testament. They had witnessed the delivering power of the Almighty in leading them from bondage to freedom and seen His miraculous protection at work. Yet, when they came to the borders of Canaan and could have entered into its rest, they drew back in fear and for forty years wandered in the wilderness. Only Joshua and Caleb made it into the promised land.

'See to it, brothers, that none of you has a sinful, unbelieving heart that turns away from the living God,' warns the writer (v.12). 'Turns away' is strong, signifying a definite action of the will that leads away from God. There are multitudes like this in the Church at present. They live as if God does not exist. The Almighty is not real to them any more.

This condition is labelled by the writer of Hebrews as having an 'unbelieving heart'. Unbelief kept a whole nation out of the promised land, and it will keep us out of spiritual blessing too. If the Israelites were excluded because they did not listen to Moses, how much more will we be excluded if we do not listen to the Son. Twice in this chapter the word 'today' is used to emphasise the fact that if in our hearts the callousing process has set in, it is imperative that we cry out to the Lord for deliverance at once. In such a state to delay is dangerous.

FURTHER STUDY

1 Cor. 10:1-13;
2 Pet. 2:20-22

1. What were Paul's warnings from Israel's history?

2. How does Peter describe the consequence of 'turning away'?

Divine Surgeon, do not withhold Your scalpel if You see that my heart has become calloused. I cannot hide my condition from You – nor do I want to. If I need a spiritual surgical operation then You have my permission to cut. In Jesus' name. Amen.

It's action that's needed

For reading & meditation – Hebrews 4:1–2
'... those who heard did not combine it with faith.' (v.2)

When the Israelites stood at the borders of the promised land they had no doubts at all that the land was there and that it contained everything God had promised. But they failed to put their belief into action and thus were turned back into the wilderness. Faith is more than mere belief; faith is *acting* upon that belief. The old Welsh theologians used to say that faith has three components: knowledge, self-committal and trust. All three have to be in operation for faith to reach its goal.

FURTHER STUDY

Num. 13:1–14:45;
Deut. 1:9–2:1

1. What was Caleb's admonition to the Israelites?

2. How did the ten view themselves?

The writer is making the point in Hebrews 4:1 that the same gospel (good news) that was given to the Israelites has been given also to us. The goal of all that God wants to do for us on this earth is to bring us from a life of spiritual striving to rest and confidence in Him.

Note the core problem with which the Israelites constantly struggled: 'Those who heard did not combine it with faith.' In other words, they heard the good tidings but they did not act upon the message. This was the underlying cause of their great failure, and is the biggest single reason why their subsequent history is characterised by so much restlessness.

And this is where we, too, will fail unless we are extremely careful. It is not enough to believe – belief must be put into action. Someone has made this comment of the Church in general: 'When all is said and done, more is *said* than done.' In the realm of faith, as in other realms, talk is cheap. What matters is action.

Father, how powerfully You put Your finger on our problems when You remind us that faith is more than mere believing. Teach me how to combine faith – true faith – with all I hear in Your Word. In Christ's name I ask it. Amen.

Entering into God's rest

For reading & meditation – Hebrews 4:3–5

'So I declared on oath in my anger, "They shall never enter my rest."' (v.3)

Many Christians seem to be confused by the idea contained in the word 'rest' as it is used in the Scriptures. The Greek word for 'rest' means 'to cease from striving and settle down'. The best way of understanding the 'rest' of which God speaks is to consider the appointing of the first Sabbath. God rested on the seventh day for several reasons, one of which was to give us a picture of what the rest of faith is. A 'rest' has been available to us from the beginning of creation, and anyone who knows what it is to cease from struggling, to hold their lives together and depend on the Lord for their daily sustenance, is, in a sense, keeping the Sabbath. God calls us to enter *His rest*, which comes from entering by faith into the nature of the One whose whole being is perfect peace and confidence.

The children of Israel were restless people, and the climax of their rebellion came when they faithlessly refused to undertake the conquest of Canaan and considered returning to Egypt. At that point God withdrew His blessing from them, and barred them – not from entering the land, but from the rest of which He had previously spoken. When eventually the Israelites arrived in the land, their rest was interrupted time and time again by marauding armies and fierce battles. Whatever rest they had was temporary and impermanent. The point was being made – the rest of God is only for those who adopt the attitude of perfect trust.

FURTHER STUDY

Psa. 55:1–6;
Exod. 33:14;
Psa. 116:7;
Isa. 28:12

1. What did the psalmist long for?

2. What did he find?

Father, we Your present-day people are so like the people of old – we prefer to struggle on our own rather than experience the helplessness of trust. Forgive us, our Father, and teach us how to truly enter into Your 'rest'. In Jesus' name. Amen.

Greater than Joshua

For reading & meditation – Hebrews 4:6–10

'For if Joshua had given them rest, God would not have spoken later about another day.' (v.8)

The more we get into the book of Hebrews the more we see the writer's familiarity with the history of the Jewish people. He works his way through the phases of Old Testament history. The time when God spoke through angels has been recognised and the superiority of the Son over angels demonstrated – the book of Genesis. Then comes the reference to Moses, when God spoke to a new nation created for the blessing of the world. The superiority of the Son over Moses is shown – from Exodus to Deuteronomy.

FURTHER STUDY

Psa. 95:7-11; 62:
1-8; 91:1;
Isa. 11:1-10

1. What did God declare?

2. What did Isaiah prophesy would be glorious?

In today's passage, we come to Joshua and the period when the Israelites entered the land under his leadership. This was a period of failure – not of Joshua, but of the people. Moses had led them out of slavery, yet not even Joshua could lead them into rest. The book of Joshua is followed by Judges, which can be summarised: disobedience, discipline and deliverance. It unfolds a history of constant restlessness and rebellion. Although Joshua was a brilliant military commander, it was beyond his ability to lead the children of Israel into the rest which God had planned for them because they had disqualified themselves by their unwillingness to believe.

Hebrews points out that a greater than Joshua is here. The Son not only leads us out of slavery but also into the Sabbath rest. No one in the universe other than the Son can stand amidst the worlds and say with the authority of heaven behind him: 'Come to me … and I will give you rest' (Matt. 11:28).

Gracious Lord, how glad I am that I have heard Your voice, that I have come to You and been embraced by Your arms. Help me to cease from struggling and experience even more deeply Your promised rest. For Your own dear name's sake. Amen.

The cure is Christ

For reading & meditation – Hebrews 4:11–13

'Everything is uncovered and laid bare before the eyes of
him to whom we must give account.' (v.13)

The writer now encourages the Hebrew believers to avoid the
error of their ancestors and seek by the exercise of determined
faith to enter into the Sabbath rest. He links this appeal to the
Word of God, described as 'living and active', and 'sharper than
any double-edged sword' (v.12).

We usually connect this statement with the Bible, but it is a
reference to the Son who is the Word of God. This can be seen
by the description that follows: the Word of God is not merely a
document, but is living and active. The words are
alive because the Word is alive – the Word that is
bigger than human words.

When the written Word – really an extension
of the living Word – is allowed to penetrate
our personalities, the Son of God goes to work
unravelling the knots in the inner being and bringing
freedom to the spirit and the soul. Often when I
have been counselling someone I have heard them
say: 'It feels as if a knot has been untied deep inside
me.' When a person experiences that, it is always a
wonderful moment for a counsellor. However, the
reason for it lies not in the words of the counsellor but in the power
of the spoken word becoming a vehicle for the living Word.

Ever since I became a minister of the gospel, I have struggled
to find the genesis of human problems. What causes all the
complexes and complications that arise in the human personality?
I still don't know all the causes, but I certainly know the cure. It
is Christ – the living Word.

FURTHER STUDY

Jer. 5:14; 15:16;
23:29;
Eph. 6:17;
Psa. 119:97-105

1. What are
some of the
descriptions of
God's Word?

2. What was
the psalmist
able to say?

**Father, what a thrill it is to know that daily as I expose myself to
Your written Word, Jesus, the living Word, is at work within me.
Untie any knots that are deep inside me and make me perfectly
whole. In Christ's name I pray. Amen.**

The throne of *grace*

For reading & meditation – Hebrews 4:14–16
'Let us then approach the throne of grace with
confidence ...' (v.16)

The writer of Hebrews now focuses on priesthood. A priest is a mediator between people and God, and in Old Testament times the priest who entered directly into the presence of God was called a 'high priest'. In the passage before us the writer, wanting to emphasise the superiority of the Son over all other priests, introduces the adjective 'great'. This *great* high priest, he says, has gone into heaven and, because of that, his readers ought to hold firmly to the faith they profess. He meant by this that they should not turn back to methods of the past which, although divinely appointed, were just illustrative and transient.

FURTHER STUDY

2 Sam. 9:1-13;
Luke 2:40;
John 1:14;
Eph. 2:7;
1 Tim. 1:14

1. How does the account in Samuel depict the throne of grace?

2. What did Paul testify of to Timothy?

The wonderful thing about Christ, the Great High Priest, he continues, is that because He has been in our condition, He is able to sympathise with our every circumstance – sin excepted. He has felt every pressure, every allurement, every pull, every temptation we are called upon to endure – and never once did He yield to them. Because of this, we can draw nigh to the throne of grace with the confidence that we are going to find One there who is fully sensitive to our problems and our needs.

Note the phrase *throne of grace*. A throne is usually thought of as a symbol of power and authority, rarely as a symbol of grace. However, because One sits on the throne who has been tempted in every way that we are tempted, authority and power are balanced by compassion and grace. No wonder we come confidently to such a throne.

Father, I am extremely thankful that the throne which seems so forbidding in the Old Testament is so inviting in the New. And the difference is all due to Jesus, Your Son and my Saviour. All honour and glory be to His name for ever. Amen.

Greatest

For reading & meditation – Hebrews 5:1-6

'You are a priest for ever, in the order of Melchizedek.'
(v.6)

One of Satan's most subtle arguments in relation to the compassionate ministry of Christ is: 'The Son of God had an advantage over you. He had no sinful nature. You are weak in this area so go on – give way. You haven't the strength to withstand. God will forgive you. After all – that's His job.'

To answer that, the writer brings to our attention the qualifications of a high priest, who first, in order to represent humanity, had to be a member of the human race. Second, his task was to offer sacrifices for sin, which separates humankind from God. Third, he was required to deal gently with the weak. Fourth, the responsibility for a high priest's appointment was God's. So sacred was the vocation that he had to be called by God and anointed.

FURTHER STUDY

Matt. 4:1-11;
Luke 22:28;
Heb. 2:18

1. How did Jesus handle temptation?

2. What did Jesus say to His disciples at the Last Supper?

Our Lord fulfilled all these qualifications. Though He was God, He humbled Himself to become human. On the cross He came to grips with the problem of sin. He experienced every temptation that comes our way. And He was appointed by God, just as Aaron was, yet with this difference: God did not say to Christ, 'You are my servant,' but, 'You are my Son – a priest for ever in the order of Melchizedek.'

In His priestly ministry – as in all other aspects of His being – our Lord is superior to all, even King Melchizedek. To apply the adjective 'great' to Christ is almost a misnomer. The correct word is never 'great' but 'greatest'. We always have to say 'greatest'.

Lord Jesus, wherever I look, in heaven or in earth, there is no one to compare with You. How glad I am that I have found You, or more correctly – You have found me. I bend my knees both in obedience and gratitude. All honour and glory be unto Your name. Amen.

'A sense of sin'

For reading & meditation – Hebrews 5:7–10

'... he was heard because of his reverent submission.' (v.7)

The refutation of the devil's argument, considered yesterday, leads us into the dark shadows of Gethsemane. There, in the garden, our Lord went through an experience of deep agony, which is described for us in the most vivid phraseology: 'He offered up prayers and petitions with loud cries and tears to the one who could save him from death' (v.7).

Years ago I used to puzzle over the fact that our Lord seemed to demonstrate more personal struggle in the garden than He did

FURTHER STUDY

Matt. 26:36–46;
Luke 22:44;
1 Pet. 3:18

1. What uncharacteristic prayer did Christ pray?

2. How many times did He make His request?

when being nailed to the cross. Then this passage in Hebrews supplied me with the answer. What affected our Lord so deeply in those private moments when He was closeted with His Father in the garden was, I believe, the fact that He faced the full misery which sin produces in the heart of the sinner. He experienced what we often describe as 'a sense of sin'. Though He was not a sinner, yet He was being exposed to the full intensity of the anguish that sin in our lives creates. He fully felt the iron bands of sin's enslaving power; His eyes filled with tears, His heart was crushed like grapes in a winepress,

and under the pressure He sweated great drops of blood. He had suffered before, but never like this. Every cell in His being cried out to be delivered, yet nevertheless His obedience remained intact.

Jesus' time of agony illustrates the fact that when we throw on God's side all our willingness, He throws on our side all His power. Hardly any thought can be greater than that.

Jesus my Lord, when I contemplate what You went through in order to save me, my heart is deeply moved. Without becoming a sinner, You tasted the agony of my sin. Such love overwhelms me. My heart is Yours for ever. Amen.

Arrested development

For reading & meditation – Hebrews 5:11–14

'Anyone who lives on milk … is not acquainted with the teaching about righteousness.' (v.13)

The writer suggests that his readers may be showing signs of arrested spiritual development. Obviously they had been Christians for years, and by this time should have been teaching others the truths of the gospel. But they appeared to have come so far but no farther. Instead of digesting solid spiritual food they were still drinking spiritual milk.

One of the greatest marks of maturity, the writer goes on to say, is the ability to distinguish good from evil. Does this mean we can have decades of Christian experience behind us and still be immature? I'm afraid it does. No matter how eloquently we can talk about our faith, if we can't distinguish good from evil, right from wrong, we are immature – period. A mistake many Christians make is to assume that age produces maturity. It doesn't.

FURTHER STUDY

Eph. 4:1-14;
1 Cor. 13:11; 14:20

1. Why did Paul admonish the Corinthians?

2. How did he describe his own development?

A school principal appointed a woman with just ten years of experience to an important administrative post. Another teacher in the school, who had worked for far longer, came to him and said: 'Why wasn't I considered for the post – I have been a teacher for twenty-five years?' The principal answered: 'You have not had twenty-five years of experience; you have had one year's experience twenty-five times.' That is what these Hebrew Christians had been doing – they had been going through the same experience again and again. Instead of marching forward they were simply marking time.

Can the same thing be said of you and me? It's a sobering thought.

Lord God, if I am suffering from this spiritual condition then shake me out of it. Help me understand that my maturity is related to how quickly I am able to differentiate between right and wrong. Move me towards maturity, dear Father. In Jesus' name. Amen.

Baby talk!

For reading & meditation – Hebrews 5:14–6:2

'Therefore let us leave the elementary teachings about
Christ and go on to maturity ...' (6:1)

Now we look at the writer's description of those who are
spiritually mature – the meat eaters, who can digest 'solid
food'. But what is 'solid food'? Obviously some of the matters he
has been writing about – the Sabbath rest, the eternal priesthood
of Christ, and so on.

The Hebrew Christians had never moved on from the elementary
things of the Christian faith – they preferred to stay on familiar
ground. What would you think of a builder who laid a foundation
for a building and then kept on ripping it up and
laying it again? This is what was happening in the
lives of these Hebrew Christians. And it is happening
in some sections of the Church.

FURTHER STUDY

1 Tim. 4:1-15;
1 Cor. 3:1-2;
Eph. 3:17-19

1. What did
Paul admonish
Timothy?

2. What did he
pray for the
Ephesians?

The three things described as 'elementary
teachings' are first, the initial act of repentance;
second, church ordinances; and third, eschatology
(the things concerning the future). These are 'milk',
says the writer to the Hebrews. Such issues need
to be addressed, of course, but *not all the time*.
When we talk about these elementary things and nothing else
then we are simply indulging in 'baby talk'. I know Christians
whose conversation never goes beyond such subjects as: Will the
Church go through the tribulation? It's time they were weaned on
to some solid food. We must not forget, however, that the low level
of Christian understanding is directly related to the low level of
Christian preaching. If we have problems in the pulpit we should
not be surprised if we have problems in the pews.

**Dear Father, if I am in need of being weaned on to more solid food
then take me through this process, I pray. You have placed the urge
for maturity within me. Now help me grow up.
In Jesus' name. Amen.**

Wills that become set

For reading & meditation – Hebrews 6:3–6
'And God permitting, we will do so.' (v.3)

We come now to what has been described as 'the thorniest and knottiest problem of the Bible': 'It is impossible for those who have once been enlightened … if they fall away, to be brought back to repentance' (vv.4,6).

What do these words mean? The most common views are: (1) It shows quite clearly that Christians may lose their salvation. (2) It was a hypothetical argument to warn immature Hebrew Christians of the reality of divine judgment. (3) It refers to people who are only nominal Christians, who show by falling away that their faith is not genuine. There have been so many differences of opinion on this passage – and by great Bible expositors – that we ought to treat all dogmatism with suspicion. The interpretation I offer, therefore, is not dogmatic, but nevertheless carefully considered.

FURTHER STUDY

2 Pet. 1:1-9;
Eph. 4:15;
2 Pet. 3:18

1. What are we to make every effort to do?

2. How does Peter describe those who do not make the effort?

I believe the key to understanding this is: '*God permitting, we will do so.*' These words imply that some will not be able to move on towards maturity because, by their continued desire to remain at their present level, their wills become set in the state of non-growth. Someone described this as 'the danger of prolonged immaturity' – of remaining in one place so long that we don't want to move on. It is perilously possible to remain so contented with immaturity that the call to maturity leaves us unmoved. If we don't set our wills in the direction of moving ahead with Christ then they can become inflexibly set in the alternative state of non-growth.

God my Father, You have my permission to stir me, prod me, challenge me, and do all that is necessary to prevent me from settling into a state of 'prolonged immaturity'. Help me keep my will moving in the direction of growth. In Jesus' name. Amen.

Rock-hard hearts

For reading & meditation – Hebrews 6:3–8

'... they are crucifying the Son of God all over again and subjecting him to public disgrace.' (v.6)

The writer goes on to say it is impossible for those who have committed themselves to Christ, if they fall away, to be brought back to repentance. There is no doubt in my mind that he is referring here to genuine believers, but I believe *a very small minority*. Note: they have been 'enlightened', have 'tasted of the heavenly gift', 'shared in the Holy Spirit', and 'tasted the goodness of the word of God and the powers of the coming age'. If these words do not describe someone who has had an encounter with Christ and the Holy Spirit then clearly words have lost their meaning.

FURTHER STUDY

Luke 9:57–62;
Matt. 24:12;
Gal. 4:9;
Rev. 2:4

1. What seemingly hard words did Christ give to would-be followers?

2. What was held against the Church at Ephesus?

If such people fall away, says the writer, it is impossible for them to be brought back to repentance. Is this impossible for them or for God? I think both. It is impossible for *them* because, having repudiated the principle of the cross by their unbelief (believing it could take them so far but no farther), their wills become so inflexibly set in the state of non-growth that they are unable to move in God's direction. It is impossible for *God* because if He permitted them to return they would demonstrate the same kind of behaviour and thus repudiate the principle of the cross all over again.

The writer's point about the rain in verses 7 and 8 is: What good does more rain do on ground that is uncultivated and thus almost rock hard? It can only mean more thorns and thistles. Do people whose wills are so set in the state of not growing really want to go on? I doubt it.

Lord God, once more I pray – do all that is necessary to prevent my heart from ever becoming rock hard. My will is Yours. Set it in the direction of continued spiritual growth. In Jesus' name I ask this. Amen.

Am I really growing?

For reading & meditation – Hebrews 6:9-12

'... show this same diligence to the very end, in order to
make your hope sure.' (v.11)

Although the writer has faced the Hebrew Christians with some
serious issues, he follows them up with the hope-building
words of today's text. He was aware of evidence that they were not
in the condition he had described, for he had seen unmistakable
signs of their love for others and their deeds of compassion – the
'things that accompany salvation'. One of the greatest evidences we
can give that we love the Lord and belong truly to Him is to put our
faith into action. 'Whatever you did for one of the least of these
brothers of mine, you did it for me' (Matt. 25:40).

FURTHER STUDY

James 2:14-26;
Col. 1:28;
James 1:4

1. What was
Paul's deep
desire?

2. What brings
maturity?

As the writer thinks of the people to whom he
was writing, he is concerned that they manifest a
fervent desire to move on in their relationship with
God. Perseverance is the hallmark of a successful
Christian life and the proven pattern for victory. The
writer points out that this is how those in the past
have succeeded, and that imitation of that principle
will enable entry into all that God has promised.

Before moving on, let's pause to ask a few personal questions:
Am I still talking 'baby talk' and drinking the 'milk' of elementary
things? Do I appear to others to show an interest in going deeper
with God though in my heart I am content with things the way
they are? Am I really growing? Unless I am greatly mistaken, the
word from the Holy Spirit to all of us at this point in Hebrews is
this – and reverently I say it – For *God's* sake grow up.

**Father, my heart responds to this challenge with fervency and
aspiration. Yes! Yes! Yes! I want to grow. And for *Your* sake – not
just my own. Lead me on to grow and grow and grow.
In Jesus' name. Amen.**

A God of character

For reading & meditation – Hebrews 6:13–18

'And so after waiting patiently, Abraham received what was promised.' (v.15)

The writer to the Hebrews now leads them into a deeper understanding of how their faith can be made strong. He takes them back to Abraham, the 'father of the faithful'.

Genesis records that God appeared to Abraham and made him a promise accompanied by an oath: 'Through your offspring all nations on earth will be blessed' (see Gen. 12:1–3). The immediate seed was Isaac, born in Abraham and Sarah's old age, but the ultimate seed was Christ. The apostle Paul said, when writing to the Galatian Christians: 'If you belong to Christ, then you are Abraham's seed' (Gal. 3:29). Christ was the seed fulfilling the covenant, and those who are Christ's are Abraham's seed. (This is 'solid food' now.)

Why did Abraham believe that God was going to bless all the nations of the earth through him? Not because he saw the promise immediately fulfilled! Twenty-five long years elapsed between the giving of the promise and the arrival of Isaac – years in which his wife, Sarah, actually passed the age of child-bearing. Abraham did not believe because he saw immediate results but because his faith rested on the character of God. A man or woman's word is no better than their character. Someone may give you their word, but if they are not a person of character they can easily break their word. All faith ultimately rests on character. This is why the Christian faith has such a powerful bedrock. Our God is more than a God of power; He is also a God of character.

FURTHER STUDY

Psa. 40:1-5;
37:7;
Isa. 25:1-9

1. What experiences did the psalmist have in common with Abraham?

2. What words of praise did the Israelites give?

God my Father, I too, like Abraham, bank on Your character. Your Word is dependable because Your nature cannot change. You can never do anything that is out of character. I bank on that with my very life. Amen.

The *anchoria*

For reading & meditation – Hebrews 6:19–20

'We have this hope as an anchor for the soul, firm
and secure.' (v.19)

The hope that one day we will enter into the presence of God
is, says the writer to the Hebrews, like an anchor for the soul
– firm and secure.

It is difficult for us to appreciate the beauty and aptness of the
figure here employed. Philip Mauro, a Bible commentator, says
the anchor referred to here is not the great iron affair we are used
to, with two huge flukes, carried at the bow and stern of modern
ships. The figure is taken from the practice that prevailed in olden
times in the harbours of the Mediterranean, where a
massive stone called an *anchoria* was embedded in
the ground near the water's edge. Sometimes a small
ship could not make its way into the harbour by
means of its sails, and in such a case a 'forerunner'
would go ashore in a little boat with a line which
would be made fast to the *anchoria*. Those on the
small ship had only to 'hold fast' to the line, and by
patient and persistent effort 'draw near' to the shore.

FURTHER STUDY

Job 11:13–19;
Psa. 112:1–8

1. What
did Zophar
assure Job?

2. What is the
result of fearing
the Lord?

The writer mixes metaphors by relating the figure
of an anchor not to a harbour but to 'the inner sanctuary behind
the curtain' – meaning the holy presence of God. Christ is there as
our 'Forerunner' and has fastened 'the rope of hope' to the divine
anchoria – the throne of God. In ancient times no one ever followed
the high priest into the Most Holy Place, but this new High Priest
– Jesus – guarantees to every believer the promise of confident
access into the very presence of the living God.

Lord Jesus Christ, my Forerunner and my Friend, how can I thank
You enough for the knowledge that one day You will bring me to
where You are. This hope is as sure and as steadfast as Your eternal
throne. I am deeply, deeply grateful. Amen.

Greater than Melchizedek

For reading & meditation – Hebrews 7:1–3

'... like the Son of God he remains a priest for ever.' (v.3)

Now we focus more fully on the mysterious and intriguing Old Testament character, Melchizedek. Reference to him occurs only twice: once in Genesis and once in the Psalms. However, here in Hebrews he is mentioned eight times, which suggests there is something very important hidden here.

Melchizedek appears to be both a king and a priest, and is described as coming from the city of Salem, the ancient name for Jerusalem (see Psalm 76:2). His name means 'king of righteousness',

FURTHER STUDY

John 8:31–58;
Micah 5:2;
John 17:5;
Rev. 22:13

1. What did Jesus declare of Himself?

2. What did Micah declare about the Messiah?

and because of his association with Jerusalem he is described also as the 'king of peace'. The fact that the writer to the Hebrews tells us he had no father and mother, and that there was no record of his ancestors, is thought by many to imply that his appearance in the Old Testament is really a Christophany – a manifestation of Christ in human form. I am not convinced of this. I believe the writer is using the silence of Scripture in relation to the history of this man to illustrate the priesthood of Christ. We cannot account for Melchizedek in the annals of history. Also, he appears to possess his priesthood in his own right, not by virtue of descent, and no record is given of him ever assuming or losing his office.

All these mystic qualities come to their ultimate fulfilment in Christ. Our Lord has no beginning and no end. He did not come out of history, like everyone else, but came into it. His priesthood is eternal – it never began and thus will never end.

God my Father, I am lost in wonder, love, and praise as I contemplate the glories of Your Son, my Saviour. He is obviously Your highest interest. May He be mine also. Amen.

When the sun comes out

For reading & meditation – Hebrews 7:4–10
'And without doubt the lesser person is blessed by
the greater.' (v.7)

The writer to the Hebrews continues to dwell upon the shadowy figure of Melchizedek in a way that some have commented is tedious. But we must remember the apostle Paul's great words: '*All scripture is inspired by God and profitable …*' (2 Tim. 3:16, RSV). There is a powerful purpose in what is being said in this passage.

The argument is very simple: the Levitical priests derived their authority from the fact that they were descended from Abraham, therefore they could never have offered any greater help than Abraham was able to offer. And because Abraham acknowledged the supremacy of Melchizedek by paying tithes to him, this meant that all succeeding priests were inferior to Melchizedek, and their priesthood to his.

FURTHER STUDY

2 Pet. 1:16-21;
1 Pet. 1:22-25

1. What did Peter testify to?

2. Where was his confidence?

The argument continues: the Levitical priests were superior to the rest of the Israelites because they took tithes from them. Levi, as the progenitor of the Levitical priesthood, was greater than all. Abraham was greater than Levi because he was the father of the whole nation, and Melchizedek was greater even than Abraham because he received tithes from him and blessed him. 'The lesser person is blessed by the greater' (v.7). Therefore, the writer argues, Melchizedek is greater than Abraham, Levi, the Levitical priests and indeed all Israel.

This is to highlight the fact that the reality – Christ – is greater than the facsimile – the Melchizedek priesthood. What need is there of candles when the sun comes out?

Father, help me to remain ever and always with a clear understanding of Your Son's superiority over all things. Wean me from everything that is marginal so that I may give myself to the Magnificent. In Christ's name I pray. Amen.

The Perfect One

For reading & meditation – Hebrews 7:11–19

'... one who has become a priest ... on the basis of the
power of an indestructible life.' (v.16)

The writer to the Hebrews now focuses on the theme of the new
order of priesthood which Christ introduced into the world,
and explains why such an order was needed. He says, first, this
new order was clearly predicted, because perfection could not be
attained through the Levitical priesthood. The word 'perfection'
here has to do with human approaches to God. The old order could
never perfectly effect such an approach because it could never
fully and effectively remove the sin which barred humankind's
way to God. Therefore the new order was in God's
mind when the old was fully in operation. Thus the
law was also provisional and was destined to be set
aside, along with the priesthood, as the old legal
system was closely related to it and turned upon it.
A change of priesthood meant a change of law.

FURTHER STUDY

John 8:42–47;
Isa. 53:9;
2 Cor. 5:21;
1 Pet. 1:19

1. What
challenge did
Jesus throw out?

2. How did Peter
describe Jesus?

Now the law forbad anyone from a tribe other
than Levi to serve at the altar. But our Lord, the
writer points out, was from the tribe of Judah. It is
clear that since the law allowed only the sons of Levi
to be priests, it had to be abrogated to make way for the One who
possessed priesthood not by virtue of descent but by the power
of an endless life. Christ is a Priest (as we saw) in the order of
Melchizedek – He had no beginning and will have no ending.

The law made nothing perfect, but Christ makes everything
perfect. He bore our sin in such a way that He bore it all away.
In Him we find *perfect* peace, *perfect* joy and *perfect* pardon.

Lord God, how clearly the deficiencies of the old system are shown
up when placed against the virtues of Your Son. In Him perfection
is personified. I am eternally grateful. Amen.

What a Saviour!

'... but because Jesus lives for ever, he has a permanent priesthood.' (v.24)

In the old order, the writer to the Hebrews tells us, a priest never took an oath because the law was but a temporary measure; it was not the ultimate divine revelation. But in Christ the permanent order has come, and therefore His ministry was confirmed by an oath.

What is being said here is this: God confirmed Christ in His office as a priest 'in the order of Melchizedek' with an oath – signifying that His priesthood would be permanent. This means there is no intention of a shutdown. Furthermore, says the writer, under the old arrangement there had to be many priests so that when the older ones died, the system could still be carried on. Christ has a permanent priesthood because He lives for ever.

The writer then summarises the whole matter by telling us that because Christ is a priest in the order of Melchizedek (One whose personality transcends all human measurement and limitations, and Who ministers righteousness and peace), He is able to save completely those who come to God through Him, *because he always lives to intercede for them* (v.25). The word 'completely' appears in some translations as 'uttermost', which gave rise to the well-known statement used by many evangelists over the years: 'Christ saves from the guttermost to the uttermost.' He takes men and women who have sunk to the deepest depths and by His grace lifts them to the highest heights. Hallelujah! What a Saviour!

FURTHER STUDY

John 17:1-26;
Isa. 53:12;
Rom. 8:31-34

1. Why is John 17 called the 'High Priestly Prayer'?

2. What did Paul affirm to the condemned Romans?

Lord God, how can I ever sufficiently thank You for all You have done for me in Christ? The depths can never be plumbed and the heights can never be scaled. I cannot fully understand it, yet I stand upon it. Thank You my Father. Amen.

Just what we need

For reading & meditation – Hebrews 7:26–28
'He sacrificed for their sins once for all when he
offered himself.' (v.27)

We ended yesterday with the thought that Christ saves from the guttermost to the uttermost. No wonder the writer begins the next sentence with: 'Such a high priest meets our need – one who is holy, blameless, pure, set apart from sinners, exalted above the heavens' (v.26). I like the way the *Living Bible* paraphrases this verse: 'He is, therefore, exactly the kind of high priest we need.' It reminds me of the lovely acrostic I once came upon: J-E-S-U-S – Jesus Exactly Suits Us Sinners.

FURTHER STUDY

Rom. 5:1–8;
Eph. 5:1–2;
John 15:13;
Titus 2:14

1. How does
Paul describe
Christ's
sacrifice?

2. How was
God's love
demonstrated?

The writer to the Hebrews simply cannot take his eyes off Christ. He is writing to buffeted, confused, persecuted Christians who are being tempted to return to the pageantry of the past, but over and over again he repeats his one theme – Jesus is just what we need. Unlike other priests, our Lord does not need to offer sacrifices every day. He has offered Himself, the perfect sacrifice, and this one offering suffices for time and eternity.

The cross is a timeless event, not simply a historic happening that occurred somewhere around AD 33. It is an intrusion of eternity into time. It is as though it is going on for ever. That is why some theologians, when speaking of the cross, refer to it as 'a contemporary experience'. Everything flows from it, everything moves towards it. From that great event all hope proceeds. The words of the writer to the Hebrews are just as applicable to us today as they were when first they were penned: *Jesus is just what we need.*

Lord Jesus Christ, just as an infant cries out for its mother and will not be satisfied with less, so my heart cries out for You. You are not just something my heart longs for – You are everything it longs for. Thank You my Saviour. Amen.

The original design

For reading & meditation – Hebrews 8:1-5

'They serve at a sanctuary that is a copy and shadow of what is in heaven.' (v.5)

The writer to the Hebrews noted the *duration* of Christ's priestly ministry – all eternity. Now he focuses on its *location* – the throne of God. Jesus, our Great High Priest, is not standing before the throne, but is *seated* there. His sacrificial work is done and the effects of His great sacrifice go on for ever. The ancient tabernacle was not an original design but a copy of the system of worship that operates in heaven. The tabernacle, as you know, consisted of three parts: the outer court which everyone could enter, the inner court which only the priests could enter, and the Holy of Holies which only the high priest could enter, and that just once a year.

FURTHER STUDY

Acts 13:32-39;
1 Cor. 6:11;
Gal. 3:24

1. What does the law do?

2. What does Christ do?

Our universe is structured similarly. At the centre – the Holy of Holies – dwells the Almighty, who by virtue of His intrinsic holiness is unapproachable. In the inner court dwell the angels, who continually minister to the Creator by their obedience and worship. In the outer court, a great distance removed, dwells the human race, stained and soiled by sin. But this is the exciting thing. Our Lord by His sacrifice on the cross opened up a way into the very presence of God – the Holy of Holies – whereby soiled sinners could pass through the open court, right past the ranks of worshipping angels, and stand before the very throne of God Himself *just as if we had never sinned*. Can anything in heaven or earth be more wonderful? If there is then I have never heard of it.

Lord God, how amazed the angels must be as they contemplate the mysteries of Your grace. It amazes me also. To be saved from hell would be enough, but to be invited into Your immediate presence is grace beyond compare. I am deeply, deeply grateful. Amen.

The new covenant

For reading & meditation – Hebrews 8:6–9

'For if there had been nothing wrong with that first covenant, no place would have been sought for another.' (v.7)

Now the writer says that Jesus, our Great High Priest, mediates a more excellent covenant than Melchizedek since it is founded on better promises. The word 'covenant' has an important place in Hebrews and appears seventeen times. It denotes a contract between two parties for achieving some object of mutual desire. A covenant between God and humanity, however, must never be thought of as a contract between two equal parties. God is always the sole initiator, and having laid down the terms of the covenant, invites people to join with Him in it.

FURTHER STUDY

2 Sam. 23:1-7;
Isa. 24:5;
54:10; 55:3

1. What was David's rhetorical question?

2. What was the basis of God's covenant?

In the covenant made at Sinai, the Ten Commandments were given as the standard set by Israel's Lord. They were perfectly valid then, as they are now. But the people found fault with them because they failed to understand them. They thought that keeping the Ten Commandments was the only way they could please God. What they could not see (though God pointed this out to them several times) was that they could not keep them in their own strength. They needed divine help; they needed a Saviour. When their efforts to keep the Ten Commandments failed they tried to lower the standards, and when that didn't work – gave up on them altogether. Isn't this what people are doing today?

God promised through Jeremiah, however, that the day would dawn when a new covenant would be given that would be infinitely more effective than the old. Thanks be to God – that day has arrived!

Most gracious and holy God, I see that though You could not lower Your standards in the presence of sin, You found a way, through Jesus, to empower me to reach up to them. All honour and glory be to Your peerless and precious name. Amen.

Inside out!

For reading & meditation – Hebrews 8:10–13

'This is the covenant I will make with the house of Israel after that time ...' (v.10)

What exactly is the new covenant? These words are spoken at the Communion service: 'This cup is the new covenant in my blood' (1 Cor. 11:25). They refer to a new agreement made not between God and us but between God and His Son. This is the thrilling thing about the new covenant: it is made between two parties who cannot fail – God and His Son, the Lord Jesus Christ. When we receive Christ, everything specified in the covenant is available to us.

There are four provisions in the new covenant that were not present in the old. (1) 'I will put my laws in their minds and write them on their hearts' (v.10). The old law was written externally; the new one is written internally. The Spirit brings the truth and puts it inside us. (2) 'I will be their God, and they will be my people' (v.10). Just as we hunger to belong to someone in the natural world, so we hunger also in the spiritual realm. Through Christ we belong to God – our spiritual identity crisis is over and our restless hearts find their home in Him.

FURTHER STUDY

Jer. 31:31;
Matt. 26:17-29;
Rom. 11:27

1. What had God promised through Jeremiah?

2. How was this covenant sealed?

(3) 'They will all know me, from the least of them to the greatest' (v.11). The knowledge of God is the most precious possession anyone can have. In Christ all can know God. (4) 'I will forgive their wickedness and will remember their sins no more' (v.12). The message the new covenant spells out most clearly is – God is not against us for our sins, but for us against our sins. The first covenant didn't work. The second one does!

Father, help me rest in the knowledge that the covenant made between Yourself and Your Son can never be broken and thus can never fail. Because the covenant is secure I am secure. Blessed be Your name for ever. Amen.

Key to effective worship

For reading & meditation – Hebrews 9:1–10

'... the way into the Most Holy Place had not ... been disclosed as ... the first tabernacle was still standing.' (v.8)

Having considered the superiority of the new covenant, the writer turns now to how worship is also made superior through the Son. We are introduced in the first five verses of this passage to the furniture in the tabernacle. But his main point is: however beautiful and wonderful the system of worship in the ancient tabernacle, it had severe limitations.

First, only the high priest could enter the Most Holy Place, and that just once a year. Second, he was obliged to offer the blood of sacrifice not only for the sins of the people but, because he also was a sinner, he had to offer a sacrifice for himself. Third, the gifts and sacrifices offered were not able to fully clear the conscience. Fourth, because the rituals in the ancient tabernacle affected only the outer person, there was no change in the inner person. The performance of a ritual such as ceremonial washing affected only the parts of the body that were involved in the performance.

FURTHER STUDY

Acts 24:10–16;
Rom. 9:1;
2 Cor. 1:12;
1 Tim. 1:19

1. What did Paul strive for?

2. What did he instruct Timothy?

One of the most important keys to effective worship is a clear conscience. Don't you find it difficult, if not impossible, to worship when you have a guilty conscience? Worshippers in Old Testament times did not have their consciences cleansed, and therefore they had no rest. Thus they had to return again and again to perform repeatedly the same rituals in an endless search for peace. How privileged we are to have our consciences made clean by the blood of Christ. It makes a world of difference to our worship.

Lord God, I see that what the ancient worshippers could never experience by ritual – a cleansed and purified conscience – is mine by redemption. May the awareness of this fact help to deepen my worship of You, this day and every day. In Jesus' name. Amen.

Nothing!

For reading & meditation – Hebrews 9:11–14

'How much more, then, will the blood of Christ ...
cleanse our consciences...' (v.14)

We focus on the better and more complete system of worship
introduced by the Son. If you grasp the writer's argument
here, I promise you it will galvanise your Christian life and add
zest to your daily living.

He says that the first system (the ancient tabernacle), depended
on the physical activity of the worshipper, and affected only the
body. Doing things for God, and being active for Him, cannot in
itself subdue the guilty conscience. The new arrangement, by
which Christians are now to live, depends not on the
work of the worshipper but on the activity of Christ
on our behalf. The ministry of Jesus, our Great High
Priest, moves through the barrier of flesh into what
we might describe as the Holy of Holies – our spirit.
Here, where the conscience resides, the value of
Christ's blood is applied. It is not our activity that
brings us peace but His activity on our behalf.

Our activity adds nothing to our acceptance before
God. We work not to be saved, but because we are
saved. Oh, if only Christians could get hold of this.
Multitudes of Christians become workaholics because they think
(erroneously) that the more they do the more God will love them.
God loves you not for what you do but because He is love. He
appreciates your work and labours for Him, of course, but that is
not the ground of your salvation. As the hymnist put it:

> *What can wash away my sin?*
> *Nothing but the blood of Jesus.*

FURTHER STUDY

Gal. 2:20;
Phil. 2:12–18;
Col. 1:27;
John 14:20

1. What did Paul
attest to the
Galatians?

2. How are we
to work out
our salvation?

**Lord God, help me lay hold of this truth and never let it go – that I
am not working to be saved, but working because I am saved. You
give – I receive. Nothing could be simpler – and nothing could be
more wonderful. Thank You my Father. Amen.**

No other way

For reading & meditation – Hebrews 9:15–22
'... he has died as a ransom to set them free ...' (v.15)

Sceptics sometimes sneeringly refer to Christianity as a 'slaughterhouse religion' because of its continual emphasis upon the death of Christ. This is the point which the writer comes to grips with here.

Without a death, he argues, it is not possible to receive the benefits of the covenant God has made. No *last will and testament* can bestow any benefits until the death of the testator. We would not be able to avail ourselves of all that God wants us to have – particularly release from a guilty conscience – unless the Son of God had died. The will drawn up by the Trinity that vouchsafes to us such great eternal benefits would be invalid without the death of the Son. In fact, death is so important that even the shadow, the picture in the Old Testament, required the shedding of blood.

There is a reason why blood drips from almost every page of the Bible – without the shedding of blood there is no forgiveness. This may be repulsive but the point is – so is our sin. The penalty for sin is death, and the remedy for that is the death of Another, One so sublime that the value of His death can be laid to the account of the whole human race. It was our blood that needed to be shed, but so great was Christ's love for us that He allowed His own blood to be shed – on our behalf. Let those who criticise the gospel try to come up with some answer. There isn't one. It took the death of the Son of God to bring us salvation. How dare we criticise it?

FURTHER STUDY

1 Pet. 1:13-19;
Acts 20:28;
Rom. 5:9;
1 John 1:7

1. How does Peter describe the blood of Christ?

2. How does Paul describe the result of the shed blood?

Jesus, Lord and Saviour, we Your children gaze at You from a different viewpoint. We see what others do not see. They are repulsed by Your cross; we rejoice in it. Help us show them what we see. For Your own dear name's sake. Amen.

The three appearings

For reading & meditation – Hebrews 9:23–28

'But now he has appeared ... to do away with sin by the sacrifice of himself.' (v.26)

It seems strange that heavenly things had to be purified by blood. Maybe, as one commentator puts it: 'The heavens have a certain defilement through contact with the sins that are absolved in them.' Whatever the reason, having offered a better sacrifice than any other priest, Christ entered into the very presence of God. His sphere of service is the true Holy of Holies, and He entered it by virtue of that one final sacrifice which He made on Calvary's cross.

In the tabernacle, the high priest went into the Holy of Holies once a year, bearing the blood of first a bullock, and then a goat. He wore a simple white robe. While he was in the Holy Place the people waited outside afraid, wondering if the sacrifice would be acceptable to God. If it was not, the whole nation would be wiped out. The high priest knew he was facing the judgment of God. Once the sacrifice was accepted, however, he returned to give the good news to the people, after divesting himself of his white robe and putting on again garments of beauty.

FURTHER STUDY

1 Pet. 3:13-18;
Isa. 53:5;
Gal. 3:13

1. What air of finality does Peter proclaim?

2. How does Galatians 3 link to Isaiah 53?

What a picture this is of the ministry of our Lord, who appeared in this world to be our Great High Priest, and who now appears in the presence of God for us. Finally He will appear to the world once again, not in humility, but in garments of majesty and glory. Let your soul feed on this thought throughout the day: He has appeared, He now appears, and will yet appear.

Lord Jesus Christ, I await Your final appearing with anticipation and joy. Day by day the Spirit unfolds Your glory to me, but my soul still longs for that day when faith will be lost in sight. Even so, come Lord Jesus! Amen.

One unchanging message

For reading & meditation – Hebrews 10:1–4

'... it is impossible for the blood of bulls and goats to take away sins.' (v.4)

Sometimes to show the superiority of one thing over another it is necessary to draw a number of contrasts. Here the writer is contrasting the finality of Christ's sacrifice for sin with the lack of finality found in the Old Testament system.

The Old Testament system of worship was not the reality; it was merely a picture, a shadow, a visual aid if you like, of what was to come. But nevertheless, one unchanging message sounded forth on almost every page of the Old Testament. Every sacrifice and offering portrayed the same truth; it was emphasised in each drop of blood, and rose to the skies in the ascending smoke of every burnt-offering – *in order for a life to be saved a life had to be given*. It was only a shadow, however, for such a system was incapable of perfecting any worshipper through its sacrifices. No worshipper was ever brought to what someone has described as 'a real and enduring fellowship with God', for none ever lost the feelings of guilt that sin inevitably brings.

FURTHER STUDY

John 1:19–29;
Isa. 53:7;
1 Cor. 5:7

1. What did John declare of Jesus?

2. How did Paul describe Christ?

To the writer of Hebrews, the very fact that the sin offerings were made continually, year after year, was proof that the old institutions, although divinely appointed, were not the final answer. Common sense ought to tell us that the blood of animals can never take away sins. Yet how many pin their hopes for salvation, even today, on shadows, instead of taking hold of the reality which is Christ. They prefer rituals instead of the Saviour. How sad.

Lord God, the heart can never be satisfied with a ritual; it is satisfied only with reality. How glad I am that I have found You. Lead others to Yourself this very day. In Jesus' name I ask it. Amen.

What God is looking for

For reading & meditation – Hebrews 10:5–10

'... I have come to do your will, O God.' (v.7)

DAY
103

God never really cared for all the rivers of blood that flowed from Jewish altars. His only interest was that they were like fingerposts, pointing to the perfect sacrifice and offering made in the body of His Son, Jesus Christ. The word 'body' figures greatly in this passage.

When God created Adam and Eve, His desire was that a human will in a human frame would choose to live in complete dependence on Him. But as you know, the first human pair chose to use their wills against God rather than with Him. Thus ever after, God had desired to see on earth a human will in a human *body* choosing to perfectly depend on Him – in all situations. When Christ came to this world He paused on the threshold of eternity and said: 'Sacrifice and offering you did not desire, but a *body* you prepared for me' (v.5). And the will of our Lord, functioning in a human body, never once acted independently. Throughout every moment of His life on earth He maintained a complete and utter dependence on the Father who indwelt Him. That is the principle that God had longed to see in the universe – the principle of trust and confidence in the Father's purposes.

FURTHER STUDY

Gal. 4:1-11;
2 Tim. 3:5;
Col. 2:20-23

1. What was Paul's concern for the Galatians?

2. What was his admonition to the Colossians?

So those who put their faith in religious rituals and ceremonies had better realise these things are of no real interest to God. What He looks for is what He saw perfectly in Jesus – a heart that is His, a life that is His, and a human will in a human frame demonstrating absolute trust in Him.

Father, You wrapped Your heart in flesh and blood and allowed it to be broken on a cross for our salvation. What need have we of ceremonies when we have a cross? Help me to keep my heart in an attitude of constant dependency and trust. In Jesus' name. Amen.

'I can't remember that!'

For reading & meditation – Hebrews 10:11–18

'And where these have been forgiven, there is no longer any sacrifice for sin.' (v.18)

The ancient tabernacle in the wilderness had a table, a candlestick – but nowhere for a priest to sit down, because the priests were required to minister continually before the Lord. But when Christ offered Himself as a single sacrifice, says the writer to the Hebrews, *He sat down* at the right hand of God to await the time when His enemies should be made His footstool.

We see illustrated here the principle of trust in the Father's purposes coming into its own. That principle once begun and adhered to in human history will inevitably result in God's will being done and all Christ's enemies becoming His footstool.

FURTHER STUDY

1 John 1:1-10;
Isa. 43:25;
44:22; 55:7;
Micah 7:18

1. What is the result of God's faithfulness?

2. What does God delight to do?

The writer reminds us again that 'by one sacrifice he has made perfect for ever those who are being made holy' (v.14). Our Lord's one final act of redemption clears our conscience of guilt and enables us to enter into true worship. This is proved by the Holy Spirit who, speaking through Jeremiah, promised all believers: 'I will put my laws in their hearts … write them on their minds …Their sins and lawless acts I will remember no more' (vv.16–17).

Just think of it – through the perfect sacrifice, our sins and lawless deeds are remembered no more. Sometimes you may be tempted to bring up those old reprehensible acts which have been forgiven and say to the Lord: 'Don't you remember what I did and those awful things I was guilty of?' He simply shakes His hand, looks at you with a smile, and says: 'No, I'm sorry, I can't remember that.'

Lord God, without Your forgiveness and the wiping out of condemnation, my heart would be filled with dread. Help me not to rake up what You have forgiven – and forgotten. In Jesus' name. Amen.

The name of the game

For reading & meditation – Hebrews 10:19–25

'... let us draw near to God with a sincere heart in full assurance of faith ...' (v.22)

This passage contains some of the most beautiful language to be found in the New Testament. But the words are a clarion call to a deeper Christian commitment. Because of the confidence we have to enter into the Most Holy Place by the blood of Jesus, and because of the continuing ministry of Jesus, our Great High Priest, three exhortations are given.

First, we are to worship 'with a sincere heart in full assurance of faith, having our hearts sprinkled to cleanse us from a guilty conscience and having our bodies washed with pure water' (v.22). This means entering into worship only after we have gained a consciousness of sins forgiven through the redemption which is in Christ. The reference here to 'having our bodies washed with pure water' is suggestive of the ritual performed at the ordination of a Levite into his priestly service (Lev. 8:6), and is intended to show that the redeemed Christian is himself a priest before God.

FURTHER STUDY

1 Pet. 1:1-9;
Rom. 15:4;
1 John 3:3

1. For what did Peter give praise to God?

2. What does hope cause us to do?

Second, we are to 'hold unswervingly to the hope we profess' (v.23). Perseverance in the Christian life is the name of the game. What God has promised He will perform – so we have every reason to keep going.

Third, we should 'consider how we may spur one another on towards love and good deeds' and 'not give up meeting together' (vv.24–25). There is no such thing as a go-it-alone Christian. Our success as individuals in the Christian Church depends largely on the functioning of others as their lives interact with our lives.

Father, as I catch these different glimpses of the purposes of redemption, my heart is on fire to discover more. Is there no end to this adventure? No, for there is no end to Thee. Amen.

Keep on keeping on

For reading & meditation – Hebrews 10:26–39

'... persevere so that when you have done the will of God, you will receive what he has promised.' (v.36)

The writer moves from exhortation to severe warning, similar to the one we looked at earlier (6:4ff.). The greatest evidence one is a Christian, the writer says, is the desire to stop sinning, and if a person continually ignores this inner urge, placed there by the Holy Spirit, they will come under divine judgment. Persistent sin soon anaesthetises the soul, and it is not long then until the attitude sets like concrete and becomes one of conscious resistance to all that has been taught. It takes a person a long time to get to this stage, but I have seen it happen several times. A person who continues to sin becomes so hardened to all they have known that they see no value in Christ's death and thus treat the blood of Christ as an unholy thing. Such an attitude will not go unpunished and, as the writer says: 'It is a dreadful thing to fall into the hands of the living God' (v.31).

Moving quickly from warning to encouragement (as was his custom), the writer applauds the Hebrew Christians for their past evidence of perseverance and tells them that having endured so much they must now watch that they do not fail in the ordinary humdrum of daily activities. 'Keep on going on' is the thrust of his final statements.

I too want to plant this deep in your souls. You who have been following the Lord for some time now through difficult and trying circumstances – keep on keeping on. You have come so far, don't even think of going back.

FURTHER STUDY

James 1:12;
1 Cor. 15:58;
Gal. 5:1;
Phil. 1:27

1. What brings blessing?

2. How did Paul encourage the Corinthians?

**Lord God, help me to keep on keeping on, no matter what kind of circumstances I find myself in. Let Your perseverance become my perseverance, Your determination my determination.
In Jesus' name I pray. Amen.**

An anatomy of faith

For reading & meditation – Hebrews 11:1–3

'Now faith is being sure of what we hope for and certain of what we do not see.' (v.1)

What is the chief component of *perseverance*, which plays such an important part in the Christian life? It is *faith*.

A tutor in my Bible college said: 'Whenever you see the word 'faith' in the Bible read 'toughness'.' Hebrews 11 gives us a list of some of the toughest people in history. They endured, or toughed it out, because their eyes were fully focused on One who never changes; nothing could divert them. The writer to the Hebrews is calling for a faith that meets life head on and is never diverted from its course of action.

But what is faith? A little boy once described it as 'believing what you know isn't true'. That is the very opposite of faith! 'Faith,' says the writer (in the only definition of faith given in the Bible) 'is being sure of what we hope for and certain of what we do not see.' Three elements are contained in this definition: a certain hope, an awareness of things not seen and strong assurance.

Hope is a strong component of faith. You can never have much faith until you are filled with a kind of divine discontent, until you are dissatisfied with the way things are. Complacency in spiritual things is so stultifying. Faith means also that one believes that there is Someone out there who can be depended upon. In other words, that God exists. Then, when we act on this conviction, we receive the same rewards as did these heroes of faith. We find the God who honoured the people in Bible times is just the same today.

FURTHER STUDY

Eph. 1:15-23;
1 Pet. 1:3

1. What does Paul pray that the Ephesians might know?
2. What have we been birthed into?

Lord God, quicken my faith until it becomes as tough and as sturdy as that possessed by the men and women of Bible days. Help me never to be diverted from any course of action which is in harmony with Your perfect will. In Jesus' name. Amen.

Faith's heroes

For reading & meditation – Hebrews 11:4–22

'All these people were still living by faith when they died.'
(v.13)

We are now presented with many illustrations of faith at work. The first listed all lived before the Flood. Abel exercised faith when he offered his sacrifice to God. He was a righteous man who pleased God, and his offering was accepted. Enoch walked with God by faith and, as someone has put it, 'walked so far that God said: 'Enoch, it's too far to go back now, so you had better come home with Me.' ' Noah, who may never have seen a ship in his life, set about building one at the command of God, and by the exercise of his faith assured the continuance of the human race.

FURTHER STUDY

Rom. 10:17;
James 1:6;
Gal. 3:6

1. Where does faith come from?

2. What are we like when we doubt?

Next are the patriarchs. Abraham's whole life is a demonstration of faith. He proved his willingness to believe God by going at His command to a land he had never seen. He did not know where he was going, but he knew with *whom* he was going, and there can be no better demonstration of faith than that. The supreme test of Abraham's faith was his response to God's request that he offer up his son Isaac. Abraham obeyed because he reasoned that God could raise the dead (Gen. 22:1ff.), and thus Isaac's figurative 'resurrection' becomes a picture of the resurrection of Christ.

Isaac, Jacob and Joseph combine to illustrate that faith is the assurance of things hoped for, the conviction of things not seen. How daring they were, and how defiant of the odds. We see at work here a faith that has changed the course of history and, if put into operation, might yet change this present age.

Father, give me this same kind of daring, defiant faith that clings to You, come what may. I came into the Christian life by faith. Now show me how to walk in it and make it work. In Jesus' name. Amen.

Seeing the invisible

For reading & meditation – Hebrews 11:23–29

'By faith he left Egypt ... he persevered because he saw
him who is invisible.' (v.27)

The writer to the Hebrews draws our attention to the faith of
Moses' parents – Amram, his father, and Jochebed, his mother.
Their action of putting Moses into a tiny cradle and setting him
afloat on the River Nile demonstrated as much faith in God as
that displayed by any of the other great names in this chapter.
The life of Moses – a life that covers 120 years – is rooted in the
faith of Amram and Jochebed, two almost unknown people and
common slaves.

What is also interesting in this passage on Moses
is that out of the many things that happened to him
during his life of faith, the writer focuses only on
two events – his leaving the court of Pharaoh and
his involvement with his people in their flight from
Egypt. Both events involved a departure, or exodus!
His departure from the court meant he turned his
back on a life of pleasure and ease because he had a
conviction that it was the unseen that mattered, not
the seen. We are told also that it was by faith that
Moses kept the Passover. Simply by obeying God he
instituted a festival that was to remain throughout
the history of the Jewish people – a symbol of the
fact that they are a people redeemed, ransomed and released
from bondage.

Moses knew what it was to hesitate, to tremble, to feel afraid,
but he knew also what it meant to trust God. And that, in the final
analysis, is what faith is all about. Faith is trusting God in the face
of every fear, every doubt, and every difficulty.

FURTHER STUDY

Exod. 2:1-10;
Dan. 3:16-18;
Acts 27:24-25

1. How did
the Hebrew
young men
demonstrate
faith?

2. What was the
basis of Paul's
encouragement
to his fellow
sailors?

**Lord God, help me see that faith does not mean there is a complete
absence of fear but is the ability to believe in the face of fear. I
would have this kind of faith permeate my soul. Grant it, dear Lord.
In Jesus' name. Amen.**

A continuous principle

For reading & meditation – Hebrews 11:30–40

'These were all commended for their faith, yet none of
them received what had been promised.' (v.39)

The writer to the Hebrews in this final section gives an
impetuous summary of persons and deeds, that is, as Dr G.
Campbell Morgan puts it, 'vibrant with power, poignant in its
account of sufferings, and challenging in its revelation of triumph'.
The phrase 'I do not have time to tell' (v.32) suggests that the list
he has given us is not exhaustive. He has illustrated faith, but he
has by no means exhausted his theme.

Unlike the other names listed in the chapter, the names in this
final list are not placed in chronological order. Yet
there *is* a system. He names five leaders from the
time of the Judges and early monarchy – Gideon,
Barak, Samson, Jephthah and Samuel. He names
only one king – David. Then he groups in one phrase
the prophets. This gives the idea of the process of
history, a continuous stream of people of faith. Faith,
it should be noted, is a continuous principle.

FURTHER STUDY
2 Chron. 20:1-12;
2 Cor. 3:5;
Job 19:25

1. What did
Jehoshaphat
confess?
2. What did
he confirm?

Then he passes to the passage in which he tells
of people who suffered greatly for their faith but
came through victorious. Every phrase is a story, every sentence a
history. He finishes with the thought that they toughed it out even
though they did not receive the promise; that is, the Messianic
promise. But we have received that promise. We *know* that the
Messiah has come. Our world has witnessed His appearance and
makes His coming the dividing point of history. How much greater
then should be our faith.

God my Father, may the fact that You have appeared in this world
in the Person of Your Son be a constant focus and trigger for my
faith, so that it grows greater and stronger day by day. In Jesus'
name I ask it. Amen.

The supreme Witness

For reading & meditation – Hebrews 12:1–2

'Let us fix our eyes on Jesus, the author and perfecter of our faith ...' (v.2)

The witness of the people of faith from chapter 11 is to serve as an inspiration but not as an example. Seeing this 'cloud of witnesses', all believers are to divest themselves of the sin that entangles and run in the self-same race. The 'sin' referred to here is unbelief – the failure to take God at His Word. That is the sin mentioned throughout the whole of Hebrews. But how do we disentangle ourselves from this cardinal sin – the sin of unbelief? By looking unto Jesus, the Author and Perfecter of our faith.

The word 'author' can also be translated 'file-leader', the one who stands at the head of a procession. We saw in Hebrews 11 some marvellous illustrations of faith – a procession that spanned the whole of Old Testament history. But now watch – one personality races past them all and moves to the head of the procession. He moves so swiftly that we can hardly catch sight of Him. Who is it? Jesus – the File-leader and Perfecter of faith. As File-leader He stands as the greatest example of faith the world has ever seen and, as Perfecter, faith finds its consummation in Him.

FURTHER STUDY

Phil. 3:1-16;
Job 17:9;
Gal. 6:9

1. What was Paul's great longing?

2. How did he depict his perseverance?

He is a further example of faith in that the endurance of the cross was the price He paid. Thus believers are encouraged, by contrast, to regard their sufferings in persecution as a small price to be secure at the end of the race set before them. Choosing the cross resulted in Christ being received on the throne. It is the same also with us.

Father, help me never lose sight of the fact that to choose the cross is to find a throne. However bad things are, they are as nothing compared to what will be. May I live day by day in the glow of this glorious truth. Amen.

Why God allows trials

For reading & meditation – Hebrews 12:3–13

"My son, do not make light of the Lord's discipline ..." (v.5)

Our Lord was so committed to His Father's will that He willingly accepted persecution from sinful people. Therefore 'Consider him,' says the writer (v.3), study carefully His life of steadfast endurance, and lean hard upon Him so that you too may be able to walk the same pathway – if this is what God wants. The Christian life, as A.C. Purdy, the Bible commentator, put it, 'is not a short dash to glory but a long-distance race, calling for endurance'. Those who have a long experience in the Christian life know that amid the joys and triumphs are many trials.

FURTHER STUDY

Job 23:10;
2 Cor. 4:1-18

1. What
was Job's
conviction?

2. Where was
Paul's focus?

Why does God allow them? One reason, says the writer, is the discipline of love. He reminds the readers that however hard they were struggling, they had not yet been called upon to shed their blood – things could be worse. This might sound glib, but think about it – it has profound meaning.

Another reason why God allows trials is to prove our sonship. No parents discipline their neighbour's children; they discipline their own. God does not discipline the children of darkness; He punishes them. Are you experiencing the disciplinary actions of the Lord at the moment? Then heed the words of the writer to the Hebrews as paraphrased by the *Living Bible*: 'Take a new grip with your tired hands, stand firm on your shaky legs, and mark out a straight, smooth path for your feet so that those who follow you, though weak and lame, will not fall and hurt themselves, but become strong' (vv.12–13).

Father, show me even more clearly that Your disciplines are not meant to disable me but to develop me. You love me too much not to correct me when I go wrong. And Your hurts are always healing. Help me never to forget this. In Jesus' name. Amen.

God's disciplinary action

For reading & meditation – Hebrews 12:12–17

'See to it that no-one misses the grace of God ...' (v.15)

Today's passage shows us that trials give us an opportunity to demonstrate to the world the adequacy of our faith. People are not impressed when we fall apart under the pressure of our troubles, but they sit up and take notice when we are able to stand up to life in a way they find impossible. So stop being weak-kneed when troubles come, is the writer's plea. How will people get the impression that Christ is our Upholder in everything if they see we are always in defeat?

The writer tells the Hebrews to 'Make every effort to live in peace with all men and be holy; without holiness no-one will see the Lord' (v.14). He turns from admonishing them previously to have an attitude of proper self-concern to urging them to have a proper concern for others also. Learn to live peaceably with everyone, he exhorts, and see to it you do not miss the grace of God or allow any bitterness to take root in your life. Bitterness is always wrong in a Christian, no matter how justified the cause may be. A bitter spirit is one of the chief causes of our problems in the Church today. It ruins relationships, paralyses potential, and makes the grace of God of no effect.

FURTHER STUDY

Eph. 4:29-32;
James 3:13-18;
Acts 8:20-23

1. How can we grieve the Holy Spirit?

2. How did Peter sum up Simon?

The writer also warns his readers to watch out for the spirit of Esau – the attitude that treats spiritual things in a lighthearted way. If we can't handle these things ourselves then we must be willing to accept the discipline of the Lord. No discipline – no development. It is as simple as that.

Father, I would not ask to be exempt from Your disciplines for I know that there are still some stubborn ways within me. You chastise me in order to change me. In Jesus' name. Amen.

Zion - the place of grace

For reading & meditation – Hebrews 12:18–24

'But you have come to Mount Zion, to the heavenly
Jerusalem, the city of the living God.' (v.22)

How can a life characterised by holiness and concern for the
welfare of others be lived? I know many who are driven by
fear in their efforts to live the Christian life. They live under the
demands of the law, which says: 'Do this – or else.'

The ancient Israelites were like this – generally they lived in
fear of the law and thus never experienced the joy of serving
God because they loved Him. The writer of Hebrews says to such
people: 'You have not come to Mount Sinai but to Mount Zion,
the place of grace.' This is his way of saying that as
Christians we have come under new management.
The law was given in an atmosphere of dread –
darkness and gloom were everywhere. Even Moses
trembled with fear. How different is Mount Zion's
message of grace. Here there is a festal gathering
consisting of angels and the assemblage of the
saints. God the Judge is there, and so are the spirits
of the righteous made perfect – the Old Testament
saints. And of course Jesus is there also, whose blood speaks
better things than that of Abel. Genesis tells us that when
Abel's blood was shed it cried out for vengeance. But does Jesus'
blood cry out for vengeance? No, it cries out for freedom and
forgiveness.

Now with all this on our side, if we fail it is because we do not
avail ourselves of our resources. That is the point the writer is
making. So if you are finding it tough, then think about your
resources and avail yourself of them. Grace ever flows.

FURTHER STUDY

Matt. 5:1-20;
Rom. 6:1-14

1. How did
Jesus relate
to the law?

2. What was
Paul's view
of the law?

Father, make this truth a living reality in my soul – that no matter
what difficulties I have to face in life, I need never run out of
resources. Your grace is always in supply. Thank You my Father.
Amen.

The great appeal

For reading & meditation – Hebrews 12:25

'See to it that you do not refuse him who speaks.' (v.25)

Today's verse – 'See to it that you do not refuse him who speaks' – reveals the ultimate purpose for which the letter was written. The Hebrew Christians to whom it was addressed were, as we have seen, wavering in their faith. They were true believers but they still hankered after the old system of worship with its pomp and ceremony, its angelic ministration, its guidance through Moses, and so on. They tended to compare the pageantry of their past with the simplicity that was in Christ. The writer knew it was not an easy thing for them to turn their backs on these splendid rituals. Thus the great appeal: 'Do not refuse him who speaks.'

FURTHER STUDY

Luke 14:15–24;
Acts 28:26–27

1. What is Jesus' teaching in this parable?

2. What did Paul remind the Jews?

This powerful injunction carries a message to the Church in every century. I hear of many churches today where the Son of God is not allowed to speak. These churches would not admit to it, of course, but they refuse the voice of Him who speaks by giving other voices greater priority than His – intellectualism, Gnosticism (bypassing Christ to get to God), and so on. If we refuse Him who speaks then all we are left with are the voices of people, bringing this emphasis or that emphasis, and all of them a million miles off the mark.

My call to the Church worldwide today is this: let us listen with bated breath to the speech of God as it is brought to us through His Son, Jesus Christ. Others in the past have not escaped the judgment of God when they refused the divine warnings. And neither will we.

Lord God, forgive us that so often we, Your people, give priority to voices other than Your own. Save us from being influenced by these other voices and help us to heed only the voice of Your Son. In His peerless and precious name we pray. Amen.

Why things are shaky

For reading & meditation – Hebrews 12:25–28

'Once more I will shake not only the earth but also the heavens.' (v.26)

God also allows trials to come because they highlight the difference between truth and untruth. They are God's way of differentiating between what passes and what is permanent. 'God is shaking the earth and the heavens,' says the writer, and he was not talking about the final shaking of the earth and heavens but something that was going on right then.

The Almighty is doing the same thing today. He is causing the foundations upon which people put their full weight to begin to move beneath their feet. In what do people put their greatest confidence? Is it not money? The financial world, from time to time, is shaken and will in the future be shaken even more.

Why does the Almighty set in operation this 'shaking' process? In order that the things that can't be destroyed by being shaken may remain – *and be seen to remain.* The words of James Russell Lowell come to mind:

FURTHER STUDY
Isa. 59:9-15;
Prov. 23:23;
12:22

1. What sad reflection did Isaiah utter?
2. What does God delight in?

Truth forever on the scaffold,
Wrong forever on the throne.
Yet that scaffold sways the future,
And behind the dim unknown,
Standeth God behind the shadows,
Keeping watch above His own.

All this ought to cause us to bow before the King of the unshakeable kingdom with thankfulness and reverential awe. And ever remember, as the writer to the Hebrews put it, that 'our God is a consuming fire'.

Jesus, Lord and Master, my allegiance is to You – and only to You. In this hour of universal shaking I am grateful that I belong to a kingdom that cannot be shaken. I am fixed to the things that are fixed. Amen.

A positive negative

For reading & meditation – Hebrews 13:1–6
'Never will I leave you; never will I forsake you.' (v.5)

The writer is trying to squeeze in everything he can by way of practical application in Hebrews 13, as if he is saying: 'God is not interested in religious ceremony. The Almighty is concerned about *life*.' For a Christian, life divides into two main areas – contact with others in the world and contact with others in the Church.

The writer begins by focusing attention on how believers should relate to the world. Make it your aim to entertain strangers, he says, and develop compassion for those who are ill-treated. It may not be easy for many to get into prisons to visit and help, but that ought not to stop us praying and supporting those who do. Christians are to have their eyes and hearts open to those who are in need around them – and to do something about their situation.

Believers must realise also the sacredness of marriage, and not allow the loose standards of the world to influence them. Then there is the danger of materialism. Christians must guard against developing an acquisitive streak in their natures and learn to see themselves as stewards rather than proprietors. Christians are able to live for Christ in a godless world because they have the firm promise that He will never leave them nor forsake them. This phrase has been described as the 'strongest negative in the whole of the Bible'. No one can make the excuse that what God asks is too hard for us to undertake. For with God with us, all things are possible.

FURTHER STUDY

Phil. 4:10–20;
1 Tim. 6:6–8;
Luke 3:14

1. What was Paul able to say?

2. What were Paul's wise words to Timothy?

Holy Spirit, shed abroad in my heart the love of God so that I can love where ordinarily I would not love. My love is not big enough to meet the needs of all who cross my path. So let eternal love flow into me and out of me. In Jesus' name. Amen.

The unchanging Christ

For reading & meditation – Hebrews 13:7–8

'Jesus Christ is the same yesterday and today and
for ever.' (v.8)

I n the Church, the Hebrew Christians should recall and be
stimulated by the faith-life of their former leaders. But so that
they should not look too closely at them and thus turn their full
attention away from Christ, the writer declares: 'Jesus Christ is
the same yesterday and today and for ever.' What Christ was to
the people of the past, He is to us today. Believers are to imitate
the faith of Christians who have gone before, which was fixed
on a changeless Christ.

FURTHER STUDY

Mal. 3:6;
Psa. 102:25-27;
James 1:17

1. What did God
confirm to the
Israelites?

2. What was
the psalmist's
conviction?

We are all conscious of the effect that change
can have upon us. Many psychologists believe that
change is one of the chief components of stress. We
drive past what we expect to be an open field, just as
it was a few weeks ago, and suddenly a complete new
building has appeared as if by magic. Alvin Toffler,
in his book *Future Shock*, argues that the quicker
things happen, and the faster life gets, the more
stress is produced because we do not have time to
adjust. He predicts that one of the greatest problems
we will have to face in the future is the problem of how to adjust
to change.

Life, if it is to be lived successfully, needs a centre of permanence,
something to which we can fasten our hopes knowing it will never
shift. Jesus Christ is that centre of permanence. What He was He
is, and what He is, He was. And what He is and was He ever will
be. This changeless Christ is the great refuge of the Christian in a
world that is caught up in constant change.

Unchanging Christ, how grateful I am that in a world of flux and
change, You are the centre of permanence. Other things may
change, but You – never. Drive this truth deep within my spirit.
For Your own dear name's sake. Amen.

Outside the camp!

For reading & meditation – Hebrews 13:9–14

'We have an altar from which those who minister at the
tabernacle have no right to eat.' (v.10)

Evidently some teachers had infiltrated the Church with a strange doctrine concerning foods. It seems there were food faddists in the Church of the first century, just as today. The point of the writer's remark is that Christianity in its truest form is a matter not of externals but of the heart, strengthened by grace.

The reference to the 'altar from which those who minister at the tabernacle have no right to eat' relates to the Old Testament sacrifice of atonement. The high priest was not allowed to eat the bodies of the animals sacrificed on the Day of Atonement. After their blood had been shed, their carcasses were taken outside the camp and burned. Jesus, who is the fulfilment of that to which the sacrifice of atonement pointed, also suffered outside the camp (ie, outside the city wall), and was treated by the people of His day as a pariah. 'Let us, then, go to him outside the camp,' the writer tells the Hebrew Christians, 'bearing the disgrace he bore' (v.13).

FURTHER STUDY

Rom. 1:1–16;
2 Tim. 1:8;
Mark 8:38

1. What did Paul proudly declare?
2. What did he encourage Timothy?

There is a shame at the heart of the gospel and it must be borne. For some it means social ostracism. For others it may mean family disinheritance. Still others find their path to professional advancement blocked because of their association with Christ. What do we do when we find ourselves in this position? We simply remind ourselves that this world is not our home. We are simply passing through. We are heading for an eternal city – the city of God.

Lord Jesus Christ, when I am asked to 'bear Your reproach', help me to do so willingly. May I gladly thrust my shoulder under Your cross and bear whatever I can of Your reproach. Amen.

The sacrificial spirit

For reading & meditation – Hebrews 13:15–17

'And do not forget to do good and to share with others, for with such sacrifices God is pleased.' (v.16)

In Christianity, externals mean very little; what goes on in our heart is what counts. This is why we are to offer to God a continual sacrifice of praise. What should we do when we don't feel like praising? We should acknowledge our feelings and then by an action of the will *choose* to praise Him anyway. Our choices, remember, are influenced by but not under the control of our feelings. Never forget that. But as believers we are expected to do more than sacrificially lift our hearts in continued thanks to God – we are to labour sacrificially for others also. 'And do not forget to do good and to share with others, for with such sacrifices God is pleased.'

FURTHER STUDY

1 Cor. 16:1-16;
Eph. 5:1-21;
1 Pet. 5:5

1. What did Paul beseech the Corinthians?

2. What did he exhort the Ephesians?

The writer's concluding words of advice are an entreaty to the Hebrew Christians to be submissive to those who have charge over their spiritual welfare. One of the ways I have learned to gauge the spirituality of believers is by their attitude to those who have authority over them. I know Christians who have been on the way for years, but who have never learned how to accept authority. They are the first to stand up in a prayer meeting and pray, but if any part of their behaviour is called into question by the leadership, they are the first also to leave. The Christian life involves much more than relating to the Authority on the throne. It involves relating also to the authorities which God has set up on the earth. You can't have one without the other.

Lord Jesus, I submit to You absolutely. Now, for Your name's sake, I can submit also to others who have legitimate authority over me. This sets me free from tyranny and oppression. In submitting to You, all the wrongs done to me become rights. I am grateful. Amen.

A prayer among prayers

For reading & meditation – Hebrews 13:18–21
'... may he work in us what is pleasing to him, through Jesus Christ ...' (v.21)

The request to 'Pray for us' (v.18) might suggest that the writer was in prison. This, together with the style and content of the letter, lead some to believe Paul was the author. We cannot be sure.

Having asked for prayer, the writer now prays for his readers, in one of the most beautifully composed prayers in the New Testament. It has often been said that the opening words – 'who through the blood of the eternal covenant brought back from the dead our Lord Jesus' – provide the only explicit reference in the epistle to the resurrection of Christ. It makes the point that our Lord's resurrection demonstrates conclusively that His sacrifice on the cross was accepted by God and that the eternal covenant has been ratified. Because of this, God now stands ready to equip us with everything good for doing His will.

This is the secret of effective Christian service. We do not have to beg God to come to our aid; He stands constantly ready to supply us with all we need to do His will. If we fail, it is not because the supplies have run out. The failure is caused by our not appropriating those supplies.

FURTHER STUDY
Gen. 9:1-16;
Rev. 4:3;
Jer. 32:40

1. Why should we rejoice every time we see the rainbow?

2. Where does the rainbow come from?

The whole prayer is wrapped around a phrase that is one of the most endearing phrases to fall upon the human ear: 'through Jesus Christ, to whom be glory for ever and ever' (v.21). That is the way God intends our lives to be lived – through Jesus Christ. Live life on your own and you won't get anywhere. Live it through Him and you will get everywhere.

God my Father, help me lay hold of this truth and never give it up – that life is not to be lived in my own strength but in the strength and power of Your Son. May I take from Him with both hands – and give with both hands. In Jesus' name. Amen.

The Surprises
of God

The final Word!

For reading & meditation – Hebrews 13:22–25

'Grace be with you all.' (v.25)

Timothy, we are told, has been released from prison, and may join the author in visiting them soon. The reference to 'those from Italy' suggests that the readers might be a group of Christians in Rome, but we cannot be entirely certain. Finally, the epistle ends with a benediction: *Grace be with you all.* This was a reminder that however challenging the Christian life may be, God provides the needed grace.

We have seen the entire thrust of the epistle is to set forth the supremacy of the Son over every other person, place and thing. He is superior to prophets, to angels, to Moses, to Aaron, to Joshua. We have seen also that through the Son there has been established a new covenant, written upon the heart and based upon personal firsthand fellowship with God. The consequence of that better covenant is a better system of worship – one in which we draw near with a true heart and a conscience that is drained and cleared of all guilt. We have a right of entry not into an earthly tabernacle but through the earthly into the heavenly, into the Holy of Holies, so that we may worship God without any mediation other than that of Jesus, our Great High Priest.

FURTHER STUDY

Rom. 16:1-20;
2 Cor. 13:14;
2 Thess. 3:18;
Rev. 22:21

1. What is characteristic of New Testament benedictions?

2. What is the final sentiment of Scripture?

The book of Hebrews, then, is all about Christ, the One who is God's final Word to humankind. There is nothing more to be said and nothing more to be added to what He has done. Jesus is God's last Word – ever.

My Father and my God, in relation to the matter of my soul, help me tune out all other voices – legitimate and illegitimate – and listen only to the voice of Your Son. May I never forget that when You speak, You speak only in Him. Amen.

'Only now and then'

For reading & meditation – Genesis 6:1–22

'So make yourself an ark of cypress wood; make rooms in it and coat it with pitch ...' (v.14)

Our new theme – 'The Surprises of God' – was triggered by a quotation from the noted theologian Frederick Buechner: 'We see God's work clearly *only now and then*.' The point he was making is that God doesn't allow us to see everything clearly all the time, but prefers to break into our lives with delightful and sometimes disturbing surprises.

Scripture is filled with accounts of God's surprises. For example, God says to Noah: 'I want you to build an ark because I have

FURTHER STUDY

Hab. 2:1-4;
Rom. 1:17;
1 John 5:4;
Gen. 5:24

1. How are we to live?

2. What is recorded of Enoch?

decided to drown everyone on the earth – with the exception of yourself and your family.' Moses walks in the desert one day and sees a bush on fire which is not consumed. He hears God speak to him, whereupon he is commissioned to be the deliverer of his people. Jesus, God's Son, is hammered to a cross and within hours is pronounced dead. He is taken down, put in a garden tomb, but on the third day He rises again.

God's surprises in our lives may not be quite as dramatic as these, but each one is significant nevertheless. These peak experiences should not be expected on a daily basis because largely God wants us to live by faith and not by sight. Perhaps we ought to put up signs when they happen: 'Warning: Unusual Peak Experiences – not to be expected daily.' They are like mountain peaks from which we can view the rest of God's more subtle work. Ascending those peaks to learn more of God's surprises is the exciting task that faces us now. This is mountaineering with a difference.

Father, while I see that I am called to live by faith and not by sight, I know also it is characteristic of You to occasionally break into my life with Your surprises. Help me not to miss them and, above all, to understand them. In Christ's name I pray. Amen.

Surprises – easy to miss

For reading & meditation – Psalm 103:1–22

'He made known his ways to Moses, his deeds to the people of Israel.' (v.7)

God occasionally breaks into our lives in surprising ways. We must not live on these surprises, but it will help us in our Christian lives if we recognise them when they come.

A deer hunter I talked to in Canada told me that although the forests are full of deer, rarely does one jump right on to the trail, and when that happens it is quite startling – as startling as an astonishing miracle or very specific answer to prayer. He also related how readily an inexperienced hunter can think he has spotted a deer, only to find he is mistaken. Like a certain hunter who, overhearing some others talking about an albino that lived in the forest, decided to search for it. One day, as he was walking through the forest, he caught a glimpse of something white. Moving slowly, he crept closer, and held his breath as he saw that what he had glimpsed was indeed large and very white. Too white. Eventually he recognised it – an abandoned washing machine!

It is easy to go through life missing God's surprises because we don't know how to spot them or, conversely, to 'spiritualise' ordinary events and read into them more than we should. Sometimes God's surprises explode in our lives like firecrackers; at other times we squint into the forest, wondering if what we see really is an albino or just an abandoned washing machine. Every one of us needs to understand the reasons why God delights to surprise us. Then we shall be less likely to miss them – or misinterpret them.

FURTHER STUDY

John 13:1-7;
16:12;
Prov. 27:1

1. What did Jesus say to His disciples?

2. Why are we not to boast about tomorrow?

My Father and my God, make me alert to the ways in which You work in my life so that I shall not miss what You are doing and thus fail to appreciate Your awesome work and Your wonders. In Jesus' name I ask it. Amen.

The light that scorches

For reading & meditation – Isaiah 21:1–17

'My heart falters ... the twilight I longed for has become a horror to me.' (v.4)

FURTHER STUDY

Luke 24:13-35;
John 20:1-18

1. What
unsuspected
surprise
followed?

2. What shocking
surprise had
these disciples
experienced?

Now we examine an aspect of God's surprises that has often bewildered His people. This is the way in which God sometimes answers our prayers by giving us more than we bargained for. Today's text presents us with a classic example. Scholars disagree as to the historical background of this text, the precise period to which it belongs, and its full meaning. Yet we can understand, I believe, enough of Isaiah's mind to enter into his experience and, to some degree, identify with the feelings that swept through his soul.

The prophet asked God for light on the situation of his day. He pleaded for insight, that he might see what was hidden from the eyes of others. And God gave him light! His prayer was answered! The darkness yielded to a growing twilight. He saw, but what he saw filled his soul with horror and caused him almost to wish he did not know what he now knew. He saw the people he loved trampled under the might of the enemy. God had answered his prayer and given him the insight he asked for, but he turned from the revelation trembling with apprehension and sick with foreboding.

This is not an uncommon experience in the Christian life. The answer we get to our prayers is not necessarily the answer our hearts desire. When we ask God for illumination, we must not complain if the light scorches at times with its fierce heat, nor be surprised that in response to our request for guidance we are shown things we might have preferred not to have known.

Father, though I may be surprised at the way You sometimes answer my prayers, help me not to be discomforted. May I be girded by the inner conviction that You do not deal with me petulantly, but purposefully. Amen.

Pain in answered prayer

For reading & meditation – Habakkuk 1:1–17

'I am raising up the Babylonians, that ruthless and
impetuous people ...' (v.6)

Christians talk a good deal about the pain of *unanswered* prayer.
But what about the pain of *answered* prayer? What about the
light that blisters and burns?

In today's passage, the prophet is confused as he observes in
the midst of his own people violence, contention, lawlessness and
injustice. And God seemed to be doing nothing about it. Obviously
he must have prayed many times about this issue for he begins his
prophecy with these words: 'How long, O Lord, must I call for help?'
(v.2). Despite his pleading, however, God had not seen
fit to answer his prayers. Quite understandably, the
prophet is deeply confused. But then his prayer *is*
answered, and God shows Habakkuk just what He
intends to do about the situation in Judah. He is going
to use the Babylonians – the most ruthless nation of
that day – to bring judgment upon His people. The
prophet is now more confused than he was before.
How could God use a pagan nation to purify His
own people? As with Isaiah, the response to his prayer caused
more consternation than having his pleas unanswered. This, of
course, led to his becoming aware of a whole new context in which
to think about God, and he emerged with a faith that triumphed
over everything – even confusion.

When God surprises you by answering your prayers in a way
you didn't expect it is not because He is being petulant; He is giving
you a greater opportunity to trust Him and thus develop a deeper
and richer relationship with Himself.

FURTHER STUDY

Isa. 6:1-13;
Matt. 8:18-22

1. What surprise
response did
Isaiah receive?

2. What surprise
response did
Jesus give?

**Father, help me see more clearly that when the answers I receive
are not what I desire, they are the stepping stones to gaining an
even deeper confidence and trust in You. In Jesus' name. Amen.**

Not the answer we expect

For reading & meditation – Luke 18:18–30

'You still lack one thing. Sell everything you have …
Then come, follow me.' (v.22)

We examine the attitude of the rich young ruler who said to Jesus: 'Good teacher, what must I do to inherit eternal life?' (v.18). Our Lord's reply was clear: 'Sell everything you have and give to the poor, and you will have treasure in heaven. Then come, follow me' (v.22). But the young man loved his wealth more than he loved God. It was the first thing in his life. That was why Jesus condemned it. Our Lord is not against people having wealth; He is only against them making wealth their god. The first place in anyone's life is God's place. The ruler, when he heard our Lord's response, might have said as did Isaiah: 'The twilight I longed for …'

FURTHER STUDY

Jonah 1:1–4:11

1. What did God do that surprised Jonah?

2. How did he handle it?

Such an experience is not peculiar to those who are unsurrendered to Christ; it happens to devoted Christians too. A minister, Thomas Champness, was appointed by his denomination to be the district evangelist to Newcastle upon Tyne, in the North of England. Hearing of the appointment, he rededicated himself to God and asked the Lord for a word that would help him carry out his task. God said this: 'If you are to concentrate exclusively on winning people to Me, you must be careless of your reputation as a preacher.' Thomas Champness had already gained a great reputation as a preacher – of which he was mildly proud. And God said: 'Give it up!' The twilight he longed for …!

We take a risk when we ask God to let us in on His purposes for our lives. Sometimes He tells us things we might prefer not to know.

God my Father, help me never to let the possibility of being surprised by You hinder me from wanting to know Your purposes for my life. For Your purposes are always best. Amen.

'A simple preacher'

For reading & meditation – 1 Corinthians 2:1-16

'My message and my preaching were not with wise and persuasive words ...' (v.4)

When we ask God for His help, we must be prepared for Him to respond in unexpected ways, and show us more than we bargained for. Yesterday we saw how the renowned preacher Thomas Champness, when appointed district evangelist to Newcastle upon Tyne, was asked by God to give up his concern about his reputation as a preacher.

Every evangelist who has a scholar's gifting knows what sacrifices he has to make for the sake of his calling. Outside the Church, the evangelist is often ridiculed as a 'hot gospeller', and inside the Church, he is often disparaged as being able only to preach the simple gospel and unqualified to teach the deep truths of the faith. Many consider evangelists to be dealers in unintelligent emotionalism, even though they may have a first-class brain.

FURTHER STUDY

Phil. 2:1-11;
3:1-14

1. What sacrifice did Christ make?

2. What sacrifice did Paul make?

I asked the wife of a great Welsh evangelist what was the greatest sacrifice her husband had ever made. She replied: 'He had a scholar's heart and could have been a university lecturer, but he heard God say to him that he must give up all scholarly ambition and be a simple preacher of the gospel.'

Some might not think that much of a sacrifice, but that would only prove they do not have the mind of a scholar. Some might go so far as to accuse God of being inconsiderate or even unjust. I can understand that, though I cannot agree with their assessment. I know enough about God, and I am sure you do too, to be certain that God always gives the best to those who leave the choice to Him.

Lord God, help me see that whatever sacrifices I am called to make in Your service they are as nothing compared to the sacrifice that You made for me. In Jesus' name. Amen.

Prayer - a risky business

For reading & meditation – Isaiah 6:1–13

'Woe to me! ... For I am a man of unclean lips ... and my eyes have seen the King ...' (v.5)

We must never deem an unexpected response from God as due to peevish impatience or irritability. It is not a question of God saying: 'You've twisted My arm for an answer. Well, here it is. Now how do you like it?' God's ways may be difficult to understand but, as we have already pointed out, petulance is never found in Him. The comment has been made that when folk ask for our opinion, very often what they really want is our praise. God will not deal with us like that. If we plead for His light, and He sees that it is appropriate to give us that light, He will not deny it – even though it hurts.

FURTHER STUDY

Psa. 27:1-14;
2 Cor. 4:6;
1 John 1:5

1. What was the psalmist able to say?

2. What can we be sure of about God?

When the desire for peace of heart and mind arose in that great stalwart of the fourth and fifth centuries – Augustine – he turned to God and asked for divine illumination on the dark problems of his way. God answered his prayer, but the first thing the light revealed was Augustine's unchastity and lack of self-control. He too could have said: 'The twilight I longed for has become a horror for me.' Augustine talks of how God's light scorched him at times and brought into awareness things that hitherto he had preferred not to look at.

The Almighty is too eager for our highest good to deny us His healing truth, and sometimes He is unable to get through to us until our hearts are found in the attitude of passionate, persevering prayer. To pray for light and illumination is a risky business, but one that is *always* well worth the risk.

Father, help me be prepared for whatever Your light reveals in me. And may I not shrink from asking for Your revelation because of the challenges that it may bring to my soul. In Christ's name I pray. Amen.

The tilt of the soul

For reading & meditation – James 4:1–17

'Come near to God and he will come near to you.' (v.8)

Sometimes God is not able to break in upon us with His healing truth until our hearts are in the attitude of passionate, persevering prayer. How often have we come to God in prayer about a concern and found that instead of answering us on that particular issue He has directed our attention to the state of our soul? This might seem a little sneaky, but think about it for a moment and you will see that God is perfectly justified in doing this. So often our concerns centre on *our* ambitions and *our* desires, and it is only when these look in danger of being blocked that we open our souls to God in fervent prayer.

FURTHER STUDY

2 Chron. 7:14;
Psa. 139:17-24

1. What must we do as well as praying?

2. How did the psalmist do this?

The Almighty will not gatecrash His way into our lives. As today's text puts it, when we draw near to God, He draws near to us. Prayer tilts the soul in the direction of God and in turn gives God an opportunity to move into the inner parts of our being. We bring to God in prayer a personal concern and He responds by saying: 'Now I have your attention, there's this other matter I want to talk to you about. To you it might not seem as important as your concerns, but it is vital to the well-being of your soul.'

We shouldn't really be surprised to discover that when we bring personal matters to God in prayer He says: 'You want to talk about *that*, but I want to talk about *this*.' Though we might prefer that He didn't change the subject, believe me, it is always His great personal love and concern for us that motivates Him to do so.

Father, forgive me for being more concerned about getting my needs met than being the person You want me to be. You are my Saviour and my Lord and thus You have the right to question me about anything. Help me get this issue straight. In Jesus' name. Amen.

No pretending

For reading & meditation – 2 Corinthians 3:7–18

'And we ... are being transformed into his likeness with
ever-increasing glory ...' (v.18)

W e expose ourselves to unsuspected possibilities when we
turn to God for illumination. He is so fiercely intolerant
of sin, so passionate for our highest good, that He will take
advantage of the tilt of our soul in His direction to tell us things
we might rather not have known. Yet to be willing to receive God's
illumination in our hearts is really the wisest thing anyone can do.
We never fully see ourselves until we see ourselves in Him. When
faced with it we may be surprised but, as we have said, there is
sometimes a good deal of pain to be experienced in
answered prayer.

FURTHER STUDY

Dan. 2:17-23;
Psa. 19:12-13

1. What did
Daniel declare
in his prayer?

2. How did the
psalmist deal
with hidden
faults?

I have found that people respond in different
ways to God's surprising answers to their prayers.
Some positively dislike the Almighty for revealing
to them more than they bargained for. One woman
said: 'I asked God for light on my problems. Instead
He pointed to the chambers of my heart and told me
there were many doors there that He did not have
access to, and when I opened them I would get the
illumination I craved.' Then she added, almost spitting out the
words: 'What kind of God acts like that?'

If we are to avoid going backwards in our Christian lives then
we must realise that once we open our hearts to God in prayer,
He is likely to make us face the locked chambers of our heart. We
can pretend to others but the Almighty will never let us pretend
to Him. In His presence smug complacency vanishes like dew in
the scorching heat of the sun.

Father, I am comforted to know that You love me too much to shield
me from the truth. Yet the revealing sometimes scorches my soul.
Help me go through with You nevertheless and no matter how
challenging Your revelation. In Jesus' name I ask it. Amen.

Walk on

For reading & meditation – John 3:16–21

'Everyone who does evil hates the light ... for fear that his deeds will be exposed.' (v.20)

Yesterday we mentioned the woman who became angry with God because He exposed her to herself. It is absurd, of course, to turn away in anger or hostility when God does this, for He only holds the mirror. The impurities are all in us.

I remember reading of a British scientist in India who became greatly troubled by the Hindu custom of drinking water from the River Ganges, considered by them to be sacred. He invited a leading Hindu priest to look at a drop of the water through a microscope to see what dreadful dangers resided there. As the priest looked through the eyepiece and saw the magnified foreign bodies, he picked up the microscope and threw it on the floor, causing it to break into a dozen pieces. It was the answer of ignorance and bigotry to the healing light. He smashed the instrument but he had not cleansed the water!

We can turn our back when God through the Holy Spirit puts His finger on something in our lives of which He does not approve, but by turning our back we have not cleansed our heart or restored our soul. There is only one thing to do when we tremble in the blinding light of some new revelation. We must march into the light with God. Pain or no pain – march on. The trembling will pass and we will prove the power of God to strengthen the weak hands and confirm the feeble knees.

FURTHER STUDY

2 Cor. 7:1-7;
Isa. 1:16;
1 John 3:1-3

1. What did Paul admonish the Corinthians?

2. What are we to do in the light of God's love?

Father, help me never to be afraid to pray for the light even though it may reveal more than I wish. And when it causes me to tremble, help me not to turn back but to walk on. In Christ's name. Amen.

The 'great surprise'

For reading & meditation – John 3:1-15

'The wind blows wherever it pleases ... So it is with everyone born of the Spirit.' (v.8)

W e look now at another of God's surprises – the way in which the Holy Spirit brings about the critical experience we call 'conversion'. Oswald Chambers said: 'The element of surprise is always the note of the Holy Ghost in us. We are born again by the great surprise.' The *Living Bible* translates today's verse: 'Just as you can hear the wind but can't tell where it comes from or where it will go next, so it is with the Spirit. We do not know on whom he will next bestow this life from heaven.'

FURTHER STUDY

John 14:15-31;
Ezek. 36:27;
1 Cor. 3:16

1. How was the Old Testament prophecy fulfilled?

2. What did Jesus promise to His disciples?

One of the greatest surprises of my life was to find myself a member of the Church of Jesus Christ. If someone had told me on the morning of the day I was converted that before the day ended I would have become a Christian, I simply would not have believed them. But that wonderful evening I sat in a mission hall in a Welsh valley and felt the Holy Spirit tug at my heart. When an invitation was given to receive Christ I walked to the front and gave my life to Him. I was born again by 'the great surprise'.

We must never forget that Christian conversion cannot happen without the Holy Spirit. Sometimes conversion is spoken of in the Christian Church as if it were human work. The word conversion is made up of *con*, meaning 'with', and *vertare*, meaning 'to turn'. Conversion is not just turning, but turning *with*. The 'with' introduces us to the Holy Spirit, and the element of the Spirit in conversion makes it a new birth. No Holy Spirit – no conversion.

Father, how can I sufficiently thank You for turning my life around? May the same Holy Spirit who saved me be ever present in my life to sanctify me. In Christ's name I ask it. Amen.

The Spirit's sovereignty

For reading & meditation – Romans 11:5–36

'How unsearchable his judgments, and his paths beyond tracing out!' (v.33)

Nothing is more revealing of the sovereignty of the Holy Spirit than when we see Him at work in bringing about spiritual conversion. Yesterday we observed Jesus pointing out that the Spirit's coming to individuals is as mysterious and unpredictable as the wind.

There is a close connection between natural and spiritual law, and our Lord often drew attention to this. To Him the connection was inevitable because the same God is the Author of both. He uses the most commonplace natural phenomenon to illustrate the most mystical of spiritual experiences and to depict the hidden operation of the Spirit of God in the regeneration of the human soul. The attributes of the wind are analogous to the workings of the Holy Spirit of God and, according to Jesus, there are at least three of them.

FURTHER STUDY

Gal. 4:1–6;
Rom. 8:16;
1 John 3:24

1. How do we know we are children of God?

2. What does the Spirit call out?

First, *the wind blows where it wills*. That means it is a sovereign element and cannot be controlled. People have learned how to control many things but they have not yet learned how to control the wind. Harness it – yes. But control it – no. Second, *we hear its sound but cannot see it*. This means it is invisible. The keenest eye is unable to detect it. Third, *we can't tell from where it comes or where it will go*. This means the course of the wind is a mystery. These three characteristics of the wind are to be seen in the ways of the Holy Spirit. He works sovereignly, secretly and mysteriously. He comes to whom He wills, when He wills, and where He wills.

My Father and my God, Your ways are beyond my comprehension but that doesn't mean I am unable to appreciate them. I join with the apostle in giving thanks that from You and through You and to You are all things. Glory be to Your name for ever. Amen.

'A man came among us'

For reading & meditation – Romans 8:1–17
'You ... are controlled ... by the Spirit, if the Spirit of God lives in you.' (v.9)

We described conversion as 'the great surprise' because it happens in the most unexpected ways and to the most unexpectant people. Just as we cannot predict the precise course of the wind, neither can we predict the Holy Spirit's course.

John Wesley was a preacher and missionary as a young man, yet did not have a personal relationship with Christ. Lecky, the historian, tells of the surprise John Wesley had when he went rather unwillingly to a meeting in Aldersgate Street, London, to

FURTHER STUDY

Matt. 4:12-22;
Acts 16:16-34

1. What were the elements of the fishermen's surprise?

2. What were the elements of the jailer's surprise?

hear someone reading Martin Luther's preface to the book of Romans. About a quarter to nine, while the reader was describing the change which God works in the heart through faith in Christ, John Wesley felt his own heart 'strangely warmed', and at that moment put his trust in Christ for salvation. He worded it later: 'An assurance was given me that He had taken away my sins, even mine, and saved me from the law of sin and death.' This strange and unexpected warming of the heart – what one biographer called 'the quarter to nine experience' – sent a moral cleansing through the soul of Britain and the world.

One county that was greatly affected by the ministry of John Wesley was Cornwall, in the West of England. Many years after Wesley had died a visitor to Cornwall commented to a local tin-miner: 'You seem to be a very temperate people here. How did it happen?' The miner took off his cap and solemnly replied: 'There came a man among us once, and his name was John Wesley.'

Father, what amazing things You can do through one soul who is deeply and wholly committed to You. I open the depths of my being yet again to the ministry and power of Your Holy Spirit. Fill me to overflowing. In Christ's name. Amen.

'Chance' encounter

For reading & meditation – Psalm 92:1–15

'How great are your works, O Lord, how profound your thoughts!' (v.5)

Often in the mornings I think to myself: today multitudes of people all over the world will be drawn into the kingdom of God – and right now most of them will be completely unaware of this. The Spirit will move towards them as mysteriously as the wind, and before the day ends they will find themselves with a new allegiance. Nothing about them will ever be the same again – except their name. Their wandering planet will find itself in a new orbit, forever caught by a Love that will not let it go.

Spiritual conversion is not a matter of chance. The Holy Spirit, who is sovereign, moves in the strangest ways to bring about the conversion of a human soul. A preacher on his way to conduct a service stepped into a shop doorway to shelter from a downpour of rain. Another man sheltered there too. Both remarked on the inclemency of the weather and, as the conversation developed, the preacher told the other where he was going. The man appeared to know next to nothing about Christian churches but willingly accepted an invitation to attend the service. He decided for Christ that night. At the end of the evening, as the newly converted man talked to the preacher, there was one thing he couldn't get over. 'Fancy turning in to a shop doorway to shelter,' he said, 'and all your life being changed because of that.'

It excites me to think that today similar 'coincidences' will be taking place worldwide. Who knows, a future 'Billy Graham' may well come into the kingdom today.

FURTHER STUDY

Luke 19:1-9;
Acts 16:11-15

1. What similar statement might Zacchaeus have made?

2. What other surprising element is recorded of Zacchaeus?

Father, what joy fills my soul as I think of the fact that every day Your Spirit is at work drawing people to Yourself. I ask that my own unconverted loved ones be touched by You too. In Jesus' name. Amen.

Sudden conversions

For reading & meditation – Matthew 7:1–24
'By their fruit you will recognise them.' (v.16)

Again today, in every part of the world, the Holy Spirit will come to people who, this morning, have no idea that before the day ends they will enter into a personal relationship with Jesus Christ. Lacordaire, the French pastor who once occupied the pulpit of the Cathedral of Notre Dame in Paris, said: 'I was unbelieving in the evening, on the morrow a Christian, certain with an invincible certainty.'

The biographer of John Duncan, a Scottish divine, wrote: 'He

FURTHER STUDY

Acts 9:1–31;
John 1:12

1. What suddenly happened to Saul?

2. How did he respond?

was the most sceptical of men who was transformed in a moment into the most believing of men. We have a picture of a strong man suddenly arrested, struck down in mid career of linguistic study and speculative daring by the realities of the unseen world; his was one of those swift upheavals of experience which attest the agency of a Higher Power working in the spirit of man.' Sudden conversions do occur; they can only be explained vertically.

Think back now to your own conversion. Did it take place in a crisis? Or was it a slow dawning of the fact that though you were lost, you were now found? Some conversions unfold like the flower to the sun – little by little. Others are a sudden leap to the breast of God. Both types of experience are valid. It is not the phenomena that surround conversion that make it valid; it is, as our text for today puts it, that 'by their fruit you will recognise them'. After all, the best evidence you are alive is never your birth certificate!

Lord God, I am so thankful for the experience of my own conversion. May the wonder of it never dim within me. It began in a miracle and is sustained by a miracle. Blessed be Your wonderful name for ever. Amen.

Saved and sobered!

For reading & meditation – Romans 1:8–17

'... the gospel ... is the power of God for the salvation of everyone who believes ...' (v.16)

The fact that some conversions are sudden and others gradual seems to bother some Christians. They believe conversions should conform to one pattern. I have often asked believers: Was your conversion gradual or sudden?

Their answers lead me to believe that about 40 per cent are gradual and 60 per cent are sudden (the findings of others may differ). Those whose conversions were gradual come from homes where from childhood they were taught to know and love Christ. They cannot tell when they crossed the line between death and life even though they know it has been crossed. Sudden conversions generally come to those who need a decisive round-about-face. A sudden conversion does not mean that the Holy Spirit comes to a person only at the moment of conversion. He will have been at work prior to that moment, but the actual commitment is clear, decisive and in some cases very dramatic.

Dr E. Stanley Jones tells how, preaching from a soapbox in a public square in Harrodsburg, Kentucky, he asked an inebriated man standing in front of him: 'Do you want to be converted?' He replied: 'I'm drunk.' 'God can save you drunk or not drunk,' retorted Stanley Jones. 'If you say so it must be so,' conceded the man as he knelt in prayer. Suddenly he opened his eyes, looked around in surprise and exclaimed: 'Why, He has saved me, and I'm drunk too.' Soon he was completely sober. God saved him and sobered him in minutes. How much more dramatic than that can you get?

FURTHER STUDY

John 4:1–29;
Acts 2:21;
Rom. 10:13;
2 Pet. 3:9

1. What are some of the factors through which the woman was being led to salvation?

2. Why were the disciples surprised?

My Father and my God, Your grace and might are beyond the power of my mind to measure. How wondrous are Your ways; how marvellous Your works. All honour and glory be to Your peerless and precious name. Amen.

Three-fifths of the way

For reading & meditation – Romans 10:1–21
'Everyone who calls on the name of the Lord will be saved.'
(v.13)

Perhaps you are one for whom this is a day of destiny. I know from my mail that many readers have not experienced a clear conversion.

If you look at today's passage again, you will see that everyone reading these lines is at least three-fifths of the way into the kingdom of God. Five important facts are clearly spelled out. (1) Everyone who calls on the Name of the Lord will be saved. (2) No one can call on the One in whom they have not believed.

FURTHER STUDY

2 Pet. 1:1-11;
Psa. 37:39;
Rom. 6:23

1. What are we to make certain of?

2. Where does salvation come from?

(3) No one can believe in One of whom they have not heard. (4) No one can hear without someone telling them. (5) No one can tell the story of Christ unless they have been sent.

Let's work our way backwards through these words of Scripture. You are reading at this moment the writings of someone who has been called by God to preach and present the gospel – fact no. 5. You have been hearing (hearing can mean the same as reading here) the message of the gospel – fact no. 4. Having heard, you now know in whom you must believe – fact no. 3. This means you are now three-fifths of the way into the kingdom. The last two steps are these: believe in the Lord Jesus Christ (this means giving up trying to save yourself and trusting Him to save you), then call upon Him in the following prayer – and you will be saved. You are three-fifths of the way there. Now take the last two steps.

Lord God, I take these last two steps in simple faith that I can do nothing to save myself but that Jesus died for me. I repent of my sin and receive Your Son Jesus into my heart as my Lord and my Saviour. Thank You that You have heard me. Amen.

Glory in the commonplace

For reading & meditation – Genesis 28:1-22

'How awesome is this place! This is ... the house of God ...'
(v.17)

Another way God surprises us is by revealing Himself in the most unexpected places, as today's passage illustrates.

Jacob had deceived his father and robbed his brother and, having obtained both birthright and blessing, made his way to his uncle's home to find a wife. Three days after leaving Beersheba he came to the hills of Bethel and, as it was evening, he settled down to sleep. Then he dreamed. He saw a ladder reaching from the ground up to heaven, on which angels were going up and coming down. In the dream God spoke to him – just as He had spoken to his father Isaac – a gracious, forgiving and promissory word. Then as dawn crept across the sky, Jacob awoke with a great sense of awe and cried: 'Surely the LORD is in this place, and I was not aware of it' (v.16). Clearly, when Jacob lay down to sleep he had no expectation of meeting God. The stirrings of his conscience almost certainly had the effect of pushing God out of his thoughts. And besides, who would expect to meet God out there on the barren hillside? Yet that was where God came to Jacob, where all the appurtenances of a holy place were wanting and we might least expect Him to speak.

God's favoured way of meeting His children is around His Word, the Bible, but this does not mean He will meet us only there. He does not wait for what we might call the 'grand moments' of life. Sometimes He surprises us by making the commonplace grand. Galilee and Glasgow are just the same to Him.

FURTHER STUDY

Exod. 3:1-22;
James 4:14

1. What commonplace task was Moses engaged in?

2. List five things that would have surprised Moses.

Father, thank You for showing me that though Your prime way of revealing Yourself to me is through the Scriptures, I can meet You also in the ordinary and unexpected places of life. You can make even the commonplace glorious. Amen.

'Crammed with heaven'

For reading & meditation – Exodus 3:1–15

'So Moses thought, "I will go over and see this
strange sight ..."' (v.3)

In the early days of my Christian life the idea of God revealing Himself through the ordinary was surprising to me. I had been taught that I must expect to find God in church and through the study of the Scriptures. 'Start your day by soaking yourself in the Word,' I was told, 'then you will not be at the mercy of subjectivity.' It was good advice, for many have been led astray by basing their conclusions about God on their subjective experiences rather than on the objectivity of Scripture. However, God sometimes surprises us by coming in the most unexpected ways. Moses was quite astonished, I imagine, to find that the bush that burned and was not consumed was God's method of getting his attention.

FURTHER STUDY

1 Sam. 16:1–23;
1 Kings 19:11–12

1. How was
David's day
changed?

2. How did God
speak to Elijah?

I am not arguing that we should abandon the usual paths to knowing God – listening in prayer, study of the Scripture, and so on. I am simply saying we should be ready for the revelation of God in the common places of life. This was the thought the poet had in mind when he penned the famous lines:

Earth's crammed with heaven
And every common bush afire with God.

It is possible to walk about blind to the glory that is around us because we do not expect to find it there. Therefore we need the discerning eye – the power to see the glory in the ordinary, to walk down familiar pathways and see unfamiliar things, and to hear the accent of Jesus in spite of a dialect.

Lord God, give me the discerning eye that discovers You in the commonplace and the unexpected. Help me understand that You come to me not only in extraordinary ways but in the ordinary too. In Jesus' name. Amen.

A muffled cry

For reading & meditation – Matthew 25:31–46

'For I was hungry and you gave me something to eat ...'
(v.35)

One can go through a wood and miss that for which one is not prepared – a deer, a fox, a squirrel – and we can miss strange stirrings in our lives also. Often it is easier to look back and see God at work in the past, because we have not learned how to look for Him in the present. Evangelicals seldom refer to today's text. Because of our emphasis on Scripture we seem a little afraid to look for God outside of the Bible. His coming to us in the ordinary is too mystical for contemplation.

I read the account of a missionary couple's visit to a slum area in Nairobi. As they entered a hut, which they described as a 'cosy refuge from the oozing and rotting garbage outside', they found a woman with an infant in her arms. The woman told them that she was unable to have children and her prayer, like Hannah of old, had been that God would give her a child. One day, a few weeks past, she had been returning home when the muffled cries of an infant sent her rushing to a pile of garbage near her house. There she found a tiny baby – cold and abandoned.
Had God answered her prayer? Taking the child first to the police to certify that it had been abandoned and not stolen, she asked to keep it. They agreed, so cleaned and warm, the child slept peacefully in her arms.

That muffled cry she believes (and so do I) was the faint reminder that the Spirit of the living Christ is everywhere.

FURTHER STUDY

1 Sam. 3:1-21;
Psa. 95:7;
Jer. 5:21

1. What confused Samuel?

2. What sometimes prevents us from hearing God?

My Father and my God, forgive me if I have overlooked the fact that even in the midst of oozing and rotting garbage You can make Your presence known. I am humbled by Your ordinariness. Blessed be Your name for ever. Amen.

Hush – God is at work!

For reading & meditation – Psalm 139:1–24

'If I go up to the heavens, you are there; if I make my bed
in the depths, you are there.' (v.8)

The Spirit of the living Christ is everywhere. This was brought
home to me most powerfully on a flight between Singapore
and Australia. I was unable to sleep properly because two
women were conversing immediately behind me. I could not
help overhearing what they were talking about, and it became
more and more interesting.

One asked the other if she had any children. Obviously at this
point a photograph was taken out and the mother replied: 'Here are

FURTHER STUDY
2 Sam. 9:1-13;
Rom. 8:23

1. What sort of
surprise did
Mephibosheth
experience?

2. What
assurance do
we have?

my children; this one here has Down's Syndrome.'
'That's amazing,' remarked the other woman. 'One
of my children has Down's Syndrome too.' As you
can imagine, the conversation really came alive. I
heard one of the women admit to the other: 'I was
very self-centred and lived for pleasure until my
baby arrived. She brought such love into the life
of my husband and myself, though, that through
it we glimpsed the love of God. We both became
Christians because of her.' 'A similar thing happened
to my husband and me,' said the other woman. 'When our baby
was born we drank to drown out the sorrow. We both became
alcoholics. But the love that flowed from our baby to us was also
the means of bringing us to Christ.'

I met God in a new way as I listened to that conversation. It's
lovely when He surprises us in our reading of the Scriptures, but
no less lovely than when He reaches out to those who need Him
through someone as special as a child with Down's Syndrome.

**Father, sensitise me to the fact that Your Spirit is present to bring
glory to Your name in everything and through everything. I do not
always know why things go wrong, but I do know that You work
through all things for good. And I am thankful. Amen.**

The ordinariness of Jesus

For reading & meditation – John 14:1–14

'Jesus answered: "Don't you know me, Philip, even after
I have been among you such a long time?"' (v.9)

Some Christians look for God only in the cloistered retreat, far
from the cry of suffering humanity, kept pure because it is
kept apart. But God comes to us in ordinary occurrences also, in
the busy press of normal life where people toil and weep, where
hearts break and hopes are buried till the resurrection morn. We
are to look for Him there as well as in the pages of Scripture.

Our Lord, as we know, was born into the intimate home life of
an artisan's family in an unsanitary village called Nazareth. He
kept Himself in customary ways: He dressed as they
dressed, spoke with a Galilean accent, knew hunger
and weariness and shared everything of their life
except sin.

In today's passage, Philip seemed to miss the fact
that the One standing before him, with whom he
had rubbed shoulders for so long, was God of very
God. Was it because Jesus looked so ordinary? Just
think of it – Philip asked *Christ* where God could

FURTHER STUDY

Mark 6:1–6;
John 1:46;
Mark 8:27–29

1. How did
the crowd
view Jesus?

2. How did Peter
view Jesus?

be seen! It does not surprise me that Philip failed to recognise
Jesus as God, for human nature is always more attracted to the
spectacular than the truly great. If God had come to earth in a
chariot of fire, multitudes would have knelt before Him. If He had
moved among people with a shining face and dazzling apparel,
aristocrats would have sought Him out. But He was born as we
are born, and so blended the sublime with the normal that only
the few saw the sublime was there. I am constantly staggered
by the ordinariness of Jesus – aren't you?

**Lord Jesus, Your humility and ordinariness overwhelm me. Teach
me not to miss the sublime simply because it is clothed in an
everyday garb. For Your own dear name's sake. Amen.**

Reach out - now

For reading & meditation – John 12:37–50

'When he looks at me, he sees the one who sent me.' (v.45)

It was because Jesus mingled the commonplace with the glorious, and came along a frequented path, that so few were able to recognise Him. The unusual and ostentatious are always more attractive than the truly great. A preacher tells how one evening he stood with a group of friends as a firework display was about to begin. While they waited, he turned and saw behind him an exceptionally glorious sunset. Excited, he exclaimed: 'Look at that!' But no one looked – they were too engrossed in watching a man lighting a common squib.

FURTHER STUDY

Matt. 11:11-19;
9:11;
John 9:16

1. What accusations were levelled at Jesus because of His 'ordinariness'?

2. What also made Him extraordinary?

God came to earth in Jesus in a particularly unspectacular way and, despite the beauty and perfection of His life, passed unrecognised. God was with humankind – and they sought Him afar. Even his disciple Philip asked Him where God could be seen. The error is not peculiar to the disciples; many make the same mistake today. They seek at a distance the God who stands before them at the door of their heart. They are waiting for a ladder to be thrown down to them from heaven while all the time Christ has descended the ladder and is right there beside them.

The Holy Spirit is, I believe, leading me to make an even more direct appeal to readers who are not Christians. So those of you who are believers, bear with me again as I invite any individuals who may not have committed their lives to Christ a few days ago to do so now. My dear unconverted friend – listen! The ladder has been let down from heaven. Reach out to Christ now. Now!

Lord God, forgive me that I have looked for You afar – but You are so near. I reach out to You now. Save me. In Jesus' name. Amen.

'Sweep under the mats'

For reading & meditation – Acts 10:1–23

'Simon, three men are looking for you. So get up and go downstairs.' (vv.19-20)

God surprises us by involving Himself in the ordinary circumstances of life, and at times the words He speaks to us seem very ordinary too. I was brought up to believe that if ever God spoke to me He would do so in the language of the King James Bible. That is why the first words I ever heard Him say came to me as a shock. I was staggered by their ordinariness. I had been a Christian only a few months when one day, while kneeling in prayer at Holy Communion, I heard God say: 'Dear Selwyn, you mean so much to Me.' The words were very plain. No 'thee's' and 'thou's', yet I have no language to describe the effect they had upon me. The fact that God had spoken to me in ordinary words reached deep into my heart and mind, to the extent that they are ineffaceably imprinted on my memory.

FURTHER STUDY

Acts 16:1-10;
Matt. 17:5

1. What ordinary words did Paul hear in his vision?

2. What was Paul's conclusion?

Note how straightforward the words appear in today's text. The Spirit said: 'Three men are looking for you. So get up and go downstairs.' The words were simple, direct, and could be spoken by anyone, anywhere, at any time.

C.H. Spurgeon, the great Baptist preacher, was fond of quoting the story of his housemaid who told him that the day she began to work for him, she knelt by her bedside and dedicated herself to keeping house for him. After prayer she asked God for a word, and this is what He said: 'Remember to sweep under the mats.' Yes, it's ordinary – absurdly so. But then God is concerned with ordinary things. Duties matter to Him as well as devotions.

Father, I confess to some surprise that such an extraordinary God speaks in such ordinary words and phrases. Yet even ordinary words that come from Your mouth become extraordinary as they are heard in my heart. I am so thankful. Amen.

Shavings of gold

For reading & meditation – Ecclesiastes 9:1–10

'Whatever your hand finds to do, do it with all your might ...' (v.10)

I remember once standing in Trafalgar Square at a time when it was crowded with holiday makers. I had been waiting for a word of direction from God over a certain matter, but although I had spent much time on my knees it had not come. But there, not in a church, but amid the fountains and the crowds, God spoke to me and gave me the direction I needed.

If we are not prepared to meet God in the commonplace we may miss many of His messages to our hearts. I read somewhere an old legend of an angel who came one evening to the brink of a river and asked the boatman to ferry him across. When they reached the farther shore, the angel rewarded the boatman with a handful of what appeared to be wooden shavings. In disgust the boatmen threw them into the river. The next morning he found a few of the shavings still lying in his boat, and examining them more closely found they were shavings of pure gold.

FURTHER STUDY

Isa. 55:1-13;
Jer. 29:11;
Psa. 145:17;
Rom. 8:33-36

1. What did God make clear to the children of Israel?

2. Of what was Paul convinced?

Life is filled with so many ordinary moments, when it might appear nothing momentous is happening. Whatever you do, don't see the ordinary moments as worthless shavings to be thrown away in pique because you have received nothing better. Look at them more closely for, as the poet John Keble put it:

If on our daily course our mind
Be set to hallow all we find,
New treasures still of countless price
God will provide for sacrifice.

God my Father, help me be more alert and ready to look for You in the ordinary and the commonplace. Give me the discerning eye that sees the difference between wooden shavings and shavings of pure gold. In Christ's name I pray. Amen.

More tragic than orderly

For reading & meditation – Ecclesiastes 1:1–18
'For with much wisdom comes much sorrow ...' (v.18)

Undoubtedly the phrase 'God's surprises' instinctively brings to mind such wonders as miracles and blessings and amazing last-minute rescues from difficult situations. But there is another side to this matter – one that is less attractive but has to be faced nevertheless. God also sends His surprises through pain. Until we are willing to look at this issue there can be no advancement in the Christian life.

Oswald Chambers wrote: 'There can be no progress in the Christian life until we face the fact that life is more tragic than orderly.' It's surprising how many Christians refuse to face this fact and, like the ostrich, bury their heads in the sand. But denial – the unwillingness to face reality – gets us nowhere. Chambers was a sharp-eyed realist and deeply aware of the agonising 'riddle' of a universe in which tragic things take place and where there are no easy answers. He often quoted these phrases from Tennyson – phrases that resonated with his own experience:

FURTHER STUDY

Job 1:1–2:13;
23:10;
2 Cor. 4:17

1. What was Job able to say?

2. How did Paul view tribulation?

> Life is not as idle ore,
> But iron dug from central gloom,
> And heated hot with burning fears,
> And dip't in baths of hissing tears,
> And battered with the shocks of doom
> To shape and use.

The surprises of God that we discover in the midst of tragedy are not always deliverance *from* but deliverance *in*.

Father, help me understand that though life in a fallen world may be more tragic than orderly, this need not lead to pessimism and gloom. For You are at work in everything. You allow only what You can use. May I see all things tragic in this light. Amen.

Voicing questions

For readING & meditation – Jeremiah 20:7–18

'O Lord, you deceived me, and I was deceived ...' (v.7)

Exactly what did Oswald Chambers mean by: 'There can be no progress in the Christian life until we face the fact that life is more tragic than orderly'? I think he had in mind two things: the tendency some Christians have to turn in another direction when confronted by unpleasant matters, and the unrealistic belief that all chaos could be eliminated if we were to exercise a strong, positive faith.

No one believes in miracles more than I, and I have witnessed enough of them to know that there is nothing God cannot do. I am also sure of this, however – sin has struck deep into the universe, and although God intervenes at times to produce astonishing miracles of deliverance, life is still 'more tragic than orderly'. And it will continue this way until Christ returns.

FURTHER STUDY

Psa. 42:1-11;
Isa. 30:20-21

1. How did the psalmist feel?

2. What has God promised?

To face life realistically means that sometimes one has to ask difficult questions. I watched the film *Schindler's List* and found myself saying: 'God, how could You have let these things happen? And to the very people who are supposed to be close to You – the Jews?' Was God upset with me because I gave voice to these questions? I think not. He wasn't upset with the prophet Jeremiah when he said: 'O LORD, you deceived me.' God would prefer us to bring our hard questions out into the open rather than pretend they are not there. God won't always answer us, but we will find, as Jeremiah found, that He rewards His sincere but confused followers with a richer sense of His presence.

Lord God, I am thankful that You are not against me for asking hard questions. Help me see that when Your answers don't come verbally they come vitally – in a deeper sense of Your presence. Thank You my Father. Amen.

Job's bar exam

For reading & meditation – Job 38:1–18
'Brace yourself like a man; I will question you, and you
shall answer me.' (v.3)

When forced by the hard facts of life to ask searching
questions of the Almighty, we will not always get answers
but we will find ourselves experiencing a fuller sense of God's
presence. Job's story is one of the greatest examples of this.

Job declared: 'If only I knew where to find him … I would state
my case before him and fill my mouth with arguments. I would
find out what he would answer me … There an upright man
could present his case before him, and I would be delivered for
ever from my judge' (23:3–7). In today's passage
God turns the tables on Job by asking *him* some
searching questions. It is as if God is saying: 'Job,
you want to plead your case before Me in the courts
of justice and ask Me some hard questions. Well,
first I have some questions for you. "Where were
you when I laid the earth's foundations? Who
marked off its dimensions …?"'

FURTHER STUDY

Isa. 40:9–31;
Psa. 89:6–9;
1 Chron. 17:20

1. What question
does Isaiah ask?
2. How might
we respond?

One after the other the questions came. Job became nonplussed
but eventually got the point: there were some things he would
never understand, and because God is who He is, He should be
taken on trust. Job emerged from the experience not with his mind
enlightened but with a deeper awareness of God than he had ever
known before: 'My ears had heard of you but now my eyes have
seen you' (42:5). Clearly he now knew God in a different way –
not intellectually but experientially. He didn't have his questions
answered but he did see God. That was enough.

Loving heavenly Father, help me reach the place that Job arrived at,
so that when answers do not come I can take You on trust. Reveal
Yourself to me as You did to Your servant Job this very day.
In Christ's name I pray. Amen.

Everything – for the best

For reading & meditation – Lamentations 3:1–26
'... great is your faithfulness. I say to myself, 'The Lord is
my portion ...' (vv.23-24)

Job came to see that God was perfectly capable of running His world, and deserved to be taken on trust. What a surprise that must have been for Job.

It brings to mind a gentle rebuke I received early in my ministry when I went to console a widow whose husband had died in a mining accident. She was left with five young children, and as I prepared for the visit I consulted my Bible college textbooks and notes for some answers on why God allows tragedy to strike our lives. I wrote down two simple points in the palm of my hand so that I would not forget them. The first was that God allows tragedy because it draws us closer to Himself. The second was that God allows tragedy because when others see us responding with courage and trust, it draws them to Himself. When I was about halfway through my prepared talk, the woman turned to me and asked: 'What are you trying to do?' I explained: 'I am trying to show how and why God has let this happen.' She paused for a moment and said: 'I don't need to understand all that. What I do need is a God who is bigger than my understanding, a God who knows so much more than me.'

That mild reproach went home, I promise you. It was one of the greatest lessons of my life. Sometimes I wonder if trying to interpret the ways of God to people becomes counter-productive. Perhaps there is more solace in simply recognising that God is bigger than we are and that we can trust Him to work out everything for the best.

FURTHER STUDY

Psa. 36:5; 89:1;
Deut. 7:1-9

1. What was
the psalmist
convinced of?

2. What did
God confirm to
His people?

Gracious Father, give me a clearer vision of Your greatness and power than I have ever had before. And help me trust You to bring all things to a good and perfect end. In Jesus' name. Amen.

Our grief – His grief

For reading & meditation – 1 Peter 2:13–25

'... Christ suffered for you, leaving us an example,
that you should follow in his steps.' (v.21)

What do we do when darkness descends on us and, despite our most passionate prayers, the Almighty fails to spring one of His surprises of deliverance? We look for the surprise in another way – a richer awareness of His presence.

Helmut Theilicke, a noted German writer and theologian, once preached a thrilling sermon in his bomb-damaged church in World War II Germany, knowing that at any moment he and his congregation might have to run for shelter from the Allied bombers. His theme was 'The God of Surprises'. Theilicke was keenly aware of tragedy when he preached that sermon, for he had personally suffered under the Nazis. As a pastor he had written to young soldiers about to die; comforted people after bombs had killed their loved ones; preached tremendous sermons week after week as explosions blew apart bits of his church. His point was: 'God not only looks down in love when we are caught up in tragedy, not only weeps with us as we are surrounded by the flames, but reaches down into the flames to offer support. And His own hands get scorched in the process.'

FURTHER STUDY

Psa. 22:1-31;
Isa. 50:6;
Luke 22:44;
John 12:20-27;
2 Cor. 12:9

1. How did Jesus respond to the challenge of suffering?

2. What did Paul discover?

Some think that God is impervious to the pains that afflict our lives. I tell you He is deeply affected by them. He hurts in our hurts. Always remember, His own family – the Trinity – have known grief too, of the greatest magnitude. He saw His own Son skewered to a Roman cross. Yes, this great God of the universe knows what it is to experience pain. Our sufferings are His sufferings.

Merciful Father, I see that Your heart too has experienced grief and pain, and indeed all our griefs are Yours. Help me to share my griefs with you. In Christ's name I pray. Amen.

Are you willing?

For reading & meditation – Mark 9:14–32

'I do believe; help me overcome my unbelief!' (v.24)

Every day television and newspapers bring reports that cannot fail to horrify – murders, accidents, abuse, and so on. Can there be any doubt that Oswald Chambers' words are true: 'Life is more tragic than orderly'?

You may even be caught up in the midst of some personal tragedy at this very moment and feel as if you are being sucked down into a whirlpool of despair. 'Now is the time for one of God's great surprises,' you may be saying to yourself. 'Let Him deliver me from the pit into which I have fallen.' But nothing happens. Your marriage and family life go from bad to worse. Your finances fail. Your sickness or disability doesn't get better. You can't find a job. Why doesn't God pull out one of His big surprises? If He is loving as He says He is, then why doesn't He do something? Why?

FURTHER STUDY

Luke 17:1-6;
1 John 5:1-4

1. What was
the request of
the apostles?

2. What enables
us to overcome
the world?

'Why?' as someone has said, 'is the easiest question to ask, but not the easiest to answer.' It's not wrong to air the question if it is vexing you, but it is preferable not to become obsessed about it. The best position to take in times of trouble is the position of trust. Though not easy, adopting the same approach to the Lord as the man in our passage today will produce amazing results in the soul: 'I do believe; help me overcome my unbelief!' The principle is this – when fullness of trust is difficult, first identify the fact that you already have some trust, then ask for more. You will receive from God only as much as you are *willing* to receive.

Lord God, help me lay hold on this principle this very day. I believe
... now help me overcome my unbelief. You are ready, I am willing.
Work now in me, heavenly Father. In the name of
Your holy Son, Jesus. Amen.

Pain – God's megaphone

For reading & meditation – 2 Corinthians 12:1–10

'Three times I pleaded with the Lord to take [a thorn in my flesh] away from me.' (v.8)

God's surprises come not only as deliverances *from* difficult situations but also as deliverances *in*. God's people down the ages have discovered that surprising things happen to them in times of great pain. C.S. Lewis's famous statement focuses the truth: 'Pain is God's megaphone to rouse a deaf world.'* He also wrote that God's primary concern is not that we be happy, but that we be holy. What is important to the Almighty, he said, is that we open ourselves to His love and pass on that love to others.

Lewis was not thinking only of physical pain, but of spiritual and psychological pain also. This was clear in his book *The Problem of Pain*, in which he dwelt on the hurt that tears through the soul when darkness descends and God seems far away. Sometimes this is the only way God can get our attention; pain becomes His 'megaphone' to rouse our inattentive spirits. Lewis, of course, was not denying the power of Christ to heal or to deliver. One has only to read his book *Miracles* to see the confidence he placed in the supernatural power of God.

FURTHER STUDY

1 Tim. 1:1–14;
Phil. 4:19;
2 Cor. 11:16–33

1. What was Paul's real life experience?

2. What was Paul's testimony?

But what do we do when God doesn't heal or respond to our predicament with a demonstration of miraculous power? We look for Him to surprise in another way – by finding a secret stair to our soul and coming to us in a way that enables us to go through the difficulties with spiritual calm. This is what it means to live by God's surprises. If the surprise doesn't come in one way it comes in another.

Holy Spirit, I see You are continually trying to unfold truth to my heart, yet I am such a dull student. Sometimes I don't hear You very well and then You have to use God's 'megaphone'. Help me become a better student. In Christ's name I pray. Amen.

The Problem of Pain by C.S Lewis copyright © C.S Lewis Pte. Ltd. 1940.

Our 'terrible freedom'

For reading & meditation – John 10:1–10

'... I have come that they may have life, and have it to the full.' (v.10)

We look now at the surprise that most people experience following their conversion when they discover that in addition to having their sins forgiven, their hearts are filled with a deep abiding joy.

Prior to my conversion I had never associated Christianity with joy. My view of the Christian life was that it was one of rigorous duty – Bible reading, prayers, doing good, and an endless round of religious services. Becoming a Christian was about as appealing

FURTHER STUDY

Hab. 3:1–19;
Psa. 30:5; 126:5

1. What did Habakkuk declare in the face of difficulties?

2. What was the psalmist's view?

to me as going to prison – mainly because I thought commitment to Christ meant giving up everything pleasurable. As I said, I have questioned many people about their spiritual conversion and, if my study is anything to go by, most people prior to their conversion think that to give their lives to God means saying goodbye to all fun and happiness. What a surprise it is, therefore, to discover that instead of experiencing less joy, one experiences more and more.

It's strange how we view God as a killjoy when really He is a 'fill joy'. Obviously, that is not His fault but ours. Our text for today tells us He gives life, and that more abundantly. Why then do we not believe it? Why are we so surprised when, having surrendered to Him, we find His words to be true? One reason, I think, is because to hold on to the concept of God as a killjoy makes it easier to justify our unwillingness to surrender to His claims. Of course, refusing to surrender is, as C.S. Lewis put it, 'a *terrible* freedom'.

Father, how thankful I am that out of all the surprises that came to me following my conversion, one of the greatest was the discovery of joy. Help me receive my birthright and live the life for which I was made. Amen.

'Glorious joy'

For reading & meditation – 1 Peter 1:1–12

'... you believe in him and are filled with an inexpressible
and glorious joy ...' (v.8)

We are reflecting on the thought that one of the great surprises new Christians experience is that they are filled with joy. But why should that be such a surprise when God clearly states that when we receive Him we will be given what Peter describes as an 'inexpressible and glorious joy'?

C.S. Lewis shared the common misconception about the Christian life before he made the great surrender. He wrote in his book *Surprised by Joy*: '... picture me alone ... night after night, feeling, whenever my mind lifted even for a second from my work, the steady unrelenting approach of Him whom I so earnestly desired not to meet. In 1929 I gave in and admitted that God was God, and knelt and prayed: perhaps, that night, the most dejected and reluctant convert in all England.'* Lewis found what all sincere converts find – that surrendering to Christ is not to be deprived of joy but to be invaded by it.

FURTHER STUDY

Acts 16:16–25;
Psa. 132:16;
Isa. 35:10

1. What is a sure sign of joy in adversity?

2. Ask the Lord to put a song in your heart today.

This joy is different from happiness, which depends on circumstances. If what happens happens happily then we are happy. Joy is a deep abiding sense that all is well, whatever our circumstances. A Roman Catholic woman who experienced a spiritual conversion said in amazement: 'Strange, but I never associated joy with God before.' Now, despite almost impossible domestic difficulties, she describes herself as 'abounding with joy'. She is joyful *in spite of*! That is real joy. If, when we come to Christ, we are surprised by joy, the surprise ought to be that we are surprised.

Father, how foolish we are to live by our misconceptions rather than by Your truth. Yet You are so gracious, so forgiving and so understanding. My gratitude knows no bounds. Help me become more trusting and more trustworthy. In Jesus' name. Amen.

*Surprised by Joy by C.S Lewis copyright © C.S Lewis Pte. Ltd. 1940.

'Tell your face about it'

For reading & meditation – Psalm 105:1–11

'... let the hearts of those who seek the Lord rejoice.' (v.3)

So many think that becoming a Christian involves giving up most of the things that make glad the human heart. Some non-Christians have told me that the mere thought of putting their feet on the Way chills their souls and they want to flee. But contrary to popular opinion, God is no killjoy. He may seem like that to those who do not know Him, but those who enter into a relationship with Him find, as the Queen of Sheba found when visiting Solomon, that 'the half has not been told'.

FURTHER STUDY

Isa. 61:1–10; 12:3; Rom. 14:17

1. What is the foundation of joy that sustains us?

2. Ask God to restore to you today the joy of your salvation.

How has this widely held illusion come about, that to enter into a personal relationship with Jesus Christ is to experience less of life rather than more? We said that one reason could be the difficulty we have in taking God at His Word, but there is another – many of us who name the Name of Christ have, somehow or another, given the impression, that the Christian life is anything but abundant and radiant. Far too often our general demeanour suggests that Christianity is a heavy load that we are carrying rather than a living faith that carries us.

A grim-looking member of a certain church paused once on the edge of a Salvation Army open-air meeting in the East End of London, and a young Salvation Army girl, hovering on the outskirts of the crowd, asked him if he was saved. Embarrassed by the question, he replied tartly: 'Of course I am.' 'Well, sir,' she advised, 'I suggest that as soon as possible you tell your face about it!' Challenging words, but they went home.

Lord God, forgive us that in a world beset by sadness we may by our own lack of faith and confidence in You add to its gloom. Help us open our hearts to more of Your joy – Your eternal Joy. In Jesus' name. Amen.

Not good 'samples'?

For reading & meditation – Matthew 5:13–20

'… let your light shine before men, that they may see your
good deeds and praise your Father …' (v.16)

Many Christians are not good samples of the faith we profess.
We claim that the focus of our lives has been shifted from
ourselves to God, yet we are chronically selfish still. We talk of the
first grace being humility, but we are so proud. We speak about a
peace that passes all understanding, and yet we are restless within.
We claim to be children of a King, yet we walk around feeling
inferior. We say that perfect love casts out all fear, yet we are as
fearful as the next person. We pray daily and ask God to forgive
our trespasses 'as we forgive those who trespass
against us', but still harbour resentments and are
no strangers to bitterness.

FURTHER STUDY

2 Cor. 6:1-10;
Phil. 4:11-12;
1 Cor. 11:1

1. How did Paul
respond to life's
circumstances?

2. What was
he able to say
to those he
wrote to?

We affirm we have a divine Father who has
numbered the hairs of our heads and is watching
over us all the time for good, and yet we worry over
everything. John Wesley once said that he could no
more worry than he could curse or swear. Many of
us, myself included, are not quite there yet. I wonder
why? We may not swear, philander, steal, get drunk,
or commit gross sins, but neither do thousands of
other people who make no claim to be Christians.

It is a terribly challenging question I am about to ask: What
does our Christianity do for us? Are we nullifying the Christian
message by contradicting by our demeanour the very truths we
try to get across to others? If Christians by definition are people in
whom Christ lives, then ought we not to be showing more evidence
that the risen Christ is alive in us?

**My Father and my God, it is no secret that I have found in You the
ultimate joy, unshakeable joy and unspeakable joy. Help me share
that secret with others. And help me not only to be alive in You but
to look alive also. In Jesus' name I pray. Amen.**

All will be well

For reading & meditation – 2 Corinthians 4:1–18

'... persecuted, but not abandoned; struck down, but not destroyed.' (v.9)

One of the reasons why such a large percentage of non-Christians imagine the Christian life to be one of gloom rather than joy is because so many of us who claim to be Christians fail to give the right impression to the world. There is no joy like the joy of being a Christian, we say, yet we are often morose. Nietzsche, the famous philosopher, said he might be more drawn to Christianity if those who called themselves Christians looked a little more redeemed.

FURTHER STUDY

Heb. 6:1-20;
Rom. 15:1-4;
1 Pet. 3:15;
Prov. 14:32

1. What do the Scriptures bring?
2. What is an anchor to the soul?

Some might feel that I am being rather hard on Christians in general and be saying to themselves: What about Christians who have fallen on difficult times? How is it possible to manifest joy when one has to face such problems as bereavement, abuse, infidelity, and so on? Does what I am saying mean that Christians have to go about wearing a fixed smile even when the hearse that is carrying a loved one to the cemetery stands at the door? No, God does not expect that and neither, it has to be said, does the world. It is legitimate to show sorrow, to cry, to feel hurt, when life gives us a hard knock. Our faith as Christians does not insulate us from feelings of hurt, grief and sorrow.

What, then, does it mean to have and express Christian joy? It means, as I said earlier, that despite whatever is happening there is an underlying sense that in the final analysis *all will be well.* Joy didn't keep the apostle Paul from being knocked down but it did keep him from being knocked out.

Father, I see that the joy You provide is not the kind that eliminates sorrow but transforms it into something else. When my joy has its roots in You then it will have its fruit, no matter what happens. I am so deeply, deeply thankful. Amen.

'Your halo is too tight'

For reading & meditation – Hebrews 12:1-13

'... Jesus ... for the joy set before him endured the cross ...'
(v.2)

How did the infectious faith of Jesus become associated with gloom, frowns and mirthlessness? It is surely one of the most tragic misrepresentations of the truth. I would not be surprised to find that Satan himself had something to do with the lie's inception, although in Britain its origin is often attributed to those fine people we call 'Puritans'. Grossly misunderstood though they were, it cannot be denied that they fostered a tradition of drabness and frowned on mirth.

Have you noticed how many comedians include as part of their stock-in-trade not only jokes about mothers-in-law but miserable Christians as well? The other evening I heard one say: 'A born-again Christian went to his doctor and complained: "I've got a persistent headache that will not go away." "Do you smoke?" asked the doctor. "No." "Drink?" "No." "Go dancing?" "No." "Philander?" "No." The doctor thought for a moment and said: 'I think I know what's wrong with you. Your halo is too tight.'

FURTHER STUDY

Neh. 8:1-10;
Psa. 16:11

1. What does
the joy of the
Lord produce?

2. In what
ways might
you express
the joy of the
Lord today?

If in any way we have contributed to the misconception that life in Christ is a dismal affair then God forgive us, because it is a travesty of our true tradition. Certainly there are some miserable Christians, but they didn't get their misery from Christianity. Most likely it was there before they became Christians, and they have never allowed the joy that Christ gives to break through. Let you and me give the lie to these misconceptions – starting today.

Father, how tragic it is that although Your joy extends to the roots of our joylessness, we are not changed by it. Forgive us and help us not only to lay hold on joy but let it lay hold on us. In Christ's name. Amen.

Our birthright

For reading & meditation – Luke 15:1–10

'... there is rejoicing in the presence of the angels of God
over one sinner who repents.' (v.10)

God makes it clear in His Word that once we become Christians then we can fully expect His own joy to invade our hearts. Unfortunately, many of us are sceptical about God's statements and have to experience what He says before we believe Him.

Another reason, we said, why we doubt that joy is the inheritance of the Christian is because Christians (some, not all) don't look very joyful. We must get it clear in our minds that joy, not gloom, is the birthright of a child of God, and is the natural way to live. We are made for joy, and if our lives are characterised by gloom there is something wrong. Joy is being blocked. When we clear away the blocks then joy comes through – automatically. If gloom does characterise our lives then we ought not to look around for the cause – we ought to look within. John 15:11 points out that Christ's joy and our joy are not two different types of joy. They are allied, not alien. '*My* joy may be in you … and *your* joy may be complete.' We are made in the inner structure of our being for His joy.

FURTHER STUDY

John 16:17-24;
17:13-18

1. What did Jesus promise would replace grief?

2. What did Jesus pray for?

Our text today pictures for us in words something of the joy that pervades heaven over the conversion of just one sinner. We referred earlier to C.S. Lewis's book *Surprised by Joy*. At the end of that book he says that his big surprise on becoming a Christian was discovering that 'joy is the serious business of heaven'. To many that is *still* a big surprise.

**Father, I am so thankful that Your joy can become my joy. You were the most joyful Person the universe has ever seen. Help me take my birthright of joy and live the life for which I'm made.
This I ask in Jesus' name. Amen.**

The divine masterpiece

For reading & meditation – Ephesians 3:1–6

'... the mystery of Christ, which was not made known to men in other generations ...' (vv.4-5)

We now look at another of God's great surprises – the Christian Church. The revelation of the Church was not imparted to the Old Testament saints for, as Paul puts it in today's passage, it was a mystery that was hidden from previous generations. What a surprise it must have been to the Jews of Paul's day to discover that Gentile and Jewish Christians were now fellow heirs of the same blessing, fellow members of the same body, and fellow partakers of the same promise.

The 'mystery' of which Paul speaks here is – when Jews and Gentiles are united with Christ they then become united with one another. In Christ, Paul tells us, the Jewish theocracy is terminated and replaced by a new international community – the Church. This is the 'body of Christ', organically united to Him, and into which both Jews and Gentiles enter, on equal terms. In the epistle to the Galatians, Paul says: in Christ 'there is neither Jew nor Greek, slave nor free, male nor female, for you are all one in Christ Jesus' (Gal. 3:28). In relation to the world we still retain our national and sexual identities, of course, but in relation to the Church those identities no longer exist.

FURTHER STUDY

Matt. 16:13-20;
Eph. 2:19-22;
1 Thess. 1:1

1. What did Jesus say to Peter?

2. How did Paul describe the Church?

Does this mean that God has no further purpose to work out through Jews and Gentiles? No, but it does mean that His highest purposes are accomplished through the Church. Tom Rees, a famous Welsh preacher, described the Church as 'the divine masterpiece'. It is. Nothing in earth or heaven can equal it.

Father, enlarge my vision of Your Church. I am so grateful that I am part of it. May the wonder of my salvation become even more apparent to me, and may it, in turn, issue forth in constant praise in my soul. Amen.

An 'open' secret

For reading & meditation – Romans 16:17–27
'... according to the revelation of the mystery hidden for
long ages past ...' (v.25)

It must have been a surprise for the first Jewish believers, having
turned from Judaism to Christianity, to discover the radical
nature of their new position in the purposes of God. This does not
mean that they lost their Jewishness when they turned to Christ,
any more than I lost my Welshness when I committed myself
to Christ. It was simply that in the Church this difference (and
others) had no significance. This was a surprise that neither Jew
nor Gentile could ever have anticipated.

FURTHER STUDY
1 Cor. 2:1-10;
Eph. 1:9-10;
3:4-5;
Col. 1:26-27
1. What has
God made
known to us?
2. How does
Paul define
this mystery?

In today's passage, Paul focuses on the subject
we looked at yesterday – the 'mystery' long hidden
but now brought into the light. The significance
of the word 'mystery' as used by Paul both in
Romans and Ephesians is somewhat different from
that of its usage in everyday English. In English
a 'mystery' is something dark, obscure, puzzling,
even incomprehensible. The sense of the Greek
word *mysterion* is different, however. Although it
still denotes a secret, it is one that can be divulged,
especially to the initiated. It is an esoteric 'mystery'
reserved for the spiritually elite. The word in its original setting
had to do with secret rites and initiations, and was used in
connection with the secret teachings of the many mystery
religions of the world at that time.

The 'mystery' of the Church, then, is a truth which is beyond
human discovery, but has been revealed by God and now
belongs to the whole Church. The 'secret' has been made open.
And how!

**Father, how can I thank You enough for sharing this 'open secret'
with me? I am grateful beyond words for the privilege of being one
of Your chosen people. I know I shall never lose this sense of
appreciation, both in time and in eternity. Amen.**

Israel is not the Church

For reading & meditation – 1 Corinthians 10:23–33

'Do not cause anyone to stumble, whether Jews, Greeks or
the church of God ...' (v.32)

Some believe that the nation of Israel is the Church – an idea based on verses such as Acts 7:38, where some translations describe the ancient Jewish people as 'the *church* in the wilderness'. But the word *ekklesia* used there by Stephen was not intended to convey the same sense as when Paul used it to denote the body of Christ – the Church; Stephen, the first Christian martyr, simply meant to convey the idea of an assembly of people. No, the Church and Judaism are not to be equated. It is true, as someone has said, that 'the Church was in the bosom of Judaism, like the unborn child in its mother's womb', but it is a mistake to regard the two as one. Our text for today makes crystal clear that the Church and Israel are different entities.

The Church is not the whole of Christendom either – as so many others believe. Ever since AD 313, when Constantine proclaimed Christianity the favoured religion of the Roman Empire, there has existed what is known as 'Christendom' – that is, the realm or domain of the 'christened'. Whatever we might think about the act of christening, no enlightened person would say that it automatically makes one fit to enter heaven. An old Cambridge professor used to say: 'When I was a child I was both christened and vaccinated, but I am afraid that neither of them took.' That, unhappily, is the state of multitudes today. They have been christened but not Christened; baptised as infants but not born again as adults.

FURTHER STUDY

John 3:1-21; 1:13;
2 Cor. 5:17

1. What differentiation did Jesus make between Judaism and the new birth?

2. What was Nicodemus' struggle with this?

**Lord God, forgive us that we have been so lax in making clear to the
world that Christendom is not the Church. Rouse us, both people
and preachers, to clarify this issue ere millions more go into
eternity resting on a false hope. In Jesus' name. Amen.**

Called!

For reading & meditation – Romans 1:1–7

'And you also are among those who are called to belong to Jesus Christ.' (v.6)

The Church is not the nation of Israel, neither is it the whole of Christendom. Today my point is: the Church is not a denomination. We speak of the Anglican church, Episcopal church, Roman Catholic church, Baptist church, Presbyterian church, Methodist church, Pentecostal church, and so on. But each of these divisions of organised Christianity is just a part or branch of the Church. The Church is far bigger than any of its branches. 'To what branch of the Church do you belong?' a believer was asked. He replied: 'I don't belong to any branch; I belong to the trunk.' The church with a little 'c' is but a part of the Church with a big 'C'.

If the Church is not Israel, not Christendom, not a denomination, then what is it? The *Westminster Confession of Faith* defines the Church in this way: '… the whole number of the elect that have been, are, or shall be gathered into one under Christ, the Head thereof, and is the spouse, the body, the fullness of Him that filleth all in all'. The Greek word for Church is *ekklesia*, and means a people who are 'called out' from the world because they belong to the Lord. Karl Barth, the well-known theologian, graphically described the Church in this way: 'The Church is like a company of citizens, rushing from everywhere – called out by the trumpet of God.' Christians are men and women who have been called out of the world to give their allegiance to the Son of God. Aren't you glad you have answered the call?

FURTHER STUDY

Rom. 12:1–5;
1 Cor. 12:27;
Eph. 1:23; 4:12

1. What term did Paul frequently use when writing about the Church?

2. What is the implication of this?

Yes, dear Father, my heart responds not in pride but humility that I heard and answered Your call. What a privilege. What a destiny. All honour and glory be to Your wonderful name for ever. Amen.

One body

For reading & meditation – 1 Corinthians 12:12–26

'For we were all baptised by one Spirit into one body ...'
(v.13)

What exactly is the Church? Let's start with a few representative New Testament definitions. 'I am not praying for the world, but for those you have given me, for they are yours' (John 17:9). 'All the believers were together and had everything in common' (Acts 2:44). 'All the believers were one in heart and mind' (Acts 4:32). 'God ... showed his concern by taking from the Gentiles a people for himself' (Acts 15:14). '... all those everywhere who call on the name of our Lord Jesus Christ' (1 Cor. 1:2). '... the church of the firstborn, whose names are written in heaven' (Heb. 12:23). '... a people belonging to God, that you may declare the praises of him who called you out of darkness into his wonderful light' (1 Pet. 2:9).

The Bible does more than define the Church however; it also describes it. 'The Church' is mentioned more than a hundred times in the New Testament, and is portrayed by many different images. The Bible does not say anything about images in the Church, but it abounds with images of the Church. It is pictured, for example, as a body, a temple, a bride, a mother, a family, a fold, salt, a loaf, a garden, a pillar, an army, a colony and a city. Paul's favourite figure of the Church, and no doubt the most powerful, is that of a body, and in the New Testament no one but he uses it. The Christian Church is a great body made up of a lot of little people who must all function properly if the body is to be kept healthy and its work done.

FURTHER STUDY

Col. 1:1–18;
Eph. 1:22–23;
4:15–16; 5:23

1. How does Paul complete his picture of the Church as a body?

2. What are the implications of this?

Father God, as part of Your body all that I have is at Your disposal. You know the needs of Your body, the Church – use me to my fullest potential to meet those needs. In Christ's name I ask it. Amen.

'His bright design'

For reading & meditation – Ephesians 1:1–14

'For he chose us in him before the creation of the world ...'
(v.4)

Differing views are expressed as to where and when the Church began. Some trace its origin to the nation of Israel, stemming from the call of Abraham. John Stott says: 'The Church is a … community of people, who owe their existence, their solidarity and their corporate distinctness from other communities to one thing – the call of God. It all began with Abraham, called by God to leave his own country ...' Others say the Church began with John the Baptist. As he was the first to baptise, and baptism in water is seen as a rite of entry into the Christian Church, they maintain it was in John's baptism that the Church had its beginning. Still others claim the Church began in the revelation vouchsafed to the apostle Paul, and quote his words in Ephesians 3:3: 'the mystery made known to me by revelation'. Most Christians, though, believe the Church was founded on the Day of Pentecost.

FURTHER STUDY
John 15:1-17;
Matt. 25:31-36;
1 Pet. 1:1-2
1. What did Jesus say about the kingdom?
2. What did Jesus assure His disciples?

Whatever our views about when and where the Church first appeared, the truth is the Church began not in time but in eternity. Our text tells us we were chosen in Christ before the creation of the world. Some theologians teach that the Church is an afterthought of God, introduced because of the rejection of His Son by the Jewish nation. But the Church is no afterthought, no addendum to the plan of salvation, no by-product of the redemptive process. The Church is, rather, a forethought. It is, as one preacher put it: 'His bright design from the very beginning.'

Father, what comfort it gives me to know that You planned my salvation before time began. I am not Your afterthought, but Your forethought. All honour and glory be to Your peerless and precious name. Amen.

A river as great as this

For reading & meditation – 2 Thessalonians 2:13–17

'... from the beginning God chose you to be saved ...' (v.13)

I have always loved the story, told by the Christian writer Ian Macpherson, of how in 1550 the Spanish explorer Vincente Pinzon found himself sailing into the mouth of what we now call the River Amazon. No European had ever charted these waters before, so Pinzon and his men did not know where they were. Mistaking South America for the West Indies, one of the ship's company suggested they had discovered an island. 'No,' said Pinzon, 'this cannot be an island; a river as great as this must drain a continent.'

'A river as great as this must drain a continent!' When one contemplates the Church of Jesus Christ and its long procession through the centuries, its increasing depth and ever-expanding width, one cannot help but feel that the source of this mighty river lies not in time but in eternity. And that is where Paul, in today's reading, traces it back to. He traces the Church, the 'Amazon', back to its source in the 'Andes' – the heart of God.

FURTHER STUDY

John 1:19–31;
Rev. 5:12–13;
13:8

1. How did John first introduce Jesus?

2. What is the song of the heavenly multitude?

If we want to trace the beginning of the Jewish nation then we must go all the way back to Abraham. If we want to trace the beginning of the human race, then we must go all the way back to Adam. But if we want to trace the beginning of the Christian Church, we must step off the platform of time and there, somewhere in the mists of eternity, deep in the heart of God, we find our eternal destiny was settled in the Lamb slain before the foundation of the world.

Father, how thrilling it is that You anticipated the fall of man and prepared in advance the great plan of salvation. Truly it can be said I was saved in eternity. Blessed be Your holy name. Amen.

Why He framed the worlds

For reading & meditation – Ephesians 3:7-21

'His intent was that now, through the church, the manifold wisdom of God should be made known ...' (v.10)

Many of the great Welsh theologians believed that the creation of the world was effected so that God might bring out of it His masterpiece, the Church. One theologian declared: 'He framed the world that He might form the fellowship.' Follow their thinking with me and see if you agree.

God knew prior to Adam and Eve's creation that they would succumb to the devil's temptation. Yet He went ahead nevertheless, because He had prepared another plan (to remain secret until the day of the apostle Paul), that would bring even more glory to Himself than if His purposes for Adam and Eve had succeeded. Undoubtedly it would have brought tremendous honour to God had Adam and Eve resisted the temptation and populated the earth with offspring who were untainted by original sin. Great though that would have been, there is now something greater: God is taking men and women who have been soiled by sin, changing them by His grace and showing them off (so to speak) to the whole universe as evidence of His manifold wisdom. Satan thought he had foiled God's purposes when he overcame Adam and Eve in the temptation. Little did he know that ahead would emerge a plan that would bring more glory to God than anything that could have been achieved in Eden.

Adam and Eve started out in innocence but they failed. We start out in sin and we are going to make it to heaven, not in our own strength, but through the mercy of God. God's grace more than matches the machinations of sin.

FURTHER STUDY

2 Cor. 3:7-18;
John 14:13; 17:4

1. What parallel did Paul draw concerning the glory of God?

2. What was Jesus able to say?

Gracious and loving Father, Your grace and power sometimes take my breath away. I see so clearly that sin is no match for Your wisdom. And I am the recipient of such matchless grace. For this I will praise You for ever. Amen.

A joy for ever

For reading & meditation – Revelation 21:9–27

'Come, I will show you the bride, the wife of the Lamb.'
(v.9)

Sir Christopher Wren, the architect of St Paul's Cathedral in the city of London, chose on his retirement to live in Camberwell, on the other side of the River Thames, where it was possible to view the cathedral, the construction of which had been his crowning glory. Erected between 1675 and 1710, the cathedral is recognised as being one of the most spectacularly splendid buildings in Britain. Sir Christopher Wren lived to be ninety, and could sometimes be seen sitting with spyglass in hand, looking out across the Thames and surveying with pleasure and pride the cathedral he had designed. What an interesting sight it must have been for those who witnessed it – the master contemplating his masterpiece. One day in the future, when the Church is complete, something similar will take place in heaven: the Master – Christ – will contemplate His masterpiece – the Church.

I am often accused of rhapsodising about the final destiny of the Church, so let me borrow the words of Paul E. Billheimer who is more down to earth in his descriptions: 'The nations of the world are but puppets manipulated by God for the purposes of the Church. Creation has no other aim. History has no other goal. From before the foundation of the world God has been working toward one grand event, one supreme end – the Church.' One of the greatest sights of heaven – for those who are there to witness it – will be to see the Master contemplating His masterpiece: the Church.

FURTHER STUDY

2 Cor. 11:1–3;
Rev. 19:7; 21:2;
22:17;
Eph. 5:25–27

1. What was Paul jealous for?

2. How will the Church be presented?

Lord Jesus Christ, my Saviour and my Lord, to be saved from hell would be enough, but to be a part of Your masterpiece is more than my mind can take in. Yet I know it to be so. And I am glad. More than glad. Ecstatic! Amen.

God's greatest surprise

For reading & meditation – John 1:1–18

'No-one has ever seen God, but God the One and Only ... has made him known.' (v.18)

Without doubt God's greatest surprise ever is His coming to this world in the Person of His Son. From earliest days, people knew the problems that sin had created in God's universe would ultimately be answered by a Word from heaven. But that the 'Word' would be God *Himself* never occurred to them. Hebrew thought used the term 'word' – as in 'Thy word', or 'the word of the Lord' – to convey the idea that the Word which the Almighty spoke was simply an expression of Himself.

FURTHER STUDY

1 John 1:1-10;
Rev. 19:13;
Gal. 4:4

1. What did John proclaim?

2. What is surprising about God sending His Son?

Though some, through divine revelation, would have grasped the fact that there was more than one divine Person in the Godhead, most of those living in Old Testament times (and all orthodox Jews today) understood God to be One. Even if they had allowed the thought to enter their minds that God would one day come to this planet Himself, it would have been instantly dismissed on the basis that it would be impossible for God to become man and still be in control of the universe.

How it must have staggered Jewish minds, therefore, to be faced with the truth, which John delineates so beautifully in this chapter, that the 'Word', whom he declares 'was *with* God' and '*was* God', took on human form and dwelt among us. Our Lord, while never ceasing to be what He had always been – true God – became what He had never been before – true man. Staggering though it may be, it is the very heart of our faith. Indeed, no one can be called a believer in the Christian faith without accepting it.

God my Father, I am so grateful that when we couldn't come to You, You came to us. Your incarnation is my salvation. Glory be to Your wondrous name for ever. I will never be able to thank You enough. Amen.

'Too wonderful for words'

For reading & meditation – 1 John 1:1–10

'We proclaim to you what we have seen and heard ...' (v.3)

When one considers carefully the words of the New Testament writers relating to the incarnation, one senses their struggle to put such an incredible fact into words. Paul says: 'Thank God for his Son – his Gift too wonderful for words' (2 Cor. 9:15, TLB). The thing that staggered the New Testament writers was that the Word really became flesh.

John found the incarnation so utterly incredible that he had to insist he wasn't spinning his account out of a fevered imagination but recounting sober fact: that 'which we have heard ... seen with our eyes ... looked at and our hands have touched' (v.1). Each statement gives added intimacy. First, 'which we have heard'. But hearing may be at such a distance that it can almost amount to hearsay; so 'which we have seen with our eyes' brings the issue nearer still. His next statement – 'which we have looked at' – is not a fleeting glance but a steady gaze. Then finally: 'and our hands have touched'.

In four statements involving three of the physical senses John endorses the fact that the Word actually did become flesh. For John saw its vital importance. If God had not come in the flesh then our salvation would not have been possible. He had to be made like us in order to save us because, as Bishop Handley Moule put it: 'A Saviour who is not wholly God and wholly man would be like a bridge broken at one end.' Let every creature gasp before such a mystery. Jesus is the heart of God wrapped in human flesh.

FURTHER STUDY

Phil. 2:1–11;
1 Tim. 2:5; 3:16
Rom. 8:3

1. How did Paul describe the humanity of Christ?

2. What was beyond all question for Paul?

Father, the unveiling in the heart of Jesus helps me see what is back in eternity. And what I see makes me grateful to my fingertips. What mercy. What humility. What grace. I am speechless at the wonder of it. Amen.

Never to be repeated

For reading & meditation – Isaiah 7:1–14

'The virgin will be with child and will give birth to a son, and will call him Immanuel.' (v.14)

The centre of the Christian faith is the incarnation: God becoming human. Other things are important but this is the central issue. People say: 'Miracles are the most important thing.' This is the miracle of all miracles – the eternal God becoming like us in order that we might become like Him. Others say: 'Teaching is what is most important.' What greater teaching could there be than to see God take on Himself the form of human flesh? We see in a flash the meaning of humility, of service, of self-giving – of everything that is good. Others say: 'Morality has the greatest importance.' God in human form is morality *par excellence*; not thundering law, but washing people's feet. Still others say: 'Nothing is more important than spirituality.' This is spirituality – Christ not aloof and lifted up but walking the earth in sandals. What about doctrine? Is this the most important thing? Our Lord took doctrine and fleshed it out in deed. He did not simply declare things, He demonstrated them – in life, in death and in resurrection.

FURTHER STUDY

Isa. 7:1-14; 9:6;
Luke 1:31;
Matt. 1:21-24

1. What are some of the titles of Jesus?

2. List several surprising things about the incarnation.

I saw a television programme about a group in India who are trying to groom their Swami to be a reincarnation of Christ. But all talk of a reincarnation of Christ is nonsense – even blasphemy. Christ became incarnate once only. Nothing like it had happened before and nothing like it will happen again. By its very nature it was the event of all events – the most surprising event in all history. And never to be repeated.

Blessed and wise God, I am so thankful that Your incarnation is the complete and total answer to human needs. No repetition is needed. Having seen You I want and need no other. Amen.

The gospel sureties

For reading & meditation – 1 John 4:1–21

'Every spirit that acknowledges that Jesus Christ has
come in the flesh is from God ...' (v.2)

The most surprising thing about the Christmas story,' said a
great Welsh preacher, 'is not that God revealed Himself to
this world but that in the revealing He chose to wear our flesh.'
At the time of the Early Church, a group of people called Gnostics
(from the Greek *gnosis*, 'to know') saw all matter as evil and could
not find words strong enough to express their loathing of the
material world in which they lived. To them the world was full
of misery, filth and uncleanness. Only spirit is good, they said;
all matter is evil. One writer says concerning the
Gnostics: 'They believed that man's spirit is a divine
being imprisoned contrary to its nature in the body,
a divine seed sown in hostile matter.'

FURTHER STUDY

Matt. 16:1-16;
John 1:49;
4:29; 11:27

To the Gnostics the idea of the incarnation, of
the Word becoming flesh, was abhorrent. To them
Jesus was not God become human, but the revealer
of knowledge that would bring salvation. So 1 John
was written mainly to combat this falsehood; in
fact John tells us in today's passage that one way to
tell if someone is speaking by the Holy Spirit is to
ask them whether they believe that Jesus Christ has come in the
flesh. Our salvation hinges on Jesus as incarnate – not merely as
a moral teacher, an inspiration or a philosopher. That, to John, was
the great issue. Over against the vagaries of Gnostic speculation
John set the vitalities of the gospel sureties, which he planted amid
the material – the Word become flesh – right down where we live.

1. What was
Peter's
resounding
response?

2. What was
Martha's
conclusion?

Gracious Saviour, You took upon Yourself human flesh and have
now elevated it into the Godhead. You came to where we are in
order to take us to where You are. How can I ever sufficiently thank
You? Receive my praise. In Jesus' name. Amen.

Good news, not good views

For reading & meditation – 1 Timothy 3:1–16
'He appeared in a body, was vindicated by the Spirit ...'
(v.16)

The fact that the Word became *flesh* is the very genius of the gospel. Take any non-Christian religion and all you will discover is a word become word. All other faiths claim that God has spoken to their founder, and to prove it they show us their books, in which often there are good words.

Christianity has the Bible, but the difference between this book and other religious books is that it is a revelation; it unfolds the fact that God has come into the world in the Person of His Son.

FURTHER STUDY

2 Tim. 3:1–5;
Titus 1:16;
Mark 7:6

1. Who was Timothy to have nothing to do with?

2. What is the hallmark of the religious hypocrite?

The Bible itself does not give us salvation – the Word become words – but the incarnation – the Word become flesh. The words of the Bible take us by the hand and lead us beyond the words to the Word – the Word made flesh. Jesus is good news; all else is good views. Every other religion is humankind's attempt to climb to God; Jesus is God's descent to humankind. Every other religion represents humankind's search for God; Jesus, the Word become flesh, represents God's search for humankind. There are many religions, but only one gospel.

Christ did not bring something a little better, a little more moral, a little more spiritual than other religions. He came to set the gospel over against human need, particularly the need of the soul. As the Son of Man He confronts the sons and daughters of men with God's offer to humankind. He Himself is the offer. The gospel lies in His Person – *He* is the good news. He didn't come to preach the gospel but that we might have a gospel to preach.

Lord Jesus, I am so thankful for who and what You are. For this determines everything. You are God's only Son. I look on You and know there is no other like You. You are the only Son and therefore the only incarnate One. Thank You my Saviour. Amen.

God takes a body

For reading & meditation – Hebrews 10:1–17

'Sacrifice and offering you did not desire, but a body you
prepared for me ...' (v.5)

In certain parts of the Church people are questioning whether
Christ was a real human being. A man I spoke to in Australia,
who had just graduated from a US theological seminary, told me
that he was presented there with three alternatives about Jesus.
First, that He was mere man. Second, that He was a phantom –
God who appeared as a man but was not really so. Third, Christ,
the second Person of the Trinity, was united with the man Jesus
at His baptism in the River Jordan and then left Him before the
crucifixion. All three of these theories have one
common goal: to obviate the difficulty of God dying
on a cross. God on a cross scandalised the ancient
world of philosophy, and it seems to be doing the
same to some religionists in our own day.

But there is an even more sinister belief
underlying these ideas, namely that matter is in
itself evil and God ineffably aloof. The question of
good and evil is not a question of spirit and matter; it
is a question of the will. The seat of evil is in the will, not in matter.
Of course matter has been affected by the evil that came into the
world through Adam and Eve's sin, but to root evil in matter, and
not in the will, is an attempt to blame evil on something other than
personal responsibility – a foolish but self-serving evasion. The
Christian faith meets us where we are – in the flesh – and offers
us redemption *in* the flesh, not *from* the flesh. We live for Christ
in our bodies, not apart from them.

FURTHER STUDY

Isa. 53:1–12;
1 Pet. 3:18; 2:24;
Titus 2:14

1. What is Isaiah
53 speaking of?

2. Where were
our sins borne?

**Heavenly Father, I am glad that You do not despise anything You
made. You made it for a purpose and that purpose is redemption.
We move in a world hallowed by Your touch and interest. I am so
thankful. Amen.**

'Gasp in wonder'

For reading & meditation – Matthew 1:18–25

'... you are to give him the name Jesus, because he will
save his people from their sins.' (v.21)

Because we couldn't climb up to God, He came down to us.
Archbishop William Temple put it like this: 'There are just
two types of religion. The one type tries to meet God at the top
rung of a long ladder; the other meets God at the lowest rung. In
the one men try to go to God, climbing up by their good deeds;
in the other, men simply allow God to save them.' The message
of Christianity is this – we do not have to climb a long ladder in
order to get to God. He comes down the ladder to us and meets us
on the lowest rung and receives us there as sinners.

FURTHER STUDY

Luke 1:1–40;
Psa. 17:7

1. What has God
done in Christ?

2. Share Jesus
with someone
who doesn't
know Him today.

This sets the Christian faith apart from all other
religions, and because of that it is revolutionary.
Judaism says: 'God loves those who keep His law.'
This means you meet Him at the top of the ladder.
Islam says: 'Pray five times a day, fast, obey Allah's
commands and you will get to God' – at the top
of the ladder. Hinduism says: 'Practise austerities,
renounce the world order, shut out everything but
the realisation of God, and you will find Him' – again at the top
of the ladder. Every religion except Christianity has this type of
approach. Only one Person dared reverse this and they crucified
Him for it – Jesus.

Nothing in earth or heaven can be more awesome, more
surprising than this – that God isn't to be found at the top of
the ladder but at the bottom. Every creature with a grain of
intelligence ought to reflect on it again – and gasp in wonder.

**Lord Jesus Christ, what can I say? I am speechless at the wonder of
Your incarnation. I am in the dust but there I find You – in the dust
before me, ready to lift me to the highest heavens. Blessed be Your
name for ever. Amen.**

In for a great surprise

For reading & meditation – Matthew 24:36–51

'Therefore keep watch, because you do not know on what
day your Lord will come.' (v.42)

O ne of God's great surprises is in the future – the second
coming of our Lord. Many have thought they knew when
Christ would return and foolishly have even given a date. But so
far all have been wrong. Today's text makes it quite clear that
Jesus will not come when we expect Him, otherwise He would
not have said 'Watch'.

There seems to be a good deal of misunderstanding about the
second coming of Christ in certain Christian circles. Some state
quite categorically that He is not coming back. Albert
Schweitzer was of this mind. Possibly before he died
he altered his view, but in his book *The Quest for the
Historical Jesus* he says that our Lord was in error
concerning His second coming. He *thought* He was
going to return to earth, claimed Schweitzer, but He
was mistaken.

FURTHER STUDY

Luke 12:35–40;
Matt. 24:27;
1 Thess. 5:2

1. What did Jesus
instruct the
disciples?

2. What will
Christ's coming
be like?

A young graduate from a liberal theological college
told me of the shock he experienced when he heard
one of his tutors say: 'Jesus somehow got the idea He
was going to come back one day, but that idea did not come from
God. Some of His ideas were from God, but some were not. The idea
of the second coming was something He thought up Himself.' What
hope is there for the Christian Church when so-called *theological*
colleges expose their students to statements such as that? I slipped
into a US church and heard a preacher admit: 'I do not believe that
Christ will ever return to this earth.' I thought to myself as I left
the service: 'My friend, you are in for a great surprise.'

Gracious and loving God, help me stay ever alert and watchful and
on tiptoe for Your coming. May I work as if You were not coming for
a thousand years, but live as if You might come today.
In Christ's name I ask it. Amen.

More misunderstanding

For reading & meditation – Philippians 3:12–21
'... we eagerly await a Saviour from [heaven], the Lord
Jesus Christ.' (v.20)

I t's strange that despite the words before us today, some professing Christians believe that our Lord Jesus Christ is never going to return to this earth. This, however, is only one category of error relating to Christ's second coming.

Two broad groups believe that Jesus has already come back. One believes that Christ returned to this earth on the Day of Pentecost. They confuse the descent of the Holy Spirit with the descent of the Son. A theologian writes: 'John [the apostle] wrote after the occurrence of the Second Advent and under the power of the abiding Presence.' It is true, of course, that the apostle penned his words under the power of the abiding Presence, for as our Lord Himself said: 'Where two or three come together in my name, there am I with them' (Matt. 18:20). His coming in the presence of the Spirit, however, is quite different to His personal and visible return, which is predicted repeatedly in Scripture. So many predictions of the second advent were made *after* Pentecost that they cannot have pointed *to* Pentecost.

FURTHER STUDY

Acts 1:1–11;
Heb. 9:28;
Luke 21:25–28

1. How did the
angels say Jesus
would return?

2. How did
Jesus say He
would return?

The other group comprises those who claim that Christ returned to this earth at the time of the fall of Jerusalem in AD 70. Without doubt *part* of our Lord's apocalyptic discourse in Matthew 24, Mark 13 and Luke 21 does refer to this event, but as one more enlightened theologian puts it: 'Part of Christ's purpose in coming to this earth is not to destroy Jerusalem but restore it.'

Lord Jesus Christ, I believe with all my heart in Your coming again to this earth. Your first coming was foretold and fulfilled, and so will Your second coming be also. I believe and wait – with confidence. Amen.

An event – not a process

For reading & meditation – 1 Thessalonians 4:13–18

'For the Lord himself will come down from heaven, with a loud command ...' (v.16)

Some say Christ will *never* come back, while others say He has *already* returned. A third view, equally erroneous, is this – Christ is *always* coming back; Christ returns in all the great events of history, in the discoveries of science, and in the major advances of civilisation. 'His second advent,' says one writer, 'is a *constant* coming – a coming in which He supervises and directs the onward march of history.'

Frank Ballard, a writer who subscribes to this same view, claimed: 'The coming of Christ is not an event, but a process which includes innumerable events, a perpetual advance of Christ in the activity of His kingdom. It has continued until now, and is still moving on, but He is truly the Coming One, for He is still coming and is yet to come.' Again, there is a sense in which this is correct: Christ is always coming into human hearts and history. Indeed, in relation to the matter of the human heart we have His own word for it. 'Here I am!' He says. 'I stand at the door and knock. If anyone hears my voice and opens the door, I will come in and eat with him, and he with me' (Rev. 3:20).

The coming of Christ into human affairs, however, is quite different from the second coming, and with so many texts in Scripture affirming this, it is astonishing that any student of the New Testament could ever confuse the two. No, Christ's second advent is an event, not a process.

FURTHER STUDY

2 Thess. 1:1-7;
Rev. 1:7;
Matt. 24:30

1. How will Jesus be revealed?

2. What will happen when He is revealed?

Father God, the coming again of Your Son to this earth gives a horizon and meaning to the whole of history. All things move to a goal – the goal of Your coming again. I am so grateful. Amen.

Is death Christ's coming?

For reading & meditation – John 21:15–25

'Jesus answered, "If I want him to remain alive until I return, what is that to you?"' (v.22)

Yet another erroneous belief is that the return of the Redeemer is to be identified with the death of the believer. 'The promise of Christ's return,' says one proponent, 'is fulfilled in the death of the Christian, and thus has changed the whole aspect of death.' Another says: 'Whenever death occurs there is the *parousia* of the Lord.' *Parousia* is 'personal presence' as well as 'arrival' in Greek. Today's passage is used by many as a basis for their belief that the second advent is Christ coming to a believer at the point of death. But can such an idea be substantiated from this passage?

FURTHER STUDY

1 Cor. 15:35-58;
John 6:40;
2 Cor. 4:14; 5:8

1. What is the promise to every believer?

2. How is this different from Christ's return?

Peter asks Jesus a question concerning the disciple John: 'Lord, what about him?' Jesus replies: 'If I want him to remain alive until I return, what is that to you? You must follow me.' At this point the evangelist adds this explanatory comment: 'Because of this, the rumour spread among the brothers that this disciple would not die.' Clearly the disciples interpreted Jesus' remark as meaning that John would live until the second coming. But John refutes this idea by saying: 'Jesus did not say that he would not die; he only said, "If I want him to remain alive until I return, what is that to you?"'

To equate Christ's return with death on the basis of this passage is to ignore the clarification made by John. In Philippians 1:23 the apostle Paul makes it crystal clear that death is not Christ coming to the believer, but the believer going to be with Him.

Lord Jesus, my Saviour and my God, the prospect that one day I will be with You quickens my spiritual pulse and moves me forward in glad anticipation. In the meantime may I stay ever faithful and alert. For Your own dear name's sake. Amen.

As ... so

For reading & meditation – Acts 1:1–11

'This same Jesus, who has been taken from you into heaven, will come back in the same way ...' (v.11)

If Christ's second coming is not something which will never happen, nor something which has already happened, nor something which is always happening – what is it? It is something which is yet to happen, as the New Testament repeatedly and emphatically asserts and as the multiplying signs around us reveal.

My point here is simply to affirm the fact that one day in the future our Lord is going to return to planet earth. It is not the fact of His coming that will surprise expectant believers, nor even the manner of His coming; it will be the moment of it. The words uttered by the angels to the disciples as He returned to heaven from the Mount of Olives, recorded in our reading today, indicate that as He went away, so He will come back. He went away visibly; He will come back visibly. He went up from earth to heaven; He will come back from heaven to earth. He left from the Mount of Olives; He will return to the Mount of Olives.

A preacher I know tells how during a visit to Israel in September 1983 he was astonished to hear of an Israeli professor of Hebrew in the University of Jerusalem who publicly professed his faith in the imminence of the coming Messiah, and who said that were it to happen in his time, he would like to go to the top of the Mount of Olives and greet Him. He said also that he would take Him by the hand and ask Him this question: 'Sir, is this your first or second visit to planet earth?' We know what His answer would be!

FURTHER STUDY

1 John 2:1-28;
1 Thess. 5:23;
1 Tim. 6:14

1. How are we to live in the light of Christ's return?

2. What was Paul's prayer for the Thessalonians?

Lord Jesus, You fulfil every promise made concerning You, and I know You will fulfil the ones that predict Your coming again to this world. I wait the fulfilment of that promise with a sure and a certain hope. Amen.

The last word

For reading & meditation – Isaiah 40:18–31

'"To whom will you compare me? Or who is my equal?"
says the Holy One.' (v.25)

O n the last day of our theme, we remind ourselves of some
of the salient points we have made as we have meditated
on God's surprises.

God's work, we said, is seen clearly 'only now and then'. The
Almighty breaks into the world and into lives with surprises
that serve as mountain peaks from which we can view the rest
of His more subtle work. We have stood together upon some of
those mountain peaks and surveyed the wonder of this most

FURTHER STUDY

Exod. 8:1-10;
15:11;
2 Sam. 7:22;
Psa. 89:6;
John 20:28

1. What did
Moses declare
to Pharaoh?

2. What did
Thomas declare?

surprising God – the way He answers prayer, the
manner in which His Spirit draws people to Himself,
the turning of the ordinary into the extraordinary,
the way He pours into our souls eternal joy, the
revelation of the Church, the glory of the incarnation
and His coming again.

I wonder how many surprises the Lord has waiting
for you. Learn to look out for them, for you never
know what God is going to do next. One can go
through life missing elusive surprises – sunsets,
deer, brooks, birds, and strange stirrings in our lives.

You can be sure of this: God's surprises will appear – watch out
for them and don't let them slip away into the unseen. Knowing
that God specialises in surprises, and that from time to time He
breaks through in surprising ways in every believer's life, makes
life an adventure. Be ready for all that God has for you up ahead,
and look out for those times when you walk around some bend in
the road or are encompassed about in darkness and the Almighty
whispers in your ear: Surprise!

**Lord God, how can I thank You adequately for the surprises of the
past and the ones that are still to come? I await the future with
expectancy and joy. May I be always alert so that I shall not miss a
single one of Your great surprises. In Jesus' name. Amen.**

Bringing the Bible to Life

There's more!

For reading & meditation – Luke 4:14–30

'... and he began by saying to them, "Today this scripture is
fulfilled in your hearing."' (v.21)

This theme came to me following intensive travel, during
which I had the privilege of talking with a number of readers.
'*Every Day with Jesus* is my lifeline,' confessed one. 'I just couldn't
get through the day without it.' 'It is my daily link with God,'
commented another.

Kind and generous things were said by many, but what
surprised and saddened me was discovering that for many this
is their *only* contact with the Bible. *Every Day with Jesus* is a good
appetiser but not a full meal; a healthy supplement
but not a substitute for regular intake from the
Bible. My message to all those whose only contact
with Scripture is through these readings is: *there's
more!* Hopefully too, those of you already engaged in
further exploration of the Bible will discover ways to
gain more when you study the Scriptures.

FURTHER STUDY

1 Tim. 4:6-15;
Phil. 3:7-11;
2 Tim. 3:10-17

1. What was
Paul's charge
to Timothy?

2. What was
Paul's desire?

Pastor Robinson, one of the Pilgrim Fathers, used
to say: 'God has much more light to break out from
His Word.' He has. When Jesus stood up in the synagogue at
Nazareth and read the passage from Isaiah He said: 'Today this
scripture is fulfilled in your hearing.' In Jesus revelation passed
from law to life, from a book to a Person. Now that Person gives
the fullest meaning to the book. The more we know of the Bible
the more we will know of Christ. Our main motivation in wanting
to understand the Bible better is not simply to gain knowledge but
to increase our knowledge of *Him*. The more we know of Him the
more love we will have for Him.

**Father, I am so thankful that in the Bible I have a book from which
light continually breaks forth. Help me discover more ways of
opening up its treasures. In Christ's name I pray. Amen.**

The inexhaustible book

For reading & meditation – Acts 1:1–11

'He appeared to them over a period of forty days and
spoke about the kingdom of God.' (v.3)

I mentioned Pastor Robinson's statement: 'God has much more
light to break out from His Word.' Can we discover something
new from the Bible each time we read it?

Yes, if my experience is anything to go by. I have been reading
the Bible on a daily basis for over fifty years and nearly every
time I tingle with anticipation for I know it will yield new vistas
and surprises. One reader, after becoming a Christian, started to
study her Bible every morning and evening. Her husband, a non-
Christian, having observed her poring over her Bible
day after day for about six months, finally asked:
'Haven't you finished that book yet?' How can you
'finish' a book that reveals the Divine Mind? Easier to
put the ocean into a thimble. John Wesley described
the Bible as 'the inexhaustible book'. It is. Today's
passage says that after His death and resurrection,
Christ appeared to some of His followers over a
period of forty days 'and spoke about the kingdom of
God'. So the revelation was not merely a physical one
but a spiritual one also – a revelation of His meaning and purpose.
Through the pages of the Bible He has been revealing Himself ever
since, continuously and inexhaustibly.

I expect this devotional aid to be exhausted of its meaning after
one reading – hence the succession of new editions. But you can
never exhaust the Bible's meaning. The inexhaustible Christ lives
in its pages, and because of that new light can always be expected
'to break out from His Word'.

FURTHER STUDY

John 1:1–18;
1 John 1:1–4;
Rev. 19:11–13

1. What does
John proclaim?

2. What is one
of the names
of Christ?

Lord Jesus Christ, the more I see in You the more I realise there is to
be seen. I am on a great adventure of discovery and growth.
My soul is alert and ready to know more of You and Your Word.
Lead on dear Saviour. I follow. Amen.

How to *make* time

For reading & meditation – Proverbs 25:15–28
'Like a city whose walls are broken down is a man who
lacks self-control.' (v.28)

Perhaps you are feeling a little threatened by the challenge of
spending more time reading the Bible. You may be thinking
that it will absorb more time than you can afford. If so, kindly I say
it, you are mistaken. *Time spent with the Bible is of incalculable
worth.* If Christ is willing to come into our lives and reveal Himself
to us through the pages of His Word, is there not something almost
blasphemous in wondering whether we can give Him time? We
must *make* time. But how can a busy person make time?

Time is made by going over one's life and pruning
out all unnecessary occupations. So spend some
moments today with God going over your days to see
what is not worthwhile. Don't cut down on essentials,
such as healthy recreation (if God assures you it is
not excessive), or family time. Look instead at such
time-wasters as watching television and reading
newspapers. Many people who have told me they
haven't 'a moment to spare' actually squander hours
like this. God does not want us to neglect anything
essential but I promise you if you prayerfully ask
Him for guidance He will help you recast your priorities and show
you how to salvage time that can be spent in connecting with Him.
There need be no tenseness in this exercise; tell yourself you are
going to use the time reclaimed for better ends.

Remember, as Christians we are answerable to God for our
use of time. Don't fritter it away. *Shape* your days. You really
can *make* time.

FURTHER STUDY

Psa. 90:1-12;
Eph. 5:15-16;
James 4:14

1. What was
the psalmist's
prayer?

2. How does
James describe
the brevity
of time?

**Father, I see that the art of making time begins with me. Help me
realign my priorities so that You have first claim on my time.
In Jesus' name. Amen.**

Once is not enough

For reading & meditation – Romans 12:1–8

'Do not conform any longer to the pattern of this world,
but be transformed by the renewing of your mind.' (v.2)

Every waking moment of our lives we are operating from one of two viewpoints – human or divine. Most of us, if we are honest, will admit that a good deal of the time we are influenced by what we read in the newspapers, hear on the radio or see on television. Human opinions tend to have a greater influence on us than those of God Himself.

The only way we can correct this is by exposing our minds more and more to His Word, the Bible. On average it takes between five and eight minutes to read the set passage and comments on any one page of *Every Day with Jesus*. Many have told me over the years that God has used His Word (and sometimes my comments) in remarkable ways to bring comfort, encouragement, guidance and illumination to their lives. If God can do that with five minutes of devotional time then think what He could do for those who would give time during the day to additional study of His Word.

As I have indicated, the reason that we allow human opinions to shape us instead of being governed by the commands and principles of the Bible is because we do not spend enough time immersing ourselves in its pages. A Christian brother remarked: 'I once read the Bible through from beginning to end just as I would read any book. Isn't that enough?' No, it is not enough. So contrary to God's will are our own ideas that we need constant exposure to the Bible for them to be corrected. Take it from me, once is not enough.

FURTHER STUDY

Phil. 4:1–8;
Rom. 8:6;
Eph. 4:23;
1 Cor. 2:16

1. What did Paul say finally to the Philippians?

2. How can we know the mind of Christ?

My Father and my God, help me understand that the continuous entrance of Your Word gives light and the continuous neglect of it brings darkness. Make me a person of the book.
In Jesus' name. Amen.

Where are we heading?

For reading & meditation – Psalm 119:81–88

'Preserve my life according to your love, and I will obey the statutes of your mouth.' (v.88)

Cardinal Newman is reported to have said: 'I read my Bible to know what people ought to do, and I read my newspaper to know what they are doing.' Which exerts the greatest influence on our lives – the newspaper or the Bible? Statistics reveal that only a small percentage of Christians read the Bible regularly. If this trend is not reversed, we will see a generation of newspaper-minded people rather than Bible-minded people – shallow and flighty rather than deep and steady.

Dr E. Stanley Jones quoted Bishop Paul Kern as saying: 'I read my Bible because within its pages (a) I find power for the ordering of my inner life, (b) it offers a way of escape from those perils which threaten our modern life, (c) in its pages are found the secret by which men walk the pathways of light and hope and freedom, (d) it assures me that man is supremely dear to God, (e) it tells me whither I am bound, and (f) it teaches me that the lesson of life is to believe what the years and centuries say, as against the hours.'

FURTHER STUDY

1 John 5:1-13;
John 20:31;
Rom. 15:4;
Psa. 119:103

1. Why have the Scriptures been written?

2. What was the psalmist's experience?

The words of that last statement came originally from Emerson; what deep insight they reveal. Those who neglect their Bible are swayed by what happens in the hours; those who know their Bibles have a perspective that enables them to see all things from God's point of view. An eagle never worries about how to cross a puddle. It operates from a higher position. So does a Christian whose worldview is based on the Bible and not on the daily newspaper.

Father, save me from becoming more newspaper-minded than Bible-minded. Help me soak myself in Scripture so that I think Your thoughts. In Christ's peerless and precious name I pray. Amen.

No ordinary book

For reading & meditation – Hebrews 4:1–13
'For the word of God is living and active.' (v.12)

Just what do we have to do to make the Bible come alive for us? Posing the question this way suggests that for some the Bible is not a living book. Many Christians have told me they are constrained by a sense of duty to read a short portion of it every day but are glad when they can turn to something more interesting. When I tell them that what they find dull and boring I find fascinating and engrossing they seem to disbelieve me. How strange that a book so forbidding to one person can be so exciting to another. So just how do we tap into the Bible's power?

FURTHER STUDY

2 Pet. 1:1–21;
Jer. 36:2;
Ezek. 1:3;
Acts 1:16;
2 Tim. 3:16

1. How did Peter describe the origin of Scripture?

2. How did Paul put it to Timothy?

First, *realise that the Bible is no ordinary book.* If you view the Bible as nothing more than the record of a group of Semitic tribes who lived centuries ago and the account of an unusual teacher by the name of Jesus of Nazareth, plus the correspondence of some of His disciples, well, it is hardly likely to arrest you. If you believe, on the other hand, that the Bible is in the most special sense the Word of God, that it is the only book God ever published, then you will approach it with a sense of awe. Sometimes when I take my Bible in my hands I find myself trembling with excitement as I say to myself: 'Here are the Almighty's thoughts put into writing. I wonder how He will use them to direct my life today.'

Our appreciation of the book will depend on whether we regard it as the word of humans or the Word of God. The Bible is God's book – His one and only published work.

Father, forgive me if my familiarity with Your book causes me to forget that it is divinely inspired. In the light of this help me come to it with reverence. In Christ's name I pray. Amen.

God's Word – God's voice

For reading & meditation – 1 Thessalonians 2:1–16

'... you received the word of God ... accepted it not as the
word of men, but as ... the word of God ...' (v.13)

Paul compliments the Christians at Thessalonica for not
merely listening to what he said when he preached to them
but receiving it as God's Word. Eugene Peterson paraphrases:
'You remember us in those days, friends, working our fingers
to the bone ... moonlighting so you wouldn't have the burden of
supporting us while we proclaimed God's *Message* to you' (v.9).
I like the phrase 'God's Message' for the Bible really is a divine
personal communication.

As you open up your Bible and realise you are
reading God's message to you doesn't it send a
tingle down your spine? Charles Swindoll says:
'God's book is, as it were, God's voice ... If our Lord
were to make Himself visible and return to earth
and speak His message it would be in keeping with
this book. His message of truth would tie in exactly
with what you see in Scripture. His opinions, His
counsel, His commands, His desires, His warnings,
His very mind.' When we start to read the Bible and realise we
are hearing God's voice then it inevitably makes a difference to
the way we evaluate it.

FURTHER STUDY

John 6:63;
Matt. 4:1-11;
24:35

1. How did
Jesus describe
His words?

2. How are
we to live?

Liberally minded Christians – those who believe that the Bible
is largely composed of human thoughts, which God uses to make
His mind known – can never be certain that they are listening to
the voice of God. Perhaps that is why people with this viewpoint
never seem to say much about the importance of reading the Bible
frequently. Why should they? They cannot be sure that it is God
who is speaking to them from His Word.

**Father, I see so clearly that my view of Scripture will influence the
way I approach it. Help me understand that it carries your message
– a message that is personal to me. In Jesus' name I pray. Amen.**

God's Word *written*

For reading & meditation – Luke 24:13–35

'... he explained to them what was said in all the Scriptures concerning himself.' (v.27)

How can we be sure that the Bible is true and absolutely reliable? Let's take a closer look at the passage before us today and see what we can learn from it.

In verse 27 we are told: 'And beginning with Moses and all the Prophets, he explained to them what was said in all the Scriptures concerning himself.' On that dramatic walk with the two on the road to Emmaus our Lord worked His way verbally through the Old Testament, which is described here as 'the Scriptures'. Later, Cleopas and his companion used the same term when they said: 'Were not our hearts burning within us while he talked with us on the road and opened the Scriptures to us?' (v.32).

As you know, the word 'Bible' does not appear in either the Old or the New Testament. Instead the word 'Scriptures' is used. This is a translation of the Greek word *graphe* which means 'that which is written'. As Christians we rely on what has been written – not merely thought or spoken but *written*. Our heavenly Father put His message into language people could understand and has preserved and protected it so that it has survived the ravages of time and comes to us with as much authority as when it was first given. I am so grateful for that, aren't you? Adam and Eve had a verbal revelation and the devil was able to persuade them they had misunderstood what God had told them. We have even less excuse than they did. God has now put what He wants us to know in writing.

FURTHER STUDY

John 2:17-22;
5:17-40;
1 Cor. 10:11

1. When did the disciples believe the Scripture?

2. What did the Jews refuse to believe?

Father, thank You that I have Your *written* Word in my hands, and that all I need to do is stand in faith on it. Amen.

God's truth

For reading & meditation – John 17:1–26

'Sanctify them by the truth; your word is truth.' (v.17)

Another reason for approaching the Bible with a sense of reverence is that it is 'God's truth'. Before us today is the longest recorded prayer of our Lord Jesus Christ, which includes: 'Sanctify them by the truth; your word is truth.' God's Word can be relied upon. It is honest, true and has integrity.

Today, in what has been called the 'postmodern society', people don't seem to have the same regard for truth as did the generations that preceded us. In the opening pages of *The Screwtape Letters* C.S. Lewis depicts the devil advising his minions that they should not talk about truth and falsehood when tempting people on earth but about what is useful or what is practical. 'That's the way to get through,' says the devil. Have you noticed that people no longer consider truth to be absolute? They often think that what is true is right today but will not necessarily be so tomorrow, whereas according to the Bible what is true today will always be true.

FURTHER STUDY

Acts 17:1-11;
2 Tim. 3:15;
2 Cor. 3:3

1. How often were the Scriptures examined?

2. What was Paul able to say about Timothy?

On a flight once, I gave a young university student my testimony of how I came to know Christ. His response? 'I'm very happy for you. That was true for you, but it may not be true for me.' This reflects the spirit of the age in which we live – truth for modern people (generally speaking) is relative. I like what James Boice, a US Bible teacher, says in his book *Can We trust the Bible?*: 'God uses His Word to accomplish His purposes whether men and women believe in the Word of truth or not.'

Heavenly Father, I live in an age of relativism when people evaluate truth by their own subjectivity rather than Your objectivity. But I am guided by Your eternal revelation – the Bible. 'Here I stand. I can do no other.' Amen.

The divine impulse

For reading & meditation – 2 Peter 1:12–21

'... men spoke from God as they were carried along by
the Holy Spirit.' (v.21)

Aman admitted: 'If I could be sure that I was reading the
unadulterated Word of God I think it would make a world of
difference to the way I came to my Bible.' How can we be certain
that when we read God's Word we are not taking in a mixture of
the human and the divine?

Today's passage tells us how the Scriptures came to be
written: 'For prophecy never had its origin in the will of man,
but men spoke from God as they were carried along by the

FURTHER STUDY

Jer. 1:1-9;
Neh. 9:30;
Heb. 1:1;
Ezek. 3:17

1. What was
Jeremiah's
testimony?

2. What did
the writer to
the Hebrews
declare?

Holy Spirit' (v.21). Though the personality of the
writers shines through their writings, the *impulse*
to write came from God and He supervised the
proceedings so that what He wanted to say was
said. When Peter wrote, 'Prophecy never had its
origin in the will of man,' I take that to mean that
Peter or Paul (or any of the other writers) did not
suddenly say, 'I think I will write to the Christians
in Ephesus today.' No, 'men spoke from God as they
were carried along by the Holy Spirit.'

The phrase 'carried along' is translated from an
ancient Greek nautical term, which was used to
describe a ship being borne along by the wind. God moved the
writers of Scripture who, without losing their own style, wrote
what He intended them to say. So what Scripture says, God says.
Once we believe that the Holy God did indeed inspire prophets and
priests, evangelists and apostles to write what He wanted to say
then it is impossible for us to treat the Bible as an ordinary book.

*My Father, quicken my spirit, I pray, so that as I take the Bible in
my hands I will sense I am communing with the Divine.
This container may be an earthly vessel but what comes through
is living water. Amen.*

'The divine current'

For reading & meditation – Colossians 3:1-17
'Let the word of Christ dwell in you richly...' (v.16)

Our appreciation of the Bible is affected by whether we view it as an ordinary book or an extraordinary book. Once we believe that God did inspire each writer, and that the Bible conveys the message of God, then our hearts will become teachable. We will come to it not thinking first of personal enjoyment but only of understanding how we may best translate its message into life.

J.B. Phillips, translator of the New Testament, said that his experience of reading a particular portion of the Bible was like 'tracing the electric wiring in an old house where the current had not been turned off'. When did you last open your Bible and feel the divine current go through your soul as you realised God was using His Word to speak directly to you? That rarely happens to those who approach the Bible as if it were an ordinary book. Scripture has spoken to the minds of people in every age, and its 'rediscovery' has been responsible for the outbreak of great spiritual revivals. Christians speak with respect of the writings of other faiths but see the Bible as belonging to a class all of its own. It is not the first among equals; there is nothing to compare with it.

FURTHER STUDY

Ezek. 37:1-14;
Jer. 5:14; 23:29;
James 1:18

1. What was Ezekiel's experience of the prophetic word?

2. How is God's Word described?

How can we help, then, but pore over it, store it in our memories, learn the route through life it has mapped out for us and regard it as a great privilege to be able to read it every day? We follow John Wesley who described himself as a man of 'one book' – God's book.

Lord God, may it be said of me too that I am a person of one book. Help me open myself to the Bible so that Christ's mind may be in my mind. This I ask in His name. Amen.

The big bonfire

For reading & meditation – 2 Peter 3:1–18

'... the elements will be destroyed by fire, and the earth and everything in it will be laid bare.' (v.10)

Scripture is not like a textbook that constantly has to be rewritten to keep up with modern findings. It contains eternal truth – not something that varies with each passing generation. Only two things on earth can be classed as 'eternal' – the people of God, and the Word of God. Everything else will ultimately be destroyed. Today's reading reminds us that one day there will be a big bonfire onto which everything material will be thrown. But not the Word of God. His truth abides for ever. And whether we allow our minds to be influenced more by the divine than the human will depend on how much time we give to absorbing God's Word.

FURTHER STUDY

Isa. 40:1-8;
1 Pet. 1:22-25;
Psa. 119:89;
Matt. 5:18

1. What was Isaiah's conviction?

2. Of what was the psalmist certain?

A Christian's home was flooded. When the water receded, an ankle-deep deposit of mud was left. The owner walked into his basement where he kept all his awards. Everything was now covered in mud. As he stood there staring in unbelief he thought he heard God say: 'Don't worry about all this stuff; I was going to burn it up anyway.'

Remembering this fact puts things into perspective, doesn't it? A story like that prompts me to give more of my mind to the things that will last for ever. This does not mean we should neglect other important matters. We can't spend all of our time reading the Bible but I am sure each one of us, with a little reprioritising, could spend more of our time studying what God has to say to us.

My Father and my God, deepen the conviction that when I come to Your book I am coming to a book that is different from every other book. May I open its pages with reverence and awe. Amen.

Loving the Author

For reading & meditation – 1 Corinthians 2:6–16

'The man without the Spirit does not accept ... things ...
from the Spirit ... they are spiritually discerned.' (v.14)

The Bible can seem dull or dynamic, depending on how well you know the One who brought it into being. Generally you have to read and understand a book in order to know the author; with the Bible you have to know the Author before you can understand the book.

A writer friend tells how a woman confessed to him that though she had read most of his books she had not found them very interesting. Some years later they fell in love and were married. Then she became one of his greatest fans. Before I became a Christian I found the parts of the Bible I read dull, boring and difficult to comprehend. After my conversion, however, all that changed. It was as if (as someone else has described it) God took the Bible up into heaven, rewrote it and sent it back to earth again. What made the difference? Knowing the Author. Things that had appeared boring and difficult to understand became interesting and clear. When you enter into a relationship with the Trinity then the Holy Spirit unveils the truths of Scripture to the mind, and what previously seemed dark and mysterious comes alive with new and surprising meaning. It is not a matter of intellect; it is a matter of illumination.

FURTHER STUDY

Heb. 12:1-11;
Rev. 1:12-18;
22:13

1. How does Hebrews describe Jesus?

2. How does John describe Him?

Today's text tells us that our natural minds are incapable of understanding the things that are of God. We need the Holy Spirit to disclose them. God has revealed His Word to us, but we need to have a relationship with Him for that revelation to be fully understood.

**Heavenly Father, deepen my relationship with You, I pray, for I see
that the more I know You the more clearly I will understand Your
Word. When I come to the Bible I need Your illumination.
Thank You Father. Amen.**

Unnecessary repetition?

For reading & meditation – Numbers 9:15–23

'Whenever the cloud lifted ... the Israelites set out;
wherever the cloud settled, the Israelites encamped.' (v.17)

This passage may seem surprising, but I have selected it because it is one of those that seemed irrelevant to me before I came to know the Author. I can remember sitting in a Sunday school class reading this passage and saying to my teacher: 'There is a lot of repetition here. If I were to write like this in one of my essays at school my teacher there would put a red line through it and say: "You have repeated yourself too often."' Over and again the statement is made that when the cloud remained over the tabernacle the Israelites stayed put; when it lifted they began to move. That point, it seemed to me, was clearly conveyed between verses 15 and 17. Why then was it made again in the following verses?

FURTHER STUDY

John 9:5; 10:7;
11:25; 14:1–6; 15:1

1. What statement of Jesus does John repeat in his record?

2. What is its significance?

Astonishingly, when I became a Christian the purpose of this passage suddenly became clear. God is telling us that when He says 'Stop' we are to stop; when He says 'Go' then we are to go. Don't we get into a great deal of difficulty because we go when God says 'Stop' and stop when He says 'Go'? Obedience is one of the most important lessons we have to learn, and some of us need to have it spelt out not only in the clearest of terms but also repeatedly before we take it in. *The Reader's Digest Condensed Bible* eliminates these repetitions and condenses the whole passage to just a few words. When God's Word is mutilated like this I can't help but feel that those responsible don't know the Author.

Father, how different words and sentences become when we are acquainted with the Author of those words and sentences. There is no knowledge of Your Word without You. Thank You Father. Amen.

The inner witness

For reading & meditation – John 14:15–31

'But the Counsellor, the Holy Spirit ... will teach you
all things ...' (v.26)

Once we have come into a relationship with Jesus Christ, the Holy Spirit helps us understand the Bible and convinces us that it is the infallible Word of God. This is not the only ministry of the Spirit, but it is a primary one.

The theologian James Packer writes about his experience as a young man at Oxford University. He was conscious that he had been converted yet different influences led him to view the Bible as nothing more than a bag of religious all-sorts. One night he attended a Bible study led by a layman who gave what he calls 'a rather esoteric exposition of one of the chapters of the book of Revelation'. Though the man said nothing about the doctrine of divine inspiration James Packer came to a sudden awareness that the whole of the Bible was truly the Word of God. He says he remembers feeling rather surprised at what had occurred.

FURTHER STUDY

John 15:18–27;
16:13;
1 John 4:6

1. How did Jesus describe the Holy Spirit?

2. How did He describe His work?

A full appreciation of what had happened came to him some years later when he was reading John Calvin's *Institutes of the Christian Religion*. In that lengthy work Calvin explains how Scripture, though written by men, comes to us authoritatively from God, and claims that every true believer gains the certainty that what he is reading is the Word of the living God. This certainty is not an emotional experience but a conscious realisation and Calvin ascribed it to what he called 'the inward witness of the Spirit'. That state of certainty governs the way I read my Bible every day of my life. How about you?

Father, how can I sufficiently thank You for bringing me not only to the point of believing Your Word but also to the point of being unable to doubt it? My gratitude just won't go into words. Amen.

'Weeds of doubt'

For reading & meditation – James 4:1–12

'Wash your hands, you sinners, and purify your hearts,
you double-minded.' (v.8)

Although knowing the Author gives us a new perspective on the Scriptures it does not necessarily follow that all doubts are instantly swept away. At the start of his evangelistic ministry Billy Graham had a crisis of confidence in the Bible which God brought him through. Brian Stiller of Canada describes his own experience in this way: 'My mind was plagued with doubts about the Bible. One night in Lausanne, at the International Congress on World Evangelism, God spoke to me, providing faith to trust the Bible to be God's Word. That was a pivotal moment. I arose with a heart of faith … and never looked back to the old doubts.'

FURTHER STUDY

James 1:1–8;
Luke 9:57–62;
1 Kings 18:21

1. What is the result of double-mindedness?

2. How did Jesus put this to those who wanted to follow Him?

In my teens I too was sceptical. One night I struggled with my misgivings, asking God to help me through the problems I was experiencing in relation to the Bible. Critics of the Scriptures had sown the weeds of doubt in my heart and they threatened to overwhelm the little faith that I had. As the dawn broke God sent His Holy Spirit as the Divine Weedkiller and all my doubts disappeared. I rose with the conviction that the Bible truly is the Word of God and I have never had a moment of uncertainty about it since.

As men and women leave liberal theological colleges unsure about the reliability of the Bible we need to pray that when they spend time with God His Spirit will assure them that His Word is true. Have any weeds of doubt grown up in your heart? God has a Divine Weedkiller available to you just for the asking.

Gracious and loving heavenly Father, if there are any doubts in my heart concerning the reliability of Your Word then pour Your Divine Weedkiller on them today. I want to be a person of faith, not doubt. Amen.

'Other people's letters'

For reading & meditation – John 16:1-16

'... the Spirit will take from what is mine and make it known to you.' (v .15)

There can be no illumination of the Scriptures without the aid of Holy Spirit. But once we come into a relationship with God through His Son Jesus Christ we are given the Holy Spirit, Who is the divine Illuminator. This is because, as we saw the other day, God's truth is hidden from the human intellect and is understood only when God reveals it. It is possible to earn a degree in theology and still not understand the Bible.

There was once a man in my congregation with a PhD in theology but after almost every sermon I preached he would come up to me and say: 'I can't understand it; you draw out from the Bible things I never knew were there.' I discovered that although he had received a high level of theological education he had never personally committed himself to Jesus Christ. He could understand the Bible's literature, its style, its history, its geography, but he could not grasp the *meaning* of Scripture, which is made clear not by education but by the Spirit's unveiling.

FURTHER STUDY

Eph. 1:1-10;
Neh. 9:20;
Amos 3:7;
2 Cor. 3:6

1. What did Paul say the letter does?

2. What did he contrast this with?

A schoolteacher who was an agnostic loved to taunt the Christians in his class by saying that the Bible makes no sense to rationally minded people. One day he happened to mention he had been reading Paul's letters and could not understand any of his statements. A young student raised his hand and said: 'Excuse me, Sir. Paul's letters were written to and for Christians. Now I can see why you are confused. That's what you get for reading other people's letters.'

Spirit of the living God, I am so grateful that You are not only the Inspirer of the Word but the Illuminator of it also. Open my eyes that I might continuously behold wondrous things from its pages. Amen.

'No full revelation'

For reading & meditation – Acts 18:18–28; 19:1–7

'... Priscilla and Aquila ... explained to him the way of God more adequately.' (v.26)

How much we owe to the ministry of the Holy Spirit can never be fully appreciated. Suppose Jesus had not sent the Holy Spirit. Just what kind of Christianity would the world have known? We would simply have had the record of the four Gospels.

If we accept for the moment that verses 9 to 20 of Mark 16 are not part of the original manuscript, then the final words of Mark's Gospel are: 'They said nothing to anyone, because they were afraid' (16:8). Although the resurrection had taken place, the disciples were bound by inner fears. They needed the power of the Holy Spirit to dissipate those fears, and that is exactly what happened when the Spirit came. As someone has put it: 'Rabbits became ferrets at Pentecost.'

From the account of events that took place at Ephesus, we get a picture of Holy Spirit-less Christianity. When Paul arrived there he sensed a central lack so his first question was: 'Did you receive the Holy Spirit when you believed?' They answered: 'No, we have not even heard that there is a Holy Spirit' (Acts 19:2). There were about twelve men in that group but what were they doing? Apparently just holding their own. Their spiritual leader, Apollos, was 'a learned man, with a thorough knowledge of the Scriptures' (18:24). Yet he knew only the baptism of John. It is one thing to be learned and have a knowledge of the Scriptures; it is another to have the Holy Spirit illuminate them. Without the Holy Spirit there is no full revelation.

FURTHER STUDY

Matt. 3:1-11;
Joel 2:28;
Luke 11:13;
24:49;
Acts 1:8

1. What did John declare?

2. What parallel did Jesus draw?

Father, how much we owe to the coming of the Spirit at Pentecost. There is no excuse for us to hide behind closed doors. We have an open road. Thank You dear Father. Amen.

Scripture's central theme

For reading & meditation – John 1:43–51

'We have found the one Moses wrote about ... about whom
the prophets also wrote – Jesus of Nazareth ...' (v.45)

Jesus Christ is the central theme of the Bible. Everything else is marginal. The whole of the Bible's message relates to God's plan of redemption through Christ, and without a knowledge of Him then it simply cannot be understood. Just as there is a road in every part of England that will eventually lead to London so there is a path in every book of the Bible that leads to Christ. All the Old Testament truths converge upon Him; all the New Testament truths emerge from Him.

In Genesis He is the Seed of the woman, in Exodus the Passover Lamb, in Leviticus the Pillar of Cloud by day and the Pillar of Fire by night, in Judges He is the Great Deliverer, in Ruth He is the Heavenly Kinsman, in Kings the Promised Sovereign, in Nehemiah the Restorer of His People, in Esther the Great Advocate, in Psalms the All in All, in Proverbs the Great Pattern, in Ecclesiastes the Answer to the Search for Meaning, in the Song of Songs the Great Lover, in the Prophets the Prince of Peace, in the Gospels the One who Seeks and Saves, in the Epistles the Great Redeemer, and in Revelation the King of kings and Lord of lords. He is the Word bigger than human words.

A man was reading his Bible on a train when a bright-faced older woman turned to him and said: 'You must love the Lord for I see you are reading His Word. I too love Him and have served Him some sixty years.' At once they became friends, drawn to a mutual friendship with the great Friend.

FURTHER STUDY

Eph. 3:1-6;
John 1:4; 8:12;
10:10;
Acts 9:1-19

1. How was the mystery of Christ made known to Paul?

2. What two things did Paul experience from the living Word?

Father, I am so thankful that I have come to a knowledge of Your Son, Jesus. He is the Key to everything. The more I know of Him the more I find the Bible makes sense. Amen.

'One, two, three, go!'

For reading & meditation – Psalm 119:17–24

'Open my eyes that I may see wonderful things in your law.'
(v.18)

Another way in which we can ensure the Bible comes alive for us is to approach it prayerfully. When you open your Bible you should be aware that the book you hold, written by men who were specially guided by the Holy Spirit, will be understood in all its richness only by those who have the same divine help. So pray before you start reading the Bible; ask God to help you to understand it.

This kind of praying can become a formality. We can easily utter a prayer without much meaning or expectation, but if we recognise this danger we can guard against it. Prayer quietens the spirit and sharpens our sense of anticipation. Rarely will the Bible speak to us if we come to it in a manner that is rushed. A little girl decided to pray for her sick father in her bedtime prayers. 'Oh Lord,' she said, 'make my Daddy better, one, two three, go!' I am sure God smiles at such a prayer but I am not so sure that He smiles if one of His mature children approaches the Bible with the same kind of petition: 'Lord, show me what You want to say to me today, one, two, three, go!' A few quiet moments of prayer before opening up the Bible will make us receptive to God's voice.

FURTHER STUDY

Psa. 119:145-152;
5:3;
Luke 18:1-8;
John 16:24

1. What was the psalmist's approach?

2. How should we prayerfully approach God's Word?

Over the years I have suggested this to many people and this is a typical response: 'I never realised that pausing to still my soul and ask for God's illumination could make such a difference.' So from today forward decide not to rush into the Bible but to quieten your heart by expectant prayer.

Father, help me to approach Your Word with quiet expectation – expectation that my weakness will become strength, my doubt become faith, my darkness become light. Thank You Father. Amen.

'Your servant speaks'

For reading & meditation – 1 Samuel 3:1–21

'Then Samuel said, "Speak, for your servant is listening."'
(v.10)

Instead of taking the Bible for granted we must quieten our soul and echo the words of today's text: 'Speak, for your servant is listening.' Far too often we come to the Word of God with this attitude: 'Listen, for your servant is speaking.' Forgive me for using an illustration I have used before but I cannot think of a better way of expressing what I am trying to convey. If you stalk through a forest you will probably see and hear very little. However, if you sit down quietly soon the squirrels will come out, the birds will begin to sing, and the whole forest will come alive.

Approaching the Bible prayerfully can become a formality, but if our hearts are sincere then the words we use in our prayers will be sincere too.

Some Christians I know try to have their daily Quiet Time on their way to work in their car. In my opinion this is not a good idea. There is nothing wrong with listening to devotional tapes or music while driving but don't let this become a substitute for your daily Quiet Time. Better to get up fifteen minutes earlier or arrive at work early and find a quiet spot (if possible) than have your concentration divided. The Bible comes alive to those who approach it with a receptive heart and it is doubtful whether that is possible in the midst of busy traffic. Now you may say, of course, that you are the exception to this. I will not argue. In my experience, however, God speaks to those whose attention is fixed on Him.

FURTHER STUDY

Psa. 130:1-8;
27:14;
Isa. 30:18

1. Where was the psalmist's hope?

2. What is promised to those who wait on the Lord?

Father, I live in a busy world when time pressures seem to get greater every year. Help me guard the time I give to You and to Your Word. This I ask in Jesus' name. Amen.

'Close the door'

For reading & meditation – Matthew 6:1–15

'But when you pray, go into your room, close the door and pray to your Father, who is unseen.' (v.6)

When I was in college training for the ministry a tutor defined prayer in this way: 'Prayer,' he said, 'is relaxed receptivity.' One of the students suggested that the word 'relaxed' was unnecessary. This triggered a long debate in which the tutor backed down and agreed that receptivity *implies* a relaxed state of mind. To be receptive, we all agreed, one must be relaxed. You cannot inscribe anything on a tense mind. Now I know that occasionally people have started to read their Bible when they have been tense and without first praying and God has used something from His Word to bring peace and comfort to their hearts. That can happen, but it is no argument for laying aside the suggestion I am making.

FURTHER STUDY

Psa. 46:1–11;
131:2;
Matt. 14:23;
Isa. 32:17

1. What was the psalmist able to say?

2. What example did Jesus set?

Lindsay Glegg, a well-known Christian figure on the British scene a generation ago and a regular reader of *Every Day with Jesus*, said to me in an interview a few years before he died: 'When I was a young man I read that if someone practised doing something for thirty days it would then become a habit. I decided that for a whole month I would never open my Bible without first bowing my head in prayer and inviting God to speak to me from His Word. That was the best habit I ever cultivated. I fixed the habit and the habit fixed me.' That attitude, beside being one of humility, had the effect of tilting his soul in the direction of heaven. It showed he was prepared to say: 'Speak, for your servant is listening.'

Father, give me the sense to approach Your Word with an attentive and listening spirit. Help me understand that if I am too busy to pause then I am busier than You intend me to be. In Jesus' name. Amen.

Put your soul on alert

For reading & Meditation – Lamentations 3:19–33

'The Lord is good to those whose hope is in him, to the one who seeks him …' (v.25)

Some time ago, after I had written about the need to have a surrendered spirit, a man asked: 'Isn't this a dangerous idea? By suggesting surrender and receptivity aren't you encouraging people to be spineless and obsequious? Surely Christianity teaches us to be strong and positive and to stand up for ourselves.' To be surrendered and receptive to God does not result in our becoming 'spineless and obsequious' in His presence. It means rather that we offer to God an alert self, but a self that is eager not for its own way but for God's way. When we yield ourselves to God we surrender all our fears. The effect of submission is not that the personality collapses or that we become less of a person. The surrendered self is not pulp; it is a person, but a person with a controlling purpose, and that purpose is to follow the Person, the Lord Jesus Christ, more fully.

Permit me to share my own testimony here. Before I open my Bible I try to free myself of all distractions and, as I enter God's presence, say to my heart: 'Be still. God is about to speak to you.' What we need to remember is this: more often than not it takes time for God's Spirit to get through to us. But time alone is not sufficient; we must be receptive too. So learn to pause before you open up the Word of God. Not all concerns will automatically dissolve. Some will snatch at your sleeve and say: 'What about me?' But as far as is possible set them aside and put your soul on alert.

FURTHER STUDY

Psa. 40:1-8;
1 Thess. 2:13

1. When did the Lord turn and hear David's cry?

2. Why did Paul thank God continually for the Thessalonians?

Father, help me to bring to the Quiet Time a heart that is surrendered. I cannot promise to be free of all concerns but I can promise to lay them aside so that You may speak to me. Amen.

Attentive listening

For reading & meditation – Matthew 13:1–17
'Though seeing, they do not see; though hearing, they do not hear or understand.' (v.13)

By approaching the Bible prayerfully we are saying to ourselves and God: 'You have my attention.' Attention and hearing are closely connected.

I once had a secretary with a very good education who nonetheless made so many mistakes that I had to speak to her about the matter. Since she left out of the letters she typed many of the things I had dictated to her I came to the conclusion that she might be slightly deaf. I put this idea to her and she agreed to a hearing test. Yet she came back with the report that her hearing was fine. Later I discovered the problem was not a hearing deficiency but a deficiency in attention. She was not sufficiently attentive to what I was saying and thus she did not hear much of it. When we are attentive little will escape us.

We might do well to remember also that when we pray for God to speak to us through His Word we are not overcoming God's reluctance but laying hold of His willingness. All His barriers are down. He longs to speak and make His Word come alive in our heart. The problem is never that God does not want to speak but that we are not listening carefully enough. Over and over again our Lord said to the people of His day: 'He who has ears, let him hear.' Surely, if we have ears then we can hear. Not so. It is not enough to have ears; we must make sure we are listening. Pausing for a moment of prayer before we open the Bible is a sign that we are ready for God to speak; we are waiting to hear Him.

FURTHER STUDY

Matt. 7:1-26;
Prov. 8:34;
Eccl. 5:1;
James 1:19-24

1. How did Jesus describe a foolish man?

2. What should we be quick to do?

Loving Father, just as sometimes I cup my ear to make sure I do not miss a sound, help me to do the same when I come to Your Word. I do not want to miss anything. Amen.

A great discovery

For reading & medITATION – Psalm 119:105–112

'Accept, O Lord, the willing praise of my mouth, and teach me your laws.' (v.108)

Some people may think it helpful to have a prolonged time of prayer before reading the Scriptures rather than afterwards. My reaction to this idea is 'No'. The suggestion of pausing prayerfully before opening the Bible is so that the mind will be stilled. This is quite different from having a lengthy time of prayer.

This advice is simply a recommendation. There have been times when I have fallen on my knees before opening up the pages of the Bible because some great concern was pressing upon me. Such occasions, however, are the exception. My rule has been: the Bible first, then prayer.

Most of the great devotional writers of the past say that reading the Bible before having a lengthy time of prayer has been the method most helpful to them. George Muller, who founded the famous orphanage in Bristol and saw the most wonderful answers to prayer, admitted that one of the greatest spiritual discoveries he ever made was to begin his prayer times with the reading of the Scriptures. For many years he used to pray first and then read the Scriptures, but when he changed his routine his prayer life developed a new dimension. He said: 'The reading of the Bible primed my spiritual pump.'

Learn to let God speak to you through His Word before you speak to Him through yours. Remember Jesus instructed His disciples: 'If you remain in me and my words remain in you, ask whatever you wish, and it will be given you' (John 15:7).

FURTHER STUDY

Psa. 116:1-19; 34:15; Isa. 65:24; 1 Pet. 3:12

1. Why did the psalmist continue to call on the Lord?

2. To whom are the Lord's ears attentive?

Father, help me from this day forward to come to my Bible prayerfully, quietly and expectantly. May my ears be inclined towards You to catch every whisper that comes from Your sacred Word. In Jesus' name. Amen.

'No news is bad news'

For reading & meditation – Isaiah 26:1–6

'You will keep in perfect peace him whose mind is steadfast, because he trusts in you.' (v.3)

Yet another way of ensuring the Bible comes alive is to approach it imaginatively. This is when we take the Bible and treat it as if it is autobiographical. In today's verse, 'mind' (in Hebrew *yetser*) can justifiably be translated 'imagination'. One translation of this verse is: 'Thou wilt keep in perfect peace him whose imagination stops at Thee.' When our imagination stops at God it works to our advantage; when it is allowed to go beyond Him it works to our ruin.

FURTHER STUDY

Rom. 8:1–6; 12:2;
Col. 3:2

1. What kind of mind experiences life and peace?

2. Where are we to set our minds on?

Almost everyone has waited for important news and experienced an unexplained delay. The news could be the result of an examination or a medical test, or confirmation of the safe arrival of a loved one in a distant land. When the expected news does not come what happens to the imagination? Unless it is kept under control it quickly runs amok. There is an old saying that no news is good news, but do we really believe that? More often than not the imagination gets to work and we find ourselves believing the opposite – that no news is bad news. I have sat with people in such circumstances and have tried to help them bring their imagination under control. It is not an easy task. The imagination when it runs wild is like an untamed horse.

What a difference it would make if, in the midst of the unknown, we could let our imagination stop at God, believing that all things are in His hands and that His purposes are best. Imagination is one of God's gifts to us but it works effectively only when it functions in harmony with Him.

My Father and my God, I function best when I work in conjunction with You. Help me understand this. May my imagination never go beyond You. In Jesus' name. Amen.

Where achievements begin

For reading & meditation – Ephesians 3:14–21

'Now to him who is able to do immeasurably more than all
we ask or imagine ...' (v.20)

A psychologist says: 'Every great achievement has to be imaged
first in the mind before it can be turned into reality.'

It was said of the first astronauts that their flight to the moon
was flown a thousand times in their imagination before they were
actually launched into space. They saw the space capsule leave the
earth. They saw the planet grow smaller and the moon grow bigger.
They saw the gauges registering all the movements of the capsule.
They saw the sun rise and set on mother earth. They saw it all,
and themselves battling with unexpected difficulties,
meeting peril with pluck and incisive judgment.
And then the return, the crowds, the cheers, and
themselves the centre and heroes of it all. They had
imaged the whole enterprise and they knew to some
degree at least how they would deal with it.

Some readers become nervous when I begin
to write about the use of imagination, and I
understand why. There are practitioners in the field
of counselling who tend to overdo the use of the
imagination by calling on their counsellees to relive traumatic life
experiences and imagine Christ to be present in them. This exercise
is thought to rid a person of the trauma of terrible memories and
bring healing to the mind. I am not convinced that is a proper use
of the imagination. But it does not follow that something which
can be misused should never be used. Again I say: imagination is
a gift from God – a gift to be used wisely, not wantonly.

FURTHER STUDY

2 Cor. 4:1-18;
Col. 1:15; 3:10;
Heb. 12:2

1. On what
are our eyes
to focus?

2. Where do we
best see the
divine image?

**Gracious Father, You have provided me with some wonderful
faculties, not least the imagination. Help me to harness it to Your
purposes, to tie it in to Your designs. In Christ's name I pray. Amen.**

Redeeming the imagination

For reading & meditation – Isaiah 65:1-10

'All day long I have held out my hands to an obstinate
people, who walk ... pursuing their own imaginations ...' (v.2)

The King James Version uses the word 'imagination' far more
frequently than more modern translations, almost always in
connection with plotting. It appears just four times in the Revised
Standard and the New International Versions. But again, these
references have to do with the use of imagination for fabricating
prophecy, planning evil acts and making idols. Because of this,
many people regard the imagination as being evil, but 1 Chronicles
28:9 uses the word in a neutral sense: 'And thou, Solomon my son,
know thou the God of thy father, and serve him with
a perfect heart and with a willing mind: for the
LORD searcheth all hearts, and understandeth all
the imaginations of the thoughts' (KJV).

Though we have to admit that the biblical use
of the word 'imagination' generally has to do with
stubbornness or plotting evil, we must not conclude
that the imagination can never be used for good. A
reverent use of the imagination can help make the
Bible come alive for us. I am surprised that more is
not made of this in Bible colleges and theological
seminaries. Soon I will show you how to apply
imagination to your reading of the Bible (something
I do regularly in my own devotional times). When you discover
this technique and develop it, I promise you that you will look at
the Bible in a new light. Our imagination may be diseased and
poisoned by sin but, like every other part of us, it can be cleansed
and redeemed and used for spiritual ends.

FURTHER STUDY

1 Cor. 2:1-16;
14:14-15;
Phil. 3:19;
Col. 2:18

1. How does Paul
link the mind
and the Spirit?
2. What is the
relationship
between
revelation and
imagination?

**Father, perhaps I have classified imagination as being merely fancy,
which has no basis in fact. But I see now that my imagination can
be redeemed. Cleanse it I pray and make it work for Your ends.
In Jesus' name. Amen.**

Imagination- its proper use

For reading & meditation – Ezekiel 13:1–16

'Say to those who prophesy out of their own imagination:
"Hear the word of the Lord!"' (v.2)

John Ruskin, the famous nineteenth-century British art critic
and philosopher, said that the noblest use of the imagination is
not to plan for the future but to call up the scenes of our Lord's
life and 'to be present, as if in the body, at every recorded event
of the history of the Redeemer'.

The first time I read Ruskin's words I was somewhat surprised; I
had always thought that the primary use of the imagination is to
look into the future. However, I have come to see that he was right;
the most commendable use of the imagination is to
go backwards; to live in the Bible, to jostle with the
disciples as they stand around the Saviour, to see the
surprise on Zacchaeus' face when the Master looks
up at him and says: 'I'd like to come to your house
for tea' (*Revised Selwyn Version!*). Or perhaps we
may choose to go back to the time of David and stand
on the hillside overlooking Jerusalem to watch him
dance before the ark of the Lord as it is being brought
to the newly conquered city of Jerusalem. All this
you can do by sanctified imagination.

FURTHER STUDY

Num. 13:1-14:12;
Prov. 29:25;
Isa. 35:4;
Job 3:25

1. How did the
spies stir up the
imagination of
the Israelites?

2. What is often
a product of the
imagination?

Have you ever used your imagination in this way?
How sad that most of us, like the prophets in the passage before
us today, use our imagination to conjure up things that are not
true and foolishly believe them to be so – disasters that will not
happen, negative events that never become fact. The proper use of
the imagination is to take true happenings and make them vivid
in one's life at the present time.

**Father, I see that imagination can work for good or ill. Teach me
more about its proper use and how I can utilise it in making Your
Word come alive more vividly. In Christ's name. Amen.**

A spine-tingling moment

For reading & meditation – Luke 24:1–12

'Bending over [Peter] saw the strips of linen lying by themselves ...' (v.12)

Through imagination we can *live* in the Bible. Dr W.E. Sangster used to say: 'There are two chief ways of reading the Bible: to read it with, or without imagination. You can read it from outside, or you can read it from inside. You can come to it in a detached fashion and always be external to the Book or you can slip inside the covers and live within the divine Word itself.' He was not saying that we must always use our imagination when we read the Bible, but that there are times when slipping into the skin of a Bible character can help make the divine Word come alive.

FURTHER STUDY

John 4:1–42;
Luke 24:13–35

1. Use your imagination to slip into the skin of the Samaritan woman.

2. Also the Emmaus road disciples.

Dr Sangster would often say to close friends: 'I am with Jeremiah at the moment. Where are you?' Or, 'I am with Ezekiel in his visions presently. Have you ever been there?' His friends would reply like this: 'Oh, I am in prison with Paul, feeling what it is like to be incarcerated but rejoicing in the fact that the Word of God is not bound.' Or, 'I am one of the ten lepers whom Jesus has cleansed and I can't wait to go back to Him to say 'Thank you'.'

Nowadays one rarely hears people talking like that. Yet in my youth my Christian friends and I similarly spent a lot of time slipping into the skin of a Bible character and imagining what it must have felt like to be that person. Today's text is a favourite. It allows us to picture Simon Peter bending over the stone slab on which Jesus had lain and seeing the strips of linen 'lying by themselves'. What a moment that was.

Lord, may I view the facts of Scripture with fascination. Help me crawl into the skin of certain of its characters, to see through their eyes, to feel with their fingers and to understand with their hearts. Amen.

Who are you today?

For reading & meditation – 1 Chronicles 29:10–20

'O Lord God ... keep this for ever in the imagination of the thoughts of the heart of thy people ...' (v.18, KJV)

My Christian companions and I used to spend time imagining ourselves to be a Bible character. When we met, we used to say, 'Who are you today?'

Over the years I have found that Christians come up with three objections when presented with the suggestion of slipping inside the covers of the Bible and living within the divine Word itself. The first is: 'It seems silly.' However, it only seems silly to those who have never tried it. Others excuse themselves by claiming they don't have a very good imagination. Yet when I question them about how they react when they are faced with some uncertainty it becomes clear that they can quickly imagine all sorts of things going wrong. They have a 'good' imagination but use it to wrong ends. A third objection is: 'Is this really a valid use of the imagination?' I believe it is. Today's verse reads in the King James Version: 'O LORD God of Abraham, Isaac, and of Israel, our fathers, keep this for ever in the imagination of the thoughts of the heart of thy people, and prepare their heart unto thee.' Imagination can be the vehicle for bad but it can also be the vehicle for good.

To take a situation recorded in the Bible and imagine yourself to be either a witness of the event or a person involved can not only be exciting but also spiritually profitable. It brings home to the heart the wonder of God's intervention in the affairs of human beings and the joy that comes through experiencing His power in our lives.

FURTHER STUDY

2 Cor. 10:1-6;
Psa. 94:11;
Rom. 1:21

1. What are we to demolish?

2. What are we to do with every thought?

Father, I know from experience how my imagination can sometimes lead me down a path I would rather avoid. Help me have a sanctified imagination, one that leads me down the path of peace. In Jesus' name. Amen.

Zacchaeus the tax collector

For reading & meditation – Luke 19:1–10

'Zacchaeus, come down immediately. I must stay at your house today.' (v.5)

I am taking two incidents from Scripture (involving today a man and tomorrow a woman) to see how we can bring them to life, using the the method I have been suggesting.

First read the story of Zacchaeus again, but this time very slowly. Raise questions in your mind as you go. Where did the incident happen? Jericho. If you have a Bible atlas, see where Jericho was situated. If you have a book about ancient Palestine, see if you can find a description of the town as it was in the days of Christ. *When* did this incident happen? Just a few days before Jesus was crucified. This means that the shadow of the cross was looming large in His vision. What about Zacchaeus himself? What is known about him? He was a *chief* tax collector. That means he was a very important person with men working under him. Clearly he had a yearning to see Jesus. Why? Was he tired of his lifestyle? Was it mere curiosity? What does a sycamore-fig tree look like? Find a picture of one.

FURTHER STUDY

Prov. 15:26;
1 Chron. 28:1-10;
Matt. 22:37

1. What is pleasing to the Lord?

2. How was Solomon to serve the Lord?

Now for the next step. *You* are Zacchaeus. Imagine yourself catching sight of Jesus for the first time. How serene He appears. Suddenly He looks up at you in the tree and your eyes meet. 'Zacchaeus,' He says, 'I must stay at your house today.' *Your house*. The Master wants to come and stay with you, a tax collector – someone whom people try to avoid. When I live this situation I can never get past the point where Jesus calls my name. From that moment on everything turns to prayer.

Gracious and loving Father, I have used my imagination many times to deepen the darkness of life's situation. Help me now to use it to deepen the wonder of this most glorious salvation.
In Jesus' name. Amen.

The spirit of infirmity

For reading & meditation – Luke 13:10–17

'… Jesus … said to her, "Woman, you are set free from
your infirmity."' (v.12)

Imagine yourself to be the woman who had a most wonderful
encounter with Jesus. Read the story slowly, raising certain
questions in your mind.

The Bible says the woman had been crippled by a spirit. Was
the spirit an evil one or was it her own spirit that was bent
and broken thus causing the deformity in her spine? In other
words, was it a psychosomatic problem? J.B. Phillips, the New
Testament scholar, thought the problem was psychological in
origin, and that her spine had become bent like a
crooked stick due to some trauma that had first
upset her spirit and then her body. How long had
she been like this? For eighteen years she had
been unable to stand up straight. Where did Jesus
meet her? In a synagogue. What did the inside of a
synagogue look like? Men were seated in one part,
women in the other.

Become that poor women in your imagination.
Feel yourself bent over as if by an iron hand. The
service is about to begin. Shssh! The first thing you hear is the
voice of the Saviour. And He is calling you by name. Oh dear. He
wants you to come to Him. You move as best as you can and drag
yourself towards Him. He puts His hands on you and suddenly
you stand up straight. Straight! You look into His eyes. He smiles
at you. Oh God, thank You … thank You. Ponder the fact that
even though outwardly you may appear to stand up straight,
inside you may be unable to do so. One touch from Jesus makes
all the difference.

FURTHER STUDY

Isa. 53:1–12;
Matt. 8:17;
Heb. 4:15

1. What does the
word 'infirmity'
mean?

2. What is
today's account
a fulfilment of?

**Heavenly Father, how can I thank You enough that with one touch
from You my crooked soul is straightened? Bring this fact home to
me as I ponder this miracle. In Christ's name. Amen.**

A lost art

For reading & meditation – Psalm 1:1–6

'But his delight is in the law of the Lord, and on his law he meditates day and night.' (v.2)

We now consider yet another way to help to make the Bible come alive – the practice of meditation. Meditation is an issue about which most Christians remain unconvinced, so it was no surprise to me when research revealed that only about 3 per cent of Christians practise the art of biblical meditation. Please note the phrase '*biblical* meditation'. This must never be confused with the type of meditation taught by Eastern religions. It is as different from those approaches as chalk is from cheese. Scripture many times declares that meditation on the truths of the Bible is of the utmost importance – today's text is just one instance.

FURTHER STUDY

Job 23:12;
Psa. 119:1–48;
John 5:39–40;
1 Pet. 2:2

1. How much did Job treasure God's Word?

2. List the verses from Psalm 119 that teach us about meditation.

If meditation is given such a high priority in Scripture why do so few engage in it? One reason is that it is time-consuming. David Ray, a US writer, describes his own attitude: 'I for one looked with suspicion on any Christian who advocated such a practice as meditation. I thought to myself, they are out of touch with reality. Give me action and work, lots of work. Let somebody else waste time staring at the end of their nose.' Then someone showed him how to let his mind focus on Psalm 46:10: 'Be still, and know that I am God.' He soon developed an increased awareness of God's presence.

People often ask me how I find topics and themes about which to write in *Every Day with Jesus*. The answer is simple: meditation. Believe me, what God has put into His Word is best considered through meditation.

Father, I know that divine life pulses through the pages of the Bible. Help me tap that power and apply it to my life through meditation. Teach me more, dear Father. In Jesus' name. Amen.

The basis of meditation

For reading & meditation – Isaiah 55:1–13

'"For my thoughts are not your thoughts, neither are your ways my ways," declares the Lord.' (v.8)

Biblical meditation is the art of taking a text of Scripture (or even a phrase) and drawing from it all the meaning and power that divine inspiration has given it.

On one occasion, after I had given a talk to a group of Christians on the theme of meditation, a man told me he was an expert on the subject because he practised meditation for thirty minutes every day. When I pressed him for more details he told me that every morning he would sit in his chair, let his mind go blank and meditate on whatever came into his mind. 'I might meditate for five minutes on my work, or my family,' he said, 'and I go wherever my mind takes me. Often I get a picture of God, and I think beautiful thoughts of Him.' I questioned him carefully on his concept of God and saw within minutes that his view of God was utterly unbiblical. He tried to get to God through his own concepts of God. His own concepts were the medium.

FURTHER STUDY

Col. 3:1–17;
Deut. 6:6–8;
Jer. 15:16;
Psa. 104:34

1. What does the word 'dwell' mean?

2. What did Jeremiah say?

The Bible is God's revelation of Himself and unless we begin there we will soon get lost. Once I heard a great Bible expositor say: 'Any idea we come up with about God which is not based on Scripture is almost certainly wrong.' Our human concepts need to be continually corrected by God's revelation of Himself as given in His Word. I was not surprised to learn that the man I had spoken to was regarded as unstable, and that he often put forward the most astonishing ideas about God. His meditation was certainty not Bible-centred.

My Father and my God, I accept that unless my thoughts are constantly corrected by Your thoughts they can go off at a tangent. I see the need for Your input, now help me understand the art. Amen.

What is meditation?

For reading & meditation – Proverbs 12:14–28

'The lazy man does not roast his game, but the diligent man prizes his possessions.' (v.27)

Practising biblical meditation involves taking a passage, a phrase or even a word from the Bible and dwelling on it for a while so that the spiritual energy contained in it deposits itself in your soul. Andrew Murray described the process: 'Meditation is holding the Word of God in your heart until it has affected every phase of your life'. It is the art of contemplation, of close and continued thought. Someone has described it as 'like gazing long at a prism of many facets, turning it angle by angle in a bright spotlight'. But perhaps the best definition of meditation is that given by a Welsh expositor, Dr Cynddylan Jones: 'It is the process by which we take the Word of God and turn it into spiritual faith and energy – taking Biblical truths and making them working realities. *Meditation is the digestive system of the soul*' (emphasis mine).

FURTHER STUDY

Psa. 77:1-20;
19:14;
Rom. 10:8

1. How did the psalmist handle discouragement?

2. What was his desire?

The purpose of meditation is to allow the Word of God to lie upon our mind and in turn pass on its power to our soul. The man or woman who reads and studies the Bible will profit tremendously. But the greatest spiritual profit comes when we meditate on what we read.

Our text for today talks about a man who goes out and catches game but is then too lazy to roast it and eat it. How sad that so many Christians read their Bible and study their Bible yet fail to grasp its full significance because they do not take that further step of meditating on it. It is akin to chewing our food but not swallowing it.

Father, I sense that here is the crux of the matter. I must go one way or the other – back to my previous habit of merely reading the Bible or on to meditating on it also. Help me dear Father. Amen.

'A second thought'

For reading & meditation – Psalm 4:1–8

'… when you are on your beds, search your hearts and
be silent.' (v.4)

Today's verse gives another definition of biblical meditation –
mulling over a biblical truth until its spiritual wisdom passes
from the mind to the heart. 'Meditation,' said A.T. Pierson, 'is
simply thought prolonged and directed to a single object.'

Non-Christians often meditate. For example, M.A. Rosanoff
worked for many years with the famous inventor Thomas Edison,
trying to soften the wax of phonographic cylinders by altering
their chemistry. Every experiment proved ineffective. Rosanoff
told how he lay on his bed night after night, trying
to mentally 'cough up' a solution. Then one night
it came 'like a flash of lightning'. 'I could not shut
waxes out of my mind,' he said, 'even in my sleep.
Suddenly through headache and daze I saw the
solution. The first thing in the morning I was at my
desk and half an hour later I had recorded in the soft
wax cylinder. This was the solution … I learned to
think waxes, waxes, waxes.'

FURTHER STUDY

Psa. 39:1-3;
119:148; 143:5
Eph. 5:26

1. What
happened to
the psalmist as
he meditated?

2. What did
the psalmist
meditate on?

If such a discovery could come through applying
meditation to the creative process, just think what
could happen if you learned to meditate biblically. Someone
writing of Rosanoff's experience said: 'It was like the unrolling of
a ball of string out of the unknown and night after night pulling it
toward his mind, not knowing what might be attached to the other
end.' 'Great matters have to be given a second thought,' said one
philosopher. Meditation is just that: giving great biblical truths at
least a second thought.

**Father, if great matters need a second thought then help me slow
down and take time to meditate on the great truths that are
enshrined in Your holy Word. In Jesus' name I pray. Amen.**

Ruminant Christians

For reading & meditation – Philippians 4:4–13

'... if anything is excellent or praiseworthy – think about such things.' (v.8)

A word which has as its secondary meaning 'meditate' or 'ponder' is 'ruminate'. Ruminant animals, such as cows, have a compartmented stomach. They digest their food by bolting it down, then later regurgitate it from the first stomach (the rumen) back into its mouth. This regurgitation process enables the food to be thoroughly digested before it is absorbed into the animal's bloodstream. Rumination and meditation, as I said, are similar words.

FURTHER STUDY

Josh. 1:1-9; 6:27; 23:3; 24:1-33

1. What was meditation linked to in God's promise to Joshua?

2. What end result is recorded?

When a Christian takes a text or a passage from Scripture, thinks about it, lets it go from the mind, brings it back again, thinks more about it, they are doing what a ruminant animal does with its food. The result is that the enriching power of the Word of God enters the soul, producing a degree of spiritual energy that otherwise could not be experienced. Just as a ruminant animal gets its nourishment and energy from what it eats through regurgitation, so a Christian extracts from the Scriptures the life of God through meditation.

To understand meditation we must realise that although we can gain a lot from the Bible by reading and studying it, we can't get the *best* from it until we meditate on it. As today's text tells us: 'If anything is excellent or praiseworthy – *think* about such things.' This thinking is not to be momentary but to occupy a significant amount of our time. Like the psalmist we should be able to say: 'Oh, how I love your law! I meditate on it all day long' (Psa. 119:97).

Father, can it be that my soul has not been enriched in the way it could have been because I have not meditated on Your Word? If this is so please help me to correct the situation. Amen.

The workshop

For reading & meditation – Psalm 63:1–11

'On my bed I remember you; I think of you through the
watches of the night.' (v.6)

By now I am sure it is quite clear that biblical meditation
involves spending time alone considering God's thoughts, not
dwelling on our own thoughts. There is a danger in rummaging
around in memories of the past. Put such things behind you and
learn to let God's thoughts become your thoughts.

Once you have grasped the concept of biblical meditation and put
it into practice, you will find your heart becoming the workshop
of an unseen Sculptor who will chisel in the secret chambers of
your soul the living forms that constitute a deeper
knowledge of Him. As a result your spiritual life will
become richer and more wonderful than you could
ever imagine.

Each time I have found myself in the presence
of someone whom I have discerned to be truly
spiritual, I have asked that person: 'Do you spend
much time meditating on the Scriptures?' Without
exception the answer has been 'Yes'. Once I asked
an elderly Welsh miner, a good and godly man,
what the secret of his spirituality was. He said he
did not regard himself as being really spiritual (deeply spiritual
people never do) and continued: 'Whatever spirituality I possess
is due in no small measure to the fact that every night before
I go to sleep I take a verse of Scripture that has come up in my
reading of the day, put it on the tip of my spiritual tongue and
suck every precious drop of fluid from it.' And he added: 'Guess
what! When I wake up in the morning the sweet taste is still
in my soul.'

FURTHER STUDY

Matt. 4:1-11;
Psa. 119:97-99;
Prov. 4:23

1. From where
do we draw
spiritual
sustenance?

2. What was
the psalmist's
testimony?

**Gracious and loving Father, I accept that I must contribute if I am to
develop spiritually. Something in me still pulls back, however. Is it
the challenge of effort or time? Help me Father. In Jesus' name.
Amen.**

The secret of success

For reading & meditation – Joshua 1:1–9

'... meditate on [the Book of the Law] day and night ...
Then you will be prosperous and successful.' (v.8)

Another benefit of meditating on the Bible is *success*. Christians who know how to meditate will (other things being equal) be successful in the tasks God gives them to do.

The book of Joshua narrates the story of how a man of proven character and ability – one of only two adults born in Egypt to survive forty years of wilderness wandering – led a nation of several thousand people across a river that had been swollen by floods to settle in their promised land. When God said: 'Moses my servant is dead' (v.2) the reins of leadership passed to Joshua. In a brilliant, divinely inspired move, he skilfully divided Canaan in half, then systematically defeated the southern armies before marching north to conquer the northern coalition. During the period this book covers, the twelve tribes defeated thirty-one armies and captured many cities.

FURTHER STUDY

Prov. 3:1–26;
8:12–14;
2 Tim. 2:7

1. How does understanding differ from knowledge?

2. How can we be wise in the ways of the Lord?

What was the secret of Joshua's great success? Mainly it was meditation. 'Meditate on [the Book of the Law] day and night … Then you will be prosperous and successful.' Continuous inner mental and spiritual discipline produced in Joshua clarity of thought, sharpness of intellect and a greater power of concentration. I am sure that Joshua's success as a leader stemmed not so much from his intuitive military ability as from his willingness and eagerness to meditate on God's Word. And remember, Joshua had just a fragment of what is now available to you and me in the pages of our full and complete Bible.

Heavenly Father, I recognise that more is needed for success than intuitive ability. Meditation sharpens and focuses that ability and makes it even more creative. I am convinced. Help me now to make a start. In Jesus' name. Amen.

Time to make a start

For reading & meditation – John 15:1–17

'I am the vine; you are the branches. If a man remains in
me and I in him, he will bear much fruit ...' (v.5)

We have seen that to read, study and memorise the Bible is
not enough. To get the most from it we must meditate on
it. What we hold in our minds very quickly affects other parts of
us – particularly the emotions and the will. Thoughts are powerful;
they are not passive. As Dr George Buttrick says: 'We dramatise
temptation in our secret thoughts thus gathering gasoline for the
devil's spark. And then we wonder why we blow up!' What we put
into our minds today will become action tomorrow. Our secret
meditations affect us – for good or for bad. We must
hold nothing in our minds that we do not want to
hold within us permanently.

The principle of meditation is a powerful one, and
can be used to help us or to harm us. When we learn
to harness it and introduce into our minds the Word
of God it goes to work, reconstructing our thought
life, realigning our wills and refocusing our emotions.
Before long others will see in us evidence of Christ's
character, for the written Word contains the power
to bring about in us the characteristics of the living Word. Just
think of it: tomorrow you can more clearly show Christ's character
to the world by what you have meditated upon today.

Once I spent a whole year meditating day after day and
phrase by phrase on the chapter before us today – John 15.
It was a remarkable experience. Though I am not saying you
should do the same, try meditating today on verse 5 and see
what happens.

FURTHER STUDY

Psa. 51:1-12;
Prov. 4:4;
2 Tim. 3:16-17

1. What does God
desire in the
inward parts?

2. Why is
Scripture
given to us?

**Father, help me apply the principle of biblical meditation to my
daily life so that as a result of meditating on the written Word
people might see the living Word. In Christ's name I ask it. Amen.**

'Dusty Bibles'

For reading & meditation – John 7:14–24

'If anyone chooses to do God's will, he will find out whether
my teaching comes from God ...' (v.17)

Another important way of ensuring the Bible speaks to us is
to surrender to the truth it reveals. Today's text could be
translated: 'He who is willing to do will know.' In a moral universe,
the key to knowledge is response. When we cease to obey the Bible
then it closes up on us. Revelation ceases.

When a person says, 'The Bible doesn't speak to me in the way it
used to,' more often than not the reason is some failure on the part
of that person to abide by the truths in God's Word. In one church I

FURTHER STUDY

James 1:19–25;
Matt. 19:17;
28:20;
Luke 11:27-28

1. What
illustration did
James use?

2. Who did Jesus
say are blessed?

pastored, two teenagers – both professing Christians
– told me that the Bible no longer seemed to make any
impact on their lives. After gently probing for some
explanation, and evasive answers, I asked them: 'Is
anything going on in your life that is contrary to
the teaching of the Word of God?' They became very
quiet and fidgety until one of them blurted out: 'Yes,
we have been doing some shoplifting.' I am glad to
say they were responsive to my counsel and asked
God to forgive them for having stolen goods. Action
followed their repentance and they returned the things they had
taken. One of those young women later became a pastor's wife and
now has a wonderful ministry teaching in a Bible college.

Shortly after I became a Christian someone wrote in my Bible:
'This book will keep you from sin or sin will keep you from this
book.' That is as true now as it was then. Dirty lives always lead to
dusty Bibles and dusty Bibles can lead to dirty lives.

**Father, help me grasp the fact that when I stop obeying, the Bible
stops revealing. Your Word has been given for belief and obedience.
May I honour it and You in all I do today. Amen.**

'Bible abortion'

For reading & meditation – Psalm 119:169–176

'Let me live that I may praise you, and may your laws
sustain me.' (v.175)

John Wallace, principal of the college I attended, used to say:
'Don't be surprised to discover that many Christians are far more
interested in interpretation of the Bible than the application of
it.' I have often thought of those words when I have come across
Christians indignant because someone has disagreed with their
pet doctrine but showing no concern about massive violations in
their lives of Scripture's commands.

Howard and William Hendricks said in *Living by the Book*:
'Observation plus interpretation without application
equals abortion.' That is, every time we observe and
interpret Scripture but fail to apply it we perform
an abortion on the Bible in terms of its purpose. The
Bible was written to transform our lives and make
us more like Christ. Once we stop applying it, it loses
its power over us. Ultimately our aim should not be
to do something to the Bible, but allowing it to do
something to us. We will never find the Bible to be a
dynamic Book if we do not obey its commands.

FURTHER STUDY

2 Tim. 3:1-14;
1 John 3:21-24;
Psa. 119:17-18

1. What
was Paul's
admonition
to Timothy?

2. What was
the psalmist's
request?

James Packer wrote: 'To know what God asks and
expects of us and not do it is worse than not knowing it at all.
God gives us His Spirit not to reveal God's mind to us apart from
Scripture and so make Scripture needless, but to show us God's
mind through Scripture by giving us personal understanding of
how the Bible bears on us and our lives.' How striking it is that the
longest psalm – before us today – celebrates the power of God's
Word in a believer's life.

**Lord God, may the prayer of the psalmist be my prayer not just
today but every day of my life: 'Let me live that I may praise you,
and may your laws sustain me.' In Jesus' name. Amen.**

Spiritual famine

For reading & meditation – Amos 8:1–11

'When will ... the Sabbath be ended that we may
market wheat?' (v.5)

I find this passage from Amos one of the most challenging in the Old Testament. Some Jews were going into the Temple on the Sabbath to join with others in the worship of God but deep down they couldn't wait for the Sabbath to be over to get back to where their real interest lay – exploiting and manipulating others in the marketplace. They got a thrill from the impact they made by cheating. Clearly they were living in contradiction of God's Word and they were warned that if they continued doing so they would suffer 'a famine of hearing the words of the LORD' (v.11).

FURTHER STUDY

Exod. 19:1-6;
1 Sam. 15:22;
Lev. 25:18;
Deut. 6:1-3

1. What is
obedience
better than?

2. What did
God promise
to those who
obey Him?

I think this means the consequence of disobedience to the clearly revealed will of God is that the time will come when we will no longer be able to hear God speaking to us. In effect God is saying: 'If you don't act upon My Word then you won't hear My Word.' As we have said before, when we stop obeying then God stops revealing. If we are not passionately concerned about doing what God asks then the Bible will become a closed book and will not provide us with the guidance, insight and comfort we desire.

I often picture Herod questioning Jesus. 'He plied him with many questions, but Jesus gave him no answer' (Luke 23:9). Previously our Lord had answered certain questions Caiaphas and Pilate put to Him. But not Herod. Why? Our Lord would not respond to someone who did not take Him seriously.

Lord God, I dread the thought that I might enter into a period of spiritual barrenness because of my unwillingness to pay attention to Your Word. But I see the possibility. Help me surrender to its truths in everything. Amen.

Response to revelation

For reading & meditation – Psalm 119:161–168

'I obey your statutes, for I love them greatly.' (v.167)

I commented that Psalm 119 (which is twice the length of the next longest psalm and ten times the average length of all the rest), celebrates the power of the Word of God in a believer's life. In today's section the psalmist states: 'I rejoice in your promise like one who finds great spoil' (v.162).

Do you share the psalmist's feelings? Does what you read provide you with as much pleasure as the discovery that you have just received a large bequest? Only when we are willing to obey the Bible will its words become treasure to us. It is one thing to search the Bible but it is another to let the Bible search us. I shocked a group of people the other day when I began my message with these words: 'I have given up reading the Bible.' I continued: 'Nowadays I am trying to let the Bible read me.'

As a young man I was taught that every time I came to the Bible I should ask myself: What can I learn about God from this passage? What can I learn about myself? Does this Scripture call for some action on my part – confession, restitution or application? Asking those questions has become a habit for me, and I find as I examine Scripture in this way the Holy Spirit lights up the Word most wonderfully. Old words take on new meanings. General statements press home a personal application. Often I am reproved and rebuked. And unless and until I respond to God's rebukes the revelation stops. The Word of God obeyed is the Word of God enjoyed.

FURTHER STUDY

Rom. 11:33-36;
Eph. 2:7; 3:8-9;
Col. 1:27-29;
2:2-3

1. What did Paul preach?

2. What was Paul's purpose?

Father, Your Word is light but I realise that the light will soon fade if I fail to walk in it. Enable me to see that obedience is a duty. Help me walk in Your ways every day of my life. Amen.

Whatever!

For reading & meditation – John 2:1–11

'His mother said to the servants, 'Do whatever he tells you.'' (v.5)

The words of our text for today should spring to mind whenever we come to the Scriptures: 'Do whatever he tells you.'

A lovely story is told of our present queen – Queen Elizabeth – that goes back to the days when she was a little girl. Her mother and father were entertaining a group of dignitaries one evening in Buckingham Palace and the little princess it seems was being ignored. She wanted to say something but nobody appeared interested. Feeling rather grieved she made her way to the centre of the room, stamped her foot on the floor and shouted as loudly as she could: 'Listen, everyone … *royalty is speaking*.' Those words should be with us every time we open up the Word of God: 'Royalty is speaking.' 'Do whatever he tells you.'

FURTHER STUDY

John 14:28–31;
15:10;
Matt. 12:50;
John 14:23;
James 1:25

1. What was
Jesus able
to say?

2. Who will
be blessed in
what they do?

Let's ask ourselves now: How large a part does obedience play in our lives? A small part? Some part? A significant part? Or is it everything? Ponder the words of our Lord's mother once again: 'Do whatever he tells you.' *Whatever*. Are you prepared to do *whatever* He tells you? If you are, then every time you open up His Word it will crackle with new surprises.

Above I mentioned a story about the then Princess Elizabeth. When she became queen she received a lovely letter from her grandmother, Queen Mary, who signed it: 'Your loving grandmother … and devoted subject'. How different and dynamic the Bible would become to many of us if only we were willing to surrender to its truths.

Father, can it be that the reason I don't see something fresh in Your Word each time I read it is that I am holding back? Help me become a devoted and obedient subject. In Jesus' name. Amen.

Sophistry's terrible toll

For reading & meditation – 2 Samuel 12:1–14

'Then Nathan said to David, 'You are the man!'' (v.7)

Something we must be on our guard against is the matter of self-deception. Count Tolstoy said: 'Lying to others is much less serious than lying to yourself.' Whether lying to oneself is worse than lying to others is a debatable issue, of course, but what we need to be aware of is the seriousness of fooling ourselves.

Is it possible for Christians to lie to themselves about evil? My experience as a counsellor tells me that it is. Some Christians can deceive themselves to such an extent that they can be guilty of violating a biblical command and still walk around feeling virtuous. This is what we find King David doing in the story before us today. He had coveted the wife of one of his soldiers, and while the army was fighting his battles he seduced her. The king described as being a man after God's own heart (1 Sam. 13:14) had committed a terrible sin but he used his reasoning to persuade himself he was innocent. Then God sent Nathan with a barbed little parable about a rich man with large flocks who stole from a poor man his one little lamb and killed it. David was so self-deceived that he saw in the story no reference to himself until Nathan's finger marked him out and he declared: 'You are the man!' The lie was exposed, the sophistry ended.

FURTHER STUDY

2 Cor. 1:1-12;
Rom. 9:1;
1 Cor. 8:7;
1 Tim. 1:5,19;
Heb. 9:14

1. What was Paul able to say to the Romans and Corinthians?

2. Why have some shipwrecked their faith?

Let us be careful that our feet do not stray onto the path of self-deception. God has given us this warning about the danger of strutting about with a drugged conscience believing a self-imposed lie.

Lord God, help me to ask the question: Am I deceiving myself? Am I walking around with a drugged conscience? Save me from the moral myopia that fails to see issues clearly. In Christ's name I pray. Amen.

Blind spots

For reading & meditation – Ephesians 4:17–32

'Therefore each of you must put off falsehood and speak truthfully to his neighbour ...' (v.25)

onsider how self-deception works. Let's assume a Christian businessman is involved in some shady practice and opens up his Bible to a verse such as the one we have before us today. Now what can he do? He can allow the Word to challenge him and decide to immediately stop what he is doing, ask God to forgive him and set about any restitution that may be necessary. If, however, his conscience is drugged by self-deception he might brush the matter aside and say to himself: 'There are many areas where I am honest. I do not cheat on my wife. I read my Bible every day. I give a tenth of my income to God's work.' He thinks of those areas of his life that are in harmony with biblical principles and gives himself a pat on the back. But he has a blind spot. He has fallen into the state of self-deception where the clear distinction between good and evil has become blurred by specious arguments that have as their end self-interest. He has allowed his conscience to become so dulled that it does not steer him in the right direction; he resembles a ship at sea with a faulty compass. And for obvious reasons a faulty compass is worse than no compass.

FURTHER STUDY

Jer. 17:1-10;
23:24;
Mark 2:8;
John 2:25

1. What does Jeremiah say about the heart?

2. What does the Lord declare?

How do those who are self-deceived become awakened to their condition? I know this: no words of mine can effect the change. All I can do is to present an argument. God alone is the One who can convict. I must therefore stop now and let the Holy Spirit take over. 'He who has ears, let him hear' (Matt. 11:15).

Holy Spirit, save me I pray from being self-deceived. Enable me to have a conscience that is sensitive to all Your principles and commands. In Jesus' name. Amen.

The five interrogatives

For reading & meditation – Hebrews 11:23–40

'They were all commended for their faith ...' (v.39)

Yet another way to make sure we learn as much as possible from the Bible is to ask questions. One of the first lessons I was taught in a course on journalism was the use of the five interrogatives: Who? What? Where? When? Why? 'Whenever you set about a writing assignment,' I was told, 'ask and answer these questions and you will probably give your readers most of the information they will want and need to know.' Some time later it occurred to me that it would be useful to apply these questions to my study of the Scriptures, and when I did so I found the Word coming alive in a most exciting way.

Hebrews 11 perfectly illustrates my point. It lists more than a dozen figures from the Old Testament but unless you ask '*Who* are these people?' and are willing to go back and read what is said about them you will not fully appreciate the strength of their faith. Each time you come across the name of someone in the Bible about whom you know little make a note to find out as much as you can about them and their background. Look in the margin of your Bible to see if there is another reference to the person concerned and if not consult a Bible dictionary. Not all the characters you come across in Scripture have something significant said about them, but many do. Exploring what the Bible says about its characters gives a greater insight into their struggles and victories. My guess is that those who find the Bible dull have not delved into it more deeply.

FURTHER STUDY

Hosea 4:6
1 Cor. 10:1-11;
15:34

1. What was Paul's concern for the Corinthians?

2. Why did he say the accounts were important?

Father, with so many ways available to me to make the Bible come alive help me utilise them all. Nothing is really mine until I receive it. Help me take in what I am discovering and put into practice.
Amen.

Who?

For reading & meditation – Psalm 88:1–18

'But I cry to you for help, O Lord; in the morning my prayer comes before you.' (v.13)

Who is the passage talking about? Did you notice in your reading of Psalm 88 that the preface draws attention to the fact that it was a *maskil* (a poem) of Heman the Ezrahite? The preface, by the way, is considered just as much part of the biblical text as the psalm itself. Ask any of your Christian friends if they know who Heman the Ezrahite was and watch their blank expressions. So how do we discover who Heman the Ezrahite was? Psalm 88 doesn't tell us. We have to go back to the historical books to find out anything about him. (A Bible dictionary will be a great help here.) Heman (according to the *IVP Bible Dictionary*) was probably 'one of the sages whom Solomon excelled in wisdom (1 Kings 4:31). He was said to be a son of Mahol, but 1 Chronicles 2:6 calls him a son of Zerah, a Judahite.' A look at the entry on Mahol informs us that 'son' may simply mean 'descendant' and that 'sons of Mahol' may be an expression meaning 'sons of the dance'. If this is the case then Heman would have taken part in the ritual of worship. Though some people might find this approach tedious there are nuggets of gold to be found.

FURTHER STUDY

Philemon;
Col. 4:14;
2 Tim. 4:10

1. Who was Demas?

2. What do we know about him?

You may wonder why the Bible mentions so many different people. The reason is this: God wants us to see the processes people went through in order to reach the conclusions they came to. Understanding that can give us an insight into how to reach our own conclusions in times of difficulty.

Father, I see there is a wise and wonderful purpose running through Your Word – even in parts where I never thought of looking. I don't want to miss a single thing when I come to Your book. Enlighten me further. Amen.

What?

For reading & meditation – 1 Samuel 15:10–35

'Because you have rejected the word of the Lord, he has rejected you as king.' (v.23)

I t is helpful to ask of a certain text or passage: Just *what* was happening in this portion of Scripture? What are the events? In what order did those events take place? What was happening to the characters? If the passage is pursuing a particular point (as in the opening chapters of Romans) then ask yourself: What is the argument? What is the writer really trying to say?

I remember applying this question to today's passage while preparing a talk on King Saul. I asked myself: What is really going on in this part of the Word of God? Here we see a king who was anointed by Samuel and who was considered by the people to be an excellent ruler. Yet Samuel, after a night of prayer, seems to dismiss him and sets his face against him. What was the cause? The key is found in verse 24: 'I was afraid of the people and so I gave in to them.' King Saul was a people-pleaser, more interested in gaining the commendation of the people than the approval of God. Hence he disobeyed God by refusing to carry out the clear command given him in verse 3: 'Now go, attack the Amalekites and totally destroy everything that belongs to them.'

FURTHER STUDY

1 Sam. 9:2;
10:1-24; 13:11-13;
18:8; 19:1;
28:7; 31:4

1. What are some of the characteristics of Saul?

2. What was his destiny?

Saul did what many of us today do also: he obeyed some of God's commandments but not all in the hope that those he kept would persuade God to overlook the ones he had not kept. From God's viewpoint, partial obedience is disobedience. And we have learned all that from our reading today simply because we were prepared to ask 'What?'

God my Father, there is so much in Your Word that can be missed unless I come to it with a questioning mind. Help me be skilful in asking appropriate, probing questions. In Christ's name I pray. Amen.

Where?

For reading & meditation – Exodus 6:1–8

'... say to the Israelites: "I am the Lord, and I will bring you out from under the yoke of the Egyptians."' (v.6)

The next question we need to ask is 'Where?' This question leads to the actual location of incidents recorded in the Bible. Where did the event take place? Many Bibles have at the back a set of maps because it is important to have some idea of the geography of Bible lands. Many Christians have no idea where events recorded in the Old and New Testaments took place.

Consider with me the passage before us today. It tells us that God appeared to Moses and reminded him of the promise given

FURTHER STUDY

Turn to a set of Bible reference maps.

1. Trace the route of the patriarchs.

2. Trace the route of the Exodus.

to Abraham that He would bring His chosen people into a land that would be theirs for all time. Thus we see the first movements in the thrilling story of how the children of Israel left Egypt, wandered through the wilderness for forty years, and finally entered the promised land. To understand the significance of this story without a map is difficult. Trace the journey and notice the route they took to leave Egypt. See how God arranged for them to cross the Red Sea at a spot where He allowed them to escape but where

He engulfed the Egyptian army in the waters. Then see how close the Israelites came to the promised land before they had to turn back because of their disobedience. Take it from me: the accounts recorded in Scripture will make a far greater impact on you if you are prepared to consult a Bible atlas.

Father, am I apathetic? Am I content to read without questioning or searching for more information? Help me not to assume anything but to search and research whenever necessary. In Christ's name. Amen.

When?

For reading & meditation – Mark 1:35–39

'Very early in the morning, while it was still dark, Jesus ...
went off to a solitary place, where he prayed.' (v.35)

Now we consider the use of the question 'When?' Obviously this has to do with the issue of time. When did the events about which we are reading take place? How do they fit in with other parts of Scripture?

Apply the question 'When?' to today's short passage. Be ready to see how asking 'When?' gives us a fuller appreciation of it. 'Very early in the morning, while it was still dark, Jesus got up, left the house and went off to a solitary place to pray.' When did Jesus pray? Very early in the morning while it was dark. There was nothing unusual about that for Jesus often rose early to pray. Check it out. If we were to leave the matter there then we would miss much of the significance. It is said that in the Gospels we have a record of what happened to our Lord in just fifty-two days of His life on earth. The particular day we read about here followed a day that had been absolutely packed with action: Jesus had taught, healed and performed many miracles. Our Lord had every reason to sleep in the following morning but what did He do? He got up early to pray. He could have said to Himself: 'I was exceptionally busy doing my Father's business yesterday so this morning I will have a lie-in.' Might we not argue like this? But so high on His list of priorities was communion with God that He got up before dawn and spent time alone with His Father.

If Jesus, who knew unclouded communion with God, needed to pray, how much more do you and I?

FURTHER STUDY

Gen. 25:12–22;
Isa. 8:19;
2 Kings 22:13

1. What did Rebekah do?

2. What should a people do?

Father, I am beginning to see how much I miss in the Bible by not asking these simple but basic questions. Help me develop the habit of probing. Once I have established the habit then it will establish me. Amen.

Why?

For reading & meditation – Luke 4:38–44

'Now Simon's mother-in-law was suffering from a
high fever...' (v.38)

There are several 'Why?' questions that can be asked of
Scripture: Why is this passage included in the book of God?
Why is it where it is? Why did that person say that? 'Why?' is
a question that probes for meaning. Let me show you how as a
result of asking 'Why?' of one particular passage I discovered a
most exciting truth.

Once while I was reading today's passage I asked myself why
Luke recorded so many cases of healing. Was it because he was a

FURTHER STUDY

2 Sam. 9:1-13
1 Sam. 20:1-42

1. Why did
Mephibosheth
describe himself
as a 'dead dog'?

2. Why did
David treat him
the he did?

doctor? Perhaps so. Then I asked myself: Why does
it say Simon's mother-in-law was *suffering* from a
high fever (v.38)? Was she really suffering? I looked
up the word 'suffering' in a concordance and found
that the Greek verb used is *sunecho*, which means
'constrained'. Why did Luke select that word? Are
there any other instances of its use? I found several,
one in Luke 8:45 ('crowding' is another translation of
sunecho) and another in Luke 12:50. Here the word
'distressed' is yet another translation of s1unecho.

Fascinated by the different contexts in which the word appears
I discovered that Paul used it in 2 Corinthians 5:14: 'For Christ's
love compels [or constrains] us.' I then began to get a picture of
an apostle who was so affected by the love of Christ that it raged
in him like a fever, pressed in on him from all sides, and made
him desperate to get to grips with the commission that he had
been given. All this came from asking the simple question 'Why?'

**Gracious Lord and Master, help me unlock the Bible through the
use of these probing questions. I know that a journey always begins
with the first step. May I take that first step today. In Jesus' name.
Amen.**

The real test

For reading & meditation – Mark 4:35–41

'They ... asked each other, "Who is this? Even the wind and
the waves obey him!"' (v.41)

Can the use of probing questions unlock the Bible for you?
Howard Hendricks of Dallas Theological Seminary recounts
how he used these questions when flying. There were eight
passengers and fifteen flight attendants when he took out his Bible
and started reading it. One of the attendants noticed and asked:
'Are you a believer?' 'I certainly am,' he said. 'How about you?' 'Yes,
I am too,' she replied with a smile.

They were soon talking about spiritual things and he asked her:
'Do you have a regular Bible study programme?' 'No,'
she confessed. 'Why not?' 'I don't know where to
begin.' As she appeared to have very little to do on
that flight he invited her to sit alongside him, took
an air sickness bag and wrote the questions we have
been considering: Who? What? Where? When? Why?
Then he invited her to read today's passage: Mark
4:35–41. Together they went through the questions:
Who were the people involved? What was taking
place in this passage? Where was it taking place? When did it
happen? Why did God include it in the Bible?

FURTHER STUDY

Job 23:1–12;
Deut. 8:3

1. What did
Job say?

2. Why not pass
some spiritual
food to someone
today?

Hendricks had rarely seen anyone get so excited about
discovering how to delve into the Bible. 'How is it,' the flight
attendant asked, 'that I have been a Christian for seven years
and nobody has ever taught me how to ask these questions of
the Bible?' That in itself is a good question. Many Christians are
starving spiritually simply because they don't know how to get a
meal for themselves. How very tragic.

**Gracious heavenly Father, I see I must not depend on this
devotional guide for my spiritual nourishment. I need much more
than it can give me. Help me also to prepare a meal for myself.
In Christ's name. Amen.**

Decision time

For reading and meditation – Psalm 95:1–11

'Today, if you hear his voice, do not harden your hearts ...'
(vv.7-8)

My last suggestion concerning how to make the Bible come alive is: explore Scripture continually and persistently. I have already made the point that if you are to grow spiritually you need much more than *Every Day with Jesus*. These notes will provide you with a good starter, but you also need to learn how to prepare a spiritual meal for yourself. For the next few days, therefore, I will concentrate on showing you how to prepare yourself to study the Bible in depth.

FURTHER STUDY

Josh. 24:1-15;
Deut. 30:19;
Prov. 8:10; 16:16

1. What did Joshua put before the people?

2. What is better than silver or gold?

First, make the decision to change. Perhaps as you have followed me through this theme day by day you have found yourself saying: 'Selwyn is right. I must do something about investigating the Bible's message for myself.' If so, good. But those good intentions must now be translated into action. What good does it do to dream about being a witness for Christ unless you start to speak to others about Your Saviour? How can you memorise a hundred verses of the Bible if you aren't willing to make the effort to learn just one? You may have some excellent thoughts about what a good marriage should be like but if you fail to watch for opportunities to encourage your partner and attend to practical matters then your vision will fail.

Far too many Christians get stuck at the stage of having good intentions and never make the decision to put these into action. It has rightly been said: 'We don't plan to fail; we fail to plan.' Now is the time to act. Say to yourself: 'I am going to change.'

Father, I don't want to stay at the stage of having good intentions. I want to move on with You and discover more of You through Your Word. Today I am deciding to change. Help me my Father. Amen.

Clear objectives

For reading & meditation – Philippians 3:12–21

'... I press on to take hold of that for which Christ Jesus took hold of me.' (v.12)

If you have decided to spend more time studying God's Word then you have my congratulations. Now set some clear objectives. Robert Mager, an education consultant, says that a well-stated objective defines where a person will be once they have achieved the intended outcome. For example, the objective I set out to achieve in writing this theme of *Every Day with Jesus* was to encourage you to spend more time with the Bible. I imagine a fair percentage of you will already be doing this and the thought of the impact this will make on your spiritual life is my reward.

What objectives can you set for yourself? One might be to get thoroughly acquainted with one or two books of the Bible. Or maybe even to work through the entire Bible in a year. Another might be to study the great doctrines of the Bible, the life of Christ, or Paul's missionary journeys. Consider prayerfully what you would like to know more deeply a year from now – your objective.

FURTHER STUDY

Luke 6:1-23;
1 Cor. 9:24-27;
Heb. 12:2;
2 Tim. 4:7-8

1. How are we to run?

2. What was Paul able to say?

'Clearly defined objectives,' it has been said, 'enable us to see truth as actions, not abstractions.' If this sounds too regimented for your temperament then consider that your goal in life may actually be to remain comfortable rather than to be conformed to Christ. Don't settle for a decaffeinated form of Christianity – one that promises not to keep you awake at night. Getting anywhere in life involves some cost. But when it comes to time spent with the Bible, the rewards far exceed the cost.

Father, something in me shrinks from challenge and change. Hold me steady as I go through the turbulence that change almost always causes. My trust and my hope is in You. Bring me through. In Jesus' name. Amen.

Be accountable

For reading & meditation – 1 Corinthians 4:1–21

'Now it is required that those who have been given a trust must prove faithful.' (v.2)

Having decided to change and set some clear objectives, what next? Devise a plan. Drawing up a specific plan will help you reach your objectives. Think through what it is going to take for you to achieve your goals. You could enrol in an evening course at a local Bible college. Or take up a correspondence course. Talk to your minister about the best ways in which you can increase your knowledge of the Scriptures. They may have the very idea that you need. You should be asking yourself such questions such

FURTHER STUDY

2 Tim. 2:1-15;
Matt. 12:36;
Rom. 14:12;
Heb. 4:13

1. What was
Paul's injunction
to Timothy?

2. Why is it
good to get into
the habit of
accountability?

as: Who are the people I should be talking to about this? What resources do I need to invest in? When and how am I going to plan time for Bible study and integrate it into my schedule?

Another important matter is to set up a system of accountability. If you decide to buy some books and study the Bible on your own then involve a friend or your spouse in checking up on you, asking questions as to how you are doing, and making sure you are keeping to your schedule. Being part of a group who are studying the Scriptures together provides its own method of accountability. A special dynamic is built up in a group, which can prove most effective. The success of the *Weight Watchers* programme is due to the concept of one person being accountable to others.

Sit down today and come up with a tentative plan of how you intend to deepen your knowledge of Scripture. But be prepared to adjust that plan as you seek help and advice from others.

Father, I know I must surrender myself to something – to the pressures around me or to the discipline of discovering more of You and Your Word. May I break with the former and close in with the latter. Amen.

Working things out

For reading & meditation – Philippians 2:1–13

'... it is God who works in you to will and to act according to
his good purpose.' (v.13)

Decisions to change, set objectives and come up with a plan will
be to no avail unless you make a start. Do you need to make
a phone call? Then do it. If you are a businessperson perhaps you
need to rearrange your schedule. Do it today. You are now at the
hardest point of all – the point of actually committing yourself
to doing what you have planned. Don't put it off. Respect yourself
enough to carry out the decision you have made.

Make a list of everything you need to do, perhaps: 1. Phone
minister for advice. 2. Work out a budget to assess
the costs involved. 3. Put starting dates in diary. One
man I know says: 'You have to take responsibility
for making choices and when you make the right
choices, ones that will result in the development
of your spiritual life, you are working out your
salvation.'

I have chosen today's text because it is often
overlooked. Many quote the words which precede
it – 'continue to work out your salvation with fear
and trembling' – and omit what comes next: 'for it is God who
works in you to will and to act according to his good purpose.' As
you make your decisions, set your objectives and draw up plans,
ask God to be right there with you to help you to follow through.
If what you plan is in accordance with His will He will pour in
His resources to assist you. He will not make the decisions for
you but He will guide you in them. If you are prepared to make
a start you can count on Him to help you finish.

FURTHER STUDY

John 8:31–47;
Matt. 7:24;
Rev. 1:3

1. What is the
evidence of
discipleship?

2. When does
the truth set
us free?

**Father, one of the encouraging things about living the Christian life
is that I am never alone. You won't do things for me, but You will do
things with me if they have Your blessing. I am deeply grateful.
Amen.**

The sin of neglect

243

For reading & meditation – Psalm 119:9–16
'I delight in your decrees; I will not neglect your word.'
(v.16)

Where would we be without the Bible? In 1621, John Rogers, a
Puritan minister, was preaching on the place of the Bible in
the Christian life. First he depicted God as telling the congregation:
'I have trusted you so long with My Word, but you have slighted it,
ignored it, and read it only when it suits you. It lies in some of your
houses all covered with dust and cobwebs. If this is the way you
treat My Word then you shall have it no longer.' He then removed
the large Bible from the pulpit and joined the congregation. After

FURTHER STUDY

Psa. 19:1-14;
119:47,72,97,140

1. How precious
was God's Word
to the psalmist?

2. What ten
things did
the psalmist
declare about
God's Word?

pausing for a while he impersonated the people by
pretending to cry to God: 'Lord, whatever You do to
us don't take the Bible from us. Take our children,
burn our barns and houses, destroy our goods, but
spare us the Bible.' Ascending again into the pulpit he
acted the part of God once more. 'Say you so? Well,
I will try you a little while longer.' Then replacing
the Bible the preacher continued acting the part of
God. 'I will watch you carefully to see how you use
it, whether you will love it more, practise it more and
live more according to its precepts.' As a result of

this dramatic portrayal the whole congregation burst into tears.
One eyewitness said that he hung a quarter of an hour on the neck
of his horse weeping before he had power to mount.

Neglect of Scripture is one of the greatest insults we can give
to its Divine Author. The entrance of God's Word brings light; the
neglect of it brings darkness.

**Father, I would emerge from these meditations with a deeper love
for You and Your Word. Help me to hide it so deeply in my heart
that it will determine my conduct and my character.
In Christ's name I pray. Amen.**

The Peak of
the Epistles

Saints in Ephesus?

For reading & meditation – Ephesians 1:1–2

'... To the saints in Ephesus, the faithful in Christ Jesus ...'
(v.1)

We begin now a devotional study of Paul's epistle to the Ephesians – which many believe to be the greatest of all his writings. Graham Scroggie described it as 'The Alps of the New Testament'.

Paul starts by claiming for himself the title which our Lord had given to the Twelve: 'an apostle of Christ Jesus'. He makes clear this privilege was granted to him by 'the will of God'. He addresses 'the saints in Ephesus, the faithful in Christ Jesus'. Saints in Ephesus? How amazing. This prosperous heathen city with its immorality was hard on saintliness. The famous Temple of Diana was one of the wonders of the world and the centre of a fertility cult. Emperor worship was also a feature of religious life, and a temple had been built to the emperor Claudius. Despite this pagan background clearly there were Christians living out their faith.

FURTHER STUDY

John 10:1-10; 1:4;
11:25;
Rom. 8:1-4

1. What contrast did Jesus make?

2. What law is Paul talking about?

The life God gives us does not depend on our environment. Christians who hid from persecution in the catacombs in Rome frequently carved on the walls the words 'Vita! Vita! Vita!' meaning 'Life! Life! Life.' The life that God imparts to us when we come to know Him enables us to rise above circumstances. 'Ephesus' for you may be a factory, an office, a school, a college or even your own home. Though the atmosphere may be an unholy one, you can rise above your surroundings through God's power. You may be environed by 'Ephesus' but you draw your life from the kingdom of God. 'Ephesus' does not govern us – Christ does.

Father, how can I ever thank You enough that no outer hell can undermine the certainty of heaven which You have given me? It's not the circumstances but the 'innerstances' that determine my life. Amen.

'A long way to go'

For reading & meditation – Ephesians 1:3

'... God ... has blessed us in the heavenly realms with every
spiritual blessing in Christ.' (v.3)

Paul's statement in verse 3 seems simple yet is positively
staggering in its implications. He is saying that in Christ we
have everything we require for our *spiritual* development and
thus we never need to look elsewhere. What a thrilling thought!

Enquiring once about a mutual acquaintance who had turned
from a life of debauchery to become a well-known gospel preacher,
I was told that he and his wife had gone over to the Baha'i faith –
which attempts to accommodate all the different religions. 'He no

FURTHER STUDY

John 14:1-14;
1 Tim. 2:5;
Heb. 12:24

1. What did
Thomas and
Philip say
to Jesus?

2. How did He
respond?

longer believes Jesus is *the* Way,' my friend remarked,
'but *a* way.' Apparently the man's wife, when asked
how she was getting on, had replied: 'We still have
a long way to go.' Sadly their weary feet now walk
a path that leads nowhere and they will never find
security until they return to the only One who can
give them true satisfaction. How pointless to worship
at the tomb of a dead religious leader – the founder
of the Baha'i faith – when one can walk the open
road with the resurrected Jesus. It seems that the
fact they 'have a long way to go' even shows on the couple's faces.
I am not surprised – outside of Jesus Christ they will never obtain
'every spiritual blessing'.

Nothing other than a complete acceptance of Jesus as the *only*
way to God enables us to experience 'every spiritual blessing'.
Anything that is not of Jesus will fail to complete us; instead it
will deplete us. In Him alone is true spiritual blessing to be found.

**Heavenly Father, I accept that now I belong to Jesus I will be
provided with all I need now and hereafter. Anything not of Him
will bring emptiness; everything from Him will bring fullness.
All honour and glory be to Your precious name. Amen.**

What's His is ours

For reading & meditation – Ephesians 1:4–5

'... he chose us in him before the creation of the world to
be holy and blameless in his sight.' (v.4)

People who have recently become Christians and are just
beginning to explore the Scriptures are often surprised to
discover that before they chose God, He chose them. And *His*
choosing took place before the creation of the world. Every
Christian I know finds this truth somewhat mind-boggling.
We freely choose God, and then we discover that He has first
chosen us.

This is termed 'divine election', and I doubt if even the most
learned theologians can fully fathom the mystery.
But we must make sure that no pride arises in our
hearts because we have been chosen in this way. It
was not our merit but our misery that led God to
focus His love upon us. Before the foundation of the
world God put us and Christ together in His mind.
Though at the time we did not exist, He determined
through the redemptive work of Christ to make us
His children, 'holy and blameless in his sight'. Surely
this is one of the most wonderful truths that has
ever been revealed.

FURTHER STUDY

John 1:1-12;
Rom. 8:15;

2 Cor. 6:18;
Gal. 4:5-6

1. What does
Paul say we
have received?

2. What are we
able to cry?

We were *predestined*, the apostle goes on to say, to be *adopted*
into the royal family of heaven. God chose us in order to adopt us.
He already had a Son but He wanted a whole family of sons and
daughters to be like Him. Our adoption means we are accorded the
same rights that Christ enjoys. In Roman law, adopted children
had the same rights as natural children. I can't understand why
God should bestow on us such a privilege – but I stand upon it.

**Father, help me see that being adopted in Your family places upon
me a high responsibility – a responsibility to cultivate the family
likeness and become more and more like Jesus. Grant that this
may be so. Amen.**

Accepted!

For reading & meditation – Ephesians 1:6

'... to the praise of his glorious grace, which he has freely given us in the One he loves.' (v.6)

These lovely words are even more beautiful when read in the New King James Version of the Bible: '... to the praise of the glory of His grace, by which He has made us accepted in the Beloved.' *Accepted* – what a gracious word. According to Scripture we were strangers – distant, defiled, soiled sinners. Yet here it is said we are accepted. How could such a change take place?

We could not effect such a change ourselves. The explanation is we have been *made* acceptable in the 'Beloved'. And we have no reason to boast about this for our acceptance is 'to the praise of his glorious grace'. I feel sorry that the translators of the NIV did not use the word 'Beloved' in this verse. Several translations in addition to the New King James Version retain the title. The designation is such a beautiful one – doing something for the heart as well as the mind and conveying the marvellous relationship between the Father and the Son. I came across these words by Catesby Paget, which put very simply the truth I am trying to express here:

FURTHER STUDY

Psa. 139:13-18;
1 Cor. 1:28-29;
John 15:16;
2 Cor. 12:9-10

1. What kind of people does God accept?

2. Say to someone today, 'I am accepted in the Beloved.'

Near, so very near to God, nearer I could not be,
For in the Person of His Son, I'm just as near as He.

We are often reminded in Scripture of the love of Jesus for others, but the title 'Beloved' implies that He also is One who is loved. That always happens. If you wish to be beloved then love. Don't ask for it – give it. Then becoming beloved will follow as night follows day.

Father, help me to be more interested in giving love than in being loved. Forgive me that so often I am inclined to reach out to others for love instead of giving it. Love in me and through me. In Jesus' name. Amen.

Too good to be true

For reading & meditation – Ephesians 1:7–8
'In him we have redemption through his blood,
the forgiveness of sins …' (v.7)

We are predestined, adopted, accepted, and now, in today's verse we find we are redeemed and forgiven. Ruth Paxson in her commentary on Ephesians *The Wealth, Walk and Warfare of the Christian* likens reading the introductory verses of Ephesians to opening up a treasure chest and running your hands over a variety of precious jewels.

Take this: 'In him we have redemption through his blood.' Can we be redeemed in some other way? The answer of course is 'No'. If Christ had not shed His precious blood then we would still be slaves to sin. To redeem means to buy back by the payment of a ransom. Our deliverance is rescue from God's judgment on our sins and the payment was Christ's blood, which He shed for us on the cross. Redemption, adoption and forgiveness all go together – a trinity of joy. Remember, the forgiveness God offers is not cheap. It cost God dearly to forgive. The sacrifice of His Son is the price God paid to emancipate us.

FURTHER STUDY

Matt. 26:28;
Heb. 9:1-28;
10:19;
1 Pet. 1:18-19

1. What contrast does the writer to the Hebrews draw?

2. How did Peter put it?

Listen to this precious phrase: 'in accordance with the riches of God's grace that he lavished on us.' Lavished! The wonder of God's generosity in forgiving us is expressed by that word. It seems incredible! Are you not surprised that you have been forgiven – that God has lavished His grace upon you? Following my conversion I found myself saying over and over again: 'How could He be so generous? He took me – even me.' It all seems so undeserved. Too good to be true. But it is true. Eternally true. Hallelujah!

Lord God, how could You be so gracious to the ungracious, so good to the not-so-good, so loving to the unlovely? Your generosity breaks my heart and yet remakes me. My gratitude just can't be expressed in words. Amen.

An eternal perspective

For reading & meditation – Ephesians 1:9-10

'... he made known to us the mystery of his will ... to bring
all things ... under one head, even Christ.' (vv.9-10)

W ill the surprises never cease? Today's verses unfold another
thrilling thought: He has made known to us the mystery
of His will. What is His will? It is to unite all things in His Son.
Does this mean that everyone will ultimately be saved? Some have
taken these words to mean that, but what Paul is talking about
here is cosmic renewal – the creation of a new order. The universe
which has been disrupted by sin will be restored and unified in
Christ. Creation will groan no more.

FURTHER STUDY

Rom. 8:20-25;
2 Pet. 3:10-13;
Rev. 21:1

1. What does
Paul say will
happen to
creation itself?

2. What are
we looking
forward to?

How this truth must have supported and
strengthened Paul as he sat imprisoned in a Roman
jail. Though his freedom had been curtailed he was
able to let his mind run back to eternity past and
on into eternity to come. The apostle had an eternal
perspective. What a difference it makes to our daily
living when we carry with us a sense of our eternal
destiny and dwell continually on the fact of what
we were, what we are, and what we shall be. How
small are our horizons. How hemmed in we are by
the things of time.

Here is a simple formula that, as you ponder it, can help
transform your days: past election and future perfection. Before
you go out into the day remind yourself of the fact that you were
chosen in Christ before the foundation of the world, then think
too of the eternal joy that awaits you up ahead. If such doctrine
does not inspire a doxology then I will be greatly surprised. If
you share Paul's perspective then I think you too will share his
feelings of praise.

**Lord God, may I be lost in wonder, love and praise as I see Your will
being realised through Your Son. Your will means well, and it
means to make me well. It is not only good but redemptive.
I am deeply thankful. Amen.**

In Christ alone

For reading & meditation – Ephesians 1:10

'... to bring all things in heaven and on earth together
under one head, even Christ.' (v.10)

Though the verse points to the future how wonderful it would be
if, right here in the present, the Church would seek to bring all
things under the one head – Christ. The Church is seeking a basis
for unity but many of the discussions about it end in disagreement
because they are attempts by one group to persuade another that
their emphasis is right. There is nothing wrong in holding on to
what we believe is true doctrine, but when we gather with other
churches then the emphasis ought to be on Christ alone.

I read the other day of a town where all the
churches gathered together to celebrate Easter
Sunday in the town's civic hall and prior to
meeting in the hall they marched through the
town in an act of Christian witness. The ministers
and clergy did something revolutionary. Those
wearing clerical collars or robes decided to lay
them aside, and as they mingled with the people
the press reported that 'it was the strangest sight'
because they could not tell the ministers from the
people. The whole group gathered not with the
expectation that people should understand their
position about Church Orders, dress, etc., but that Christ alone
should be the focus of their meeting. God's purpose in the future
is to unite all things in Christ – and in Him alone. There is no
better plan. When we say Christ-and-something-else we divide;
when we see Christ and Christ alone we unite. Only when He
is the centre can true unity be known.

FURTHER STUDY

Matt. 11:27;
John 13:3;
Col. 1:20

1. What evidence
is there that
Jesus was aware
of bringing all
things together?

2. How did God
bring all things
together?

**Lord God, how grateful I am for this one purpose and one plan – to
unite all things in Christ. May that purpose be worked out not only
in eternity but also here in time. In Jesus' name I pray. Amen.**

'Doomed to be saints'

For reading & meditation – Ephesians 1:11–12

'In him we were also chosen ... in order that we ... might be
for the praise of his glory.' (vv.11–12)

Paul falls back on thoughts he has already introduced: 'chosen',
'predestined', 'the purpose of his will'. Is this tautology? No, it
is the ramp he uses to bring us face to face with the truth that
we have been brought into a relationship with God 'for the praise
of his glory'. The very first Bible I had given to me was from my
pastor, the man who led me to Christ. He wrote in it these words:
'To the praise of His glory'. When I first read those words I was
moved to tears. That Bible was so well used that it fell apart after
two years, but the words inscribed on the flyleaf
have lived on in my heart.

FURTHER STUDY

Rom. 15:1–6;
John 15:5–8;
2 Cor. 3:7–18

1. What does
Paul say about
the glory of
the Lord?

2. How did
Jesus say we
can reveal the
Father's glory?

What does being predestined for the praise of
His glory mean? It means that our primary aim is
to bring glory to God by our life and with our lips.
With our lives we live out His commands, and by
our lips we give Him praise. Let us be clear about
this: we are here not to advance our glory but *His*.
We are destined for this, says Paul, appointed for this
purpose from the very beginning.

An elderly African chief, when commenting
on this verse in a group Bible study, said: 'We are
doomed to be saints.' It was a slip of the tongue. He meant, of
course, destined to be saints. We are destined to live Christ's way
since 'All things were created *by* him and *for* him' (Col. 1:16). We
are made to think like Christ, act like Christ, love like Christ. To
live any other way is to deny our destiny.

**God my Father, how grateful I am that I am destined and appointed
to be in Christ – to think like Him, act like Him, love like Him. Since
this is my destiny I shall pursue it – by Your grace. In Jesus' name.
Amen.**

'This signet from God'

For reading & meditation – Ephesians 1:13–14

'Having believed, you were marked in him with a seal, the promised Holy Spirit ...' (v.13)

Don't miss Paul's use of pronouns here, as he moves from 'we' (v.12) to 'you' (v.13). The 'we' refers to himself as a Jewish believer, and the 'you' to the Gentile believers he is addressing at Ephesus. He is anticipating the theme of Jew and Gentile becoming one in Christ, dealt with later. When you believed, he tells his Gentile readers, you were marked with a seal, the promised Holy Spirit.

What does it mean to be sealed with the Spirit? A seal is a mark of ownership, an external sign that an object has become someone's personal property. There is no outward sign to show a person is a Christian (other than a radiant life) but there is an inward sign – the seal of the Holy Spirit. This is God's pledge that we have become His personal responsibility. Our being sealed with the Spirit guarantees that the inheritance God has promised us will become ours. The word translated 'deposit' (*arrabon*) is used in modern Greek for an engagement ring. Just as an engagement ring is a sign that marriage will take place so the Holy Spirit is an assurance that God will complete the good work He has begun in us. We have a taste now – the banquet comes later. Heaven awaits us, but we have a little bit of heaven to go to heaven in.

I love the way Eugene Peterson paraphrases this verse in *The Message*: 'This signet from God is the first installment on what's coming, a reminder that we'll get everything God has planned for us, a praising and glorious life.'

FURTHER STUDY

2 Cor. 1:18–22;
John 6:27;
1 Cor. 9:2

1. What does Paul affirm to the Corinthians?

2. What was Jesus able to declare?

Father, I am thankful that You have not only given me the promise of an eternal inheritance but a foretaste of it also. Help me realise that what I enjoy now is but a small sample of that which is to come. Amen.

Knowing God better

For reading & meditation – Ephesians 1:15–17

'I keep asking that … God … may give you the Spirit …
so that you may know him better.' (v.17)

I t is very striking,' says the commentator Geoffrey B. Wilson,
'that Paul never congratulates his readers on their faith, but
always thanks God for it.' Paul recognised that their conversion
was a demonstration of God's almighty power. But he not only
viewed them as a cause for gratitude; he also saw them also as
standing in constant need of his prayers. We tend to think of Paul
as a great preacher but he was a great pray-er too. Here he unfolds
for us the thoughts that nourished his prayer life. All effective

praying is rooted in biblical thought. I have never
yet met a person powerful in prayer who did not also
have a high view of Scripture. The one is the outcome
of the other.

Paul says of his prayers for the Ephesians: 'I keep
asking …' He did not pray for them just once, but kept
asking God that He would give them the spirit of
wisdom and revelation so that they might know Him
better. Wisdom is the heightening of our thinking
faculties. But we need revelation also. As we wait
before God He gives us insights which are not our
own. And for what purpose? That we might know
Him better.

What greater purpose can we have in life than getting to know
God better? The message of philosophy is: 'Know yourself.' But
philosophy never says: 'Know God.' We can never know ourselves
without knowing God. And our knowledge of God comes not as a
result of striving to know Him but from letting Him reveal Himself
to us. We know because we are known.

**Lord God, help me know You better. Give me the spirit of wisdom
and revelation that opens my heart to a deeper knowledge of
Yourself, for to know You is to love You. In Jesus' name I pray.
Amen.**

Three thrilling thoughts

For reading & meditation – Ephesians 1:18–21

'I pray also that ... you may know ... his incomparably great power for us who believe.' (vv.18-19)

Paul continues his prayer for the Ephesians by asking God that the eyes of their heart might be enlightened. He prays that they will understand three things. First, that they may know the hope to which they have been called. John Calvin said: 'Hope is no other than the expectation of those things which faith has believed to be truly promised by God.' What is the hope to which we have been called? We are called to Christ, to faith in Him, to joy, to freedom, to peace and coming glory.

Paul's second request is that they might know the riches of Christ's glorious inheritance in the saints. This refers specifically to what God has to give us in the future although we experience something of it now. As we saw in verses 13 and 14, the Holy Spirit is God's pledge that the inheritance He has promised will be given to us, and His presence makes us increasingly aware of the riches that are ours for ever.

Third, Paul prays that they might know the amazingly great power of God which was demonstrated most clearly when Jesus was raised from the dead. This is important because it is the 'power that is at work within us' (3:20). Just think: that same power is at work in our lives. Why is it, then, that we do not feel its effects more often? Can it be that we do not avail ourselves of it in the way we ought? How foolish to be given access to the greatest power in the world and not to draw on it. Resurrection power is available to us. Let's be sure to use it.

FURTHER STUDY

Psa. 62:1-12;
Rom. 8:11;
1 Chron. 29:12

1. What two things had the psalmist heard?

2. What impact does resurrection power have on us?

Father, help me never to forget that I live in the strength of the power that raised Jesus from the dead and lifted Him to the highest heavens. Show me how to appropriate it continuously.
In Jesus' name. Amen.

Spiritual cerebral palsy

For reading & meditation – Ephesians 1:22–23

'And God placed all things under his feet and appointed him to be head over everything for the church ...' (v.22)

Having touched on the truth that Christ has been exalted to the right hand of God, Paul continues by saying that the One to whom everything in creation has been made subject has been appointed Head of the Church, and therefore all the powers in the universe are under the authority not only of Christ but also the Church.

A boy of about ten once handed me a Bible and announced: 'Scripture says God gave His Son twice. The first time is mentioned in John 3:16. But do you know the second time?' As I was unable to answer him he drew my attention to today's text, which in the Authorised Version reads: 'and gave him to be the head over all things to the church'. It was a lesson I have never forgotten. Though a denomination may appoint a person as their head, there is only one Head of the Church – Christ.

The next words Paul uses baffle many: 'the fulness of him who fills everything in every way' (v.23). Does this mean God fills Christ as He fills all things? Or does it mean the Church fills Christ and He is incomplete without it? I think it means that the Church is the fulness of Christ, because He fills it. So if our Lord fills the Church why is His power and presence not manifested in the same way that it was when He was here on earth? The problem is not with the Head; the problem is with the body. Sometimes it seems as if the Church is suffering from spiritual cerebral palsy because the body does what the Head doesn't want.

FURTHER STUDY

Col. 1:15–20;
Eph. 4:15; 5:23;
Col. 2:16-19

1. How does Paul describe the supremacy of Christ?

2. How does Paul depict those who go off on tangents?

Lord God, forgive us that so often we, Your body, fail to carry out the instructions given by the Head. May there be greater co-ordination between us and our Saviour. In Jesus' name we pray. Amen.

Alive yet dead

For reading & meditation – Ephesians 2:1–2

'As for you, you were dead in your transgressions
and sins...' (v.1)

As we move into chapter 2 we experience a startling change: we plunge from the heights of redemption to the depths of ruin, from the pure air of heaven to the putrefied atmosphere of the pit. A striking contrast is drawn between what we are 'in Christ' and what we were before we invited Him to be Lord of our lives. Paul encourages his readers to take a look at what they were in order that they may become more grateful for what God has done for them and appreciate His grace more fully.

Prior to salvation, we 'were *dead*,' says the great apostle, 'in [our] transgressions and sins.' When I was a young Christian I used to puzzle a great deal over this, wondering how unbelievers could be described as 'dead' when clearly they looked very much alive. I thought of all the non-Christians I knew who seemed to enjoy life to the full. To some degree the problem was solved when I read Herbert Spencer's definition of death: 'cessation of correspondence with environment'. When a flower ceases to correspond with the environment for which it was made – soil

FURTHER STUDY

Rom. 8:1–8;
Ezek. 18:20;
Rom. 6:23;
James 1:15

1. What contrast does Paul make?

2. How does James describe the path from conception?

and water – though it continues to exist for a while it is dead. It is the same with the soul. Those who do not correspond with the soul's true environment – God – may have existence but they don't have spiritual life. They are as unresponsive to God as a corpse and are under the control of the devil. Life without God is a living death, and those who exist without Him are dead while they live.

Father, to be in You is to be alive – alive to the full, to my very fingertips. My heart overflows with gratitude for the privilege given me to be alive in Christ. Now there will be no more death. I am alive for *evermore*. Amen.

But!

Paul reminds us of one more unpleasant truth about ourselves. Eugene Peterson paraphrases Ephesians 2:3: 'We all did it, all of us doing what we felt like doing, when we felt like doing it, all of us in the same boat. It's a wonder God didn't lose his temper and do away with the lot of us' (*The Message*).

Peterson's contemporary language captures the apostle's thought that in our sinful state we did what we did because we enjoyed doing it. Not only were we sinners, we *delighted* in our sin. The more we think about our mutinous condition the more we have to agree that 'It's a wonder God didn't lose his temper and do away with the lot of us.'

Well, why didn't He? 'But because of his great love for us, God, who is rich in mercy, made us alive with Christ even when we were dead in transgressions – it is by grace you have been saved' (vv.4–5). Over and against our desperate condition these words break upon us like sunshine streaming through stormy clouds. We were rebellious, defiant, insubordinate, objects of wrath, *but* God had mercy on us. 'But.' A book I read in my youth entitled *The Buts of the Bible* described this 'but' as 'the hinge on which we swing from ruin to redemption'. It is indeed a glorious 'but'.

Always keep these two states in mind: what we were and what we are by grace. To think only of what we were leads to depression. To think only of what we now are leads to pride. To think of both leads to humility.

FURTHER STUDY

Lam. 3:1-23;
Psa. 103:17;
108:4;
Micah 7:18;
Titus 3:5

1. What never fails and is new every morning?

2. What question did Micah pose and what was his response?

Father, help me to keep things fully in perspective and to remember that it was Jesus my Saviour who wrought this change in me. Keep me free of pride and also free of depression. In Jesus' name. Amen.

What God has done

For reading & meditation – Ephesians 2:6–7

'And God raised us up with Christ and seated us with him
in the heavenly realms ...' (v.6)

Can anything be more wonderful? God has made us alive with Christ (v.5), has raised us up with Him (v.6a), and has seated us with Him in the heavenly realms (v.6b). These three actions, say many commentators, are linked to three great events in the life of our Saviour: the resurrection, ascension and exaltation. Those who recite the creed will be familiar with these words: 'The third day He rose again from the dead, He ascended into heaven and He sits at the right hand of God the Father.'

However, Paul is talking here about Christian believers. He is reminding us that God has raised us and seated us with Christ. This is the thrilling message of the New Testament: by virtue of our union with Christ we actually share in the resurrection, ascension and exaltation of our Lord. This may be meaningless mysticism to some, but to me it is a glorious fact. We share with Christ His privileges.

FURTHER STUDY

Acts 7:51-60;
Mark 16:19;
Luke 22:69;
Phil. 2:9

1. What did Jesus declare before Pilate and Herod?

2. What did Stephen see?

A Christian businessman had on his desk a motto: 'Keep looking down.' A friend commented: 'Shouldn't it read 'Keep looking up?'' 'No,' said the businessman, 'I'm already seated with Christ on the throne, and my task is to look down and see everything beneath my feet.'

God's purpose in granting us these wonderful privileges is so that 'in the coming ages he might show the incomparable riches of his grace, expressed in his kindness to us in Christ Jesus' (v.7). The glory always goes not to the one who is saved but to the One who saves.

Father, as I understand more each day of Your purposes I see that they go beyond creation to recreation – the redemption of us who spoiled Your first creation. We are the testimony to Your grace. Thank You Father. Amen.

By grace are you saved

For reading & meditation – Ephesians 2:8–9

'For it is by grace you have been saved, through faith ...'
(v.8)

Today's statement is a cornerstone of evangelical belief. It was Martin Luther's great conviction, C.H. Spurgeon's favourite truth, and the first of John Wesley's famous *Forty-Four Sermons* is based on it. Let's scrutinise in turn each of the three key words.

What do we mean by *grace*? An old definition is: 'the free unmerited favour of God'. Nothing in us gave rise to God's kindness towards us. The initiative was with Him. When you first came to Him (if you have) you came because He drew you. Grace drew you and grace keeps you. Most people think we are *saved* only from the penalty of sin, but we are being saved from the power of sin also. Through God's grace we can overcome such evils as jealousy, lust, greed and pride. From these and all other sins there is salvation here and now. At the heart of *faith* lies the idea of trust. Faith is the venture of the whole personality in trusting One who is worthy.

Am I talking today to someone who is not yet saved but now feels strangely stirred by God? Then God's gift of faith is being offered to you. God waits for you to open your heart to Him, and when you do He will by an act of grace – undeserved mercy – lift you out of sin and give you a new life. Nearly 2,000 years after the New Testament was first written this is still the heart of the gospel. With jubilation I repeat Paul's words: 'By grace you have been saved, through faith.'

FURTHER STUDY

Rom. 5:1-15;
Acts 15:11;
Rom. 3:24; 11:6

1. What has grace freely accomplished?

2. When is grace no longer grace?

Father, it seems incredible but true that in the ages to come You will have nothing more beautiful to show than the products of Your grace. We are to be the showpiece of Your riches. My heart is humbled dear Father. Thank You. Amen.

'God's work of art'

For reading & meditation – Ephesians 2:10

'For we are God's workmanship, created in Christ Jesus to do good works ...' (v.10)

Salvation is entirely the result of grace. It is something we receive. Now Paul balances this truth with the fact that we have been saved *for* good works. 'We are God's workmanship,' he cries – His work of art, His masterpiece – 'created in Christ Jesus to do good works.'

This makes clear the Christian position with regard to good works – they do not produce salvation but they are the product of salvation, of His 'workmanship'. Jesus Christ begins by changing us. He starts with the person and then His new creation takes on a new power. Just as a fish was created to swim and a bird to fly so a Christian has been created to demonstrate the power of God – by good works. 'Good works,' says John Stott, 'are indispensable to salvation – not as its ground or means, however, but as its consequence and evidence.' And according to Paul we are *destined* to bring forth good works, 'which God prepared in advance for us to do'.

FURTHER STUDY

Heb. 10:24;
James 2:14-26;
Matt. 5:16;
Titus 2:7

1. What are we to consider?

2. What example was Titus to set?

We return to the point we made earlier – we are destined to do certain things. What things? Actions that reveal our love, our faith, our forgiveness, and so on. Deeds that express hate, fear, self-centredness, guilt and suchlike are sand in the machinery of human living, whereas Christlike acts oil the mechanisms. God has pre-ordained what we should do. We can live against that destiny or we can live with it and for it. If we go with it we experience spiritual health; if we go against it we experience spiritual ill-health.

Father, I see I'm destined to be like Jesus – to love like Him, give like Him and act like Him. When I walk in His ways I make progress; when I walk in some other way I stumble and fall. Help me be more like Jesus. Amen.

Bad news - good news

For reading & meditation – Ephesians 2:11–13

'But now in Christ Jesus you who once were far away have
been brought near through the blood of Christ.' (v.13)

It is important to remember the deep divide between Jews and
Gentiles when Paul wrote this letter. Verses 11 to 22 deal with
divisions of race and culture. Gentiles were despised by the
Jews for being outside God's covenant; Jews were despised by
Gentiles for their spiritual arrogance and claim to be the only
people whom God loved.

Paul encourages his Gentile readers in Ephesus to remember
the great change which divine grace had brought about in their
condition and to reflect on their new standing with
God and their new relationship with Jews who shared
their faith in Christ. They had no past connection
with Christ (unlike the Jews who looked for a coming
Messiah), had been excluded from citizenship in
Israel, looked upon as foreigners to the covenants
of the promise, and were without hope and without
God in the world. One commentator sums it up: 'They
were Christless, stateless, friendless, hopeless and
godless.' That is the bad news.

But now comes the good news: 'In Christ Jesus you
who once were far away have been brought near through the blood
of Christ.' The spatial language used here – far and near – was
common in the Old Testament (see, for example, Deut. 4:7 and Isa.
49:1). How has this nearness to God been accomplished? Through
one means alone – *the blood of Christ*. Thus the integrating point
for Jew and Gentile is spiritual, not political. Outside of Christ there
can be no lasting relationship between Jew and Gentile.

FURTHER STUDY

Phil. 3:15-21;
Luke 10:20;
1 Pet. 1:4;
Gal. 3:26-28

1. What are we to
rejoice about?

2. What does
the citizenship
of heaven
mean for us?

God my Father, how wonderful it would be if everyone could see
this truth – that unity is achieved not through political means but
through You and Your Son. Help me make this truth more
widely known. Amen.

All one in Christ

For reading & meditation – Ephesians 2:14–15

'For he himself is our peace, who has made the two one …'
(v.14)

History shows that no treaty ever made can bring opposing groups into a state of permanent peace. It can help restrain hostile activity but it can never remove the will to war. The heart of peace is not an 'it' but a 'He'. God is our peace. He is working to unite men and women not by the reconstruction of human society but by the construction of an alternative society, as Paul shows so clearly in this passage.

How does God achieve lasting and meaningful peace between Jew and Gentile? First by destroying the barrier, the dividing wall of hostility. When Paul wrote these words the wall around the Temple which excluded the Gentiles was still standing but, as Armitage Robinson expressed it: 'It still stood but it was already antiquated, obsolete, out of date, so far as its spiritual meaning went. The sign still stood but the thing signified was broken down.'

And how did God break down the dividing wall between Jew and Gentile? Paul tells us it was 'by abolishing in his flesh the law with its commandments and regulations … to create in himself one new man out of two' (v.15). The law 'abolished' was not the moral law but the ceremonial law. Jesus, by His death on the cross, set the ceremonial law aside with all its rules and regulations. He has designed a new humanity, not by making a Jew into a Gentile, or making a Gentile into a Jew, but by reconciling both Jew and Gentile to Himself. All are on the same level at the foot of Christ's cross.

FURTHER STUDY

Col. 2:1-15;
Heb. 7:18; 8:13;
10:1; 12:27

1. What has Christ done with the written code of regulation?

2. What has been introduced?

Lord Jesus, You are our peace. Around You we unite. You have made it pos-sible for Jew and Gentile to be one, as we belong inseparably to You. Keep us close to You and to each other. For Your name's sake. Amen.

Proclaiming peace

For reading & meditation – Ephesians 2:17–18

'He came and preached peace to you who were far away and peace to those who were near.' (v.17)

Through His death our Lord Jesus Christ has abolished the law and brought into being a single new humanity. This, of course, relates only to those who are in Christ, and is the reason why Paul now draws attention to the fact that Christ came and *preached* peace.

Some think the preaching of peace here refers to Christ's public ministry but, as many commentators point out, peace was made at the cross and therefore the announcement of peace could not

FURTHER STUDY

Rom. 9:30–10:13;
Col. 3:11;
1 Pet. 3:8

1. How does Paul contrast the Jew and the Gentile?

2. What unites them?

take place until after the crucifixion. It is interesting to note that the first word Jesus spoke to the disciples after His resurrection was: '*Peace* be with you' (Luke 24:36). I believe Paul thinks that Christ preaches through the lips of His followers. 'It is a truly wonderful fact,' says John Stott, 'that whenever we proclaim peace it is Christ who proclaims it through us.' The preaching of this peace applied alike to those who were afar off (Gentiles) and to those who were near (Jews). As each group embraced the good news of the gospel they found a twofold unity – unity with God and unity with each other. One and the same Spirit was at work in both groups, giving both continuous access to God.

It is one thing to be reconciled to God but it is another thing to have continual access to a Father who can be approached without fear. How wonderful that God makes no distinctions. He welcomes each one of us who believe in Him equally, regardless of our background.

Father, how clear it all is – humility towards You produces humility towards one another. To be at peace with You is to be at peace with each other. Help us turn the ideal into reality. In Jesus' name. Amen.

God's dwelling place

For reading & meditation – Ephesians 2:19–22

'In him the whole building is joined together and rises to become a holy temple in the Lord.' (v.21)

Paul exclaims that Gentile believers 'are no longer foreigners and aliens, but fellow-citizens with God's people and members of God's household' (v.19). In other words, they are no longer refugees because now they have a new kingdom and a new home.

Perhaps the most exciting picture in this passage is that of the Church. Though the word 'Church' is not mentioned, that is the thought behind the phrase 'a holy temple in the Lord'. Paganism had set up a magnificent temple in the centre of Ephesus for the worship of the goddess Diana. Judaism also had its Temple in Jerusalem, dedicated to the worship of the one true God. Paul now places before the Ephesian Christians the thrilling truth that Christianity too has a temple of which Jesus Christ Himself is the chief cornerstone. Upon the divine foundation of the apostles and prophets (not necessarily themselves as persons, but the instruction that came through them) God lays one living stone upon another – those who come to faith in Him.

A sense of permanency is given by the words in verse 22: 'to become a dwelling in which God lives by his Spirit.' A *dwelling place* is not a temporary abode where the Spirit comes and goes. He will 'be with you for ever' Jesus promised the disciples (John 14:16). This truth that the Church is the lasting dwelling place of God's Spirit is the most beautiful thing imaginable. He does not come and go depending on our moods or emotions. He is with us – permanently.

FURTHER STUDY

Psa. 118:15–24;
Matt. 21:42–44;
Acts 4:8–12;
1 Pet. 2:4–8

1. How did Jesus describe Himself?

2. How does Peter describe the implications?

Father, the fact that we, Your people, are the dwelling place of God in the Spirit is something I can hardly take in. What more can I have? What more do I need? Let that truth embolden me I pray. Amen.

Suffering for the cause

For reading & meditation – Ephesians 3:1

'For this reason I, Paul, the prisoner of Christ Jesus for the sake of you Gentiles ...' (v.1)

So far Paul's thoughts have been so occupied with the scope of God's salvation that he has had no time for self-reference. But here he remembers where he is, and why. 'I [am] the prisoner of Christ Jesus for the sake of you Gentiles,' he says. A prisoner of Christ? But wasn't Paul a prisoner of Rome? In one sense he was but in a higher sense he saw himself as the captive of Christ. His imprisonment was part of an eternal purpose, 'for the sake of you Gentiles'.

FURTHER STUDY

Phil. 1:7-13;
Col. 4:2-18;
2 Tim. 1:8,16; 2:9

1. How did Paul view his imprisonment?

2. What did he ask prayer for?

Paul was incarcerated in Rome because of fanatical Jewish opposition to his mission to the Gentiles. He had been arrested in Jerusalem following the uproar caused by the false charge that he had taken with him into the Temple an Ephesian believer, Trophimus (Acts 21:29). The Jews set their faces against Paul for his interest in the Gentiles, and it is probable that the theme of the epistle to the Ephesians – an undivided humanity – had been his topic on many previous occasions. Acts 22 records that when Paul addressed a Jewish audience they listened quietly until he told them that God had sent him to the Gentiles (v.21). They then shouted: 'Rid the earth of him! He's not fit to live!' (v.22).

Without doubt Paul's Roman imprisonment was the direct result of his obedience to God's call to preach to the Gentiles. How many of us are willing to suffer for what we believe? After a little bit of persecution most of us, if we are honest, are guilty of retreating into silence. How sad.

Father, forgive me if I shrink in the face of persecution and hold back from saying what needs to be said. Give me tact, wisdom and grace to say what I know You would have me say. Amen.

Fellow heirs!

For reading & meditation – Ephesians 3:2–6

'This mystery is that through the gospel the Gentiles are heirs together with Israel ...' (v.6)

Paul assumes that his readers had heard something of the commission given him by God to become an apostle to the Gentiles and of the mystery revealed to him. A 'mystery' in Scripture is something that is understood only by those whom the Holy Spirit enlightens.

Paul has already briefly mentioned the content of this mystery in Ephesians 2:19: the fact that Gentiles had become equal members with Jewish Christians of the one Church of God. All racial barriers had been broken down and all the blessings promised to the Jews were now shared by the Gentiles. This was something that had been disclosed by Christ to Paul and the other apostles. Although the Old Testament indicated that the Gentiles would be blessed, as Paul himself reminded the Romans (Rom. 15:9–12), what was not understood was that as a result of God's grace Jews and Gentiles would share the same inheritance as fellow heirs, and that they would belong to the same body – the Church.

> **FURTHER STUDY**
>
> Heb. 1:1-4;
> Rom. 8:17;
> Gal. 4:7; 3:29
>
> 1. What does it mean to be an heir?
>
> 2. What does it mean to be a co-heir?

When Paul wrote that Gentiles were 'heirs together with Israel, members together of one body, and sharers together in the promise in Christ Jesus' (v.6) he made a really radical statement, for every day the pious Jew thanked God that he was not born 'a woman, a leper or a Gentile'. A new concept of society had emerged that embraced everyone who trusted the Lord for salvation and saw all believers as one family of God in Christ Jesus. In this new creation everyone who belongs to Jesus is a fellow heir!

God my Father, thank You for this revolution that You have brought about through Christ. Yet in some places Your Church seems to struggle with this concept. Cause all barriers to fall, I pray. Amen.

A psychological trick?

For reading & meditation – Ephesians 3:7–9

'Although I am less than the least of all God's people,
this grace was given me ...' (v.8)

God not only revealed to the apostle Paul that Jew and Gentile were to be incorporated into Christ and His Church on an equal footing but also that He had commissioned him to be His ambassador in making this truth widely known. Clearly Paul regarded this as a tremendous privilege. Grace and power had been given him to proclaim this message in the face of Jewish hostility even though he regarded himself as 'less than the least of all God's people'.

FURTHER STUDY

1 Cor. 15:1–11;
1 Tim. 1:12–17;
Gal. 2:20;
2 Cor. 5:16–21

1. How does Paul describe his former self?

2. How does he describe his transformation?

A liberal theologian said at a lecture I attended once that Paul's claim to be 'less than the least of all God's people' revealed what a low opinion he had of himself. He went on to argue that Paul was here resorting to a psychological trick in order to gain affirmation. As I listened to this explanation I fumed inwardly as it is obvious that Paul used the expression 'less than the least' not because he was looking to others to boost his ego but because he remembered what he had been in the past.

Review his record for a moment: he had been a blasphemer, a persecutor, and had been directly involved in the murder of Stephen – the first Christian martyr. While Stephen was being stoned to death he stood by, holding the coats. Grace had changed him but he never forgot the depths from which he had been delivered. No, it was not veiled humility that led Paul to say he was 'less than the least'. He made that comment because that was how he saw himself – as a trophy of grace.

Father, help me also never to forget the pit from which I was rescued. Whatever I am now it is all because of Your grace. May the humility that characterised the great apostle be in me also. In Jesus' name. Amen.

The divine masterpiece

For reading & meditation – Ephesians 3:10

'His intent was that now, through the church, the manifold wisdom of God should be made known ...' (v.10)

Paul tells us that one of God's intentions in forming the Church is to reveal to the rulers in the heavenly realms the many-splendoured wisdom of God. Some believe that the term 'rulers and authorities' refers to worldly political powers, but that is easily refuted when one looks at the phrase: 'in the heavenly realms'. Paul is talking here about cosmic intelligences – angels and demons. Satan and the fallen angels must stand amazed as they contemplate how God has overcome the effects of the first creation by the redemption He secured for the new creation. If they thought God's purposes had been foiled in the Garden of Eden they failed to understand the versatility of divine wisdom, which has taken humanity far beyond the purposes of the first creation. It would have been wonderful to see Adam rise from innocence through temptation into perfect holiness, but now God takes people who are *sinful* and makes them pure by His grace, which even overcame the otherwise insurmountable barrier dividing Jew and Gentile.

FURTHER STUDY

James 3:13-18;
Prov. 3:19;
Rom. 11:33;
1 Cor. 1:25

1. What are the characteristics of earthly and unspiritual wisdom?

2. What are the characteristics of heavenly wisdom?

No wonder the late Tom Rees, a famous evangelist, called the Church 'the divine masterpiece'. The Christian community is like a prism through which the light of God's wisdom shines, breaking up into myriads of different colours, each one demonstrative of the fact that eternal wisdom is more than a match for sin and Satan. The devil and his fallen angels are discomfited by it. The good angels stand in awe of it. Nothing can outwit God.

Lord God, how marvellous are Your ways. You surprise angels and demons by Your shrewdness and versatility. And I am part of that demonstration of divine wisdom. Thank You my Father. Amen.

Purposed - and accomplished

For reading & meditation – Ephesians 3:11

'... according to his eternal purpose which he accomplished
in Christ Jesus our Lord.' (v.11)

Today's verse has deep meaning. In Jesus, purpose became
accomplishment, the idea became fact, the Word became
flesh. Throughout time, men and women have purposed and
have come short of that purpose. Once God purposed to redeem
humanity through Jesus Christ at the close of the fulfilment of
that purpose Jesus could say, 'It is finished.' Note '*It* is finished', not
'I am finished.' Verse 11 is one of the most decisive verses in the
whole of Scripture. In all other faiths there is verbal anticipation;
only in Christianity is there realisation. Everything
God purposed, Jesus accomplished.

FURTHER STUDY

Exod. 9:16;
Acts 2:23;
Rom. 8:28;
John 19:30;
Heb. 10:10

1. What is
included in
God's eternal
purposes?

2. What is
finished?

A missionary says that he often told people of
other faiths: 'If you can find God some other way
than in Jesus then come back and tell me about it.' A
Hindu took him up on that, saying, 'I have found God
in myself.' During the conversation that went on for
some time he confessed to having so many sins in
his life that often he would contemplate suicide. The
missionary said to him: 'I can take you to hundreds
of people in this city who were guilty of the same
sins as you but through Christ they have been
forgiven and cleansed and now no longer live the way they did.'
The Hindu said, 'There you win. I have found no one who found
God in themselves to have power over sin.'

Other faiths may hope they get what they are wanting –
forgiveness and power to overcome sin. But only in Christ is the
great purpose of God accomplished. There is no other way.

**Lord Jesus Christ, just as God's purposes were accomplished in You,
may the divine purposes also be accomplished in me. Outside of
You there is nothing but barrenness; in You there is nothing but
realised accomplishment. I am so grateful. Amen.**

An ambassador in bonds

For reading & meditation – Ephesians 3:12–13

'In him and through faith in him we may approach God
with freedom and confidence.' (v.12)

The priesthood of all believers' expresses the fact that everyone
has the right to approach God through His Son Jesus Christ
without using an intermediary – one of the great doctrines of the
sixteenth-century Reformation. This is not to deny the function
of ministers in the Church, but to affirm the privilege accorded
to all believers to have direct access to the Father through Christ.
Paul is referring to this right when he says: 'In him and through
faith in him we may approach God with freedom and confidence.'
Are we so used to the freedom of access Christ has
given us that we take it for granted?

Paul concludes this chapter of his epistle as he
began (3:1), by drawing attention to the suffering
he had experienced because of his commitment to
the Gentile cause. But *my* sufferings, he says, are
your glory. He is suffering in prison for their cause,
he is their ambassador representing them – an
ambassador in bonds – standing firm for the truth
that they are to be included in God's new society.
Clearly Paul saw the Church as central to God's
purposes and to his ministry – and he was prepared
to suffer for what he believed.

FURTHER STUDY

1 Pet. 2:1-10;
Rev. 1:6;
Heb. 4:16;
10:19-22

1. What was
the privilege
of the priest?

2. What do
we now have
confidence
to do?

Permit me to ask you a personal question: How central to
your life and service is your concept of the Church? Do you pray
regularly for it? Even more to the point: Would you be willing
to suffer for it? Perhaps the old saying is true: 'We do not really
believe anything until we are willing to suffer for it.'

**Father, I see so clearly that the Church is central to Your purposes.
May it become central to my purposes also. Make me more active in
prayer that Your Church might become all You want it to be. In
Christ's name. Amen.**

Powerful praying

271

For reading & meditation – Ephesians 3:14–16
'I pray that out of his glorious riches he may strengthen
you with power through his Spirit ...' (v.16)

The best way to discover the concerns of a fellow Christian is to
listen to them pray. We all pray about those things that matter
most to us. The hymnist put it like this: 'Prayer is the soul's sincere
desire, uttered or unexpressed.' Paul was a great preacher but, as
I said earlier, he was a great pray-er also.

What prompted the great apostle's prayer? It was the thrilling
truth that he had been discussing – the revelation given to him
by God that all things are reconciled in Christ. Great praying is

FURTHER STUDY

Phil. 1:1-6;
Col. 1:3;
1 Thess. 1:1-3;
2 Thess. 1:11-12

1. How did Paul
always pray?

2. What was
his motivation
in prayer?

always inspired by biblical truth. As I pointed out
earlier, great pray-ers are people who fill their minds
with Scripture. What is Paul praying for? He prays
that his readers might be given the strength of the
Spirit, the abiding presence of Christ, the rooting of
their lives in love, the knowledge of Christ's love in
all its dimensions, and the fulness of God Himself.
What a prayer!

Don't you wish you could pray for people like
this – with prayers filled with deep biblical content?
I certainly do. The way to develop such a prayer life is easy to
understand though difficult to adopt. To do so we must soak
ourselves, as Paul did, in the great truths of Scripture, so that
when we pray our thoughts are guided by the issues that are most
central to the growth of our own and other people's spiritual lives.
The more Scripture we have in our minds the more powerful will
be our prayers. Powerful praying is biblical praying.

**Father, help me allow the truths of Your infallible Word to run
through my mind constantly so that I might deepen the content and
power of my praying. This I ask in Jesus' name. Amen.**

Love in four dimensions

For reading & meditation – Ephesians 3:17–19

'... to grasp how wide and long and high and deep is the love of Christ, and to know this love ...' (vv.18-19)

The apostle Paul knew that when the saints understand that the love of God is as wide as the universe, as long as the ages of eternity, as deep as the abyss from which He redeemed us and as high as the throne of God itself, there is just no way they can be overcome by gloom. I am convinced that nothing makes a Christian more secure than to know that they are loved with a love that is greater than any human love.

Often I have made this point and I make it yet again: none of us have been loved in the way our hearts crave. Wives, your husband is not enough. Husbands, your wife is not enough. Young man, young woman, your best friend is not enough. There are longings to be loved within you that only God can meet for He is the one who put those longings there in the first place.

Time and time again when people say their problem is they do not love God enough I say to them: 'No, that is not your problem. Your problem is you do not know how much you are loved.' In a way Paul is saying the same thing here, I think, for he knows that the more the Ephesian converts comprehend this great love, which stretches from one part of the universe to another *and will never be taken away*, the more the converts will be established in the faith. What Paul prayed for back there in Bible days I pray for you today – that your roots may go down into the fact that you are loved by the world's greatest Lover and nothing can ever separate you from it.

FURTHER STUDY

Job 11:7-8;
Rom. 8:35;
2 Cor. 5:14

1. How are the things of God to be measured?

2. What is the extent of Christ's love?

Lord God, thank You for reminding me of this great and wonderful fact that I am loved with a love than can never take away. I drop my anchor into the depths of this reassuring and encouraging revelation. In Jesus' name. Amen.

Free to give

For reading & meditation – Ephesians 3:20–21

'Now to him who is able to do immeasurably more than all
we ask or imagine ...' (v.20)

No limitation can be placed on God's resources. In this
magnificent doxology, one of the greatest in the Bible, Paul
expresses the truth that God's ability to provide surpasses our
asking and even our thinking. God does not just hear our words;
He is able to hear our unspoken thoughts also. How encouraging
this is. Aren't there times when we long for something to happen
in our Christian life but we can't put it into words? God can read
those unspoken thoughts and, what is more, He responds to them.

FURTHER STUDY

Job 42:2;
Matt. 19:16–26;
Luke 1:37;
Isa. 43:13

1. What
was Job's
conviction?

2. What did
Jesus tell the
disciples?

But it doesn't finish there – '*Immeasurably more
than all we ask or imagine.*' These words almost
transcend language and may leave us speechless
and in awe. This is because, says the apostle, 'his
power ... is at work within us' (v.20). Not *on* us
but *within* us. Something is going on inside each
Christian all the time. The Spirit is at work pleading
for our co-operation so that He might be allowed to
demonstrate how great God is. If there is full co-
operation then God's hands are untied. He is free
to give – and how!

The final ascription is: 'to him be glory in the church and in
Christ Jesus throughout all generations, for ever and ever!' Glory
in the Church and glory in Christ Jesus are not temporary; they
are to last for ever. There will never be a time when the glory fades.
After such a climax there is nothing for Paul to add except 'Amen'.
He had said all that could be said about redemption. The rest could
only be commentary.

**God my Father, my own heart says 'Amen' also. And this is not just
an intellectual assent but a vigorous affirmation of my faith. Thank
You Father. In Jesus' name. Amen.**

Walk on

For reading & meditation – Ephesians 4:1

'As a prisoner for the Lord, then, I urge you to live a life worthy of the calling you have received.' (v.1)

The apostle now begins to emphasise that we should show our indebtedness by the way we walk. Divine truth only becomes fruitful as it is translated into life.

You will notice that Paul does not dragoon his readers into submission but appeals for their obedience – a characteristic of all good Bible teachers. 'I urge you,' he says, 'to live a life worthy of the calling you have received.' Beware of those who thunder from the pulpit in commanding terms: 'Do this,' or 'Do that.' That is not the way to address the children of the King. Notice also that the apostle makes his appeal for them to live a life worthy of their calling only after he has made that calling crystal clear. Again, a mistake many Bible teachers make is to cajole their hearers into walking correctly before giving them a clear doctrinal perspective. In some parts of the Christian Church a growing problem is that experience is being emphasised over doctrine. One reader passed on to me a tape in which I heard a preacher say: 'I am not interested in what you believe; I am more interested in how you walk.' Really?

FURTHER STUDY

1 John 2:1-6;
2 Tim. 2:15;
1 Pet. 3:15

1. What did Paul exhort Timothy?
2. What should we always be prepared to do?

Surely the more clearly we understand our faith the better we will live it. The calling which is wholly of God comes first and a corresponding walk is looked for as the fitting consequence of that calling. Walking without an awareness of what is involved in our calling leads to legalism. Walking in the light of our calling leads to freedom.

Heavenly Father, now that I have surveyed with Paul the wealth and wonder of my calling as a Christian, teach me how to walk in a manner worthy of it. In Christ's name I pray. Amen.

Five foundation stones

For reading & meditation – Ephesians 4:2–3
'Make every effort to keep the unity of the Spirit through the bond of peace.' (v.3)

How do we live a life worthy of our calling? In today's verses the apostle tells us such a life is characterised by humility, gentleness, patience, mutual forbearance and love.

Humility was something the world in which Paul lived had little time for, regarding it as 'the crouching submissiveness of a slave'. Into this world Jesus had come, demonstrating humility by washing His disciples' feet. None was more gentle than Jesus. The word 'gentle' is often translated as 'meekness', which unfortunately has the connotation of weakness. Gentleness denotes strength that is under control. Patience is longsuffering – the willingness to put up indefinitely with difficult circumstances or irritating people. Mutual forbearance is the kind of tolerance that God shows towards us and without which no group of people can live together in harmony. Love is thinking more of others than oneself. When these five foundation stones are in place then, and only then, do we have the basis for enjoying spiritual unity.

FURTHER STUDY

2 Cor. 13:1-11;
Phil. 1:27;
Col. 2:2

1. What was Paul's appeal to the Corinthians?

2. What did Paul want to know about the Philippians?

Paul's exhortation to 'make every effort to keep the unity of the Spirit through the bond of peace' must be seen in this context. When we allow the indwelling Holy Spirit to cultivate these five cardinal virtues in us then keeping the unity of the Spirit will really be effortless. Remember, the unity of Christ's body has already been secured through the Holy Spirit. We are called simply to keep it, which we will as we cultivate these qualities.

Father, I recognise that the unity of the Spirit has already been secured. My task is to maintain it. Establish these five foundation stones firmly in my life I pray that I might demonstrate that unity. In Christ's name. Amen.

'No splits'

For reading & meditation – Ephesians 4:4–6
'There is one body and one Spirit ...' (v.4)

Paul now describes the unique basis of God-given unity, emphasised by the use of the word 'one', which occurs seven times: one body, one Spirit, one hope, one Lord, one faith, one baptism, one God. Most probably these words were originally part of an early confession of faith.

First, *one body* – the one Church of Jesus Christ. Not only the people who go to church but all those who belong to God through faith in His Son. Second, *one Spirit*. Just as the members of our physical body are joined together and function as a united whole so the unity of Christ's members in the Church is realised through the one Spirit who indwells them. Third, *one hope*. All Christians have the same hope of our heavenly inheritance. What can be more binding than the knowledge that we will all share in Christ's glory?

Fourth, *one Lord*. No other person has the right to claim to be the head of the Church. In Him alone is salvation to be found. Fifth, *one faith*. Because there is only one Lord there can only be one faith, one way of salvation. Sixth, *one baptism*. Our one faith is visibly confessed in one baptism. Seventh, *one God and Father of all*. The Church can no more be multiplied than our one God and Father can be multiplied. Thus the unity of the Church is as indestructible as God Himself. A local church may be split through warring factions or disagreements, but it is as impossible to split the Church invisible as it is to split the Godhead.

FURTHER STUDY
1 Cor. 8:1-6;
Mark 12:28-31;
Psa. 83:18

1. What perspective does Paul put on idols?

2. What did the psalmist want the people to know?

Father, how sad it is when a congregation splits. But it is comforting to know that though the separation of Your people hurts the reputation of Your Church it cannot destroy its essential unity. I am so thankful for that. Amen.

Every member ministry

For reading & meditation – Ephesians 4:7–10
'But to each one of us grace has been given as Christ
apportioned it.' (v.7)

In today's passage Paul shows that the unity of the Church doesn't mean uniformity. There can be variety. Different gifts are distributed in the body by the grace given to us in Christ.

When God created our bodies He knew what He was doing. He gave us two ears to hear in stereo, two eyes for peripheral vision; every part of our body has a different purpose. Likewise God knew what He was doing when He created the body of Christ, the Church. He created a body with different parts and gifts.

FURTHER STUDY

Matt. 25:14-28;
Rom. 12:1-8;
1 Cor. 12:12-31;
4:7

1. What is Jesus
teaching in
the parable of
the talents?
2. What is Paul
teaching in
his epistles?

Every single member of the Church has a gift! If you don't know what that gift is then you need to have a talk with your pastor. Those who have not yet discovered how they are gifted by Christ tend either to envy other people's gifts or attempt to do something for which they are not gifted. The gifts God has given to His people are the direct result of Christ's ascension into heaven, says Paul. Eugene Peterson in *The Message* puts it like this: 'He climbed the high mountain. He captured the enemy and seized the booty. He handed it all out in gifts to the people.'

Paul points out by way of parenthesis the truth concerning Christ's incarnation: He descended from heaven to earth and then ascended from earth to heaven. He has been exalted that He might take regal sway and provide His people with the grace and gifts they need.

**Father, thank You for not only saving me but for gifting me also.
Help me to discover the gift or gifts You have given me so that I will
function in Your body with maximum effectiveness and
minimum weariness. In Christ's name. Amen.**

God's training team

For reading & meditation – Ephesians 4:11–13

'... to prepare God's people for works of service, so that
the body of Christ may be built up ...' (v.12)

Paul now concentrates on God's gift of individuals whose
ministry is to build up Christ's body, namely apostles, prophets,
evangelists, pastors, and teachers.

Some believe that the ministry of apostles and prophets
ceased a few decades after Pentecost. That is not my view. The
first apostles had seen the risen Lord and been commissioned
by Him to preach the gospel, but the ministry of apostles and
prophets has continued throughout the entire life of the Church.
An apostle goes ahead to pioneer and plant. A
prophet brings the Word of God and applies it
to specific situations. An evangelist enlarges the
Church both by presenting the gospel and by
inspiring others to reach out to their non-Christian
friends. A pastor cares for the flock and a teacher
instructs them. Christ has given the Church five
'ministry gifts' to equip believers for service and
to help them become mature in the faith.

In verse 13 Paul uses the phrase 'unity in the faith'.
What is the difference between that and the unity of the Spirit?
We already possess unity in the Spirit; we move towards unity in
the faith. The unity of the Spirit has been achieved for us through
the work of the one Spirit. We, however, have to achieve the unity
of the faith through careful interaction with each other. How
wonderful it would be if, when discussing aspects of our faith with
one another, we kept in mind the old maxim: In things essential
unity; in things unessential, charity.

FURTHER STUDY

2 Thess. 1:1–5;
Heb. 6:1;
2 Pet. 1:5–6;
Heb. 5:14

1. What was Paul
able to give
thanks for?

2. What is for
the mature?

**Father, help us all to see more clearly that the prime purpose of the
ministry gifts You have given to Your body is that they might teach
us to minister. We languish because of this lack.
Help us Father. Amen.**

'No prolonged infancies'

For reading & meditation – Ephesians 4:14–16

'Then we will no longer be infants ... blown here and there
by every wind of teaching ...' (v.14)

One reason why so many in the Church are immature is because the ministry gifts are not being exercised. Any local church that does not seek to equip its members for service and lead them towards spiritual maturity is not functioning in accordance with biblical principles. I suggest every local church's mission statement should include wording along these lines: 'We see our prime task as teaching our members to serve Christ and bringing them to spiritual maturity.'

FURTHER STUDY
1 Cor. 14:13-20;
3:1-2;
Heb. 5:12;
1 Cor. 13:11

1. What was
Paul's rebuke to
the Corinthians?

2. What was he
able to say?

Otherwise the result is spiritual infantilism. A church where most of the members are like unstable children and have no settled convictions is a church that is lacking in spiritual leadership. I love Eugene Peterson's paraphrase of verses 14 and 15 in *The Message*: 'No prolonged infancies among us, please. We'll not tolerate babes in the woods, small children who are an easy mark for imposters. God wants us to grow up, to know the whole truth and to tell it in love – like Christ in everything.'

Next notice Paul's insistence on speaking the truth *in love* (v.15). 'Truth becomes hard if it is not softened by love,' said E. Stanley Jones, 'and love becomes soft if not strengthened by truth.' Love *with* truth is the right formula. God wrapped His truth in love and we called Him 'Jesus'. In Jesus, love speaks, acts and thinks. He is love in action. When we are in Jesus and speak the truth in love then we grow up in *every* way into Him – spiritually, mentally, emotionally, volitionally, socially.

Father, help me face this matter of spiritual infancy. You have opened to me the possibility of growth. Help me yield to the process, with nothing held back. And above all, teach me how to speak the truth in love. Amen.

The struggle to say 'Yes'

For reading & meditation – Ephesians 4:17–19

'So I tell you this, and insist on it in the Lord, that you must
no longer live as the Gentiles do ...' (v.17)

We have been called to be a *holy* people. The apostle knew
that the subject of holiness causes many people to switch
off. So he prefaces his remarks with the statement: 'I tell you this,
and insist on it in the Lord.' Insisting on what he was about to say
meant it was a non-optional issue. 'In the Lord' signified that the
message came not from Paul but the Lord.

The instruction 'you must no longer live as the Gentiles do'
might sound confusing, especially as Paul was writing to Gentiles.
What he was saying was: 'Don't live the way those
around you live.' It was essential that the Ephesian
Christians understood the difference between where
they had come from and where they now were. To
help them Paul embarks on a graphic description
of the state of their minds before conversion. Their
minds were darkened, he tells them, until the laser
beam of Christ's light cut through that darkness,
which was due to ignorance and ignorance to the
hardening of their hearts.

'Hardening of their hearts' suggests that wilful
stubbornness is the underlying cause of the
human condition. There is a deliberate refusal on
the part of people to allow God's light to penetrate their minds.
It is not so much that we are born sinners but that we choose
to remain sinners. We don't believe because we don't want to
believe. Hardness of heart leads to darkness of the mind, and
that to deadness of the soul. And all because we simply will not
say 'Yes' to Jesus.

FURTHER STUDY

Heb. 12:1-14;
Lev. 11:45;
2 Cor. 7:1;
2 Pet. 3:11

1. What are we
to make every
effort to do?
2. What is the
relationship
between
holiness and
happiness?

**Father, I am so thankful that I was enabled by Your Spirit to say
'Yes' to Jesus. It was this that brought light into my mind and life
into my soul. I am grateful beyond words. All honour be to
Your name. Amen.**

Off with the old

For reading & meditation – Ephesians 4:20–24
'... put off your old self ... corrupted ... put on the new self,
created to be like God ...' (vv.22-23)

'Y ou, however, did not come to know Christ that way' (v.20) does not convey Paul's meaning as clearly as it might. *The Message*'s paraphrase is better: 'But that's no life for you. You learned Christ! My assumption is that you have paid careful attention to him, been well instructed in the truth, precisely as we have it in Jesus' (vv.20–21). There is truth but there is also truth *in Jesus*.

When Paul says 'the truth that is in Jesus' (v.21) he is implying

that the substance of Christian teaching is Christ. He is the Alphabet out of which God frames all we need to know on the route to spiritual maturity. Becoming a mature Christian involves much more than learning biblical doctrines; it involves knowing Christ who is the subject of those doctrines. John Stott points out that 'Christ himself is the Christian's teacher, even when that teaching is given through the lips of his teachers.'

Since we no longer have the excuse of ignorance (because our minds have been enlightened) we must put off everything that has any connection with our old way of life. And not only must we put off those old clothes; we must also put on new clothes – the character of Christ. We usually wear clothes to suit the occasion – casual wear at a party, more formal attire at a wedding or a funeral, and so on. Similarly now that we are in Christ we should wear the clothes that suit our new position. And the clothes we should wear are the clothes of His character.

Father, save me from becoming someone who wears the clothes of Christ's character on some occasions only; help me wear them all the time. Off with the old – on with the new. This shall be my life motto. Amen.

A strong challenge

For reading & meditation – Ephesians 4:25–28

'Therefore each of you must ... speak truthfully to his neighbour, for we are all members of one body.' (v.25)

Do you tell lies? Then stop it, says Paul. Christians should be known as tellers of truth. In ancient Ephesus truth was not regarded as important. But that was no reason for Christians to adopt such a viewpoint. Paul saw lying as causing offence. When Christians lie to one another it sends a shudder through the body of Christ.

Sinful anger must be put away too, instructs the apostle. How can we be angry and yet not sin? When we are angry at nothing but sin. Sinful anger is anger that is motivated by such things as pride, malice and the desire for revenge. Christian anger is caused by *grief* at the bad things that people do and not a *grudge* at what is happening to us. The psalmist expressed this godly anger when he said: 'Indignation grips me because of the wicked, who have forsaken your law' (Psa. 119:53).

FURTHER STUDY

Psa. 37:1–8;
Prov. 14:17;
Eccl. 7:9;
Matt. 5:22;
James 1:19

1. What does anger lead to?

2. What does a quick-tempered man do?

We must be careful too, Paul warns, that we do not let the sun go down upon our wrath. He is not saying that we should wait until sundown before we deal with our wrath but that we should not nurse it. The old maxim 'Never go to bed angry' is a good one. Anger not only curdles the soul; it also gives the devil a foothold. Satan loves to linger around people who are angry, and if the anger is not dealt with then he quickly moves in.

Christians must not steal either. Stop stealing and start working, admonishes the apostle. Not only to get money to live but to get money to give to others. In other words, don't be a burglar, be a benefactor.

Loving Father, Your Word cuts deep into the very fabric of my soul. Help me be honest, free of all unrighteous anger, and someone who gives to others. In Jesus' name I pray. Amen.

Watch your language

For reading & meditation – Ephesians 4:29–30

'Do not let any unwholesome talk come out of
your mouths ...' (v.29)

Paul reminds the Ephesian Christians of the power of the tongue. Watch what comes out of your mouth, says the apostle, and make sure that your words are wholesome and edifying.

I have heard Christians say some terrible things to each other. Harsh comments, swearing and vulgarities should not come from a Christian's mouth. The tongue is the most difficult part of the body to bring under control, says James in the third chapter of his letter, and when a Christian resorts to cursing or swearing to make a point they show by their words just how little control the Holy Spirit has in their life. Some time ago I came across this by Will Carleton:

FURTHER STUDY

James 3:1-12;
4:11;
Titus 3:1-2;
Psa. 34:13

1. What analogy
does James use?

2. What was
Titus to remind
the people?

Boys flying kites haul in their white-winged birds,
You can't do that when you are flying words,
Thoughts unexpressed fall back dead,
But even God can't kill words after they are said.

We grieve the Holy Spirit when we allow our tongues to run away with us and use words that blister instead of bless. Why is He grieved? Because we show by our words that we do not take the issue of purity as seriously as we should. He is, after all, the *Holy* Spirit. And He is grieved by anything that even borders on the unholy. So the next time you feel like using a swear word or making a vulgar remark, remember that the *Holy* Spirit is listening and that bad words bring great grief to Him.

God my Father, help me use language that helps and does not hurt, that heals and does not hinder. Forgive me if I have hurt You, Christ and the Holy Spirit through anything I have said. In Jesus' name. Amen.

A striking contrast

For reading & meditation – Ephesians 4:31–32

'Be kind and compassionate to one another, forgiving each
other, just as in Christ God forgave you.' (v.32)

It would be difficult to find another text in Scripture filled with
such ugly words as verse 31. Reading them brings a chill to the
spirit: 'bitterness, rage and anger, brawling and slander … malice.'
They are like dark clouds but in the next verse it seems as if the
clouds part and the sun shines through again with warmth and
light: 'Be kind and compassionate to one another, forgiving each
other, just as in Christ God forgave you.' What beautiful language.

Bitter people have a crabby spirit which often reveals itself on
the face, giving rise to the expression 'sour puss'.
Those who are filled with rage have deep down
within them a smouldering anger. Brawling is the
action of those who like to quarrel, and slanderous
people are those who destroy the reputation of
others behind their backs. Those with malice wish
harm on others and plot against them, seeking to
bring about their downfall. There is no place for
these things in the Christian life. Instead, as Paul
says, we should be kind to one another. You will
never regret being sympathetic and kind. Almost
every one of us has regrets in life, but no one has
any regrets about being kind.

FURTHER STUDY

2 Pet. 1:1-7;
1 Cor. 13:4;
2 Cor. 6:6

1. What does a
look of kindness
show?

2. Think of
kindness and
demonstrate
it to someone
today.

We are to forgive one another also, just as in Christ God forgave
us. How does God forgive in Christ? Lightly? No, it cost Him the
death of His own dear Son. It costs to forgive, as I am sure you
know. But we must offer forgiveness even though it has to be
tendered through nail-pierced hands.

**Father, I see that I am to forgive as I have been forgiven –
generously, wholeheartedly and fully, with no conditions attached.
Help me understand that if I do not forgive I break the bridge over
which I myself must pass. Amen.**

Losing and finding

For reading & meditation – Ephesians 5:1–2

'Be imitators of God, therefore, as dearly loved children ...'
(v.1)

Now we are instructed to be imitators of God in compassion. Imitators of God? What a startling expression. How can we do as we have been directed? Eugene Peterson's *The Message* paraphrases verse 1: 'Watch what God does and then you do it.' Children learn how to behave by watching their parents. Christians learn how to behave by watching what God does and then doing it themselves.

This raises the question: What is the one thing above all others that characterises God? People will have different opinions but permit me to tell you what I think it is – the spirit of self-sacrifice. One of the most profound laws of the universe is: 'Whoever finds his life will lose it, and whoever loses his life for my sake will find it' (Matt. 10:39). And does this law hold good for God as well as humankind? 'By all that God requires of me, I know that He Himself must be.' God obeys every law He makes for us.

FURTHER STUDY

John 15:1-13;
Gal. 1:4;
Titus 2:14;
1 John 3:16

1. How is the greatness of love demonstrated?

2. What ought we to do?

The greatest of all became the servant of all in the Person of His Son. Jesus was not a moralist imposing on humanity a moral code. He was a revealer of the nature of reality. He revealed that God is self-giving love. No wonder our Lord's sacrifice on Calvary is described by Paul as 'a fragrant offering and sacrifice to God' (v.2). This, then, is what it means to imitate God: giving ourselves up for others. Nothing in all the universe is greater. The principle of self-giving is firmly planted in the heart of the Deity; it must also be firmly planted in us.

Father, the world's emphasis on the need to realise oneself seems tawdry when placed against this amazing revelation of self-giving. I must lose myself in order to find myself. Help me grasp this. Amen.

No self-indulgence

For reading & meditation – Ephesians 5:3-4

'But among you there must not be even a hint of
sexual immorality ...' (v.3)

As the apostle tells us in these verses, we should separate ourselves from all that is unholy. There must be no sexual immorality or greed among those who are God's people, not even a hint of it.

The gist of Paul's argument, based on the opening verses of this chapter, is: don't allow love to turn into lust. I once heard a preacher define the difference between love and lust as: 'Love can always wait to give; lust can never wait to get.' A young girl who was a believer was pestered by her fiancé – also a believer – to have a sexual relationship before marriage. She responded to his plea 'But I love you' with words similar to those I have just quoted: 'If you loved me, really loved me, then you could wait to give. What you are saying is not 'I can't wait to give but I can't wait to get.'' That brought the young man up with a start and led to the end of the engagement.

FURTHER STUDY

James 1:22-27;
Prov. 13:3; 21:13;
1 Pet. 3:10

1. How do
we deceive
ourselves?

2. What makes
a good day?

What is more, sex is not something to even joke about, continues the apostle, but a cause for thanksgiving. He is thinking, of course, about sex within the marriage bond. The world loves to joke about sex but Christians have a responsibility to shun such coarse humour. Self-sacrifice is the hallmark of a believer, not self-indulgence. In Ephesus, a centre of sexual vice and debauchery, these words might have sounded like a thunderclap. They might sound like that right here in the twenty-first century too. But this is what God says. We ignore His words at our peril.

**Father, You raise the standards high but You provide the power to
keep them also. Help me cut out of my life all that dishonours Your
name. Instead may I to live a life characterised by
constant thanksgiving. Amen.**

'Empty words'

For reading & meditation – Ephesians 5:5–7

'Let no-one deceive you … for because of such things
God's wrath comes on those who are disobedient.' (v.6)

Paul says that Christians should live a life free of immorality
because of the fact of judgment. Immoral people may get
away with their behaviour in this world but they will reap the
consequences in the world to come.

The words he uses are among the most sober in Scripture: 'No
immoral, impure or greedy person … has any inheritance in the
kingdom of Christ and of God' (v.5). The kind of person to whom
the apostle is referring here is the one who has given themself
over to an immoral way of life, one who is obsessed
with sex and is greedy for more. Such a person Paul
describes as an 'idolater' – a worshipper of eroticism.

'Let no-one deceive you with empty words,'
continues the apostle, meaning: don't be taken in
with religious smooth talk. There were false religious
teachers in Paul's day who argued that sins of the
body in no way affected the state of the soul. Those
that Paul seems to have had in mind were the
Gnostics (Knowing Ones) who thought they knew
better than God.

FURTHER STUDY

1 Tim. 1:1-7;
4:1-5; 6:3-5;
2 Tim. 4:1-5

1. What did
Paul urge
Timothy to do?

2. What charge
did he give
to Timothy?

Our world is filled with 'knowing ones' also – people who
teach that God is too good to keep anyone out of heaven and that
everybody will make it there in the end, though they might have
to pass through some period of refining. Such teaching must be
condemned as 'empty words'. The truth is: the wrath of God falls
on the disobedient. Avoid partnership with such people, we are
told. We may have to associate with them, says Paul, but we must
not become partners with them.

Heavenly Father, help me pause for a moment of self-examination
to ensure that there is nothing going on in my life that is deserving
of judgment. Keep me clean, keep me pure, and keep me from
all evil. In Jesus' name. Amen.

The great unmasking

For reading & meditation – Ephesians 5:8–14

'For you were once darkness, but now you are light in
the Lord.' (v.8)

Today we have yet another reason for avoiding an immoral
lifestyle: we have been delivered from darkness and are now
'light in the Lord'. Paul begins: 'For you were once darkness.' The
problem of living in darkness is that it pervades you and you
become darkness. You become what you habitually think about
and do. The result of such darkness is appalling moral degradation.

The opposite is also true: 'now you are light in the Lord.' You
are not merely in the light, you are light. As you live in the light
you become light. A Christian has been described as
'someone who lets the light come through'. But to live
in the light we have to adopt the proper attitude to
those who are in darkness. We must expose deeds
of darkness to the light. Doesn't that sound rather
judgmental? Do we need to set out to expose every
act of wickedness we come across? No, I don't think
that is meant. Paul is saying that the more God's
light shines through our lives the more deeds of
wickedness will be exposed, by the light that shines
in us and through us.

FURTHER STUDY

John 12:27–36;
Acts 13:47;
Phil. 2:15;
1 Thess. 5:5

1. What has
the Lord
commanded?

2. What are we
to shine like?

At times it may become necessary verbally to condemn and
expose evil, but the main thrust of Paul's argument is that the
light shining through Christians shows up by contrast the evil that
crosses our path. It is light that makes everything visible. Darkness
hides ugliness; light reveals ugliness. Evil needs to be unmasked,
sometimes verbally – by our lips – but always vitally – by our lives.

**Father, I see I have a responsibility to expose evil, sometimes by my
lips but always by my life. Help me avoid judgmentalism and yet
unmask evil. In Christ's name. Amen.**

Managing time

For reading & meditation – Ephesians 5:15–17

'Be very careful, then, how you live ... making the most of
every opportunity ...' (vv.15–16)

Wise people, says the apostle, are those who make the
most of every opportunity. In other words, they are good
managers of their time. Some translations actually use the word
'time' instead of 'opportunity' because the Greek word *kairos* has
the meaning of a limited period of time, a fitting or opportune
time. 'Redeeming the time' is the wording used in the New King
James Version. Discipleship, it seems to me, ultimately amounts
to what we do with our time.

FURTHER STUDY

Eccl. 2:17-22;
Psa. 90:12;
Col. 4:5;
1 Cor. 7:29

1. What so often
robs us of time?

2. What are
we to make
the most of?

In the book *Managing Your Time* Ted Ensgtron
and Alex Mackenzie refer to an announcement that
once appeared in a USA newspaper: 'Lost yesterday,
somewhere between sunrise and sunset, two golden
hours, each set with sixty diamond minutes. No
reward offered, for they are gone for ever.' Do you
manage your time well? Do you know the difference
between the urgent and the important? If so, you are,
says Paul, a wise person.

Wise people also find what the Lord's will is
for their lives. Someone has put it like this: 'To follow our own
will is pure foolishness; to follow God's will is pure wisdom.'
How do we discover the will of God? Nine-tenths of God's will
for our lives is revealed in Scripture – the revealed will of God.
Only one-tenth is not revealed. And the key is this: the more we
understand the revealed will of God the more clearly we will
understand the unrevealed will of God. Do what you know you
should do and you will receive guidance concerning what you
don't yet know.

**Father, forgive me for the times I have pleaded to know Your
unrevealed will when I have not taken the trouble to get to know
Your revealed will. Help me correct this in the future.
In Jesus' name. Amen.**

Keep being filled

For reading & meditation – Ephesians 5:18

'Do not get drunk on wine ... Instead, be filled with the Spirit.' (v.18)

Paul's exhortation to be filled with the Spirit is a command to be obeyed, not simply the mention of an experience to be enjoyed. The verb 'be filled' in the Greek is in the present continuous tense so the words are best translated 'be being filled with the Spirit'.

People have different ideas about how we are filled with the Spirit. Some think the gift of the Spirit is part of our conversion experience; others maintain the Spirit can be imparted at conversion but that usually the gift comes later. The issue is really whether or not the Spirit is filling you now. As Billy Graham admits: 'I need to be continually filled with the Spirit because there are holes in my soul through which He easily leaks out.'

But why does Paul warn: 'Do not get drunk on wine' before directing the Ephesians to 'be filled with the Spirit'? One interpretation of the words is: 'Do not be drunk with wine but be drunk with the Spirit.' But that is not what Paul is saying. Dr Martyn Lloyd-Jones pointed out that wine is not a stimulant but a depressant: 'It depresses the highest centres of all in the brain ... they control everything that gives ... self-control, wisdom, judgment, discrimination ... everything that makes a man be at his very best and highest.' If we are truly filled with the Spirit our faculties will not be depressed but stimulated – to behave as Jesus did. Being filled with wine leads to debauchery, being filled with the Spirit leads to discovery.

FURTHER STUDY

Luke 4:1-14;
Acts 2:4;
4:31; 11:24

1. How did Jesus return to Jordan?

2. How did Jesus return to Galilee?

Heavenly Father, help me examine my soul in the light of what I have read today to see whether my experience of the Spirit is up to date. Help me to keep being filled. In Jesus' name I pray. Amen.

Speak, sing, submit

For reading & meditation – Ephesians 5:19–21
'Speak to one another with psalms, hymns and spiritual songs.' (v.19)

When we allow the Holy Spirit to continually fill us, says Paul, we will speak for Him, sing for Him and submit for Him. What does it mean to speak for Him? When we speak to one another with psalms, hymns and spiritual songs we both edify one another and glorify God.

The picture we have in verse 19 is of a church giving members the opportunity to speak to one another about the things of God, as the Spirit directs them. A church where the members are unable to do this is not following the biblical pattern.

FURTHER STUDY

1 Cor. 14:1-15;
Psa. 81:1;
Isa. 30:29;
James 5:13

1. What did Paul say he would do?

2. What is James' exhortation to the happy?

Spirit-filled believers also sing for Him. Singing and making music must come from our hearts and be directed to the Lord. Think, for example, of Psalm 95, which begins: 'Come, let us sing for joy to the LORD; let us shout aloud to the Rock of our salvation.'

Most of us have no difficulty in responding to the Spirit's invitation to sing and speak for Him, but what about submitting for Him? Ah, there's the rub. Submission to one another out of reverence for the Lord is not always easy, and there is no doubt without the Spirit's assistance it would, on occasions, be well nigh impossible. Perhaps because of the natural tendency we all have to put ourselves first, one of the most evident signs of being filled with the Spirit is displaying the same humility that characterised our Lord and honouring each other more than ourselves for His sake. How wonderful it would be if we were as ready to submit as we are to speak and sing.

Father, help me display the meekness of Christ, not only when I speak or sing but when I am called to submit. May I keep before me the pattern of the Lord Jesus in all this. Amen.

God's word for wives

For reading & meditation – Ephesians 5:22–24
'Wives, submit to your husbands as to the Lord.' (v.22)

Being filled with the Spirit helps us relate properly to one another in the home. Paul focuses on the relationships of husband and wife, parents and children. He begins with the relationship of the wife to the husband: 'Wives, submit to your husbands as to the Lord.' Many women cringe at the word 'submission'. I am not surprised. Some of the teaching given on submission makes me glad I am not a woman.

Submission is not absorption into a man. God does not call a woman to be a non-person in the name of submission. Neither is it appeasement, with the wife doing everything her husband tells her in order to pacify him. What if he asks her to sin? Is she to obey in order to keep the peace? Of course not. But aren't women called to submit to their husbands 'in everything' (v.24)? Yes, in everything except sin. If it were otherwise this command would be inconsistent with teaching given elsewhere in the New Testament. What, then, is submission? It is a willingness to yield to her husband's authority and to support his leadership whenever that leadership does not lead to sin.

FURTHER STUDY

Col. 3:15-25;
1 Tim. 3:11;
Titus 2:4;
1 Pet. 3:1-7

1. What are the older women to teach the younger?

2. What example does Peter give?

Notice Paul's words: 'submit ... *as to the Lord.*' In my experience if a woman has problems submitting to her husband she has problems also in submitting to the Lord. Just as the Church is called to submit to Christ so is a woman to her husband. This may not be popular teaching in today's world, but the issue is not if it suits us but whether or not it is what God asks.

**Father, help us in this day when biblical teaching is viewed as out of date to honour You and Your Word in everything. The world's way has never been Your way. Help me understand that.
In Christ's name I pray. Amen.**

God's word for husbands

For reading & meditation – Ephesians 5:25–27
'Husbands, love your wives, just as Christ loved the church and gave himself up for her ...' (v.25)

What are husbands commanded to do in relation to their wives? They are to love them – in the same way that Christ loves the Church. How does Christ love the Church? First, He *sacrificed* Himself for her. If a man does not demonstrate a willingness to sacrifice himself on behalf of his wife then there is little hope for that relationship. Husbands, are you willing to sacrifice your own pleasure to give pleasure to your wife? If not, then you are failing to follow in the footsteps of Christ.

FURTHER STUDY

1 Pet. 3:7-12;
Gen. 2:23-24;
Prov. 5:18

1. How are husbands to treat wives?

2. What happens when they don't?

Second, He is the initiator of love. Why does the Church love Christ? He poured His love into us and our hearts flamed in response. 'We love *because* he first loved us' (1 John 4:19). This does not mean that a woman cannot initiate love but that, generally speaking, this is a man's function. A man is designed to initiate; a woman to respond.

Third, He continuously seeks to beautify her. He is at work all the time attempting to make the Church holy, cleansing her from defilement, and one day He will take her to Himself 'without stain or wrinkle or any other blemish' (v.27).

What a beautiful picture this is. It portrays the Saviour nurturing His Church to make her radiant for the time when He will come back and claim her. Likewise, God wants every husband to dote on his wife, to think up endless ways in which he can minister to her and make her happy. Since this is how Christ relates to His Church, this is how husbands should relate to their wives.

Father, once more I pray that You will help us to avoid being brainwashed by the world and to take to heart Your age-old truths. And not merely take them to heart but put them into practice. In Christ's name I ask it. Amen.

'Not just good friends'

For reading & meditation – Ephesians 5:28–33

'In this same way, husbands ought to love their wives as their own bodies.' (v.28)

Many commentators have struggled with the opening sentences of this section: 'Husbands ought to love their wives as their own bodies. He who loves his wife loves himself' (v.28). The cause of their difficulty is the sudden transition from the theme of Christ's love to self-love. Why does Paul descend from the elevated level of Christ's love to the low level of a man's love for himself? Perhaps because though we may find it difficult to comprehend the deep love that Christ has for His Church we can grasp the love we have for ourselves. And this love is never condemned in Scripture. We are even to love our neighbour as much as we love ourselves (Lev. 19:18). From a lifetime of observation – personal and general – if a man loved his wife as he loved himself there would be far fewer problems in marriage. 'After all, no-one ever hated his own body,' says Paul (v.29). If you doubt that, go to a gymnasium where men are working out and count the number of times they look in the mirror.

Clearly this exhortation for a man to care for his wife as his own body is given by Paul because in marriage a man and his wife have become 'one flesh' (v.31). And this mystery of two becoming one in sexual union is a picture of the relationship that exists between Christ and His Church. Let it stagger you if you will, but our relationship with Christ is as intimate as a man's physical union with his wife. We are not just 'good friends'. We are one with Him. *One.*

FURTHER STUDY

John 17:1-26;
15:9-17;
Rom. 8:35;
Gal. 2:20

1. What was the last statement of Jesus' prayer?

2. What picture did Jesus draw of oneness?

Father, help us to submit to You fully and absolutely. When we do so then the matter of how we are to relate to each other will be resolved more easily. In Christ's name I ask it. Amen.

Fathers and children

For reading & meditation – Ephesians 6:1–4

'Children, obey your parents in the Lord, for this is right.'
(v.1)

Children, Paul commands, must obey their parents, and particularly fathers must not exasperate their children. Why are children to obey? Paul gives two reasons: first, it is right; second, it is one of the Ten Commandments, given by God to Moses on Mount Sinai. When Paul says 'this is right' he means there is a rightness about a child obeying their parents because it accords with biblical teaching, it is plainly reasonable and part of the universal scheme of things.

FURTHER STUDY

Prov. 22:1–6; 1:8;
6:20;
Col. 3:21

1. What is the responsibility of parents?

2. What are fathers not to do?

Before we are qualified to have authority over others we must first learn to obey. Most children will one day become parents themselves, and no parent can effectively wield authority until they have learned how to live under authority. Psychologists have observed that once people who have not learned to obey find themselves in a position of authority over others, they tend to use that authority in an abusive way. One of life's great axioms is: 'To rule one must first learn to obey.'

Parents have a duty also: they must not exasperate their children but bring them up in the instruction of the Lord. The art of child development is firmness without harshness. A child's personality is as delicate and as fragile as a flower and it is so easy, unless love and wisdom are the guiding principles, to crush that developing persona and thus prevent it from blooming in later life. Sadly many adults fail to reach their potential because of damage done to them in the developmental years.

Father, help us put the rearing of our children on a higher level
than the rearing of animals or the cultivation of flowers.
Impress on all of us who are parents the delicacy and
importance≈of this task. Amen.

Transforming the mundane

For reading & meditation – Ephesians 6:5–8

'Slaves, obey your earthly masters with respect and fear ...
just as you would obey Christ.' (v.5)

Paul's next word is to slaves and their masters. According to
William Barclay there were about sixty million slaves in the
Roman Empire at the time the apostle was writing. Paul must have
sensed that the liberation of slaves would not come in his lifetime,
no matter how much he might have campaigned for this, and
sought instead to give spiritual guidance regarding the situation.

His message to the slaves, therefore, is this: slavery can be
transformed. But how? By serving one's master as one would serve
the Lord: 'Obey ... *just as you would obey Christ*.'
Paul urges slaves not to play up to their masters by
working only when their owner's eye is on them but
to see themselves as the slaves of Christ, doing the
will of God from the heart. These words are more
profound than they might appear, and doubtless
those slaves who read them would have come to see
themselves not merely as slaves of an earthly master
but as servants of God, endeavouring to please Him.

FURTHER STUDY

Col. 3:22–25;
1 Tim. 6:1;
Titus 2:9;
1 Pet. 2:18

1. What
was Paul's
exhortation to
the Colossians?

2. What
was Peter's
instruction?

This principle can be applied to all the tasks
we undertake in life – especially those that are
mundane. When we understand that a Christian's
duty is to do everything as unto the Lord then even such boring
tasks as housework or garbage collecting can be transformed. A
street cleaner I knew in the Yorkshire city of Sheffield – a fine
Christian man – kept the streets he had charge of scrupulously
clean. 'I do it,' he explained, 'as if Jesus Christ were to walk down
these streets every day.'

Father, help me see that everything I do – everything – is to be done
as unto You. Give me the perspective that views the mundane as a
ministry and looks upon the boring as blessed.
In Jesus' name. Amen.

No favourites with God

For reading & meditation – Ephesians 6:9

'... he who is both their Master and yours is in heaven,
and there is no favouritism with him.' (v.9)

Paul had some wise words of advice for those who were slave
owners. First: 'Treat your slaves in the same way.' In other
words: 'Hear what I have said to the slaves about treating you
respectfully and work on showing the same attitude towards them.'

Second: masters are not to threaten their slaves. No doubt Paul
had in mind the practice common among slave owners of warning
their slaves: 'If you don't do exactly what I ask then you will be
severely punished.' One commentator claims that 'punishment was
accepted in the Empire as the only way to keep slaves
under control'. There are times when punishment is
necessary, but to threaten people constantly is not a
good way of motivating them. This is something that
should be recognised by every parent.

Paul's next point is even more powerful: 'You and
your servants are both under the same Master in
heaven. He makes no distinction between you and
them' (Eugene Peterson, *The Message*). No doubt
most slave owners felt superior to their slaves and above them
both in status and intelligence. But Paul seeks to narrow that
divide by reminding them that they share the same Master –
the Lord who is in heaven. However fawned upon a slave owner
might have been by his slaves, he would not receive the same
sycophantic treatment from the Lord Jesus Christ. With Him
there is no discrimination. He treats everyone the same and has
no favourites. He loves each of us as if we are the only one there
is to love.

FURTHER STUDY

Acts 10:30-35;
Job 34:19;
Matt. 5:45;
Gal. 2:6

1. What did
Peter declare?

2. What position
did Paul take?

**Father, how can I thank You enough for the love the Trinity has for
me? It is so personal and so profound. Nothing in me gave rise to it
and nothing in me can extinguish it. I bow in adoration at Your feet.
Amen.**

A call to arms

For reading & meditation – Ephesians 6:10–12

'Finally, be strong in the Lord and in his mighty power.'
(v.10)

Paul's teaching concerning submission – first to Christ and then to others who are in positions of authority – might give rise to the idea that Christianity produces passive people. It does the very opposite; it produces people who are able to stand strong in the Lord. Submitted to Him and obedient to all legitimate authority we gain a power that leads us to be unwavering. Note Paul's words carefully: 'Be strong *in the Lord*.' An organism can expend as much as it takes in and no more. Receptivity is a law of life. When we are in the Lord we take in His strength and therefore we are able to stand up to anything.

Verse 10 is a transitional verse that takes us into the final section of Ephesians. In this concluding section we move from considering the wealth and walk of the Christian to the matter of spiritual warfare. It is a clear call to arms. We move from the home to the battlefield and find ourselves in hand-to-hand combat with the forces of darkness. Whatever our views on pacifism, there is no room for a *spiritual* pacifist in the kingdom of God. Our

FURTHER STUDY

2 Cor. 10:1–5;
1 Tim. 1:18; 6:12;
2 Tim. 2:4

1. What are the weapons of our warfare able to do?

2. What did Paul instruct Timothy to do?

adversary is the devil and his minions – spiritual forces in the heavenly realms. Dr Martyn Lloyd-Jones in his commentary on this verse asked the pointed question: 'Have we become so psychological that the devil has been forgotten?' Psychological conflicts ought not to be ignored but we must never forget that often our biggest struggle is not with them but with the devil and his forces.

Father, help me not to make too much of the devil, but not to ignore him either. Give me the wisdom and power I need to combat his dark forces. In Christ's name. Amen.

'Dressed to kill'

For reading & meditation – Ephesians 6:13–17
'Therefore put on the full armour of God ...' (v.13)

To withstand the devil we have to *stand*. Shaky Christians are an easy prey for the devil. To stand effectively against the devil we must put on the full spiritual armour of God. Not one piece is to be discarded. Paul compares it to the six pieces of a Roman soldier's battlefield equipment.

First, the belt of truth. Paul is thinking not just of truth *per se*, but the truth that comes from God. The devil is a liar, and when we stand against him with the truth of God's Word his lies are seen for what they are. Second, the breastplate of righteousness, which protects us when we rest in the merits of Christ's redeeming work for us on the cross and rebut the devil's accusations by reminding him that all our sins have been blotted out. Third, the shoes of peace, which give us a firm foothold so that we can stand against the devil, free from the natural fear we have of one so strong and powerful. Fourth, the shield of faith – the protection that comes from believing the mighty promises of God. Fifth, the helmet of salvation, with which we hold up our heads in confidence and joy, knowing we are saved. Lastly, the sword of the Spirit which is the Word of God. All the other parts of the armour are defensive; this is offensive. God's Word has great cutting power. It is sharper than a two-edged sword. But it is only effective as we use it.

The Christian's armour is really Christ in His totality. Put on Christ and we are more than a match for the devil.

FURTHER STUDY

Rom. 13:1-12;
2 Cor. 6:7;
1 Thess. 5:8;
Heb. 4:12

1. How does Paul describe the armour to the Romans?

2. What are we to carry in our right and left hands?

Father, thank You that You have not left me at the mercy of the devil. Help me to take Christ in His totality and to be found always clothed with His armour. This I ask for His glory. Amen.

Spirit-guided praying

For reading & meditation – Ephesians 6:18

'And pray in the Spirit on all occasions with all kinds of prayers and requests.' (v.18)

Is prayer a part of the Christian's armour or something additional to it? No, it is not separate but undergirds our whole approach to spiritual warfare. This is because every one of us is prone to self-dependency, and it is very easy to think of the energy we expend when we put on the armour of God as something for which we take credit. But as John Stott points out: 'Equipping ourselves with God's armour is not a mechanical operation; it is in itself an expression of our dependence on God, in other words, of prayer.' Nothing is more powerful than prayer for reminding us that we are dependent on God. Prayer makes us aware that unless God comes to our aid we are sunk.

Spiritual warfare requires a special kind of prayer – *in the Spirit*. How do we pray in the Spirit? By asking God to show us precisely what we should pray about. As the Commander-in-Chief of spiritual forces He knows the key points of the battle on which prayer should be concentrated, and because of this, Spirit-guided prayers are necessary.

We are to pray *on all occasions*. This means utilising the power of prayer whenever we can. Our prayers also should be 'of all kinds'. They should take various forms – sometimes petitioning, sometimes powerfully interceding, sometimes praising. Then, like good soldiers, we must be always alert so that we will not be overtaken by the enemy. Finally, we are to keep on praying for each other continually. Put on the armour but put on also prayer.

FURTHER STUDY

Luke 18:1-8;
1 Chron. 16:11;
Matt. 26:41;
1 Thess. 5:17

1. What is Jesus teaching in the parable of the persistent widow?

2. What did Paul exhort the Thessalonians?

Heavenly Father, thank You for reminding me that equipping myself with the armour of God is not a mechanical operation. The armour is to be put on with prayer. Help me never to forget this. In Christ's name. Amen.

'Pray for me please'

For reading & meditation – Ephesians 6:19–20

'Pray ... that I will fearlessly make known the mystery of the gospel ...' (v.19)

Paul asks his readers to pray for him. 'Pray also for me,' he pleads (v.19). 'Pray that I'll know what to say and have the courage to say it at the right time, telling the mystery to one and all, the message that I, jailbird preacher that I am, am responsible for getting out' (Eugene Peterson, *The Message*). Paul was aware that the strength he needed came not only from his own prayers but the prayers of others also. What deprived lives we live because we do not pray enough for ourselves and are too proud to ask others to pray for us.

FURTHER STUDY

Rom. 15:23–32;
1 Thess. 5:25;
2 Thess. 3:1–5;
Heb. 13:18

1. What did Paul request prayer for?

2. Pray for a spiritual leader today.

To my shame there was a time when I would never ask anyone to pray for me because I thought it was an indication of weakness. I came to see, however, that it was not so much that as pride. God dealt with me over this and now it is easy to ask you, my dear readers, to please pray for me as I write, preach, travel and teach people the things of the faith.

Paul describes himself in these verses as 'an ambassador in chains' (v.20). He rejoiced in being Christ's ambassador even though he was in prison in Rome. Clearly he yearned to preach the gospel: 'Pray ... that I will fearlessly make known the mystery of the gospel.' Dedicated disciples long above everything to be loyal to their Lord. When Billy Graham was asked by Larry King, an American television interviewer, how he would like to be remembered after his death he replied: 'That I preached the gospel without compromise and fear.' Great believers always do.

Heavenly Father, I may not be a great preacher but I want to be a great Christian. Help me take every opportunity that comes my way to tell others of Your love. In Jesus' name I ask it. Amen.

Godliness at its highest

For reading & meditation – Ephesians 6:21–22

'Tychicus, the dear brother and faithful servant in the Lord,
will tell you everything ...' (v.21)

Paul's letter to the Ephesians seems to have been dictated to his
friend, Tychicus. At this point it is thought Paul took the pen
from Tychicus and wrote these final words of greeting with his
own hand, as he did to the Galatians and Colossians.

Tychicus may well have been a member of the community at
Ephesus. Certainly he was an Asian (see Acts 20:4). And clearly
he was a young man in whom Paul had a great deal of confidence.
To his description here in Ephesians of Tychicus being a 'dear
brother and faithful servant in the Lord' Paul adds
in Colossians that he was also a 'fellow-servant' (Col.
4:7). Some are faithful and devoted to the work they
do for God but they could not be described as 'dear'.
They are so absorbed in being faithful ministers
that they have no time for brotherliness. Then some
are 'dear brothers' who get on well with everybody
but are not faithful servants. They cultivate friends
but they do not convert them. Then again there are
those who are dear and faithful but not good 'fellow-
servants'. They cannot work with others. Tychicus
was all three 'in the Lord'.

FURTHER STUDY

Acts 20:1-5;
2 Tim. 4:10;
Col. 4:7-9;
Titus 3:12

1. What did
Paul sadly say
about Demas?

2. Why did Paul
send Tychicus to
the Colossians?

He was also a man Paul could send on his errands. 'I am
sending him ... that he may encourage you,' says Paul (v.22). How
typical of Paul to think of encouraging others when he himself
stood in need of encouragement. When we need encouragement
ourselves but our thoughts are occupied more with how others
can be encouraged then this is godliness at its highest.

**Father, will I ever reach this place – the place of thinking more of
others than I do of myself? Forgive me that I am so self-centred.
Move me on to higher ground I pray. In Jesus' name. Amen.**

Bestowed from above

For reading & meditation – Ephesians 6:23

'Peace to the brothers, and love with faith from God
the Father ...' (v.23)

Paul's penultimate statement to his readers at Ephesus is filled
with words that contain deep spiritual meaning: peace, love
and faith. Peace is a word he has used several times before. 'Grace
and *peace* to you from God our Father and the Lord Jesus Christ'
(1:2). 'For he himself is our peace, who has made the two one and
has destroyed the barrier, the dividing wall of hostility' (2:14). Paul
longs that in the midst of a city which was a centre of iniquity and
thoroughly pagan the hearts and minds of the Ephesian Christians
would be kept in perfect peace.

FURTHER STUDY

John 20:19-22;
14:27;
Gal. 6:16;
Phil. 4:7;
1 Pet. 5:14

1. What are we
to let the peace
of God do?
2. Share the
peace of God
with someone
today.

His wish for them also is that they would be
people who loved. Peace and love belong together;
peace is the heart being at rest and love is the spur
that others might come to know that same perfect
peace also. To these two qualities is added faith. Paul
does not say peace and love *and* faith, but peace and
love *with* faith. Most commentators believe that the
faith Paul is thinking of here is not something the
Ephesians needed to be given but something they
already had. One of them says: 'Faith they had;
Paul's prayer was that love might be connected to it.'

Peace and love, when combined with faith, become
a powerful formula for effective Christian living. These qualities
come down from the Father and the Son. They can be demonstrated
on the horizontal level only as they are bestowed from above, and
they are bestowed only on those who are willing to receive.

**Father, I see that what happens on the horizontal depends on the
vertical. I can only give what I receive. Today I open my heart to
receive heaven's gifts. Grant me Your peace and love with faith.
In Christ's name. Amen.**

'The favour of God'

For reading & meditation – Ephesians 6:24

'Grace to all who love our Lord Jesus Christ with
an undying love.' (v.24)

Paul began his letter with the word 'grace' and ends with the
same word. Paul was constantly talking about grace. The word
appears over and over again in his epistles. Why did he make so
much of grace? I think it was because he realised that although
he had been one of Christ's fiercest enemies and an abuser of the
Church, God had demonstrated grace towards him and turned
him from a persecutor of Christ to a preacher of the gospel. 'But
by the grace of God I am what I am,' he said when writing to the
Corinthians (1 Cor. 15:10).

But here he is thinking not so much of God's
grace in redeeming the Ephesians as His grace in
upholding and strengthening them. Grace means
'the favour of God' and his thought is that the same
favour that saved them might also keep them. They
lived, after all, in a city in which grace was sorely
needed if they were to demonstrate to others the
power that could enable them to live blameless lives
despite their circumstances.

FURTHER STUDY

Phil. 4:10-19;
2 Tim. 2:1;
1 Tim. 1:14

1. What was
Paul's advice
to Timothy?

2. What
was Paul's
testimony?

In his final words he characterises the Ephesian Christians
as being people who were not only loved by Jesus but who also
loved Him: 'Grace to all who love our Lord Jesus Christ *with an
undying love.*' As I conclude these meditations on Ephesians I
borrow Paul's final words and address then to you: 'Love mixed
with faith be yours from God the Father and from the Master,
Jesus Christ. Pure grace and nothing but grace be with all who
love our Master Jesus Christ' (Eugene Peterson, *The Message*).

**Father, thank You for inspiring Paul as he wrote to the Ephesians.
Inspiration was given to him and through that inspiration has now
come to me. To you be all the honour, the glory and the praise.
Amen.**

The Grand Design

A book for today

For reading & meditation – Revelation 1:1–2

'The revelation of Jesus Christ, which God gave him to
show his servants what must soon take place.' (v.1)

During different periods of history, different books of the Bible
have come into prominence. St Augustine turned to Genesis.
Martin Luther focused on the book of Romans. The book for today,
I believe, is the book of Revelation.

Revelation is a prophecy about things *soon* to take place. The
Greek word here translated 'soon' is *tacheos*, which also means
'quickly'. Our English word 'taxi' best gives the flavour of the Greek
word (even though there is no linguistic connection). When we
shout 'Taxi!' there is a sense of immediacy.

The book is not the revelation *of* John but the
revelation of Christ *to* John. The primary purpose
of the book is not to provide us with a timetable
for the future but to remind us of the glories of our
all-conquering Christ. Is not this precisely what
the Church needs – a vision of the power, authority,
and supremacy of our glorious Saviour? The people
of God, set as we are in the midst of a hostile
environment, need to concentrate on the fact that
Jesus is *Lord*. The Church rises and falls in relation
to its concept of Christ. 'A Church with its back to the
wall fighting for survival,' says John Stott, '*must see Christ*.' Notice
the words: 'The revelation of Jesus Christ, *which God gave him*.'
Elsewhere in the New Testament it is Jesus who reveals God; here
the roles are reversed. Now God is revealing Jesus. Can anything
be more spiritually motivating than to see our Saviour 'uncovered'
in all His glory?

FURTHER STUDY

Dan. 2:19-23;
Acts 2:29-36;
Col. 1:15-20;
2 Pet. 1:16-18

1. For what
does Daniel
praise God?

2. How does
Paul describe
the supremacy
of Christ?

**My Father and my God, may I be open to all that You want to show
me of Your Son, for although I know Him, there is so much more of
Him to know. Reveal more of Him to me in the days that lie ahead,
dear Father. In Jesus' name. Amen.**

The message

For reading & meditation – Revelation 1:3

'Blessed is the one who reads ... this prophecy ...those who hear ... and take to heart what is written in it ...' (v.3)

A special blessing awaits those who read or hear words of the book of Revelation and 'take to heart what is written in it'. Our text indicates that it was not only to be read by individuals, but also meant to be read aloud in the churches. The immediate aim of Revelation was to encourage persecuted Christians so that they could face the difficult days that lay ahead. The chief aim was to support those oppressed believers by showing them that though evil would be allowed to continue, it would do so only because it would contribute to God's eternal purposes. *This was the message that was to be taken to heart.*

FURTHER STUDY

Josh. 1:7-9;
Psa. 1:1-6;
Matt. 7:24-27;
Rom. 10:5-13

1. What are both Joshua and the psalmist required to do?

2. What is Paul's essential confession of faith?

Unfortunately many approach the book of Revelation only to find keys to unlock the future. Will the Church go through the tribulation? Is there to be a millennium of peace on the earth? How will everything come about? These are legitimate but not the first questions that should be asked of Revelation. The most significant questions are: Is Jesus Lord of the universe? Are all things proceeding according to the divine plan? Is there an horizon to history? The answer is a resounding 'Yes'. Of more importance than establishing a particular theory of Revelation is that we grasp its underlying message, namely that Jesus Christ has control of the universe, and that when ultimately all is revealed, history will prove to be His story. When we catch a glimpse of the grand design on the right side of the tapestry we can face anything!

Heavenly Father, please help me for it is so easy to miss the wood for the trees. Save me from becoming so interested in the symbols in this book that I lose sight of the Saviour and fail to take its underlying message to my heart. Amen.

The magnificent Christ

For reading & meditation – Revelation 1:4–5

'John, To the seven churches in the province of Asia:
Grace and peace to you ...' (v.4)

The book of Revelation contains a number of great themes, the first being the glory of our Lord Jesus Christ. It finds a powerful focus in this first chapter. John, instructed by an angel to write to the seven churches in Asia, opens with a greeting found in many New Testament letters: 'Grace and peace to you ...'

John's greeting is not from himself but from the triune God. How wonderful to be greeted by the Trinity! First, the Father, 'who is, and who was, and who is to come'. Next, the Holy Spirit, as expressed by the term 'the seven spirits before his throne'. But isn't the Spirit one, not seven? Archbishop Trench wrote, 'The Holy Spirit is being depicted here not so much in His personal unity as His manifold energies. Though the Spirit is indeed one, He ministers to each of the seven churches at one and the same time.'

But it is our Lord Jesus Christ who is given the fullest description, and is presented to us first as 'the faithful witness' – the One who during His ministry here on earth never failed to present God's truth. Next, He is called 'the firstborn from the dead', meaning that He is the first of an order which others can follow. John's final description of our Lord is that of 'ruler of the kings of the earth'. A church facing uncertainty, ostracism, and perhaps even persecution, will do well to remember that kings and rulers, though they may not realise it, are themselves being ruled. Our Lord is for ever the King of kings.

FURTHER STUDY

Psa. 89:26-29;
John 18:33-37;
1 Tim. 6:12-14;
1 Pet. 1:1-2

1. How did Jesus testify before Pilate?

2. How does Peter link believers' lives with the Trinity?

Heavenly Father, thank You for the reminder that no matter how things appear, Your Son is in charge of the march of the moments. Help me never to forget this. In Christ's name. Amen.

Loved! Loosed! Lifted!

For reading & meditation – Revelation 1:5–8

'To him who loves us and has freed us ... by his blood,
and has made us ... priests to serve his God ...' (vv.5-6)

Consideration of Christ's glory inevitably leads John to heartfelt praise of his Lord. He loves us, says John. That is how it all started. We could not resist the overtures of One who showed us such amazing affection. He has 'freed [or loosed] us from our sins'. The King James Version reads: 'Unto him that loved us, and washed us from our sins.' Both translations are admissible. We are washed first and then loosed, or freed. D.L. Moody once trenchantly remarked that Christ did not wash us and then love us;

FURTHER STUDY

Exod. 19:5-6;
Eph. 1:3-10;
1 Pet. 2:9

1. What spiritual
blessings are
ours in Christ?

2. How does
Peter describe
the Church?

He loved us and then washed us. Anyone could have loved us after we had been washed; only Christ could have loved us before we were washed. He has lifted us, continues John, and made us kings and priests to serve God. The mitre as well as the crown adorns our brow. As kings, God means us to reign over sin and self, and as priests, to represent the world before God and bind it by the chains of believing prayer to His feet. Loved! Loosed! Lifted! What a thought to prime the pump of praise in our hearts.

There is still more. This glorious One is going to return some day, and those who pierced Him will bewail their lost opportunity of salvation. His own people, however, knowing He is the Alpha and Omega – the beginning and the end – will rejoice at His coming. A little girl in Sunday school, when asked why Jesus was described as the Alpha and Omega, said: 'Because He is the Alphabet out of which God puts together all His promises.' He is.

Father, I am so grateful to You for loving me, loosing me and lifting me. Thank You too for putting a mitre as well as a crown on my head. All praise and honour be to Your glorious name. Amen.

A secret stair

For reading & meditation – Revelation 1:9–11

'On the Lord's Day I was in the Spirit, and I heard behind
me a loud voice like a trumpet ...' (v.10)

J ohn's account of the revelation he received was written from the
island of Patmos to which he had been banished because of the
word of God and the testimony of Jesus'. We are not told exactly
why he was exiled, but John's great influence in the Church might
well have seemed a threat to the Roman authorities.

Picture him there on that lonely island. He was an old man,
and his banishment almost certainly involved hard labour. He
tells us that he is a 'brother and companion in the suffering and
kingdom' (v.9), but his exile must have seemed more
like the sharing of Christ's suffering than the sharing
of His kingdom. However, Rome was powerless to
sever John's contact with the throne of God. Though
he was on Patmos, he was in the Spirit – his heart
and mind were caught up in the contemplation of
God. And he was to be given a vision of the King and
His kingdom that would transform not only his own
life, but the lives of countless others who, down the
centuries, have studied his words. It was the Lord's
Day when he received his revelation, we read.

FURTHER STUDY

Ezek. 1:1-3;
Acts 14:21-24;
Phil. 3:4-11;
1 Tim. 1:14-17;
2 Tim. 2:9-13

1. How does
Ezekiel's
experience
compare with
John's?

2. What are
Paul's losses
and gains?

Think about these contrasting phrases: 'I ... was on
the island of Patmos ... on the Lord's Day I was in the
Spirit.' 'On the island' he was in exile, but 'in the Spirit' he touched
the glories of another world. Nothing can stop God getting through
to us no matter what the circumstances. The Almighty is always
able to find or, if necessary, construct a secret stair to our soul.

**Father, how reassured I am to know that nothing can ever stop Your
Word being transmitted to my heart. I am so grateful that no matter
how difficult the circumstances, heaven's mail always gets through.
Amen.**

The vision

For reading & meditation – Revelation 1:12–16

'... among the lampstands was someone 'like a son of man,'
dressed in a robe reaching down to his feet ...' (v.13)

A voice like a trumpet commands the apostle to write what he sees on a scroll and send it to the seven churches in Asia. When John hears the voice he says: 'I turned round to see the voice that was speaking to me.'

When John turns he sees Christ standing amid seven golden lamptstands – symbols of the seven churches. The Saviour is wearing a robe that reaches down to His feet, has a golden sash around His chest, His head and hair are white as snow, His eyes

FURTHER STUDY

Ezek. 1:24-28;
Dan. 10:5-11;
Matt. 17:1-2;
Acts 22:6-11

1. Compare
John's vision
with those
of Ezekiel
and Daniel.

2. Compare
Paul's account
with Matthew's.

like a blazing fire, His feet as bronze, His voice is like the sound of rushing waters, His face is as the sun, in His right hand He holds seven stars, and from His mouth comes a sharp double-edged sword. What an astonishing sight it must have been.

Clothing defines role, and here our Lord is represented as a priest (Exod. 29:5), the One through whom we have access to God. The head, eyes and face speak of His character. No one is more pure in character than our Lord. The feet of bronze indicate His ability to crush His enemies underfoot. His voice, like His appearance, commands attention. The seven stars represent the angels (or leaders) of the seven churches, and the sword is symbolic of the sharpness of His Word. This is no longer the Socratic Christ reasoning with Pharisees and Sadducees, no longer a crucified Christ nailed to a cross. No greater description of Christ is to be found anywhere in the Word of God. This is the picture of Christ I always hold before me when I pray.

Lord Jesus Christ, Son of Man and Son of God, may this vision of
Your glory so fill my heart that it will transform every part of me,
especially my prayer life. In Your precious name I ask it. Amen.

'What you have seen ... write'

For reading & meditation – Revelation 1:17–20

'I am the Living One; I was dead, and behold I am alive for ever and ever!' (v.18)

It is not surprising that the vision of the glorified Christ causes John to fall into a dead faint. The hand which held the seven stars is placed upon him, and the voice like the sound of rushing waters says: 'Do not be afraid.' John soon revives, and his fear abates as he realises he is in the presence of his Creator – the First and the Last – who tells him: 'I was dead, and behold I am alive for ever and ever! And I hold the keys of death and Hades.'

Then John is instructed: 'Write … what you have seen' (v.19). If you will permit a personal reference here, these were the words God used in 1965 to start me on a writing career. I came to the Scriptures looking for a directive to confirm the desire growing within me to begin writing daily Bible notes, and this was the message that sealed it. The Spirit quickened those words to my heart. Ever since that time I have been trying to write what I have seen.

FURTHER STUDY

Isa. 41:4,8–10;
44:6–8;
Rom. 6:9–10;
1 Cor. 15:54–57

1. What does
'the First and
the Last' tell us
about Jesus?

2. How has
Jesus removed
the sting of
death?

The vision sets John on the task of making known the mystery of the seven stars and the seven golden lampstands – the seven stars being the angels (or leaders) and the seven lampstands the seven churches. How thrilling it must have been for John to realise that there was a correlation between what happened to the seven communities of faith he knew so well and the movements of heaven. It will help us as we face the future to remember that nothing can ever happen on earth that is not anticipated in eternity.

Father, I have started with this vision of Christ; help me never to let it go. May He fill my mind and dominate my life in the same way that He dominates this book. For His name's sake. Amen.

The three Rs

For reading & meditation – Revelation 2:1–7

'Yet I hold this against you: You have forsaken your first love.' (v.4)

We turn now to the next great theme – the Church. We are called to have fellowship with others. The revelation of Christ is not just for John, but for the seven churches in Asia. Why *seven* churches when we know there were at least ten? The seven churches stand for all churches.

The first church addressed is that in Ephesus. Our Lord introduces Himself as the One 'who holds the seven stars in his right hand and walks among the seven golden lampstands'

(v.1) as if to say: 'I am your Chief Pastor … the One who sees all and knows all.' The letter opens with a commendation, followed by a condemnation and concludes with a command. First the commendation: 'I know your deeds' (v.2). The believers in Ephesus were faithful, industrious and toiling to the point of exhaustion. But although our Lord commends them for this, they are condemned because they have left their first love. What good is duty without devotion? Hearts that had once been on fire with love for the Lord had now chilled.

Then comes the formula for recapturing that lost love: remember, repent and return. The Ephesians were to remember the way things had been, what had happened to chill their affection, to repent of it, and return to a close relationship with the Saviour. If they did not, they were told, their lampstand would be removed. There is little point in a church continuing to function or even exist if there is no love in it, for where there is no love there can be no light.

Lord God, forgive us that our light shines so dimly in the world because we love so weakly. Help us to remember how things once were, to repent of our lost love, and to return to a close romantic relationship with You. In Christ's name. Amen.

Fearful but faithful

For reading & meditation – Revelation 2:8–11

'Do not be afraid of what you are about to suffer ...
Be faithful, even to the point of death ...' (v.10)

The second letter is addressed to the church in Smyrna. If love was the key word for the Ephesians, the key word for the believers in Smyrna was *suffering*. At the time Revelation was written (probably about AD 95), Smyrna was the pride of Asia. It is still thriving, and is known today as Izmir.

Great suffering was to fall upon the church at Smyrna, and our Lord begins by reminding them that He is 'the First and the Last, who died and came to life again' (v.8). This is always the manner in which our Lord seeks to comfort His people in times of distress; He reminds us that all things are under His control. Christ was well aware of their poverty (probably the result of the refusal of Smyrna's citizens to do business with Christians), and also the slander they received from the Jewish community. But He encourages them to continue being faithful, promising them an eternal reward, a crown of life – a term used to describe the wreath or trophy awarded to the victor at the games. The suffering Christians of Smyrna needed to know that a trophy of victory awaited them in eternity.

Sadly, many face martyrdom even today. More Christians were martyred for their faith in the twentieth century than in the previous nineteen centuries combined. The prospect of being forced to give up one's life for the cause of Christ is not pleasant, but for a Christian death is not the end; it is the prelude to a new and joyously endless life.

FURTHER STUDY

John 16:33;
1 Thess. 1:2-10;
2 Thess. 1:3-10;
1 Pet. 4:12-19;
1 John 2:12-14

1. For what does Paul commend the Thessalonians?

2. How does Peter encourage his readers?

Father, wherever Your children are being persecuted or are under threat of death, give them a special supply of Your grace, I pray. Deliver them from fear and help them stand firm for You no matter what. In Christ's name I ask this. Amen.

A church fight

For reading & meditation – Revelation 2:12–17

'Repent therefore! Otherwise, I will ... come to you and ...
fight against them with the sword of my mouth.' (v.16)

We reflect now on the words of our Lord to the church in Pergamum. At the time of these letters, this city was known as a strong centre of emperor-worship and idolatry, 'where Satan has his throne' and 'where Satan lives' (v.13). Our Lord's key word to this church was truth. In Pergamum there was conflict between truth and error.

To this church Christ reveals Himself as the One who has 'the sharp, double-edged sword' (v.12). This shows His power to defeat false doctrine. St Augustine said that Christ's double-edged sword consists of the Old and New Testaments, adding: 'We need both if we are to overcome error.' Though false doctrines were circulating in the church in Pergamum, many still held fast to the truth, one member having been martyred for his refusal to renounce his belief (v.13).

The error accepted by some at Pergamum was similar to that of Balaam's day. Compare Numbers 31:16 with Numbers 25:1–9. Balaam suggested to Balak, king of Moab, that young Moabite women should seduce the men of Israel and persuade them to worship idols, knowing that such behaviour would bring down upon the Israelites the wrath of God. What Balaam was to ancient Israel, the Nicolaitans were to the church in Pergamum. Christ's face is always set against a church where error is propagated and sin is tolerated. If such a church doesn't repent then it will have a fight on its hands (v.16). This type of fight should be strenuously avoided.

FURTHER STUDY

Psa. 26:1-12;
1 Cor. 15:1-5;
Gal. 1:1-12;
1 John 4:1-6

1. What is Paul's message to the Corinthians?

2. How does John advise his readers?

Lord Jesus Christ, who can win a fight against You? May we Your people set our faces against every kind of sin so that You do not have to set Your face against us. For Your own dear name's sake. Amen.

A holy people

For reading & meditation – Revelation 2:18–29

DAY
315

'Nevertheless, I have this against you: You tolerate that woman Jezebel, who calls herself a prophetess.' (v.20)

Christ addresses the church in Thyatira, which appeared to be flourishing spiritually, with good works, love, service, faith and perseverance. Our Lord introduces Himself to this church as 'the Son of God, whose eyes are like blazing fire and whose feet are like burnished bronze' (v.18). Despite its pleasing appearance, a pernicious sin was destroying this church. They needed, therefore, to see Christ as the One whose eyes burned with the fire of righteous indignation against sin, and whose feet were capable of trampling them to powder.

The operative word to the church in Thyatira it was *holiness*. Although quite clearly the church manifested a number of graces, holiness was not one of them. A woman in the church was acting like Jezebel, the wife of Ahab (see 1 Kings 16:31), and encouraging Christians to practise immorality and eat food sacrificed to idols.

FURTHER STUDY

Lev. 19:1-8;
1 Cor. 5:1-13;
1 Pet. 1:13-16

1. How does Paul deal with immorality in the Church?

2. According to Peter, what is the cost of our holiness?

The Christ of the piercing eyes and trampling feet will deal with any church where immorality is practised. He may tolerate things for a while, but you can be sure judgment will eventually come. He promises that those who do not repent will experience spiritual death and, dare I say it, perhaps even physical death. When there is repentance, however, and the church shines as a light in a dark world, then Christ will be seen as the morning star who, as one commentator puts it, 'is the assurance of the coming dawn when lamplight will be swallowed up in the light of eternal day'.

God my Father, how we need this emphasis on holiness in an age when almost anything goes – even in Your Church. Give us a new vision of holiness and help us all become a more holy people. In Jesus' name. Amen.

Wake up!

For reading & meditation – Revelation 3:1–6

'But if you do not wake up, I will come like a thief … you will not know at what time I will come to you.' (v.3)

To the church in Sardis, Christ introduces Himself as the One 'who holds the seven spirits of God and the seven stars' (v.1), referring to the manifold energies of the Holy Spirit. Why does our Lord begin by laying emphasis on the ministry of the Spirit? Because this was their greatest need – *life*.

Clearly the church at Sardis had gained a reputation for being a lively centre of witness, but the outward appearance was deceptive. Christ saw them as being nothing more than a morgue with a steeple. All those around would have regarded the church at Sardis as a flourishing, active, successful church – all except Christ. 'Wake up!' is our Lord's command to them. 'Strengthen what remains and is about to die' (v.2). The church at Sardis was desperately in need of revival. In all the other churches Christ finds something to commend, but for this one there is only condemnation. A few were still thriving spiritually, and to them Christ promises His presence in a powerful way (v.4). However, in the main the church was dead, a spiritual graveyard.

How true this is of some of today's churches which have a name for being alive but do not allow the Holy Spirit to work in their midst; they have ceremony but no life, pageantry but no Pentecost. These churches need to 'wake up'. If the Holy Spirit is not welcomed and allowed to have His way in a church then it no longer functions as a church; it is merely a club.

FURTHER STUDY

Isa. 52:1-6;
Rom. 13:11-14;
1 Cor. 2:12-16;
Eph. 5:8-14;
1 Thess. 5:4-5

1. What does Isaiah call on the people to do?

2. What does Paul urge the Ephesians to do?

Gracious and loving Father, help us open our hearts to the whole Trinity – Father, Son *and* Holy Spirit. Let there be no 'missing member' in the Church of the twenty-first century.
In Jesus' name I pray. Amen.

A global perspective

For reading & meditation – Revelation 3:7–13

'See, I have placed before you an open door that
no-one can shut.' (v.8)

The church in Philadelphia receives almost unqualified
commendation. Our Lord informs them He is the 'holy and
true, who holds the key of David' (v.7). The image of a key is
used because Christ is to open for them a door of opportunity:
'See, I have placed before you an open door that no-one can shut.'
Opportunity therefore best summarises our Lord's message to the
Philadelphia church.

What was this open door? Probably *evangelistic* opportunity.
Philadelphia was strategically placed for going to
Mysia, Lydia and Phrygia. In *Letters to the Seven
Churches*, Professor Ramsey likens those in the
church at Philadelphia to 'archers, bow bent, and
ready to thrust arrows deep into the heart of the
interior'. The believers were not strong (v.8), and
faced great opposition. But through the door opened
to them they would go out and bring others in, some
of whom were at present their fiercest antagonists.
A church of little strength was to become mighty in
winning souls to Christ and would be established as an immovable
pillar in the temple of the new Jerusalem, the city of God (v.12).

FURTHER STUDY

Isa. 52:7-10;
Matt. 16:15-19;
Rom. 15:14-21;
Col. 4:2-6;
2 Tim. 2:8

1. What was
Paul's ambition?

2. What was
Paul's gospel?

Today's Church needs to hear the message of love, suffering,
truth, holiness and life. It needs also to see that it has a greater
opportunity to preach the gospel than at any other time in history.
Radio, television, the internet – all are open doors. We must go
through those doors with a global perspective and say with John
Wesley: 'All who perish are in our parish.'

**Father, forgive us that in an age when there is a communication
explosion we are so slow to use our opportunities to present the
gospel. Forgive us, restore us, and quicken us, we pray.
In Jesus' name. Amen.**

You make me sick!

For reading & meditation – Revelation 3:14–22

'So, because you are lukewarm – neither hot nor cold –
I am about to spit you out of my mouth.' (v.16)

Our Lord's seventh and final letter is addressed to the church in Laodicea. Christ presents Himself as 'the Amen, the faithful and true witness, the ruler of God's creation' (v.14). The church needed to see Him as the One who remains constant in the midst of flux. A change for the worse had taken place in the Laodicean church – they had become spiritually lukewarm. Christ feels nauseated – its people make Him sick. Our Lord tells them: 'I wish you were either one or the other!' (v.15). Our Lord prefers cold Christianity to the lukewarm variety!

FURTHER STUDY

Prov. 8:32-36;
Isa. 55:1-7;
2 Cor. 1:19-22;
Heb. 12:5-11;
James 5:7-9

1. What invitation is given by Isaiah?

2. Why does God discipline us?

Laodicea was wealthy, famous for its manufacture of black woollen clothing, lukewarm supply of water channelled from hot springs, and special eye ointment. Though the believers considered themselves rich, Christ tells them they are 'wretched, pitiful, poor, blind and naked' (v.17). Despite abhorring lukewarm Christians, our Lord still loves His people and counsels them to come to Him in earnest repentance. How compelling is Christ standing at the door of His own Church seeking readmittance (v.20)?

You will have noticed that at the end of each of His messages to the churches Christ exhorts them to hear what the Spirit is saying. This need to pay attention is emphasised because we are such bad listeners. We hear the words but we don't get the point. To hear what the Spirit says and not apply it to ourselves is one of the greatest tragedies that can befall us. Let's make sure it doesn't happen.

Father, I tremble lest in hearing I still fail to hear. Help me understand the point of everything You say to me and apply it to my soul. I ask this in the Saviour's precious name. Amen.

Our God reigns

For reading & meditation – Revelation 4:1–3

'Come up here, and I will show you what must take place after this.' (v.1)

The next great theme of Revelation is *worship*. In the first three chapters, Christ is seen only in the company of His Church. Some would prefer to move from chapter 1, with the magnificent Christ, to chapter 4, with marvellous worship, without having to negotiate the flawed Church. But, as Eugene Peterson says: 'Christ is not apart from the gathered, listening, praying, believing, worshipping people to whom He is Lord and Saviour. It is just not possible to have Christ apart from His Church.'

In today's verses John observes a open door in heaven, and once again he hears the trumpet-like voice calling him to come. As he does, the first thing he sees is a rainbow-encircled throne 'with someone sitting on it' (v.2). A vision of the heavenly throne sustained the Old Testament prophets Isaiah (Isa. 6:1), Ezekiel (Ezek. 1:26; 10:1), and Daniel (Dan. 7:9). Why a throne – God's throne? In Bible times a monarch reigned from his throne. It was the symbol of authority. By giving a vision of His throne, God seeks to reassure His people that no matter what happens on earth, the final seat of authority is in heaven.

FURTHER STUDY

Psa. 45:1-6;
93:1-5;
Dan. 7:9-10;
Luke 1:29-33

1. For what does the psalmist praise God?

2. What does the angel promise Mary?

The early Russian Communists used to say: 'We will depose the kings from their thrones on earth and then we will depose God from His throne in the sky.' Not so, says the writer to the Hebrews: 'Your throne, O God, will last for ever and ever' (Heb. 1:8). Other thrones may be toppled, but not God's throne. Our God reigns – eternally.

Lord God, how reassuring it is in an age when so many thrones have been toppled to know that Your throne will never be overturned. It is from everlasting to everlasting. Thank You my Father. Amen.

Nothing more wonderful

For reading & meditation – Revelation 4:3–4

'And the one who sat there had the appearance of
jasper and carnelian.' (v.3)

In John's vision not only the throne captivated his attention,
but the One who sat upon it. Stretching words to their limit, he
compares the appearance of the throne's occupant to that of 'jasper
and carnelian'.

The NIV Commentary says: 'Since God dwells in unapproachable
light and is One whom no one has seen or can see, He is described
in terms of the reflected brilliance of precious stones.' Light,
scientists inform us, is full of colour, all colours, but our eyes
are unable to fully detect them. One commentator
explains it like this: 'A 'precious' stone, selecting
certain colours out of the air and intensifying
them, shows us the deep colour that is in light all
the time.' It was from this colour-laden throne, we
must remember, that the command 'Let there be
light' first went forth (Gen. 1:3).

On earth light is often filtered through polluted
air, and rarely do we see colours as they really are.
Then we pick up a precious stone and glimpse a
brilliant blue or a glorious green and stand in awe
once again. Something similar happens to us as we
draw near to God's throne to worship; the light from this rainbow-
encircled throne bathes our souls so that holiness, grace, truth and
love shine with their true colours. It is in the act of worship that
the qualities God has so graciously given show up most clearly,
most sharply. Only in His light can we see – really see. I tell you,
nothing illuminates and enriches the soul more than worship.

FURTHER STUDY

2 Chron. 5:12-14;
Psa. 36:5-9;
John 1:1-9;
2 Cor. 4:4-6

1. What song
and what light
filled Solomon's
Temple?

2. What does
John say about
'true light'?

Father, I can only feebly comprehend the impact that the worship of
You has upon my soul. Right now I draw near to worship You.
Please draw near to me. In Jesus' name. Amen.

Worship – the right response

For reading & meditation – Revelation 4:5–8

'From the throne came flashes of lightning, rumblings and peals of thunder.' (v.5)

On the significance of God's eternal throne, Eugene Peterson says: 'The throne of God – the fact of the throne, and the fact of God enthroned – is the supreme revelation of the Bible. All rejection is rejection of divine government, all peace comes from an acceptance of God's right rule in His universe.'

John observes before the throne 'what looked like a sea of glass, clear as crystal' (v.6). To get close to the throne, worshippers must pass through this 'crystal sea', which suggests that they have to be cleansed and sanctified before they can draw near. Some think worship involves simply going into the country and thinking about God. But true worship involves first a purifying. 'Without holiness no-one will see [or worship] the Lord' (Heb. 12:14).

In addition to the representative people around the throne mentioned in verse 4 (probably the twelve patriarchs and the twelve apostles), John sees representative animals (v.6). These four creatures represent aspects of creation: the lion, nobility; the ox, strength; the one with a human face, wisdom; the flying eagle, swiftness. Hebrew patriarchs, Christian apostles, human beings, animals, birds – all surround the throne as a testimony to the fact that they are what they are because God is Who He is. God desires that all creation worship Him, not because He is egotistic, but because, as C.S. Lewis finely put it, worship is the right response to such a creator.

FURTHER STUDY

Psa. 51:7-12;
148:1-14;
2 Cor. 6:14-7:1;
Heb. 10:19-23

1. What does the psalmist summon creation to do?

2. Why does God call for our purification?

Father, as I reflect on the wonder of your creation, I want to echo the words of Francis of Assisi: 'All creatures of our God and King, lift up your voice and with us sing.' As I contemplate your glory my heart truly *sings*. Amen.

Dazzling splendour

For reading & meditation – Revelation 4:9–11

'You are worthy, our Lord and God, to receive glory and honour and power ...' (v.11)

As the living creatures are giving glory, the twenty-four elders fall down before the throne and worship Him who lives for ever. The elders remove their crowns and place them before Him who sits on the throne, acknowledging that God alone is worthy of ultimate praise and worship. Aloud they cry: 'You are worthy, our Lord and God, to receive glory and honour and power, for you created all things, and by your will they were created and have their being.'

FURTHER STUDY

1 Chron.
29:10-13;
Psa. 8:1-9;
Rom. 1:21-25

1. How does
David praise
the Lord?

2. What
exchanges do
'fools' make in
their worship?

New Christians often ask: Why does God want us to worship Him? Is it because He can't function without the compliments of His creation? No, we become better for having worshipped, for in the act of worship our personalities are made healthy. C.S Lewis said that as we worship we complete ourselves; we become all that we were meant to be. Another commentator says: 'God is the centre of all things. We worship so that we live in response to and from this centre, the living God. Failure to worship consigns us to a life of spasms and jerks, at the mercy of every advertisement, every seduction. If there is no centre there is no circumference. People who do not worship are swept into a vast restlessness ... with no steady direction and no sustaining purpose.'

The only way to go in a universe that was called into being by the Word of the Creator is the way of worship. If we do not know how to worship we do not know how to live.

Father, I accept that unless I know how to worship I remain a stunted soul – incomplete. Teach me to worship You in spirit and in truth, I pray. For if I do not worship I do not truly live. Help me my Father. In Jesus' name. Amen.

Why unanswered prayer?

For reading & meditation – Revelation 5:1–8

'Then I saw a Lamb, looking as if it had been slain,
standing in the centre of the throne ...' (v.6)

In the midst of the glory of the rainbow-encircled throne, John becomes aware that in the right hand of Him who sits upon it is an unopened scroll, sealed with seven seals. A mighty angel shouts: 'Who is worthy to break the seals and open the scroll?' (v.2). When no one comes forward John finds himself overcome with emotion. 'I wept and wept,' he says, 'because no-one was found who was worthy to open the scroll or look inside' (v.4).

Commentators disagree as to the meaning of the scroll. It is more important, though, to watch what happens after Christ opens it. One of the elders says to John: 'See, the Lion of the tribe of Judah ... is able to open the scroll' (v.5). John lifts his eyes, expecting to see a lion, but instead he sees a Lamb 'looking as if it had been slain'.

What are we to make of this – a Lamb who is a Lion? Christ, God's Lamb, possesses all that is necessary for our redemption. Though He has the gentleness of a lamb, He has also the strength of a lion. The moment the Lamb takes the scroll, heaven breaks into jubilation, and the living creatures and the twenty-four elders fall down before Him. Each one has a harp, and a golden bowl full of incense representing the prayers (presumably unanswered) of the saints. One commentator suggests that the biggest problem people cry out to God about in their prayers is this: 'Why, Lord, do You permit evil to continue?' It is something that here on earth we will never fully understand.

FURTHER STUDY

Psa. 73:1-28;
74:1-23;
Rom. 15:8-12;
Heb. 7:20-28;
2 Pet. 3:1-7

1. How does the psalmist resolve the problem of evil?

2. How does Paul outline God's plan?

Father, I recognise that this cry arises from time to time in my own heart too. Why do You allow evil to have such seemingly unhindered sway? I am thankful that though I may not fully understand, You give me grace to fully stand. Amen.

A song *par excellence*

For reading & meditation – Revelation 5:9–10
'And they sang a new song: "You are worthy to take the
scroll and to open its seals ... you were slain ...'" (v.9)

Songs are mentioned throughout Scripture. At creation the
morning stars sang (Job 38:7). Moses sang (Exod. 15:1).
Miriam sang (Exod. 15:21). Deborah sang (Judg. 5:1). David sang
(2 Sam. 22:1). Mary sang (Luke 1:46). Jesus and His disciples sang
(Matt. 26:30). Paul and Silas sang (Acts 16:25). Singing cannot be
repressed in the people of God. But nowhere in the Bible do we find
a song like this – a song not merely about the goodness of God, but
a specific song of redemption. And it is described as a *new* song. In

FURTHER STUDY

Psa. 96:1-13;
98:1-9;
Acts 20:28;
Heb. 12:22-24

1. What is the
scope of the
psalmist's
'new song'?

2. How does the
writer to the
Hebrews portray
Mount Zion?

the Old Testament a new song celebrated a new act
of divine deliverance or intervention and that is its
purpose here. Heaven now has a song *par excellence*
– a song about the ransom paid for sinners by the Son
of God Himself.

In Revelation 5:6 – 'a Lamb, looking as if it had
been slain' – we find the assurance that the marks
of our Lord's suffering will be seen in heaven for all
eternity. As the old hymn puts it: 'Those wounds, yet
visible above [are] in beauty glorified.' The highest
note of worship surely must be the fact that we have
been washed in Christ's blood. In this angels cannot
join us for they have not been redeemed.

Notice in verse 10 the phrase 'a *kingdom* and priests'. Three times
this phrase occurs in Revelation, because in Christ we are lifted
(as we saw earlier) not only to the dignity of priesthood but also
to the splendour of royalty. We have a crown on our head as well
as a censer in our hand.

**Gracious and loving heavenly Father, how can I ever sufficiently
thank You for the honour You have bestowed upon me? May I show
myself worthy of such honour. For Your own dear name's sake.
Amen.**

'O Yes'

For reading & meditation – Revelation 5:11–14

'The four living creatures said, "Amen", and the elders fell down and worshipped.' (v.14)

Five songs are sung in the worship depicted in Revelation 4 and 5. The first is adoration of the being of God: 'Holy, holy, holy is the Lord God Almighty, who was, and is, and is to come' (4:8). The second is about God's creative power (4:11). The third – new – song is to Christ, the Lamb of God (5:9–10).

The fourth song (5:12) begins like the third, uses the ascription of the second, but is sung by 'many angels'. They focus their praise on the Lamb but their praise can only be objective. In the words of an old hymn: 'Angels never knew the joy that my salvation brings.' The fifth song (5:13) joins together the blessings of creation and redemption and is sung by the whole of creation. Imagine hearing every voice in creation being lifted in adoration of God and the Lamb!

The last word that we hear as we contemplate this wondrous worship is 'Amen'. Eugene Peterson in *The Message* translates the word 'Amen' as 'O Yes'. He calls it 'the last word in worship', and says: 'Amen means 'Yes'. It is the worshipping affirmation to the God who affirms us. When we come to God in worship we are immersed in God's Yes, a yes that silences all our no's and calls forth an answering yes in us. We respond to His yes by saying yes.' How wonderful it is when a congregation responds to someone's prayers with a vigorous 'Amen'. Sadly, the practice seems to be dying out in many modern-day churches, but I'm glad it is still practised in heaven.

FURTHER STUDY

1 Chron. 16:36;
Psa. 103:19-22;
Heb. 1:4-14;
1 Pet. 1:10-12

1. In what ways does the psalmist describe angels?

2. How is Jesus superior to God's angels?

Father, as I see the whole universe engaged in worshipping You and listen to their songs of praise my heart wants to join in. I do so now – heartily. I worship You dear Father. O Yes.

Evil is doomed

For reading & meditation – Revelation 6:1–2

'Its rider held a bow, and he was given a crown, and he rode out as a conqueror bent on conquest.' (v.2)

We consider now another great theme of Revelation – our Lord's victory over evil and how we overcome it. If the magnificent Christ who towers over everything in Revelation 1 is so powerful, why does evil still wreak havoc? Will evil eventually be vanquished?

It is largely from here on that interpretations of Revelation differ. One group (preterists) see it applying only to the first century. Another group (historicists) take it as describing the long chain of events from John's day to the end of time. A third group (futurists) place events outlined in the book primarily in the end times. A fourth group (idealists) view it as containing symbolic pictures which trigger the imagination and enable us to feel more powerfully the impact that Jesus Christ makes on history. My purpose is to focus on its *overall* message and apply it devotionally, which does not depend on adopting a particular view.

FURTHER STUDY

Psa. 149:1-9;
Rom. 6:8-14;
1 Cor. 15:20-28;
Col. 2:13-15;
Heb. 2:14-18

1. How does Jesus defeat the last enemy?

2. Why did Jesus share our humanity?

Chapter 6 begins with John's description of the first of the seven seals being opened by the Lamb. The voice of one of the living creatures cries 'Come', whereupon John sees a white horse on which sits a rider with a bow in his hand who is given a crown. This rider, a warrior bent on conquest, is most likely a representative of Christ (see also 19:11) who is first in the battle against sin and evil. The word 'evil' is the word 'live' spelt backwards. Sin has blotted the universe by taking life and turning it into evil. Christ is bent on turning it back again.

Father, I am so grateful that You are not content to wage the battle against evil from Your throne. You sent Your Son into the rough and tumble of it. He is always the first on the field of battle. Help me not to be afraid of joining in. Amen.

Right use of the Spirit

For reading & meditation – Revelation 6:3–8

'When the Lamb opened the second seal, I heard the
second living creature say, "Come!"' (v.3)

Yesterday we looked at the first of the famous 'Four Horses of the
Apocalypse' – the white horse – which may represent Christ,
who is first on the field in the battle against evil. As the white
horse recedes from John's vision he observes the opening of the
second seal, and the appearance of a bright red horse and its rider.
The fact that the rider was given power to take away peace, and
was given a large sword, clearly indicates that he was involved
in waging war. War is evil, no matter how it may be rationalised.
'Our Lord,' says one commentator, 'does not sit on
the red horse – ever.'

When the Lamb opens the third seal a black
horse appears, whose rider holds in his hands a pair
of scales. From the context, these are symbolic of
famine, which too is a terrible evil. Who has not sat
appalled at the sight of the victims of famine, who
feature so frequently on our television screens, with
their bloated bellies and spindly limbs? When the
fourth seal is opened a pale horse appears whose
rider is named Death. This horse and its rider are
symbolic of sickness and epidemic disease.

These three horseman stand for three of the
greatest evils in the world – war, famine, and sickness which leads
to death. What is being said here is that Christ has set His face
against them and will ultimately overcome them. Whatever form
of evil you encounter today be assured of this: your Lord is there
ahead of you riding into battle against its forces.

FURTHER STUDY

Isa. 11:1-5;
Luke 21:12-19;
John 11:17-27;
16:1-11

1. What,
according to
Isaiah, will
the Messiah
accomplish?

2. What
promises does
Jesus give
Martha?

**My Father and my God, forgive us that we Your people are more
ready to enjoy the thrill that the power of Pentecost produces in us
than we are to use it in the battle against evil. Forgive us and
restore us. In Jesus' name we pray. Amen.**

Never 'No longer'

For reading & meditation – Revelation 6:9–11

'They called ... "How long ... Lord ... until you judge the inhabitants of the earth and avenge our blood?"' (v.10)

The chief manifestations of the evil that has filled this world are identified. However, as we said, because our Lord is first on the field of battle against evil and is 'bent on conquest' (6:2), we can rest assured that evil will ultimately be overcome.

With the opening of the fifth seal another kind of evil is exposed – the evil of religious persecution. John sees under the altar the souls of those who had been slain because of their commitment to God's Word, and hears them crying out: 'How long?' This indicates the sacrificial nature of the martyrs' death. It is probable that they are described as being 'under the altar' because that is where the blood of animals sacrificed on the altar was poured out (see Leviticus 4:7).

Why does God allow His people to be persecuted? We know that He is not powerless to deliver them. Why, then, are they allowed to suffer? This is a question for which there is not a complete answer here on earth. Though we have some explanations, such as the fact that we are tested through suffering and that tribulation produces patience, we will have to wait until we get to heaven for the full answer. What we do know, however, is that our Lord is filled with compassion for those who suffer and, after giving the martyrs a white robe – a symbol of blessedness and purity – they are told to 'wait a little longer' (v.11). The mark of the faithful is that they hold on. They may cry 'How long?' but they never cry 'No longer.'

FURTHER STUDY

Psa. 79:1-13;
119:81-88;
Matt. 5:10-12;
2 Cor. 4:7-18;
James 1:2-4,12;
1 John 4:13-18

1. How does the psalmist pray?

2. What promise does Jesus give His disciples?

Father, I praise You that though You do not always remove trials You always provide sufficient grace for me to bear them and carry on. For this I am so grateful. Amen.

No peaceful co-existence

For reading & meditation – Revelation 6:12–17

'For the great day of their wrath has come, and who can stand?' (v.17)

The opening of the sixth seal by the Lamb brings about a great cataclysm – the shaking of the cosmos. Everything falls apart. There is chaos. No one can stand upright. Many regard this as depicting the end of the world, but it can also be seen as a graphic picture of a natural catastrophe which causes those not standing firm in Jesus Christ to topple into despair. The seals have introduced: war, famine, death, religious persecution and now catastrophe.

The images in this passage terrify, striking the imagination with tremendous force. That is exactly what they are intended to do. Evil is exposed in all its hideousness and, having seen it exposed, we should find it impossible to co-exist peacefully with it. Some Christians stubbornly refuse to open their eyes to evil lest it disturb their quiet reflections. Christians, however, must be realists who face things as they are, and there is no better book than Revelation to make us do that. The graphic descriptions are designed to shock, to make us recognise reality, to help us have no illusions about the depravity and evil that exist in the midst of God's fair creation. The book of Revelation brings everything out into the open; there is no glossing over matters, no sugar-coating of the bitter facts.

The chapter ends: 'Who can stand?' The answer is obvious – no one. Those who live by evil shall perish by evil. Evil has the smell of death upon it. It may prosper for a time but its end is certain.

FURTHER STUDY

Gen. 6:5-22;
Mark 13:1-8,
24-25;
Heb. 12:25-29;
1 Pet. 3:18-22

1. Why did God flood the earth?

2. What cannot be shaken?

Father, I see from these graphic depictions that You want to stir up a righteous anger in me against all forms of depravity. Help me not to be reconciled to evil but to resist it in every way I can. For Jesus' sake. Amen.

More than a match

For reading & meditation – Revelation 7:1–8

'After this I saw four angels standing at the four corners
of the earth ...' (v.1)

We see here angels at work. They can stand. They are not
intimidated by evil. The issue seems so important that for
a little while there is a delay in the opening of the seventh seal. The
point being made is that angels are not intimidated by the three
evil horsemen for, from their special vantage point in heaven, they
see the whole scheme of Providence remaining intact.

John observes four angels holding in check the four winds to
prevent them blowing on the earth and causing great destruction.

FURTHER STUDY

Mal. 3:1-4;
Matt. 4:1-11;
Luke 22:39-43;
Acts 12:5-11;
Eph. 1:13-14

1. How did
angels minister
to Jesus?

2. How did
an angel help
Peter?

As he watches, another angel appears, crying out in
a loud voice: 'Do not harm the land or the sea ... until
we put a seal on the foreheads of the servants of our
God' (v.3). The number of those who were sealed, John
says, is 144,000. Bible scholars vary in their opinion
as to who these and the 'great multitude' in verse 9
are, and the relation between them. But it is quite
clear that they are God's servants, all of them, both
Old Testament and New Testament alike. All God's
believing people are sealed. The 144,000 (12 squared
then multiplied by the cube of 10) need not be taken
literally. Most numbers in Revelation are symbolic,
and this number signifies completeness.

This must be linked to the question at the end of Chapter 6: 'Who
can stand?' Well, for one thing, angels can stand. And for another,
God's people can stand. When evil is unsealed, the Christian is
sealed against it by the Holy Spirit. This sealing fortifies us against
the unsealing.

**Father, I know that You are more than a match for evil. Nothing can
successfully work against Your purposes. I draw confidence from
this, dear Lord. Help me always to view things from this
perspective. In Christ's name I pray. Amen.**

An argument against evil

For reading & meditation – Revelation 7:9–17

'And they cried out in a loud voice: "Salvation belongs to
our God, who sits on the throne ..."' (v.10)

John hears the number of those who are sealed against evil but
when he looks, it is 'a great multitude that no one could count'.
The 144,000 and the great multitude are one and the same – all
servants of God. Throughout Revelation John uses poetic forms and
language, and repetition of ideas was common in Hebrew poetry.
It is designed to show that the hearts of all God's servants in both
the Old and New Testaments are sealed against evil. Though evil
may harm their bodies it cannot harm their souls.

The people John writes about are not only sealed
but exuberant, because they know that evil cannot
harm them spiritually. Thus they sing. It seems
wonderful that the people of God can still sing in
the face of evil. There is a charming passage in a
book by Henry Adams entitled *Mont St Michael*
which describes a pompous theologian attacking a
brother who belonged to the Order of Assisi over
some of his simple beliefs. It reads: 'When the
theologian attacked the Brother by the usual formal
arrangement of syllogisms, the Brother, taking out a
flute from the folds of his robe, played his answer in
rustic melodies.' Music and song are sometimes the
best argument we can muster against the attacks of evil.

FURTHER STUDY

Psa. 146:1-10;
Isa. 35:1-10;
Mark 13:22-27;
Luke 12:4-7;
Acts 16:22-34

1. How does
Isaiah describe
the joy of the
redeemed?

2. How do Paul
and Silas face
up to evil?

The robes of the multitude had been washed and made white
in the blood of the Lamb. This most precious imagery of being
washed in Christ's blood is being omitted from some modern
hymn books but thankfully not from the hymn book of heaven.

**Father, in a day when our faith is being called by some 'an abattoir
religion' because of our emphasis on the shedding of the Saviour's
blood, help us to remember that nothing else could have
cleansed us. For this we are eternally grateful. Amen.**

'Reversed thunder'

For reading & meditation – Revelation 8:1–5

'Then the angel took the censer, filled it with fire from the altar, and hurled it on the earth ...' (v.5)

The opening of the seventh seal brings us to the next great theme of Revelation – the power of prevailing prayer. When the seventh seal is opened there is silence in heaven for the space of about half an hour. Why? In order to *hear* the prayers of God's people. We are about to see, as someone has put it, that 'more things are wrought in heaven and earth through prayer than this world dreams of'.

Then silence gives way to action. As John watches, an angel comes before the throne of God, mixes the prayers of God's people with incense, combines them with fire, and hurls the censer over the ramparts of heaven so that it falls to earth. When it reaches the earth there are peals of thunder, rumblings, flashes of lightning, and an earthquake. The prayers which had come up before God and had been purified and set on fire by God's Spirit return to earth with tremendous force. George Herbert had a beautiful phrase to describe this. He called it 'reversed thunder'.

Sometimes when I pray for the Church and the world I wonder if prayer makes much difference. How wonderfully reassuring it is to learn that prayer is heard, purified, and re-enters earth like 'reversed thunder'. Have faith to believe that the prayers you offer for the needs of the world are being heard and, after having been mixed with the fire of God's Spirit, fall back to earth. What an exciting concept: today, as every day, earth will be shaken spiritually by the prayers of God's people.

FURTHER STUDY
Psa. 141:1-2;
Luke 18:1-8;
Rom. 8:26-27;
1 Tim. 2:1-8;
James 5:16-18

1. What assurance does Paul give the Roman Christians?

2. On what basis does Paul encourage Timothy to pray?

Father, I am so grateful for the reassurance that when I pray for the needs of the world You not only listen but take my words, mix them with the fire of Your Spirit and put them to work. Help me to intercede more. In Jesus' name. Amen.

The part prayer plays

For reading & meditation – Revelation 8:6–12

'Then the seven angels who had the seven trumpets
prepared to sound them.' (v.6)

The seven angels who were standing before the throne, and apparently waiting for their moment, prepare to sound their trumpets. A trumpet is a symbol of proclamation. Over and over again in the Old Testament the trumpet was used to call people to battle or to proclaim a religious festival. Here the trumpets are sounded to herald what God does in answer to prayer, and so to alert us to our part in His purposes. God wants to enlist our prayers in the battle against evil. He could work without us, but such is His regard for His people that He wants to involve us in the fight.

FURTHER STUDY

Joel 2:1-14;
Luke 5:32
Acts 17:22-31;
20:20-21;
1 Thess. 5:6-9,
16-18

1. What warning and what promise does Joel give?

2. Describe Paul's preaching in Athens.

Christian author Paul Rees wrote *Don't Sleep through the Revolution*. That, in effect is what the trumpets are saying: be alert to the fact that you have a part to play through prayer in God's programme of judgment and discipline.

The first four trumpets, when sounded, initiate great disasters on the earth: a third of the earth is burned up, a huge burning mountain is thrown into the sea, a great star blazing like a torch falls from the sky, and the sun, moon and stars lose a third of their light. The trumpets sound out not just doom but warning. These judgments, like the plagues in Egypt (Exod. 8–11), are meant to show God's wrath against evil and alert men and women to the fact that He is active. Personally I am convinced that through natural disasters that occur in the world God is trying to bring people to repentance. And we, God's praying people, have a part in this.

Father, the more I see how prayer plays such a major part in Your universe, the more responsibility I feel to step up my prayer life. Help me to place a greater emphasis on prayer. In Jesus' name. Amen

A new way of seeing

For reading & meditation – Revelation 8:13; 9:1-12

'And out of the smoke locusts came down upon the earth and were given power like that of scorpions ...' (v.3)

Before the fifth trumpet sounds an eagle is seen flying and calling out: 'Woe!' (8:13). How strange. It is as if God, knowing the human tendency to make light of judgment, breaks into the sequence with something that throws us off our guard.

The fifth angel sounds his trumpet and precipitates a plague of terrifying locusts. A huge hole is opened up in the earth's surface and the locusts start moving with a deafening noise, attacking people. They are armed like scorpions, shaped like horses, crowned

FURTHER STUDY

Psa. 83:1-18;
Amos 5:18-24;
Matt. 3:1-12;
Luke 11:37-52

1. Why did the psalmist call down judgment?

2. Why did Jesus pronounce judgment?

like kings, have faces resembling human ones, hair like women's, teeth like lions', and their bodies are covered in armour plating. Will such creatures plague the earth? Of course not. Here again our imagination is being stirred, and the recasting of Joel's locust prophecy (Joel 1–2) – is intended to show the terrible consequences of a life that resists the overtures which God in His mercy makes. Only the repentant are saved from the awful horrors of sin's consequences.

The introduction of the figure of Apollyon (the Destroyer called the angel of the Abyss, or bottomless pit) in verse 11 makes the picture even more nightmarish. Again I emphasise that these pictures are meant to send the adrenaline through our spiritual system and enable us to see truth through new eyes. A great deal that is found in Revelation is found also in other parts of the Bible. There is not all that much that is new in Revelation, just a new way of saying it.

My Father and my God, I am seeing truth through new eyes. How tragic is a life that resists the advances of divine grace. I am so thankful that Your love has won my heart. All honour and glory be to Your worthy name. Amen.

Shouting through pain

For reading & meditation – Revelation 9:13–21

'The rest of mankind that were not killed by these plagues still did not repent ...' (v.20)

Though there is a seventh trumpet to be sounded, the sixth trumpet is the last to herald a warning for the inhabitants of earth. A voice comes from the altar saying: 'Release the four angels who are bound at the great river Euphrates' (v.14). Their task is to kill a third of humanity. How? They have a cavalry of 200 million fire-breathing, snake-tailed, lion-headed horses. Once again these images are to stir our imagination.

The voice John hears at the sound of the sixth trumpet comes from the 'altar'. This, as we saw, is where the Church's prayers are processed and fiery answers returned to earth. Trumpet six, like the others, is sounding out the warning of God's wrath against sin in response to His people's prayers that evil should not go unpunished and that justice might prevail.

Verse 20 says: 'The rest of mankind that were not killed by these plagues still did not repent.' Multitudes in every age witness all kinds of disasters and still refuse to hear God's voice sounding through them, calling people to repentance. One person has said: 'The judgments of God are not just retributive but remedial; they are designed to bring us from sickness to health, from sin to repentance.' C.S. Lewis put it best: 'God whispers to us in our pleasure, speaks in our conscience, but shouts in our pains.'* If people will not hear the voice of God in their pains, what hope is there that they will listen to Him in the midst of their pleasures?

FURTHER STUDY

Psa. 115:1-8;
Isa. 44:9-20;
Luke 10:10-16;
11:29-32
Acts 19:18-20
2 Pet. 3:3-9

1. What is the Word of the Lord according to Isaiah?

2. How does Peter raise the hopes of his readers?

Father, I stand amazed at the grace that continues to woo men and women despite their resistance and stubborn commitment to independence. But with all my heart I cry: 'Continue speaking, dear Lord.' Many may yet respond. Amen.

*The Problem of Pain by C.S Lewis copyright © C.S Lewis Pte.Ltd. 1940.

A time for everything

For reading & meditation – Revelation 10:1-4
'Seal up what the seven thunders have said and do not write it down.' (v.4)

During the interlude between the blowing of the sixth and seventh trumpets John introduces another theme – the importance and power of godly witness. In chapters 10 and 11, this New Testament truth is presented in a way that once again stirs the imagination.

From heaven a mighty angel descends, whose face is like the sun, who is clothed in a cloud, crowned with a rainbow, and bestriding ocean and earth on legs that are like great columns of fire. When he shouts the heavens echo his words with seven thunders. In his hand he holds a small open scroll. Angels are often portrayed as effeminate figures, but not so the apocalyptic angels. They are strong and powerful with, as one commentator puts it, 'hell in their nostrils and heaven in their eyes'. John is about to write down the words he hears but he is forbidden by the angel.

Relating this vision to our witnessing, it shows that our responsibility to witness must be balanced by judgment of what to say and what not to say. Holding back is as much a part of Christian witness as telling out. Jesus, on the Mount of Transfiguration, told His disciples: 'Don't tell anyone what you have seen, until the Son of Man has been raised from the dead' (Matt. 17:9). There are other occasions in the Gospels when Jesus also forbad people to tell what they had experienced. This was because they needed to know a simple but important truth, namely that there is a time to speak and a time to keep silent.

FURTHER STUDY

Isa. 43:10-21;
Luke 24:45-49;
Mark 5:37-43;
Acts 16:6-10

1. To what is Israel called to be a witness?

2. To what were the disciples called to be witnesses?

Father, You have taught me in Your Word that there is a time for everything. Help me in my personal witness not only to know what to say, but what not to say. In Jesus' name I ask it. Amen.

Bitter sweet

For reading & meditation – Revelation 10:5–11

'Take it and eat it. It will turn your stomach sour, but in your mouth it will be as sweet as honey.' (v.9)

John is now commanded to take the little scroll that was in the angel's hand and eat it. The prophet Ezekiel had a similar experience (Ezek. 2:8–3:3). Eating a book suggests assimilating it, digesting it, taking it all in. Before we can truly tell out the good news of the gospel we must internalise it. If we fail to do this our witness is nothing more than 'gossiping about God'. A true witness is someone who has absorbed the Word of God into their spiritual system so that they can share it naturally with others.

John is told by the angel that when he eats the scroll it will be bitter to his stomach but sweet to his taste. Almost every child of God will know this experience. The Word, when it enters our mouth, is as honey to our taste, but so often, when the word we share with others is resisted, we feel in the pit of our stomach the sourness of rejection. Jeremiah took hold of God's words with great delight, but later, when the people refused to accept what he had to say, he cried: 'The word of the LORD has brought me insult and reproach all day long' (Jer. 20:8).

The Word is sweet when it comes to us from God, but when rejected by those we share it with it turns to bitterness inside us. It is not that we are bitter because of the rejection, but we experience the bitterness that comes with rejection. But whether it is rejected or not, the Word must be shared. 'Prophesy again,' John is told. The work of witness is not optional.

FURTHER STUDY

Isa. 6:8–13;
Jer. 11:18–23;
Matt. 10:1–16;
Acts 13:38–52

1. What bitterness did Isaiah and Jeremiah experience?

2. What mixed receptions did Jesus' disciples meet with?

Father, Your Word tells me that perfect love casts out fear. May Your love so permeate my life that it will overpower every fear – particularly the fear of rejection. I ask this through Jesus' name. Amen.

'Mightily Assured'

For reading & meditation – Revelation 11:1
'Go and measure the temple of God and the altar, and count the worshippers there.' (v.1)

This fascinating chapter presents us with a picture of God's people being spiritually assured. When I was young it was a fashion among some Christians to write after their name 'M.A.', which stood for 'Mightily Assured'. This somewhat deceptive practice came into disrepute but, looked at from our present standpoint, every Christian is such an 'M.A.' The image of the temple being measured can be taken as the assurance that our work of witness does not go unnoticed.

FURTHER STUDY

1 Kings 19:9-18;
Rom. 8:9-17;
Heb. 2:10-13

1. What assurance did Elijah receive?

2. What assurance does Paul give?

John sees the Temple in Jerusalem and is told to measure it and count the worshippers there. The Temple was by this time just a memory as it had been destroyed by the Romans in AD 70. In this vision the Temple – the 'measured' place – represents the community of God's people gathered together who enjoy the security of perfect order. In the Church the dimensions are specified. There is an order that is inviolate. The battle lines against the world, the flesh and the devil are clearly drawn. We know what to pray for (1 Tim. 2:1–15) and how to pray. We know how the Church is to be governed, how it is to evangelise, and how it should represent itself to the world. We are also given the guarantee that where two or three come together in Christ's Name, He will be in their midst (Matt. 18:20).

How wonderful that in the midst of our chaotic world there is a measured place to which God's people can retreat. There, as one poet puts it: 'We kneel how weak, we rise how full of power.'

Father, how encouraging this is. In the midst of a chaotic world You have provided for me a measured place. May this image strengthen me so that I remain steadfast, unmovable, always giving myself fully to the work of the Lord. Amen.

The witnessing dynamic

For reading & meditation – Revelation 11:2–6

'And I will give power to my two witnesses, and they will prophesy for 1,260 days, clothed in sackcloth.' (v.3)

The worshipping community of Christians is protected by a holy order, but the 'court of the Gentiles' is not. There holy things, and those who witness to them, are treated with derision. Similarly, consider how difficult it is to speak of the things of Christ in the workplace compared with discussing them in church.

Again, Revelation strikes our minds with imaginative pictures. Two unnamed witnesses emerge here, both wearing sackcloth to emphasise the seriousness of their message. Who they represent is open to speculation, but the astonishing things they can do (vv.5–6) suggest the two symbolised the witness of God's people through the ages, and also witnessed Christ's glory on the Mount of Transfiguration – Moses the lawgiver and Elijah the reformer. The law is the revelation of God's truth; reformation is its application.

The two witnesses proclaim their message in the world as long as it survives. They prophesy with remarkable power for 1,260 days (about the 42 months mentioned in verse 2 as the time of great distress). They have power to shut up the sky so that it will not rain, turn the waters into blood and strike the earth with plagues. This seems to indicate that witness is backed by both heaven and earth. This telling image of the two witnesses shows that knowing God's law and applying it to our daily lives is the dynamic behind all Christian witness. There can be no true witness if either knowledge or application is omitted.

FURTHER STUDY

Deut. 30:11-20;
Psa. 119:17-32;
Mal. 4:4-6;
Matt. 11:7-19;
22:34-40

1. What choice did Moses give Israel?

2. What does Jesus say about the greatest commandment?

My Father and my God, quietly something is being burned into me: the work of witnessing is one of Your highest priorities. Help me know Your law, apply it to my life, then share it with others. In Jesus' name. Amen.

A tide about to turn?

For reading & meditation – Revelation 11:7–12

'But after the three and a half days a breath of life from God entered them …' (v.11)

The two witnesses are suddenly attacked by a beast which rises from the pit, overpowers and kills them. Their bodies lie exposed on the streets for three and a half days and are refused burial. There appears to be great jubilation on the part of the inhabitants of the earth as they see them put to death.

Christians are not surprised that witnessing comes to such an end. The world has a long history of rejecting God's truth. In the West, ever since the Enlightenment, generally speaking, people

FURTHER STUDY

2 Chron.
34:1-33;
Psa. 14:1;
80:1-19;
Acts 3:12-26

1. Why does the psalmist plead for revival?

2. What is the condition for 'times of refreshing'?

have rejoiced as they have sought to replace God's truth with human reasoning. The conclusion of the past centuries has been in effect: 'Moses and Elijah are dead … no longer will we be reminded of the need to toe the line spiritually and morally.' We live in an age when much of the world holds that there is no such thing as objective truth. People argue: 'My truth is as good as yours.' Intellectuals celebrate the dethronement of truth and the enthronement of reason.

Is this the way of the future? Not necessarily. Though dead, the two witnesses come to life again (v.11), and before the seventh trumpet is blown, they disappear in a cloud as Moses and Elijah did during the Transfiguration (Matt. 17:5). All this symbolises the work of Christian witness throughout the ages. At times it appears to have been overpowered and brought down to death, but always it rises again by way of revival or reformation. I believe revival is on the way.

Lord God, grant that this may be so. Turn the tide of spiritual oppression and rejection of Your Word by a visitation from on high that will revive Your Church and bring a powerful witness to the world. In Christ's name I ask it. Amen.

Longsuffering mercy

For reading & meditation – Revelation 11:13–14

'Seven thousand people were killed in the earthquake …
the survivors … terrified … gave glory to … God …' (v.13)

The work of witness takes place between the sixth and seventh trumpet blasts. It is as if the Spirit breaks in and interrupts the proceedings to assure Christians they are not forgotten, nor deprived of the presence and power of the Lord. The messages these trumpets heralded were given in answer to the prayers of God's people for justice and truth, and the desire to bring people to repentance. As the two witnesses are being caught up to heaven, a severe earthquake causes great fear to fall on the people of the earth.

The first six trumpets are sounded to alert the world to the judgment of God. Those who have still not repented will face the third woe introduced by the seventh trumpet – a woe from which there will be no appeal. Trumpets one to four demonstrate God's power over the world that men and women inhabit. Trumpets five to seven show us God's power over people and His prerogative to damn those who remain unrepentant.

FURTHER STUDY

Gen. 18:16–33;
Dan. 4:28–37;
Rom. 1:18–20

1. Why did Nebuchadnezzar glorify God?

2. How does godlessness manifest itself according to Paul?

While a certain sadness affects us when we see God damn the unrepentant, we should remember that He always gives people plenty of time to repent. Yet if they are not willing to hear the first six trumpets they will be unlikely to heed the seventh. By that time their hearts will be so hardened that they will not believe, no matter what happens. God has gone to great lengths in His universe to reveal Himself to those who desire to know Him. Those who want to know Him – really want to know Him – will find Him.

Father, how good You are to the men and women of this world. In longsuffering mercy, not willing that any should perish, You continue to speak. All honour and glory be to Your wonderful name. Amen.

The two maximums

For reading & meditation – Revelation 11:15–18

'The kingdom of the world has become the kingdom of our Lord and of his Christ ...' (v.15)

The sounding of the seventh trumpet presents us with a picture of the final display of the majesty of God. The scene is of the end of all things when the offer of mercy will be withdrawn, and the kingdom of this world becomes the kingdom of our Lord and His Christ. The twenty-four elders fall on their faces before God and raise their voices in thanksgiving and praise. Those who pray 'Thy kingdom come' will one day see their prayers answered. The kingdom comes in answer to the prayers of the Church. We must never forget that. Our praying has more influence in the world than we will ever realise here on earth.

FURTHER STUDY

Deut. 32:1-4;
Psa. 145:1-21;
Acts 28:30-31;
Eph. 6:18-20;
Heb. 10:32-39;
James 2:12-13

1. For what does the psalmist exalt God?

2. What kinds of prayer does Paul talk about?

We know that this is speaking of the coming of Christ because of the phrase 'who is and who was' (v.17). In other parts of Revelation Christ is referred to as the One 'who is, and who was, and who *is to come*' (1:4; 4:8). Now the One who is to come has come. The song of the twenty-four elders shows that ultimately God's character will be vindicated and that none of the redeemed will be able to say that God is not just.

Our praying should not only be for the redemption of the penitent but also for the punishment of the impenitent. C.S. Lewis expressed it like this: 'The evil man must not be left perfectly satisfied with his own evil ... it must be made to appear to him what it rightly is – evil ... that sooner or later, the right should be asserted.'* Sound prayer will focus on the demonstration of God's maximum justice with maximum mercy.

Father, when I think about the evil that is in the world You know I am tempted to pray sometimes for maximum justice with minimum mercy. Deliver me from this wrong perspective. Help me to see all things from Your point of view. Amen.

*The Problem of Pain by C.S Lewis copyright © C.S Lewis Pte.Ltd. 1940.

War in heaven

For reading & meditation – Revelation 11:19; 12:1-12

'She was pregnant and cried out in pain as she was about to give birth.' (v.2)

In Revelation, one moment we are looking at the end of all things and the next we are plunged back into another phase of time. Through a rift in the temple of God John sees the ark of the covenant – the symbol of God's presence. This sighting is accompanied by lightning flashes, thunder, and an earthquake, interpreted elsewhere in Scripture as signs that God is resident in heaven and active. All this provides the setting for the next theme of Revelation – the clash between the kingdoms of earth and the kingdom of God.

A pregnant woman appears and suddenly cries out in the pain of childbirth. At that moment a dragon with seven crowned heads is poised to devour the emerging male child. As soon as He arrives in the world He is snatched up to God. Following this John observes a war breaking out in heaven, when the dragon is dislodged and cast down to the earth. At this a loud voice is heard in the heavens announcing the dragon's defeat.

FURTHER STUDY

Josh. 10:1-15;
Matt. 2:1-20;
Eph. 6:10-17;
1 John 3:7-10

1. How does Paul define the spiritual battle for believers?

2. Why did the Son of God 'appear'?

John reminds us that the woman and the dragon are 'signs' that point to something else (vv.1,2). But what? We are being carried back here to the beginning of the story of salvation – the nativity. For what purpose? To enable us to grasp more clearly that the coming of our Lord to this world meant the beginning of the end for the dominion of our adversary, the devil. This is the nativity as seen from an eternal perspective: not a baby in a manger attended by wise men but a child in a cosmos attacked by a dragon.

Lord Jesus Christ, how blind this world is to the real reason for Your coming. How it must grieve You to see Your incarnation so misunderstood, so commercialised and sentimentalised. Forgive us and help us, dear Lord. Amen.

No room for pacifism

For reading & meditation – Revelation 12:13–17

'When the dragon saw that he had been hurled to the earth, he pursued the woman who had given birth ...' (v.13)

The defeated dragon (Satan), having been bounced out of heaven, turns his fury on the woman who brought the child into the world. She symbolises the nation of Israel from whom Christ came. As she is given wings to fly into the desert, the dragon pursues her and ejects a cataract of water in an attempt to drown her, but the earth opens up and swallows the water. Thwarted, the dragon goes off to make war against the rest of her offspring: 'those who obey God's commandments and hold to the testimony of Jesus' (v.17). As the devil is unable to attack Christ he attacks those who follow Christ.

FURTHER STUDY

1 Sam. 17:41–50;
Eph. 3:2–13;
Col. 1:9–14;
1 Pet. 5:8–12

1. What does Paul say is God's intention for the Church?

2. What is Peter's counsel?

Some Christians I have come across don't believe in a personal devil. They need to know, however, that the devil believes in them. Christians are poised between two kingdoms – the kingdom of this world and the kingdom of Christ. Whether we like it or not we are involved in spiritual warfare. Whatever our view may be concerning pacifism in relation to the affairs of this world, there is no room for pacifism in the kingdom of God. Scripture tells us: 'For we wrestle not against flesh and blood, but against principalities, against powers ...' (Eph. 6:12, AV). Many Christians get no further than the first four words of that statement: 'For we wrestle not ...' But we must not be alarmed by all this talk about warfare and fighting. Our Lord is more than a match for the devil. He that is in us is greater than he who is in the world (see 1 John 4:4).

Heavenly Father, I accept that I am involved in a war whether I like it or not. But the outcome of this war is already settled. I am so thankful. Help me play my part. In Jesus' name. Amen.

One Jesus

For reading & meditation – Revelation 13:1–4

'And the dragon stood on the shore of the sea.' (v.1)

The deeply disappointed dragon obviously needs another strategy. To wage war against 'those who obey God's commandments and hold to the testimony of Jesus' (12:17) a plan needs to be devised that will discourage them from obeying God and disillusion them about their Christian faith. Two beasts come from the underworld to assist him, one from the sea, the other from the land (v.11).

The beast that emerges from the sea is at first glance a fearsome-looking creature, but one commentator suggests that a closer look reveals that it is nothing more than a patchwork job assembled from leftover parts of a leopard, a bear and a lion. The beast's seven heads and ten horns with ten crowns suggest that power is of its very essence. If there is one thing the devil lusts after more than any other thing, says Michael Wilcock, it is omnipotence.

What we are seeing here in symbolic language is the anti-God state which derives its power from Satan. For the Christians of John's day that meant the Roman Empire, but every succeeding generation knows its equivalent. Paul, in Romans 13:1, indicates that there is no authority except from God. God has ordained that the world should be run under a system of authority, but often the devil has perverted political systems and used them to intimidate and frustrate the followers of Jesus. Christians are called to uphold all that is right, but we serve another king and another kingdom, one Jesus.

FURTHER STUDY

Isa. 14:12–15;
Matt. 22:15–22;
Luke 4:1–13;
Rom. 13:1–7;
1 Pet. 2:13–17

1. How did the devil tempt Jesus?

2. How did the Pharisees set out to trap Jesus?

Father, I pray for the politicians who govern my country.
I recognise that politics is a field where Satan delights to roam.
Help us to be aware of his tactics and combat him through powerful,
persevering prayer. In Christ's name. Amen.

Are you listening?

DAY 346

For reading & meditation – Revelation 13:5–9

'He who has an ear, let him hear.' (v.9)

The emergence of the beast from the sea is an imaginative way of drawing attention to political power struggles. Christ has come to establish a kingdom (the rule of God), and as Christians our first allegiance is to that kingdom. We are to obey the laws of the state (Rom. 13:1), but when they clash with the laws of God then we are free to disobey. One commentator says: 'If the devil's design is to separate our behaviour and our belief from the rule of God, politics will be a field in which he deploys his picked troops.'

The beast, we are told, 'was given a mouth to utter proud words and blasphemies' (v.5). When a political system adopts the attitude 'I am God' and seeks to get its people to worship it as such then there can only be one word to describe it: blasphemous. Everyone has the right to discern, as Michael Wilcock puts it, 'between the state functioning *under* divine authority and acting illegitimately *as* divine authority'.

Verse 3 said: 'One of the heads of the beast seemed to have had a fatal wound … but had been healed'. The pattern of politics throughout history has been the death and resurrection of ideas. Christians must be careful that their interest in politics does not lead them to worship at its shrine. Our trust must be in the blood of the Lamb; we must stay faithful to Him. It is so easy not to hear what we don't want to hear, hence John's use of our Lord's saying: 'He who has an ear, let him hear.' Are you listening?

FURTHER STUDY

Matt. 24:15–25;
Acts 4:18–31;
12:19–24;
2 Thess. 2:3–12;
1 Pet. 1:17–21

1. How did the Early Church pray?

2. Of what did Paul warn the Thessalonians?

Father, living as I am in an age when men and women appear to put more faith in a political system than they do in You, help me maintain my trust in You and in Your atoning blood. In Jesus' name. Amen.

Get its number

For reading & meditation – Revelation 13:10–18

'He exercised all the authority of the first beast ... made the earth ... worship the first beast ...' (v.12)

The way of the beast is to kill off opposition; the way of the followers of the Lamb is to endure it. The beast that arose from the sea represents Satan's covert bid to get into power politics; he seeks thus to interfere with all that is right, just and true. The land beast, however, is different. He looks like a lamb but has the voice of a dragon. 'The beast from the sea,' says Michael Wilcock, 'is Satan's perversion of society; the beast from the land is his perversion of Christianity.' Notice the Christlike quality of the second beast; it is said to be 'like a lamb'. However, it is an imitation of Christ and its speech betrays its origin.

Any church that encourages people to seek salvation in a system rather than in the Saviour is not a true church of Christ but an agency of the devil. Such churches may appear to have God-given power, and their leaders may speak with authority, even producing miracles and thus deceiving people. 'There is, in fact, no part of life,' warns one commentator, 'in which deceit is more prevalent than in religion.'

How do we protect ourselves from such charlatans? Again John puts his answer in an imaginative way: get its number. The number he gives is 666. All kinds of theories have been propounded as to the meaning of this number. The number, though, does not stand for any person; it is the number of the beast – the religion that makes a great spiritual show but subtly turns our eyes away from the true Christ.

FURTHER STUDY

Matt. 24:3-14;
Mark 13:20-23;
John 10:1-13;
2 Cor. 11:4-15;
1 John 2:18-27

1. What deception does Jesus warn against?

2. How did Paul test false apostles?

Father, enable me to look at all things through eyes that see to the heart of issues. Help me discern the confidence tricksters that pose as Your servants, and above all keep me faithful and true to You. In Jesus' name. Amen.

The power of worship

For reading & meditation – Revelation 14:1–5

'... before me was the Lamb, standing on Mount Zion ... with
him 144,000 who had his ... and his Father's name ...' (v.1)

We have been seeing how a Satanic trinity infiltrates the
political world to vie against the kingdom of God, and
deflect our worship from the One we cannot see to the things
we can see. This invasion might be alarming but not invincible.
The dragon was overcome by Michael and his angels, the sea
beast can be countered and the land beast seen for what he is.
The Satanic trinity is matched by three visions showing the
forces of good that are at work behind the scenes.

FURTHER STUDY

Psa. 96:1-13;
Isa. 12:1-6;
Col. 3:15-17;
Heb. 13:15-16

1. Outline the
psalmist's
invitation to
worship.

2. How far does
Isaiah's song of
praise extend?

The first vision is that of the Lamb leading worship.
The 144,000 referred to here represent the Church.
The number is symbolic of all God's people. This
vision of the Lamb leading worship depicts one of
the most exciting scenes in the whole of Revelation.

In a world where political ideologies clash with the
interests of Christ's kingdom it might seem strange
that Christians should consider their first focus
the worship of God. Some would put work before
worship. But the Lamb leads us into worship so that
our work might be more profitable and effective. The
best workers for the kingdom are those who know
how to worship. Worship first, work second. Nothing happens in
worship, some might think, but that is where they are wrong. From
the worship of God we come refreshed, inspired, reinvigorated
to do God's work in the world. 'Excessive activism,' says Charles
Brutsch, 'is typical of those who do not live by grace.' Worship is
not a waste of time; it is time best made use of.

**Father, help me make worship my highest priority and, even
though the needs of the world are great, help me not substitute
work for it. Make me a worshipper first and a worker second.
In Jesus' name. Amen.**

The power of preaching

For reading & meditation – Revelation 14:6–13

'Then I saw another angel flying in mid-air, and he had the eternal gospel to proclaim ...' (v.6)

Besides worship, another support system which Christians enjoy is that symbolised by the three flying angels. The word 'angel', as you know, means 'messenger', and the message conveyed here is threefold.

The first angel speaks of salvation by grace – 'the eternal gospel'. The second angel speaks of Babylon, which stands for a world system that is in rebellion against God. The third angel brings a powerful challenge and proclaims that those who identify with Babylon will share its fate. Just as the Lamb standing with the 144,000 on Mount Zion represented the support system of worship, so the flying angels represent the power of preaching and proclamation. After all, what is preaching? It was defined by one great Welsh preacher, Dr Cynddylan Jones, in this way: 'Preaching is the act in which the gospel of God is proclaimed, the downfall of all that resist Him is announced, and the call to repent is encouraged.'

In a world preoccupied with wars, treaties, alliances and scandals, the need for sound preaching is greater than ever. Some might think that with so much in the world demanding our attention, there is little time left for preaching. We must make time for it. In a new millennium our need is not for clever talks on current events but a renaissance of good Bible-based preaching. Though we need to take note of what our politicians and statesmen are saying, our greater need is to hear regularly from God.

FURTHER STUDY

Rom. 10:14-17;
1 Cor. 1:17-25;
1 Tim. 4:1-16;
2 Tim. 1:8-14

1. What is Paul's message to the Corinthians?

2. What are Paul's instructions to Timothy?

Father, thank You for the many faithful preachers You have set in Your Church who tell us what You have to say about what is happening, and remind us of Your eternal plans. May their number increase. Amen.

Divine pruning

For reading & meditation – Revelation 14:14–20

'... seated on the cloud was one "like a son of man" with a crown of gold on his head and a sharp sickle ...' (v.14)

The third support system that Christians enjoy in the midst of a world dominated by the devil is that of having their lives pruned spiritually under the direction of the Divine Gardener. In today's passage we see 'one 'like a son of man" (which can be taken to mean Christ – see Dan. 7:13) sending his angels to reap. The first reaps a harvest from the earth, the second comes out of the temple with a sharp sickle and is instructed by a third angel to gather grapes from the earth's vines. Although this picture obviously relates to the end times (see Matt. 13:30,39), and the judgment of the ungodly, I want to take this word picture and relate it to the way in which God works to prune His people.

FURTHER STUDY

Isa. 63:1-9;
John 15:1-8;
2 Cor. 13:14;
Gal. 5:16-25;
2 Thess. 2:13-17

1. Why does the Father prune the vine?

2. Meditate on Paul's exhortation to the Thessalonians.

How many of us realise that every day God is at work in our lives? 'Everything we do, no matter what we do, however common and little noticed our lives, is connected with the action of God and is seed that becomes either a harvest of holiness or a vintage of wrath,' says one writer. That thought encourages me tremendously. God, Christ and the Holy Spirit are at work guiding me in holy living, supervising my days, watching over me, prompting me, leading me, influencing me for good so that out of my life comes a crop of grapes that delights the palate of the Divine Gardener.

These three support systems may seem very feeble when compared with the power of the dragon and his beasts, but they have kept the Church alive throughout the centuries.

Father, how grateful I am that the Trinity seeks to guide my footsteps through the world and bring honour and glory to You out of all that goes on in my life. Blessed be Your name for ever. Amen.

The exodus

For reading & meditation – Revelation 15:1–4

'... and sang the song of Moses the servant of God and the song of the Lamb ...' (v.3)

Seven angels with their seven plagues, poured forth from seven bowls, introduce us to the next theme of Revelation – divine judgment. The desire for judgment is deeply embedded in God's people. 'How long, O LORD? Will you forget me for ever? … How long will my enemy triumph over me?' (Psa. 13:1–2). Hurting people cry out for justice. And who can blame them? Justice is not always to be found on earth. What about heaven? That God is just can be deduced from the words found in verse 1: 'God's wrath is completed.' He dispenses justice with a full measure.

John observes 'those who had been victorious over the beast … They … sang the song of Moses … and the song of the Lamb' (vv.2–3). Prior to the outpouring of great judgment the scene once again is that of worship. Only in the context of worship can the affairs of God be understood. Seven angels prepare to dispense judgment while a congregation sings a hymn. But what a hymn!

Notice the words 'the song of Moses *and* the song of the Lamb'. Two songs of Moses are recorded, in Exodus 15 and Deuteronomy 32. The hymn in verses 3 and 4 chiefly echoes the first of these songs, in which the people rejoice because of the exodus from Egypt. But great though that was, there is an even greater exodus which our Lord spoke to Moses and Elijah about on the Mount of Transfiguration (Luke 9:30–31) – the deliverance of men and women such as you and me from the penalty and power of sin.

FURTHER STUDY

Exod. 15:1-13;
John 3:16-21,
31-36;
Rom. 9:14-24;
12:17-21

1. What is the keynote of the song of Moses?

2. Who is saved from condemnation by Jesus?

Father, I praise You for the deliverance from Egypt, but I praise You even more for the deliverance You wrought for me at Calvary. Because of it I am saved from the penalty of sin, the power of sin and, one day, its presence. Amen.

A just God

For reading & meditation – Revelation 15:5–8; 16:1–7

'After this I looked and in heaven the temple ...
was opened.' (15:5)

The Temple that we saw opened in Revelation 11:19 comes once again into view. This time, however, it is filled with smoke symbolising the glory of God. From this place – the scene of awesome holiness – the seven angels, their bowls filled with God's wrath, leave to execute judgment on the impenitent. Some of these judgments are similar to the plagues that afflicted the ancient Egyptians.

The first angel pours forth a plague of painful sores on those who have the mark of the beast. The second angel empties his bowl into the sea, whereupon it turns into blood. The third angel does the same to the rivers and springs of water and they too become blood. Once again our imagination is being stirred to show us that God's judgments are directed against anything that prevents His people worshipping Him. The Egyptians were not judged because they were particularly evil but because they tried to prevent Israel from worshipping God. The negotiations between Moses and Pharaoh had one theme – worship: 'Let my people go, so that they may hold a festival to me' (Exod. 5:1–3).

FURTHER STUDY

Ezek. 43:1-5;
Matt. 23:29-36;
John 5:24-30;
Eph. 5:3-7

1. For what does Jesus say 'His generation' will be held accountable?

2. Who will not inherit the kingdom of God?

Notice the reference to the altar (Rev. 16:7). Earlier we saw the saints crying out for vindication from the altar (8:3). God's response at that time was to give a warning. Now, however, there is no warning. This is crunch time; the final judgments are at hand. All voices speak with approval of what God is doing. There can be no argument, for everything that God does is just.

Father, there are many reasons why I worship You and why You are worthy to be praised, not the least of them being Your perfect justice. I too join in the company of those who adore You for the perfection of Your character. Amen.

Nothing can stop worship

For reading & meditation – Revelation 16:8-21

'The fourth angel poured out his bowl on the sun, and the
sun was given power to scorch people with fire.' (v.8)

The fourth angel empties his bowl over the sun, which is given
power to scorch people. But those burned by the heat do not
repent. People who harden themselves against God become harder
still when judgment falls. The fifth angel pours out his bowl on
the throne of the beast causing his kingdom to be plunged into
darkness. Again human hearts are hardened.

The sixth angel pours out his bowl on the Euphrates and causes
the river to dry up. Some see mention of the Euphrates in verse
12 and of Armageddon in verse 16 as references to
the final battle when the nations in the north of
the Middle East make their way to Israel. This is
because Armageddon means 'hill of Meggido', a site
a few miles southeast of Haifa. The seventh angel
pours out his bowl into the air whereupon there is
cosmic chaos.

As this battle is referred to again a little later, let
me take you back to the vision of the worshipping
congregation who provided the setting for the
outpouring of these seven plagues (15:1-4). Judgment
is inevitable on anyone or any system that interferes with divine
worship. The greatest evils are the prevention or subversion of
worship. All divine judgment, whether it is visited now or in the
future, has within it the energy of wrath against anything or
anyone who interferes with the true worship of the Deity. Worship
is such an important issue to God (and should also be to us) that
He will not tolerate anything or anyone who seeks to subvert it.

FURTHER STUDY

Amos 8:1-10;
Rom. 2:5-9;
Heb. 10:19-31;
Jude 3-19

1. What subverts
Israel's worship
according
to Amos?

2. Why did Jude
write his letter?

Father, seeing what worship means to You I feel sad that so much of
my time with You is spent in asking for things rather than adoring
You for who You are. Help me worship You in spirit and in truth.
Amen.

The great prostitute

For reading & meditation – Revelation 17:1–5
'Come, I will show you the punishment of the great
prostitute, who sits on many waters.' (v.1)

Now we come to what one commentator describes as 'the
plainest and the most obscure section of Revelation'. There is
more clarity in the symbolic language used here than elsewhere,
yet more mystery accompanies this section also. Once again note
the statement that with the seven angels and their seven plagues
'God's wrath is completed' (15:1). The completion of this judgment
is seen in the overthrow of the woman on the beast, or the great
prostitute as she is known here. Chapter 17 deals with her

FURTHER STUDY

Gen. 11:1-9;
Eph. 4:17-24;
James 4:4-8;
1 Pet. 2:11-12

1. How does
Paul describe
the 'new self'?

2. What is
James warning
against?

destruction, and chapter 18 is a song on the same
subject. Story followed by song is reminiscent of
Exodus, and reinforces the thought that judgment is
visited in order that worship may be better enacted.

John sees a woman dressed in costly clothing
riding on a scarlet beast with seven heads and
ten horns and covered with blasphemous names.
A title is written on her forehead: 'Mystery,
Babylon the Great …' (v.5). Babylon has been
mentioned before (14:8; 16:19), but now we have
a clear explanation. Babylon is the world, not in a

physical sense but in a spiritual sense – the system that seeks
to set itself up independently of God. To flirt with the world is
to live dangerously. 'Everything in the world,' says John in his
first letter, ' – the cravings of sinful man, the lust of his eyes
and the boasting of what he has and does – comes not from the
Father but from the world' (1 John 2:16). We live in the world
but we must watch that we are not of it.

**Heavenly Father, help me heed the warning You are bringing before
me today. Give me the discernment and power I need to walk
through the world without being of it. In Christ's name I pray.
Amen.**

'The prince of this world'

For reading & meditation – Revelation 17:6–18

'I saw that the woman was drunk with the blood of the saints … of those who bore testimony to Jesus.' (v.6)

When asked why she created such bizarre characters, the writer Flannery O'Connor replied that 'for the near-blind you have to draw very large simple caricatures'. The appearance of the great prostitute is more than a warning about sexual infidelity; it is intended to open our eyes to the terrible influence of a godless world.

A prostitute takes men to bed merely for the joining of bodies. By such means both prostitute and client are demeaned. Prostitution says that love can be purchased and sexuality is nothing more than appetite. The seven heads and ten horns signify the evil principles we encounter every day. Everyone looks for meaning in life and the great prostitute says: 'You can find it in me. Come to my bed … there you will find purpose, love, everything your soul longs for.'

We must not think of the world as just an evil influence, for behind it is an evil intelligence. Jesus referred to the devil as 'the prince of this world' (John 14:30; 16:11). The spirit of Satan in the world seeks to attract people away from the worship of God to the worship of pleasure, sex, drugs, and so

FURTHER STUDY

Exod. 32:1-6,25;
Prov. 7:1-23;
1 Thess. 4:1-12;
2 Tim. 3:1-5

1. What is the penalty for ignoring wisdom?

2. What kind of life pleases God?

on. Every time I read Revelation 17, the words of John from his first letter ring in my mind: 'Do not love the world or anything in the world … The world and its desires pass away, but the man who does the will of God lives for ever' (1 John 2:15–17). I can understand why we need John's bizarre caricature. Without it we would not see things so clearly.

Father, protect my soul from being invaded by the spirit of the world. I long to be like Your Son, who said: 'The prince of this world comes but finds no foothold in me.' I pray this in and through Christ's precious name. Amen.

Destined for destruction

For reading & meditation – Revelation 18:1–24

'With a mighty voice he shouted: "Fallen! Fallen is
Babylon the Great!"' (v.2)

In Revelation 18 another angel comes from heaven with a glory
that far outshines the colourfulness of the prostitute and
announces her downfall. However attractive and appealing the
spirit of the world may be, its annihilation is sure.

In verse 4 another angelic voice is heard issuing a warning to
God's people not to be caught up in the spirit of the world. This is
followed by another exposé of the great prostitute's evil wiles. It
is interesting to note that the longest laments over her demise are
uttered by the merchants and sea traders (vv.11–19).
Through worshipping her they gained everything
their hearts were set on yet finished up with nothing.
It was not just their business ventures that collapsed
but also their religion – of self-interest.

Finally another angel is seen (v.21) who takes up a
huge boulder and throws it into the sea, whereupon
all becomes calm. The distinctive feature of this
scene is that whereas previously all destruction has
been accompanied by great noise, the end of Babylon,
the great prostitute, occurs in fearful stillness and
silence. The music dies down, the sound of the
workman's hammer is heard no more. No more
bartering, no more trading, no more leisure, industry
or relationships. The enormous boulder, the size of a millstone,
drops beneath the surface of the sea and it is as though Babylon
had never been. Be warned: there is no point in joining forces with
the world. It is destined for destruction.

FURTHER STUDY

Eccl. 2:1–11,24–26;
Luke 12:16–21;
16:10–15;
Acts 19:23–27;
1 Tim. 6:6–10;
James 4:13–5:5

1. Why is the
author of
Ecclesiastes so
disillusioned?

2. What leads
to contentment
according
to Paul?

**Heavenly Father, if I am ever tempted to join forces with the world
help me to remember that it is destined for destruction. May I be on
my guard so that nothing draws me away from You. In Jesus' name
I ask this. Amen.**

Ringing Hallelujahs

For reading & meditation – Revelation 19:1–10

'After this I heard what sounded like the roar of a great
multitude in heaven shouting: "Hallelujah!"' (v.1)

In contrast to the silence of Babylon's downfall, this chapter
opens with the roar of a great multitude shouting 'Hallelujah!'
Its timing is exactly right. Many commentators have pointed out
that the four Hallelujahs in this section are not to be understood
as gleeful rejoicing at the demise of wickedness or seeing the
impenitent punished, but as an act of praise to the God whose
ways are perfect.

The first Hallelujah (v.1) celebrates the judgment that a just
God visits on the great prostitute. The second (v.3)
expresses gratitude for her eternal incineration.
Her smoke, we are told, 'goes up for ever and ever'.
The third Hallelujah (v.4), prefaced by an 'Amen', is
expressed by the twenty-four elders, and the fourth
(v.6) is a tremendously powerful congregational
response to the call for worship issued by a voice
from the throne (v.5). The great multitude go on to
shout that the wedding of the Lamb is about to take
place when the Bridegroom will take His Bride and
enter into an eternity of shared joy and love.

How delightful it is to turn from the cheap and
gaudy attire of the great prostitute to focus on the
fine, bright, clean linen of the Bride's wedding garment (v.8). This
is a dress she has been given to wear, by God Himself. What a
wedding it will be when the Bride – the Church – is joined to the
heavenly Bridegroom. We often hear the expression 'wedding of
the year'. That will be the wedding of eternity.

FURTHER STUDY

Psa. 147:1-20;
Song 2:3-13;
Isa. 61:10-62:5;
Rom. 11:28-36;
2 Cor. 11:1-2

1. What causes
the people of
God to sing
'Hallelujah'?

2. What gives
rise to Paul's
doxology?

**My Father and my God, to be saved from sin and have a home in
heaven is far more than I deserve. But to be wedded to Christ is
something I find almost mind-blowing. It seems too good to be true.
But I know that it is true. Thank You my Father. Amen.**

We win!

For reading & meditation – Revelation 19:11–21
'I saw heaven standing open and there before me was a
white horse, whose rider is ... Faithful and True.' (v.11)

Another theme emerges in verse 9 – the end of all things. This section begins with the angel prompting John to write of the blessedness of those who are invited to the marriage supper of the Lamb. When John hears the voice of the angel he falls at his feet to worship him, but he is rebuked for his mistake. Though we may admire angels, we are not to worship them. The statement which forms part of the angel's reply – 'the testimony of Jesus is the spirit of prophecy' (v.10) – is to be understood, I believe, as meaning that all true prophecy in some way has to do with Jesus.

FURTHER STUDY
Gen. 3:14-15;
Psa. 2:1-12;
110:1-7;
Col. 2:9-15

1. How does
Jesus fulfil
these psalms?

2. How does
Paul see Jesus
as Victor?

We move from a wedding to a war, and we see once again our Lord riding on a white horse, victoriously robed, leading the armies of heaven into battle against the beast and the false prophet. Comparing Revelation 19:20 with 13:14, the false prophet is almost certainly the beast from the earth. The battle ends with these two enemies, who have caused so much havoc in the world, being thrown alive into the lake of burning sulphur, and those who followed them being destroyed by Christ's sword.

It is predicted from the early pages of the Bible that evil will ultimately be eliminated, and here we see its death throes. A new Christian became discouraged as he read in Genesis of the entrance of evil into the world. Quickly he turned to Revelation to see how it all ends. Coming to today's passage he breathed a sigh of relief and exclaimed: 'Thank God we win!' We do.

Father, I am grateful that I am on the winning side. Your victory is my victory. May I walk through life conscious that though at times it appears some battles are being lost, the outcome is certain and secure. We win. Amen.

The thousand-year reign

For reading & meditation – Revelation 20:1–6

'And I saw an angel coming down out of heaven,
having the key to the Abyss ...' (v.1)

DAY
359

Why was Satan not consigned with the beast and the false prophet to the fiery lake? None of the speculations I have ever read makes much sense. It's a question best left until eternity.

In today's passage we see, however, that Satan is bound for a thousand years, during which the earth enjoys a period of peace. This period of a thousand years is one of the most controversial aspects of Revelation's prophecy. If you want to know how a person interprets the book of Revelation you simply ask them for their view of the thousand-year reign. You will then get a good idea of their approach to the rest of the book. Generally, people hold one of three views. The first group are the pre-millennialists who believe that Christ's coming takes place before the thousand-year reign. The second group are the post-millennialists who believe Christ's coming takes place after it. The third group are the a-millennialists who believe the thousand-year reign is not literal but symbolical. One thing we can all agree on, I think, is that the millennium has not yet arrived for Satan is alive and well and living on planet earth.

FURTHER STUDY

Job 1:6-12;
Isa. 9:2-7;
Matt. 12:22-29;
Rom. 16:17-20

1. What sort of reign does Isaiah envisage?

2. Why did Jesus cast out demons?

No matter what our view of this thousand-year reign, every one of us can be encouraged by the knowledge that Satan and his evil influence will one day be suspended and then eliminated from the world. A friend of mine likes to calls himself a pan-millennialist. 'Everything,' he says 'is going to pan out all right in the end.'

Loving heavenly Father, I rejoice that there is an horizon to Satan's history. You will allow nothing and no one to defeat Your purposes. I am in the hands of Someone who knows the end from the beginning, and for that I am deeply grateful. Amen.

The great white throne

For reading & meditation – Revelation 20:7–14

'When the thousand years are over, Satan will be released from his prison ...' (v.7)

John tells us that when the thousand-year reign is over, the devil will be released from his prison and allowed to go free for a time to deceive the nations. The result of this will be the final battle of the ages, which has been referred to before as Armageddon. The scenes in Revelation are not necessarily presented in chronological order. Some regard Gog and Magog as symbolic of all nations which resist God's rule, and the battle as an attack on the new Jerusalem, the focus of Christ's kingdom. Others believe Gog and Magog are people from the far north (see Ezekiel 38–39), long-time enemies of Israel who are gathered for the final overthrow. The battle ends with the defeat of the invading army, and Satan being consigned to the lake of burning sulphur.

FURTHER STUDY

2 Chron. 20:1–30;
Matt. 19:28–30;
Luke 10:17–24;
1 John 3:11–14;
4:16–18

1. Why did the 72 rejoice?

2. Why did Jesus rejoice?

Following this, John depicts what is often referred to as the 'Great White Throne Judgment' when all humanity will be resurrected and brought before God for final sentencing. This final judgment will be made according to what is found in books containing the deeds, both good and bad, of all people, and a further book, the book of life, containing the names of those who trusted in the saving work of Christ.

People are sent to hell because they have not come to Christ. Billy Graham explains it like this: 'People don't go to hell just because they are bad; neither do they go to heaven just because they are good. They go to either of the two places according to their relationship to Jesus Christ.'

Lord Jesus Christ, how glad I am that I have settled the question of my eternal destiny. I am in You and You are in me. Thus I am safe not only for time but for all eternity. I am deeply grateful. Amen.

What a prospect!

For reading & meditation – Revelation 21:1–8

'Then I saw a new heaven and a new earth, for the first heaven and the first earth had passed away …' (v.1)

John's final theme is heaven. And how it dazzles us. One commentator says of it: 'It is as if we have passed through a series of … rooms in each of which one window looks out on eternity … and now we step out and find ourselves in the open air.' There is to be a new heaven and a new earth. Creation is the first word and the last word of the Bible.

The cataclysmic effects of sin have reached to the utmost parts of the universe, but there is to be a cleansing and a reconstruction based on our Saviour's work on the cross. Heaven is not the end of all things but a new beginning. C.S. Lewis, writing in *The Last Battle*, put it beautifully: 'All their life in this world and all their adventures in Narnia had only been the cover and the title page; now at last they were beginning Chapter One of the Great Story which no one on earth has read, which goes on for ever, in which every chapter is better than the one before.'*

A city comes into John's view, 'prepared as a bride beautifully dressed for her husband' (v.2). Heaven is pictured as a beautiful community living in harmony and ready to receive God's love. When John is given the command 'Write this down, for these words are trustworthy and true' (v.5) he is receiving confirmation of the promises made to us throughout the Bible, namely that heaven is a place open to all who trust in Christ and barred to those who remain impenitent. Nothing could be more sobering yet at the same time more exciting.

FURTHER STUDY

Isa. 65:17-25;
Rom. 8:19-25;
2 Cor. 5:17-18;
2 Pet. 3:10-15

1. What picture of the future does Isaiah present?

2. How does Paul envisage the future?

My Father and my God, I see that in heaven I am to be caught up in an eternal story where 'every chapter will be better than the one before'. There will be no more death, no more crying, no more sorrow, no more pain. What a prospect. Thank You Father. Amen.

The Last Battle by C.S Lewis copyright © C.S Lewis Pte.Ltd. 1956.

The gates of pearl

For reading & meditation – Revelation 21:9–27

'The twelve gates were twelve pearls, each gate made of
a single pearl.' (v.21)

There is some disagreement among Christians as to whether the
New Jerusalem is an actual city or a symbolic representation
of the Church in its eternal state. Either way it is breathtakingly
exciting. We have seen already that here God dwells with His
people (v.3), and the next thing John shows us is that the city is
awash with light (v.11). God's first act of creation was to make
light. It is light, too, that floods the new creation. A wall surrounds
the city with twelve gates on which are written the names of

the twelve tribes of Israel. Its twelve foundations,
adorned with precious stones, have written on them
the names of the twelve apostles.

The image that transfixes my mind is that found
in today's text verse: 'twelve gates … each gate made
of a single pearl'. A pearl, it has been discovered, is
the product of pain. When the shell of the oyster is
pierced by a microscopic worm or a speck of sand
immediately the resources of the tiny organism rush
to the spot where the breach has been made. It then
exudes a precious secretion in order to close the
breach and save its life. If there had been no wound

there would be no pearl. Pearls are healed wounds.

Can you see what the gates of pearl are saying to us? The
entrance to the New Jerusalem is secured through the pain
which our Lord endured for us on the cross of Calvary. Now those
wounds are healed. We cannot scale those jasper walls. We must
go in at a gate, and the gate is a pearl.

**Lord Jesus Christ, my Saviour and Redeemer, I see that in heaven
there is to be an eternal reminder of Your sacrifice for me on
Calvary. It is a truth I never want to stop thinking about, here and
in eternity. Thank you dear Master. Amen.**

'Eternal nutrients'

For reading & meditation – Revelation 22:1–5
'... the Lord God will give them light. And they will reign for ever and ever.' (v.5)

Here again the images recall those found in the Old Testament. The springing of the water of life from God's throne reminds us of Ezekiel's vision (Ezek. 47:1–9). Joel and Zechariah refer to it in their prophecies also (Joel 3:18; Zech. 14:8). This miraculous river, in fact, flows through the whole Bible and suggests abundance of life and fertility.

On either side of the river is the tree of life bearing all kinds of fruit, and yielding its fruit every month. This picture, I think, is intended to show that we will be dependent on God for our life in eternity in the same way that we are dependent on Him now. The nutrients we need for our eternal existence will come from Him. Our lives will be watered by the river of God and ripen into exotic fruit.

FURTHER STUDY

Psa. 46:1–11;
John 7:37–39;
Gal. 3:13–14;
1 John 3:1–3

1. In what does the psalmist put his confidence?

2. What does Jesus promise believers?

We will *serve* also. Heaven is not a place of everlasting repose. There will be activity – *joyous* activity, I imagine. Darkness will be a thing of the past. No more dark nights of the soul. The Lord God will be our light. One writer believes we will never truly see light until we see it in heaven. He puts it like this: 'The light of heaven is not the blur of a 40-watt bulb hanging naked in the night. It is *colours*, light that reveals the specific hue and texture of everything in creation. In that light we see not only objects but also their dazzling light-charged beauty.' Best of all, of course, our eyes will be focused on the Lamb. We may glance at each other but our gaze will be upon Him.

Father, the more I ponder the glories of heaven the more eager I am to go there. But all in good time. I have a work to do for You down here on earth. Let me not shirk the responsibilities of time because of my contemplation of eternity. Amen.

Continuing in the right

For reading & meditation – Revelation 22:6–11

'... let him who does right continue to do right; and let him who is holy continue to be holy.' (v.11)

As the visions come to an end John again falls at the feet of the revealing angel in an attitude of worship. The angel rebukes him for his misplaced devotion. 'Do not do it!' he says. 'I am a fellow-servant with you … Worship God!' (v.9). How sad it is when we become more interested in the messenger than the message. This frequently happens in church life. Those who reveal the truth often become more popular than the revealed God.

Eugene Peterson suggests that some people treat the book of Revelation in the same way; they become so interested in what is happening that they forget God. 'They lose themselves,' he says, 'in symbol hunting, numbers, speculating with frenzied imaginations on times and seasons despite Jesus' severe stricture against it (Acts 1:7).' It is Christ's revelation we are to be taken up with, not the revelation of anti-Christ or the end of the world.

Along with the worship of God the angels command urgency: 'Do not seal up the words of the prophecy … because the time is near' (v.10). The urgency expressed in Revelation 1:1 is there also at the end. However blessed, encouraged and enlightened we are by reading these words 2,000 years after they were first written, we must not forget they had a special meaning for the churches of John's day. The book still speaks to us today, of course, and we are to use its message to help us continue to do right, to continue to be holy. That is its main purpose for us.

Father, save me from becoming so preoccupied with dates and seasons that I miss out on the real meaning of all You are saying to me, namely that I must remain faithful and obedient to Jesus Christ. In His precious name I pray. Amen.

'Come Lord Jesus'

For reading & meditation – Revelation 22:12–21

'He who testifies to these things says,
"Yes, I am coming soon."' (v.20)

Revelation ends, as it begins, with Jesus Christ. He is the coming One, the Alpha and Omega, the Root and Offspring of David, the Bright and Morning Star. Twice in these last few verses our Lord reminds us that He is coming soon (vv.12, 20), for those whose robes have been washed; only they will have the right to enter through the pearly gates of the holy city.

The Spirit and the Bride also urge His arrival on the world's scene. They too say 'Come.' Those who have not tasted of the water of life and whose souls ache with thirst are urged to come to Him who one day will come to this world (v.17).

We dare not close without considering the warning that anyone who takes away from this book or adds to it will be refused entrance to the holy city (v.19). If we believe that what God has said in this book is not sufficient and we make additions of our own, or if we believe its demands are not to be taken seriously, then we put ourselves at great risk spiritually. The safest position is to take God at His Word, trust in Christ's sacrifice for us on Calvary, and wait with earnest expectation for His coming. I believe we are very close to Christ's coming now. There is not much time left.

FURTHER STUDY

Jer. 11:1-5;
1 Cor. 1:4-9;
Heb. 9:24-28;
2 Pet. 1:19-21;
Jude 24-25

1. What was Jeremiah's response to God?

2. Meditate on Jude's doxology.

The final statement is a promise of grace. Grace means strength, divine enabling. There is no better way of gaining strength for the days ahead than to ponder the truths in this book. How else could John finish his book than with the simple affirmation 'Amen', *O Yes?*

Father, thank You for what You have shown me these past weeks of the glories of Your Son, my Saviour. Help me not to be taken up with times and seasons but with Him. I face the future with confidence knowing that all things are in His hands. Amen.

More one year devotionals by Selwyn Hughes

Each compact devotional contains a whole year's worth of daily readings, covering six specially selected themes from *Every Day with Jesus*.

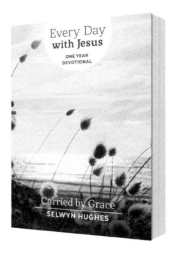

Carried by Grace
Includes these issues:
Prepared, The Call, Our True Identity, Pursued by Grace, Standing Strong and Bringing Down Giants.

ISBN: 978-1-78259-062-0

Price **£7.99**

A Fresh Vision of God
Includes these issues:
The Vision of God, From Confusion to Confidence, The Beatitudes, The Power of a New Perspective, The Corn of Wheat Afraid to Die and Heaven-Sent Revival.

ISBN: 978-1-85345-121-8

Price **£7.99**

Continue to be inspired by God.
Every day.

Confidently face life's challenges by equipping yourself daily with God's Word. There is something for everyone...

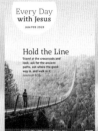

Every Day with Jesus
Selwyn Hughes renowned writing is updated by Mick Brooks into these trusted and popular notes.

Life Every Days
Jeff Lucas helps apply the Bible to daily life through his trademark humour and insight.

Inspiring Women Every Day
Encouragement, uplifting scriptures and insightful daily thoughts for women.

The Manual
Straight-talking guides to help men walk daily with God. Written by Carl Beech.

To find out more about all our daily Bible reading notes, or to take out a subscription, visit **cwr.org.uk/biblenotes** or call 01252 784700. Also available in Christian bookshops.

 Printed format Large print format 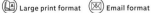 Email format Ebook format

Discover more about CWR, our ministry, training and all our resources at cwr.org.uk

For you
and your church

With FREE online resources

paraclesis
Coming alongside others

Paraclesis: Journeying Together

This six-week church programme provides a fresh perspective on pastoral care within your whole church by helping people to come alongside people.

paraclesis.org.uk    **Currently only available in the UK**

TRANSFORMED (LIFE)

TRANSFORMED **LIVING**

Transformed Life and Transformed Living

Using Ephesians 1–3, Transformed Life explores questions of our identity, purpose and belonging. **transformed-life.info**

Focusing on Ephesians 4–6, Transformed Living explores how we can live in the light of what Christ has done for us. **transformed-living.info**

Both programmes are ideal for the whole church, small groups and individuals and each programme lasts for seven weeks.

40
days with
JESUS   **40 Days with Jesus**

A post-Easter resource, for individuals, small groups and churches. At the heart of this six-week church programme is an invitation to actively explore the accounts of the risen Jesus.

40days.info

Courses and seminars

Waverley Abbey College

Publishing and media

Conference facilities

Transforming lives

CWR's vision is to enable people to experience personal transformation through applying God's Word to their lives and relationships.

Our Bible-based training and resources help people around the world to:
• Grow in their walk with God
• Understand and apply Scripture to their lives
• Resource themselves and their church
• Develop pastoral care and counselling skills
• Train for leadership
• Strengthen relationships, marriage and family life and much more.

Our insightful writers provide daily Bible-reading notes and other resources for all ages, and our experienced course designers and presenters have gained an international reputation for excellence and effectiveness.

CWR's Training and Conference Centre in Surrey, England, provides excellent facilities in an idyllic setting – ideal for both learning and spiritual refreshment.

CWR Applying God's Word to everyday life and relationships

CWR, Waverley Abbey House,
Waverley Lane, Farnham,
Surrey GU9 8EP, UK

Telephone: **+44 (0)1252 784700**
Email: **info@cwr.org.uk**
Website: **www.cwr.org.uk**

Registered Charity No 294387
Company Registration No 1990308